Mathematics, Teachers and Children

Mathematics, Teachers and Children

A Reader

Edited by
David Pimm
at the Open University

HODDER AND STOUGHTON
LONDON SYDNEY AUCKLAND TORONTO
in association with the Open University

British Library Cataloguing in Publication Data

Pimm, David
Mathematics, teachers and children.
1. School. Curriculum subjects:
Mathematics. Teaching
I. title
518′.7′1

ISBN 0 340 48756 9

First published in Great Britain 1988
Second impression 1991

Typeset by Gecko Limited, Bicester, Oxon.
Printed in Great Britain for Hodder and Stoughton Educational, a division of Hodder and Stoughton Ltd, Mill Road, Dunton Green, Sevenoaks, Kent, by Page Bros, Norwich.

Contents

Preface

The 1980s have seen a resurgence of interest in mathematics education in the UK at a number of different levels. Not least among the influences was the publication of the Cockcroft Report (HMSO, 1982). Nationally, there have been a number of changes which have markedly affected the mathematical education that schoolchildren receive. The secondary examination system and what (and how it) should be assessed have come in for radical criticism and reform, changes which are still percolating through the educational system. At the very time of writing, there is considerable uncertainty and anxiety about how the current government's Education Bill (including proposals for a national curriculum and a national age-specific system of testing) will affect mathematics education. In all of these public educational discussions, mathematics appears as a key example, endowed with a (possibly overvalued) status unmatched by any other school subject with the possible exception of English.

The largest single change has had to do with how the mathematics curriculum has been perceived, the move being from a description in solely content terms (the addition of two-digit numbers, multiplying fractions, the solution of quadratic equations, etc.) to one stressing mathematical *thinking*. In particular, this involves paying more attention to mathematical processes (such as generalising, modelling and estimating) in addition to the overt mathematical content. 'Problem solving' and 'mathematical investigation' are two terms which have gained considerable currency in connection with pupil involvement in situations that allow or encourage mathematical thinking. As a consequence, the primary focus of this reader is varied aspects of problem solving and problem posing in mathematics in a school setting, which is becoming a key area of interest at both primary and secondary levels.

The majority of the articles have been specially commissioned for this reader, the remainder being reprinted from books and journals. The authors are practising teachers, advisory teachers and lecturers in tertiary education. The collection is divided into four separate sections, and each one has a brief introduction outlining the articles within it. While no article will deal with just one of these areas, this categorisation provides a means of signalling the intended focus. The sections are entitled:

Classroom Issues
Social, Political and Personal Issues
Mathematical Issues
Mathematical Education Issues.

The first one contains accounts by teachers of work they have carried out in their classrooms. The second section attempts to explore some of the wider social and political issues which impinge on teachers on the one hand, while other articles in it examine the personal, individual struggles of teachers endeavouring to change their own classroom behaviour. The third section focuses on the fact that it is *mathematics* teaching and learning that is the central concern of this reader. It therefore includes articles dealing with some influential aspects of mathematics itself. The final section expands upon some of the issues under examination by the emerging discipline of mathematics education, exploring, among other things, aspects of research about both pupils and teachers.

This reader is published as part of the Open University course ME234 *Using Mathematical Thinking*, and the chosen articles reflect the course's content, emphasis and preoccupations. The main force of the course concerns teachers reflecting on their own teaching as a means of enhancing their own professional development. Underlying all of these articles is a belief in the importance of exploring and working on issues which arise from the varied attempts to teach and learn mathematics in a classroom setting.

David Pimm
Milton Keynes
September 1988

Acknowledgments

The publisher would like to thank the following for permission to reproduce material in this volume:

The Mathematical Association for Chapter 1 'A question of balance' by Barbara Jaworski from *Mathematics in School*, **16**(2), March 1987, pp. 7–10, Chapter 9 'Asian children in schools' by Valerie Emblen from *Mathematics in School*, **15** (5) November 1986, pp. 26–9 and **16** (1), January 1987, pp. 7–9; The Association of Teachers of Mathematics for Chapter 2 'Some infants' work' by Maureen Gratton-Kane from *Mathematics Teaching*, **108**, pp. 2–3, Chapter 4 'Towards a problem-solving school' by Bob Smith from *Mathematics Teaching*, **111**, pp. 7–11, and **112**, pp. 2–6, Chapter 12 'Hidden messages' by Jenny Maxwell from *Mathematics Teaching*, **111**, pp. 18–19, Chapter 13 'Politics of percent' by Dawn Gill from *Mathematics Teaching*, **114**, pp. 12–14 (also by permission of the author ©), Chapter 17 'Opening-up' by Anne Watson from *Mathematics Teaching*, **115**, pp. 16–18, Chapter 19 'Tensions' by John Mason from *Mathematics Teaching*, **114**, pp. 28–31, Chapter 31 'Investigating investigations' by David Wheeler from *Mathematics Teaching*, **106**, pp. 24–5 and the letter on p. 69 from *Mathematics Teaching*; Basil Blackwell for Chapter 3 'Chairs for bears' by Marilyn Metz from *Micromath* **1**(3), 1985, pp. 8–9; Times Newspapers Ltd for Chapter 14 'Looking for relevance: can we let them decide?' by Barbara Edmonds and Derek Ball from *TES* Extra, 19 October 1986, the extract on p. 69 from the article 'Anodyne Report Angers Minister' by Ian Nash from *TES*, 25 February 1987; *The Computing Teacher/Logo Exchange* vol. 5, 9, May 1987 published by The International Council for Computers in Education for Chapter 21 'On the mathematical nature of turtle programming' by Uri Leron; Ellis Horwood Limited, Chichester for Chapter 23 'Modelling: what do we really want pupils to learn?' from *Teaching and Applying Mathematical Modelling*, ed. J. S. Berry *et al.*, 1984; Thomas J. Cooney/The Association for Supervision and Curriculum Development, Alexandria, Virginia for Chapter 28 'Teachers' decision making' by Thomas J. Cooney from *Mathematics Education Research: Implications for the 80s*. Copyright © by ASCD. All rights reserved; the SMILE Centre for Chapter 30 'Imagery, imagination and mathematics classrooms' by John Mason, based on his article 'I is for imagery' in *Investigator*, no. 9, pp. 8–9; Husmo-Foto, Oslo for the illustration on p. 58; Cambridge University Press for the diagram and exercise on p. 59 taken from School Mathematics Project, *Advanced Mathematics Book 1*, 1979; Geoff Franklin for the photograph on p. 69; Paul Brown/*The Guardian* for the extract on p. 69 from the article 'Row as maths CSE examines arms spending', 14 June 1988; Century Hutchinson Ltd for the photograph and text on p. 183 taken from *Tackle Windsurfing* by Glenn Taylor, published by Stanley Paul and Co. Ltd, 1982; the Board of Trustees of the Victoria and Albert Museum for the illustration 'A Pair of Cranes' on p. 237; Harvester Press Ltd/Birkhäser Boston Inc. for the diagram on p. 254 from *The Mathematical Experience* by P. J. Davis and R. Hersh published by Harvester Press Ltd, 1981; the Controller of Her

Majesty's Stationery Office for the extracts from the report *Better Mathematics* in Chapter 11; Mr L. J. Hordern for the photograph on p. 309 of an item from the Hordern collection of puzzles; *Petit x* for the cartoon sequence on pp. 231–5 which first appeared in French in issue no. 12, pp. 76–79, 1986; Ray Hemmings for the photographs in Chapter 25; John Harris for the photographs appearing in Chapter 4.

The editor would like to thank Sheila Hirst for her assistance in preparing much of the photographic material to be found in this volume. He would also like to thank Liliane Beaulieu, Reynand Dreyer, John Poland, Rosamond Sutherland and David Wheeler for their work on the translation of the Balacheff cartoon sequence on pp. 231–5.

All other material has been specially commissioned for this Reader and is reproduced by permission of the Open University copyright department.

SECTION I

Classroom Issues

THOUGHTS ON INVESTIGATIONS.

Sowing the seeds . . . .

How much do I say to get them started?
Now I'd like you to think about...

Watching Ian and Simon

Ian's writing, what's Simon thinking?

Looking over Halina's shoulder

How can I get them to generalise?

Drawing together the threads

They've found such a variety of ideas to pursue, its such a shame we haven't time.

Introduction

In Britain, the teacher is (currently) responsible for choosing and providing the mathematics education of pupils. The following seven articles offer accounts of what it is like 'being there', each exploring certain aspects of the problem-solving and investigating themes which comprise the central concern of this collection. Barbara Jaworski starts from the much-examined (if conceptually far from coherent) paragraph 243 of the Cockcroft Report, and explores what might be an appropriate balance between discussion, investigation and practical work on the one hand, and exposition, consolidation and practice on the other. In particular, she indicates how interrelated these areas are, and that 'the discussion lesson' or 'the practical lesson' are aberrations and should not be seen as ends in themselves.

In the second article, Maureen Gratton-Kane explores how a variety of everyday occurrences in an infant school can be used as the starting point for mathematical investigation. Marilyn Metz documents some of her very young pupils' involvement with the notion of variable, a useful conceptual tool to achieve their desired ends. Her short piece hints at the intended import of Bruner's often misquoted hypothesis that 'any subject can be taught effectively *in some intellectually honest form* to any child at any stage of development' (*The Process of Education*, Harvard University Press, 1963, p. 33: my emphasis).

Bob Smith uses problems from the social world of his middle school pupils as the vehicle for both their intellectual engagement, and the development of their problem-solving skills and interrelated aspects of personal qualities such as autonomy, perseverance and cooperation. Christine Shiu reports her use of some of the documented research literature on pupils' misconceptions about decimals. She shows how diagnostic assessment allowed her a clearer view of some of the beliefs of her pupils about both the specific mathematical concepts, and, more generally, how they saw mathematical problems involving the material world beyond the classroom. Both Bob Ansell's and Dave Pratt's articles relate to the use of the microcomputer to manipulate data, both computationally and in a graphical form, but also to its ability to provide a more realistic experience of what mathematical modelling of a situation can involve in an open-ended setting.

The age of pupils working on problems in these accounts varies from infant to upper secondary level, but in some ways the commonalities are more striking than the dissimilarities. These include pupils being engaged in their own tasks of various sorts, with the problems arising from a variety of sources. Another common theme is one of personal engagement and commitment, together with the pupils' own use of mathematical ideas, tools and procedures to help them.

1

A question of balance

Barbara Jaworski

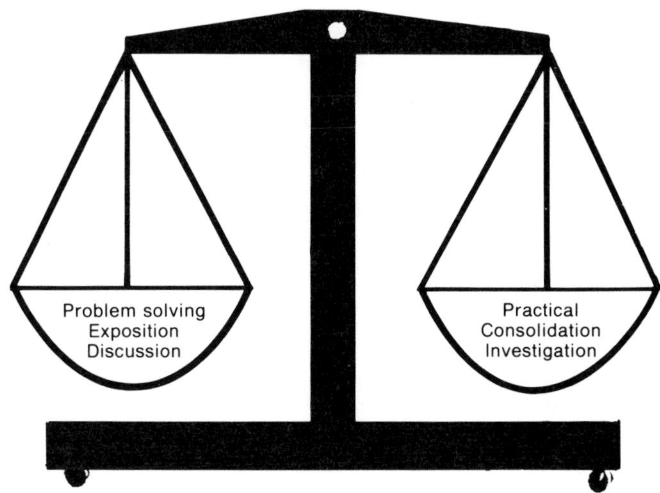

Mathematics teaching at all levels should include opportunities for
- exposition by the teacher;
- discussion between teacher and pupils and between pupils themselves;
- appropriate practical work;
- consolidation and practice of fundamental skills and routines;
- problem solving, including the application of mathematics to everyday situations;
- investigational work.

Paragraph 243 (above) is probably the most well known section of the Cockcroft Report,[1] yet its content is still a worry for many teachers. As much as *how* to incorporate all of these elements into mathematics lessons, there is the question of *balance* – how much of each, and how often?

Initial inertia

Exposition by the teacher, followed by consolidation and practice by the pupils, has long been a model for the teaching of mathematics in many schools. Its perpetuation has had a lot to do with its safeness, because:

it is familiar – many teachers were themselves taught by that model;
it is expected – many pupils have been brought up to regard it as the right and proper mode of teaching;

one's colleagues use it – safety in numbers;
discipline and control are well defined and relatively easy to achieve.

On the other hand, *investigation* and *discussion* are everyday words which are hard to relate to classroom mathematics. Discussions fit into literature classes or social studies classes, but what constitutes a discussion in the mathematics class? What are the pupils to investigate – number puzzles perhaps? How should this be fitted into the limited time available to cover a demanding syllabus?

Practical work is yet another worry. Resources are all too scarce to equip every classroom with a lot of apparatus. In any case, what apparatus is actually required, and what does one do with it? How is it possible to prevent it from being stolen without locking it away and thus making it inaccessible?

It is easy to continue with such questions without getting very far; perhaps justifying inertia because it all seems too confusing and difficult or perhaps thinking that there must be a magic formula somewhere around but worrying because you have not found it.

There is no magic formula. Each individual teacher has to develop their own way of working and define for himself/herself what the different aspects of paragraph 243 actually mean for their classroom. It is quite frightening when put like this, but it is nonetheless true. However, there is experience around which can help in providing ideas to enable a teacher to make a start. It is making this start which is the first hurdle to overcome.

Getting started

In order to illustrate ways of incorporating discussion, investigation and practical work into mathematics lessons, I shall give an example of a series of four lessons which actually took place with a first-year class of 32 pupils in a comprehensive school.

It was the pupils' second term in the school. The purpose of the lessons was two-fold:

1 To introduce some elementary notions of algebra.
2 To continue to encourage pupils to think mathematically, to articulate their own ideas and to listen to and respect those of others, and to negotiate meaning.

The first objective included a desire to avoid the aridness of traditional algebra teaching; to help the pupils see meaning and purpose behind the introduction of symbols rather than simply accepting their use and learning the conventions. James and Mason[2] discuss these ideas at some length with reference to examples of pupils working in a way similar to that described below. To quote them:

> Behind the formal symbols of mathematics there lies a wealth of experience which provides meaning for those symbols. Attempts to rush students into symbols impoverishes the background experience and leads to trouble later.

The second objective was ongoing. The teachers wanted to establish a way of working as early as possible so that it would become natural as the pupils moved through the school. They were prepared to put as much emphasis on this way of working as on the content of the lessons at this stage.

Lesson one

The first lesson began with the teacher presenting the pupils with three formations of Cuisenaire rods, which they were asked to describe.

Black			
W	R	R	R

Blue					
R	R	R	W	W	W

Blue					
R	W	R	W	R	W

Work had been done in previous lessons on giving clear descriptions and being precise about meaning. The following descriptions were some of those offered:

'The black rod has a white followed by three reds.'
'. . . a white at one end, and three reds all together . . .'
'. . . a blue rod with three reds and three whites.'
'Those two are the same.' (number 2 and number 3)
'No, they're arranged differently. It's white and red alternately.'
'There's the same number of each though.'
'. . . a white and a red three times.' (number 3)

There was some debate about the description, 'a white and a red three times', and whether the black rod's pattern could be described in this way too. Some pupils contended that the arrangement did not matter, but others felt that it was an important part of the description. Someone said:

'If we were describing it for someone who couldn't see the patterns, just saying three red and a white wouldn't be enough.

For this part of the lesson the pupils had been grouped around a table in the centre of the room, some sitting, some standing, others kneeling up on desks in order to see. The teacher's contribution at this stage had been one of management.

'Can you see from there James?'
'What do **you** think Tamla?'
'Hold on for a moment Andrew, I didn't quite catch what Kim said.'

This whole class discussion lasted for about 15 minutes, with a large proportion of the pupils making contributions. The teacher then asked pupils to return to their places, to draw a diagram for each of the three patterns in their exercise books, and write a description of each diagram; thus consolidating the ideas from the discussion. These written descriptions were then available for the teacher to monitor at a later stage as evidence of each pupil's thinking.

During the discussion, some conversation had been about the relative sizes of the rods. There was agreement that calling a white rod 'one' (i.e. one unit) seemed to be a good idea, so that a red rod would be 'two', a black would be 'seven' and a blue rod would be 'nine'. It follows that three reds and three whites together would make nine, which is the same as the blue rod. Implicit in this sameness is the notion of length, and later some pupils referred to the length of the rods when using the numbers. Other pupils talked about area, e.g. the area of the blue rod is 9 square cm. When asked what area they were talking about they pointed to the area covered by the rods on paper. Others referred to the volume of the rods. Clearly they felt that the numbers were strongly associated with some physical property of the rods.

In writing their descriptions some pupils had used a form of shorthand. Someone had written

Black = **White** + **Red** × 3

When the teacher asked why they had done this, there were replies that it was 'simpler to write', 'shorter', 'easier to understand'. The teacher then invited *everyone* to spend a few minutes trying to write a shorthand version for their descriptions. A few of these were then copied by the teacher onto the blackboard. They included

3**R** + 1**W** (black) **Blue** = 1**R** + 1**W** × 3 3**R** f.b. 3**W**

Blue=**R**, **W**, **R**, **W**, **R**, **W** ×3**R**$\xrightarrow{f}$ × 3**W**

3**R** + 3**W** = 1**B** in length

(f = followed, f.b. = followed by)

As the blackboard filled up with such contributions, there was avid discussion about their merits (or otherwise).

Someone said,

'. . . couldn't **R**, **W**, **R**, **W**, **R**, **W** be written as **R**, **W** × 3?'

Someone else said,

'. . . that might mean 3**R**, 3**W** . . .'

A lot of people believed that **R**, **W**, **R**, **W**, **R**, **W** was the clearest. Others said it was too long. The teacher asked,

'What if you had a hundred of them?'

Tamla said (of **R**, **W** × 3),

'It could be mistaken as 1 red followed by 3 whites.'

This was acknowledged,

'Yes, it might only be the white times three.'

One boy, Erik, had introduced a complex notation involving the use of arrows which he explained in detail to the class, leaving them extremely impressed at his invention.

The class was then invited to comment on the various abbreviations, in pairs.

'Tell your partner what you think.'

There was a buzz of talk as pupils compared their versions and discussed those written on the board. As the teacher wandered around listening to conversations, it appeared that two boys were talking about football. One said to the other,

'. . . if the final result is QPR 3, Bristol Rovers 3, does it matter what order the goals were scored in?'!!

As the lesson was nearing an end, the teacher drew everyone together again and asked them to write their preferred version for homework and explain why they thought it was best, for each of the three cases.

Lesson two

The second lesson began with the teacher reminding the class about their work in the previous lesson, summarising the discussion in the lesson and the pupils' written homework, and in particular remarking on the notation **R, W** × 3 and its possible interpretations. She suggested that the numbers of the rods might be helpful in checking that the shorthand description made sense, and illustrated with some examples, e.g.

> **R**, **W**, **R**, **W**, **R**, **W** with numbers would be 2, 1, 2, 1, 2, 1. Some people had used + instead of comma, and so their version would be 2 + 1 + 2 + 1 + 2 + 1. This adds up to 9, which of course is the length of the blue rod.

The class was split into six groups with five or six people in each, and each group was provided with a box of Cuisenaire rods. The teacher asked them to work on fitting patterns of rods to the orange rod.

> 'For each pattern that you find, agree on a shorthand description and write this down. Then try fitting the numbers to your shorthand and see if this makes sense.'

It was a noisy lesson, but everyone in the room was involved. The status of commas and arrows was discussed – what do you do with the numbers if they have commas between them? Some pupils drew boxes, or used brackets for grouping items. It was very interesting to note how different groups organised their working. James said:

> 'We agreed for one of us to draw a pattern, and then we pass the paper around and everyone writes a shorthand for it . . . if they can!'

Other groups worked individually or in pairs and then compared and pooled their results. The diagram shows a sample from one group:

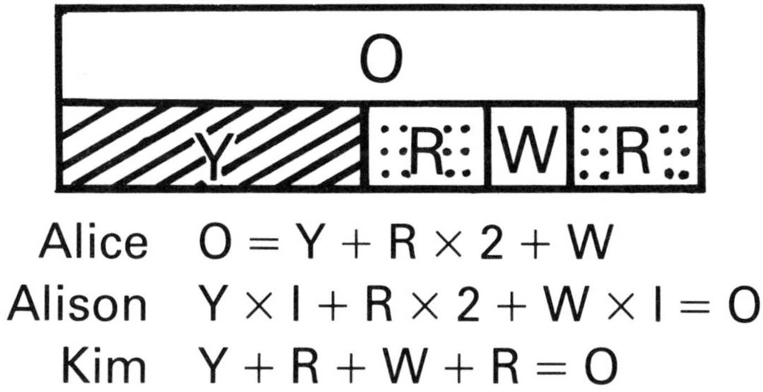

Lesson three

In the third lesson the teacher started off by giving everyone a sheet of questions on which they were asked to work individually. This asked them to draw patterns to illustrate such notation as

$$\mathbf{R} + \mathbf{W} \times 3 \quad \text{and} \quad (\mathbf{R} + \mathbf{W}) \times 3$$

and to write notation for patterns such as

Orange					
R	R	W	W	R	R

or

Orange			
Purple	W	Purple	W

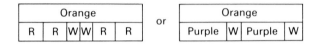

She wanted to find out what sense each person individually was making of these ideas, and made this explicit to the pupils. They recognised the purpose of the exercise, and there was silence in the room as they each worked at their sheet.

After this brief exercise she gave pairs in the classroom a pot of Cuisenaire rods, and a sheet of paper on which was written:

Investigate – ways of making a frame with Cuisenaire rods to fit around a square picture – the frame should be one rod deep. Start with the one below:

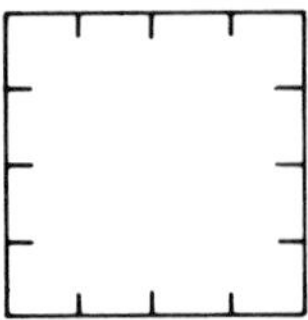

What colours can you use?
What is the minimum number of rods possible?
What is the total length of rods in the frame?

Most pairs started by fitting rods physically around the square. The teacher asked them to record their results using diagrams and notation. A great variety of possibilities was emerging. They all seemed to be of length 20.

> 'They'll all be the same won't they, because it's the same frame, isn't it,' someone said.
> 'What do you mean by the same frame?' said the teacher.
> 'They're all frames for the same picture, aren't they?'

The teacher asked what would happen if they changed the picture.

> 'What if you have a smaller picture, or a larger one? What would the frame length be for a 3 by 3 picture for example, or for a 5 by 5 picture?'

This proved to be motivating.

Comments which were heard included:

> 'The numbers are going up by 4.'
> 'It's like the four times table.'
> 'You multiply 5 by 5 and then you add 4.'
> 'No you don't, it's 4 times 5, then add 4.'

As predictions were produced, the teacher asked pupils to write down what they thought and to try to explain what they saw. Fierce competion emerged between two groups who thought they could see a rule to explain their numbers. As each one produced a version, the other tried to produce a counterexample to it, which meant that a lot of modification was taking place. The room was in motion as pupils moved around comparing and discussing results. There was a general feeling of excitement and discovery. One girl wrote:

> I think the rule for the perimeter of a picture frame would be you find out what size the picture is, say 4 × 4, you go up one say 5 then times it by itself leaving you with 5 × 5 = 20.

Then she put a cross by the side of this, and wrote:

> I think the rule is, say you had a 4 × 4 square, you +1 to the 4 then times the answer by 4 because there is 4 sides. 4 + 1 = 5, 4 × 5 = 20.

She had seen that her original prediction was in error and so had modified it.

Someone else had written, at the end of an explanation:

6 × 4 + 4 = 28
↓ blocks in row ↓ sides ↓ corner pieces

S × 4 + 4 = answer
↓ sides ↓ number of sides ↓ corners ↓ total

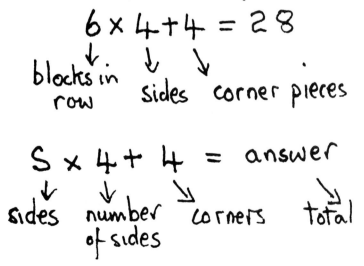

Both of these pupils were working towards the general. Although the first girl expressed her rule in terms of a particular case, it was only one step away from applying it generally. Whereas the second girl, after looking at the 6 × 6 square, wrote down a statement in terms of the side *S* of any square. Other pupils had produced different general statements, such as:

> Add one to the side, then multiply by four.

Add up all the sides, then add four for the corners.

Some pupils had extended the problem to produce general statements for rectangles as well.

It was interesting to observe pupils using letters for *specific* unknowns in setting up patterns of rods, such as

$$\mathbf{O} = \mathbf{R} + 3 \times \mathbf{W} + \mathbf{G} + \mathbf{R}$$

and for *generalised* unknowns as in length of frame of a square of side S is

$$S \times 4 + 4.$$

Dietmar Küchemann[3] says of this,

> It is perhaps more fruitful to regard these two interpretations as 'different sides of the same coin' as it seems likely that in many algebra problems children will flip from one interpretation to the other, depending on which is momentarily more convenient.

In conclusion

As a result of these three lessons the teacher felt that it would be appropriate to talk to the pupils about some of the conventions of formal algebra, such as precedence of operators and use of brackets. She planned a lesson in which she would talk herself about some of the interpretations which are possible of different notations, of the need for standards, of conventional forms of expression, referring to examples from pupils' work such as Erik's arrows, and to the discussions which had taken place. She then planned to ask pupils to work with a calculator, guessing the results of a number of expressions, such as $2 + 3 \times 4$ or $(2 + 3) \times 4$, then keying them in and testing out their predictions. Finally she hoped to relate this back to the Cuisenaire rod patterns. Why should rules such as

> Multiply by four and add four.
> Add one and multiply by four.

give the same results?

As well as this mathematical agenda she hoped to comment on ways of writing down their predictions and the results of testing them, and on the effect of continued demands for teacher attention. She wanted them to have more confidence in their ability to continue with their work without constant reassurance, and in consequence leave her with more time to spend where it seemed to be most needed.

Degree of balance

The balance of the elements of Cockcroft 243 was not explicitly a consideration in planning these lessons, although it might usefully have been so. In *Teaching Styles*[4] the authors remark,

> We do not necessarily expect every topic to include opportunities for all of the items (of Cockcroft 243) . . .

They go on to suggest that a helpful exercise might be to consider where any of these items would usefully occur in the lessons planned.

However, it is interesting to note where these elements were present in the lessons described above.

Discussion was evident throughout at a number of levels.

The discussion at the beginning of the first lesson concerned the whole group, and was managed by the teacher. Not everyone took part. Does this mean that not everyone was involved with the ideas?

At the end of the first lesson pupils discussed their interpretations of the shorthand, in pairs or in larger groups. This time, everyone was involved. The teacher could listen in to some of the conversations, but could not hope to hear all that was said. Is this important?

In the second lesson the pupils worked in groups for almost the whole lesson, and during this time, as far as the teacher could ascertain, the talk was about the activity and the mathematics involved – forming patterns, writing down shorthand versions, and justifying and checking them. Pupils discussed their ideas together, and with the teacher whenever the teacher joined a group.

Investigation took place in exploring the various patterns of rods which had the same length as an orange rod, and finding ways of representing them in symbol form; in working on the possible frames for square pictures; and in exploring with a calculator what results were obtained for a variety of numeric expressions.

At the basis of the investigative work were the Cuisenaire rods. These enabled the pupils to feel and see patterns which represented patterns of numbers. In describing the patterns of rods and relating these to the numeric values associated with the rods, pupils could get a feel for algebraic notation and the need for being precise and unambiguous. This provided groundwork for the teacher to talk to them about conventional notation and why this is necessary. **Practical apparatus** is very often useful in this way as a physical embodiment of mathematical ideas.

Exposition by the teacher happened at a number of levels:

in setting up activities, giving instructions and comments to the class at various points;

at the beginning of the second lesson where she summarised activity and discussion from the previous lesson and commented on it;

in the fourth lesson where she talked to pupils about algebraic conventions.

Pupils consolidated ideas at various points by writing down for themselves what they thought and understood about an activity in which they had been involved. In particular, a homework was devoted to this. In the second lesson pupils were given a chance to practise writing expressions to describe patterns; in the third lesson to practise problem-solving skills such as predicting and testing; and in the fourth lesson to practise their use of a calculator.

Problem solving occurred explicitly where pupils were asked to find the length of the frame for a given square picture, and implicitly wherever a question was posed to which an answer had to be found. Teachers sometimes worry about the difference between problem solving and investigation. Problem solving happens in tackling questions in a text-book exercise. Usually this is restricted to finding a particular answer to some question related to a particular topic under consideration. Solving the problem of what Cuisenaire rods can be fitted to an orange rod is more open-ended. There are many solutions. Sometimes a problem may have no solution. Perhaps one distinction between problem solving and investigation is that part of the investigative process involves exploring what problems to solve.

A significant feature of these four lessons was that at most times it was possible to identify more than one of the elements of paragraph 243. In general these elements do not take place in isolation. Very rarely is it possible to say that a lesson was a 'discussion lesson', a 'practical lesson', or an 'investigation lesson'. Exploring ideas, making predictions, testing out findings, convincing other people all support the learning process. Apparatus helps to illustrate and clarify ideas, and is often challenging in its own right in motivating exploration. Teacher exposition provides information and guidance when and where this is needed.

One way to begin the weaving of these elements is to incorporate them little by little. Do not try to get a whole class discussion going if pupils are not used to it. Invite them to talk in pairs for five minutes about what you have just been saying to them. This gives everyone a chance to say something and get used to talking about the mathematics themselves. Similarly, do not try to set up a major investigation. Find some small idea that you could ask them to explore in groups for perhaps 15 minutes, and then talk with them about it afterwards. The pupils as much as the teacher need to be introduced gradually to new ways of working and become accustomed to what is involved and expected.

Notes

1 Cockcroft, W. H. (1982) *Mathematics Counts*: HMSO.
2 James, N. & Mason, J. (1982) 'Towards Recording', *Visible Language*, XVI, 3.
3 Küchemann, D. (1981) 'Algebra', in *Children's Understanding of Mathematics*, ed., Hart, K. John Murray.
4 *Teaching Styles* (1984): Association of Teachers of Mathematics.

Barbara Jaworski was head of mathematics in a comprehensive school; she is now Lecturer in Mathematics Education at the Open University.

2

Some infants' work

Maureen Gratton-Kane

A common sight in most infant classrooms is the picture of the teacher with her young charges gathered close, usually seated on a carpet, or cushions; listening; contributing ideas and discussing the subject of the moment, their physical closeness adding a richness to the thoughts and experiences which they uninhibitedly share.

These sessions – perhaps more generally associated with children recounting their 'news' or with story-telling – can also be the starting point for mathematical investigations.

A simple idea gleaned from such an occasion can arouse the interest of the whole class and be the source of lively discussion. This is the point at which I have found it most fruitful to invite volunteers to pursue problems meriting deeper investigation.

One might expect that the same children would always undertake these challenges, but in actual fact I have found that the subject matter is a strongly influencing factor, plus, of course, the attraction of other activities in progress in the classroom.

The school, its pupils, furniture and general equipment have, in their time, provided a wealth of mathematical experiences. Pupils derive all the benefits of working closely in a small group; sharing skills, intuition, creativity and motivation. Teacher support is ever present but discreet, and the general procedure if investigators are perplexed, or uncertain at some point about how they should proceed, is to seek a 'carpet' discussion when the problem is aired to all the pupils in the class, who, having knowledge of the subject matter from the earlier discussion, are invited to offer suggestions. Likewise, the results and any recording the children may have produced as a result of an investigation will be discussed with everyone in the class, providing a further opportunity for sharing experience, developing confidence and showing competence.

How many lunch boxes can be fitted onto the middle and bottom shelves of the cupboard?

This investigation was undertaken by Jason, Robin and Adam, all top infants. This practical problem arose after I observed that the children were being careless and untidy with their lunch boxes.

For the purpose of the investigation I allowed the boys to use lunch boxes of standard dimensions; irregular sized boxes were disregarded. The shelves were emptied and every class member was invited to estimate how many boxes the shelves would hold. The written estimates were placed in a sealed jar until the conclusion of the work, although the majority were wildly inaccurate.

This problem did not involve a great deal of thoughtful deliberation, more the ability to work co-operatively in a practical situation. Various reports have stressed the importance of pupil/pupil discussion and of children developing independence in working at mathematics rather than asking for help at every stage. There was much evidence of this type of working in this situation. After experiment they discovered that 16 boxes could be left on the bottom shelf and 14 on the middle shelf, i.e. 30 packed lunch boxes each day. All three boys when questioned had made a mental calculation of 16 add 14 in the following way:

> 16 add 10 makes 26, and four, makes 30.

They volunteered the information that during the school week a total of 150 boxes could be left on the shelves. This calculation (5×30) was done quickly by Jason and Adam using this method:

> 30 add 30 makes 60, so twice that makes 120, and that leaves us with 30, so add that on and that makes 150.

The boys did not talk a great deal about what they were doing. They worked well together as a team in finding the best way to store the boxes. I asked them if they could record pictorially what they had discovered. It was this part of the work which caused them problems. Each boy insisted on seeking his own solution.

Robin made a small template of a lunch box and drew around it the required number of times, placing the template on two drawn shelves which were too long for the required number of boxes. He then drew the dimensions of the cupboard to fit his representation and erased the length of shelving not required.

Jason drew a cupboard and, finding that the shelves were too long, left gaps in between his representations of the boxes.

Adam took a long, narrow strip of paper. He folded it in a concertina fashion and drew the outline of a box on the front paper face. Unfortunately his own co-ordination was too clumsy for him to have the skill to cut his outline accurately and his first attempt ended up as several badly cut small pieces of paper. With the help of a better co-ordinated friend the desired result was achieved and he was able to show me representations of 30 boxes of identical size in one long strip. He then cut off the number of boxes required for the middle shelf and made the necessary adjustment to the remaining strip for the bottom shelf. He then drew the outer dimension of the cupboard around the box representations.

The boys each wrote about their discoveries, although they collaborated on sentence construction and spelling. Their work was available for future reference in a special book.

How many tiles will be needed to cover an outlined part of the classroom floor, if the new tiles are only one-quarter of the size of one of the older tiles?

Several children have tackled this and similar problems concerned with area. I am particularly interested in the procedures adopted by two different pairs of children in solving this problem.

Firstly, Karen and Mark. These children selected a section of the floor where the tiles are lifting and drew a line around an area six tiles by three tiles. They:

- cut a piece of large squared graph paper to the same shape;
- divided the squares on the top row into sections;
- numbered along the top row of large graph squares 0, 4, 8, 12, 16, 20, 24;
- announced that the answer was 3 sets of 24 and that '3 sets of 20 made 60, add 3 sets of 4 which made 12, 60 and 12 made 72'.

The calculations were made rapidly and mentally and checked as a matter of form on a calculator. (It is interesting to note how many children mentally calculate addition by adding firstly all the tens and then adding on the units.)

Secondly, Russell and Alison tackled a similar problem, but adopted a totally different strategy for solving it. On this occasion I controlled the problem by marking an area of the floor two tiles by four tiles. They had lengthy discussion beforehand and needed considerable encouragement to begin any plan of action. Russell decided that he would support Alison's plan first and that if they did not get an answer, she could support him in his method of tackling the problem. Alison and Russell found an answer by adopting the following strategy.

- Alison took a piece of chalk and placed a large cross in one of the squares. She then went to a section of the floor not being used and drew around four tiles. At this point Russell gently remonstrated with her and said that they could draw on a piece of paper the number of new tiles required for each old tile. Alison was uncertain about this and so Russell agreed to continue his support for her method of working.
- Alison continued this procedure for all eight tiles, until
- she had eight adjoining tiles marked with individual crosses and eight sets of four tiles each marked on the floor.
- Alison then added each individual tile in each set until she reached 32 – that, she said, being the number of new tiles she would need.

I asked Russell how he would have liked to tackle the question. He replied that he would have let Alison put a cross in each tile but each time that she did this he would have put a column of four Unifix cubes in a box. I asked him what he would do with the Unifix cubes in the box. He replied that he would rearrange them into columns of ten to make counting easier, e.g. 10, 20, 30 and two more makes 32. 'It's quicker that way,' he insisted.

Are both feet of each pair the same length?

Initially this was presented to the class as a subject for discussion. Several children knew that their feet were different lengths because they recalled a conversation between a shop assistant and their parent when the last pair of shoes had been purchased.

Karen and Lisa enthusiastically undertook this assignment. This may have been because they instinctively knew what to do and sensed that certain types of recording, at which they are competent, would meet with approval.

They asked class members, individually, to remove their shoes, and then they drew the outline of each foot onto thin card. With great concentration they used a centimetre rule and accurately measured the length of each outline, recording the measurement on the appropriate outline. They had a brief discussion about the results, and then decided to record this information in three sets:

- a set of people whose feet were the same length;
- a set of people whose left foot was longer than their right foot;
- a set of people whose right foot was longer than their left foot.

Another short discussion between Lisa and Karen was followed by a request for graph paper. They proceeded to draw a bar graph. When this had been completed Lisa uttered a sound of exasperation. She had noticed that she had incorrectly recorded one person too many as having feet of the same length. This was explained to me and I asked them what they felt they would like to do about it. Without hesitation they elected to draw the graph again. This time it accurately recorded what they had found out.

They wrote a record of this work and used the graph as a basis when writing questions for their peers to answer. For example: How many more people are there with two feet the same length than people with the left foot longer than the right?

The two pupils completed this assignment without any teacher intervention. In fact it could be argued that there was mismatch between pupils and work, for it did not present them with any challenge, the pupils using ritualised actions triggered off by certain deeds which then followed a pattern so repetitious that nothing happened to disturb the train of events that had been triggered off. But, as stated in the ATM book *Notes on Mathematics for Children*,

> Not all action is thus. There are actions which we take which involve some kind of triggering that invokes some known skills and yet which still may imply a conscious awareness of the possibility of change.

This possibility existed for these two pupils.

Maureen Gratton-Kane is a teacher in an infant school in Cornwall.

3

Chairs for bears

Marilyn Metz

Once upon a time – to start as all good fairy-tales should – there was a class of top infants who had a floor turtle and an Apple II computer. They enjoyed working with Logo, and sometimes wrote procedures. This is the story of how the first procedure with an input came to be written.

We had been working in class around a story which involved a café, and the children decided to use the turtle to draw some furniture. Jola drew a chair and proudly took it to show another class. It was much admired, and the teacher there asked her if she would draw chairs for the three bears for her class. Enthusiastic about this idea, Jola first wanted to define a procedure for her original chair. She had not written procedures before, so we worked on this together, 'playing turtle' and chalking out the drawing on the floor. In this way Jola planned the turtle moves on paper, and then defined her procedure, which was:

```
TO CHAIR
PD
FD 90
BK 90
BK 90
FD 90
RT 112
LT 20
FD 90
RT 98
LT 10
FD 90
PU
END
```

When Jola told me about the suggestion that she should draw chairs for the three bears, the obvious thought in my mind was 'Do I introduce the idea of inputs to a procedure now?' The class had only been using Logo for three or four months, and many of the children, including Jola, were still very much at the stage of investigative play. Also, the concept of variable does not normally appear in the mathematics curriculum for infants. There were some children, however, who had taken to writing procedures rather like ducks to water, and the opportunity of offering the class a pervasive mathematical idea seemed too good to ignore. Jola's interest in the three chairs had grown easily from something she had done, and would enable her to contribute something of her own to work in another class. What more natural opportunity would I have?

The next question I asked myself was 'How do I do it?' I did not want to restrict the idea to Jola alone, and I was not sure how many of the rest of the class would be either interested, or able to use the idea in their own work. So I chose a Friday afternoon (our most relaxed time) to ask Jola to tell everyone about her chair and about the proposed chairs for the bears. The children found it easy to see that they could draw chairs of other sizes with other procedures, but I explained that Logo would allow them to write just one procedure which could then produce a chair of any size. I offered to show anyone who was interested how they could do this.

Next came the direct teaching. I did not want to use Jola's procedure as the example, because I wanted that procedure to be edited by the children. So I worked at the computer, defining a procedure to draw a line:

```
TO LINE :LENGTH
FD :LENGTH
END
```

I used an empty box to represent the name of the variable LENGTH, and the children put multilink cubes in the box, to the value of the length of the line they wanted drawn. We tried out lines of several different lengths with the floor turtle. Jola found this difficult, but clung to trying to understand it. David and Sarah were more comfortable with the idea and offered to help Jola edit her original procedure. Together we

looked at the first line, and edited it to read: TO CHAIR :SIZE ('Draw a chair the size that I tell you'). We discussed briefly which inputs we would need to change, and David saw clearly that the first command, FD 90 would need to become FD :SIZE. I then left Jola to complete the editing with David's and Sarah's help and to let me know when she had finished. Walking away, I was sure that the children needed to be on their own to do the editing, but I was not sure what I would return to!

When I was called back by the children, I was delighted to see that they had edited the procedure perfectly, :SIZE replacing all the numerical inputs to FORWARD and BACK, and I told them so. They had not tried it out yet, and as we all gathered round the floor turtle there was a lovely feeling of excitement and achievement. I suggested that first we try to run the procedure CHAIR; this gave the error message 'NOT ENOUGH INPUTS TO CHAIR'. I explained that by not putting a number in the box named SIZE, there was not enough information to make the procedure work. Next we tried CHAIR 90, Jola's original chair, and compared the new drawing with her previous one. Suggestions now came thick and fast from the children, aimed at producing the three chairs for the three bears. CHAIR 70 became Mother Bear's chair, and CHAIR 40 was Baby Bear's. The children realised that there was no need to stop there, and we tried CHAIR 1 (not a great success because it was too small for us to see properly). CHAIR 4 was much admired, and someone suggested it might be the right size for an ant. A little later on, we tried CHAIR 999, but were not successful: the paper we used was much too small, and all the classroom furniture got in the way!

It was a long time before other procedures with inputs started to be written regularly, and this did not surprise me. I am still pleased that I intervened so directly. I am sure that Jola found the idea extremely complex; she did not use it again for a long time. But her helpers, Sarah and David, did gain an initial grasp of the idea, and subsequently wrote both graphical and non-graphical procedures with two inputs. Sarah worked with Elizabeth to create a procedure for writing letters:

```
TO COX :NAME :NAME4
PR SE [TO] :NAME
PR [WE HOPE YOU LIKE YOUR]
PR SE :NAME4 [LOTS OF]
PR [LOVE FROM ELIZABETH]
PR [AND SARAH XXXX]
PR [CLASS 1]
END
```

This procedure proved quite useful for sending greetings to teachers who had babies, or even to me on my birthday!

I realise that luck played an important part in the success of the three chairs. Jola's original procedure contained the same value of 90 as the input to all the FORWARD and BACK commands. My decision to intervene, and to introduce the concept of variable, was definitely influenced by my awareness of this. If this had not been the case things would have been much more complicated, and I doubt that the bears would have had their chairs just then. In fact, after the chairs were drawn, Abarna, Jola and Shanthi drew a bed for one of the bears, and tried very hard to edit the procedure so that there would be beds for everyone. Their procedure was:

```
TO BED
FD 90      RT 80
BK 40      FD 90
LT 100     BK 90
RT 20      BK 40
FD 30      BK 10
FD 70      END
```

Even though Jola had begun to see how the input to her CHAIR procedure worked, to do the same with the BED procedure would have been much harder. It would have been possible to edit this procedure to take an input if the children had been able to perceive their original inputs to FORWARD and BACK as multiples of ten. But this idea was too complicated for them, and we had to make do with just one bed.

While some of the children wrote complex procedures with variables, others never used the idea at all. My intervention illustrated a little of the potential of Logo to the class, and thus made it available to those children who would like to explore it.

As I mentioned before, the concept of variable is not usually part of an infant's experience of mathematical ideas. And yet some of these young children demonstrated convincingly that they were able to understand and use this concept in graphical and non-graphical Logo work. It may be that, in our anxiety to give children basic arithmetical skills in their early years of school, we are in danger of neglecting the richness of the children's own mathematical knowledge. Mathematical development in the infant school is too often seen as linear, and we ignore the mathematical awareness that children bring to the classroom. One of the basic premises adhered to by teachers creating a language environment is that it shall be rich and exciting. Do we hold this premise to be as important when we provide the mathematical environment for the same children? I think the answer is often, sadly, no. But I also believe that, by using Logo with young children, teachers will feel able to enrich the mathematical thinking of their pupils and, as Papert suggested, help them to become mathematicians.

Marilyn Metz was mathematics coordinator in an infant school; she is now Senior Lecturer in Education at Goldsmiths' College, University of London.

4

Towards a problem-solving school

Bob Smith

Part 1 Listening to Katie

> 'It was good fun being able to organise something yourself . . . like normally teachers just organise everything . . . and you know . . . it's good fun for *you* to decide what *you* want to do.'

Katie is in the first year of our 10–13 middle school. When she spoke I knew it was an important moment. I'd never really thought about it quite like that before. Yes – we do organise absolutely everything. We organise all the supporting structures within the school, the whole learning experience right down to a particular time on a particular day. Katie had just been involved in organising an 'It's a Knockout' competition for her year and in deciding on stalls for the school fair. She'd obviously enjoyed herself. The fair was run by the school as a whole, working through the 'school council', composed of representatives from each of the 18 classes. The planning, organisation and running was completely in their hands – it was a problem for the whole school to solve. Here are the minutes that started it all.

School Council Minutes. 23 October
In this week's meeting it was decided that we would have organising groups for the fair.

These are the different groups – one group to sort out the money, one group tidying up, and one group to organise where the stalls will go. There are still some things which you have to discuss with your class and find out their views. These are – do you want a School Fair? Do you want a Rag Day? How much should a Rag Day cost? Are the public allowed in? Should it go on after school?

There were also some decisions made on the actual fair. These are – each class must narrow their ideas for stalls to the three best ideas to be brought to school council next week.

Oct 24: John Harris's class 1H (10-year-olds)
Open area – a double circle of children. Their rep reads out the minutes and they begin to discuss:

> People might have something on after school. – People might pinch money. – I don't think 5p is enough. – It will get dark early in November. – We might get drunks in! – We could have somebody on the door. – Every child could have five tickets to sell. – Let's have a disco until five o'clock. – Who is going to supervise it? – Are we having a snack?

Help! John and I exchange glances – it is amazing how they cut across each other's thoughts – it seems individuals are clearing their own minds of questions and possibilities – they aren't able to store them up and listen to other people's ideas. They aren't aware of the niceties of discussion groups. Very tempting to say 'Can we please stick to one point at a time.' 'Now what about . . .' I think if John hadn't been there I would have said something. Maybe if I hadn't been there John would have said something. It certainly is a support to have two of you there in moments of uncertainty! After twenty minutes Katie ended the discussion with a good deal of frustration showing: 'I think we ought to have a rag day, pay 10p to wear our own clothes, have it in school time, on the same day as the fair and invite the public.' She spoke very precisely, leaning forward in her chair – it was quite stunning – all five variables rolled into one proposition. Would that have emerged if either of us had intervened and imposed our own structures?

The idea of a fair began three years ago at a staff meeting on finance. Derek suggested a fair, not for parents, but just for children. Finance group planned it all and organised the event – children coming in at the next level down. The following year school council was asked to take it on board. Of course there was still a good deal of teacher support and teacher ideas, and in a sense finance group was still in overall control. The money side was completely controlled by teachers and the secretarial staff – there wasn't enough trust to let children have this area on their own. This year was different: I want to give you some further glimpses of what went on.

Oct 30: Minutes of School Council Meeting

There is probably going to be a disco for each year on separate nights and so we have a disco committee. The three ideas originally suggested must now be narrowed down to the two favourite stalls but keep the third one as a reserve. The people organising each of the stalls in your class must fill in the sheets provided at the meeting. If two ideas are the same, the older year gets priority. If the idea is in the same year then the best organised is the one we will use. Pony rides were suggested by 2L and 3W. We think it is a good idea but would like more information.

I was very unhappy about the first of their criteria to choose between identical proposals – the older year gets priority. But I chose to keep quiet. I really hate this kind of solution which is one that has come up on other occasions like planning a rota for the tennis courts etc. The argument is: 'you'll all be third-years sometime', and there is a good deal of social pressure on the other years to say nothing and accept it.

Nov 6 (11 am): School Council Meeting

The pony experts have been invited to attend and they get a thorough examination: Where will you have it? What will you do if it's wet? Won't it make a mess of the field? What about safety? What about insurance? Are your mums coming?

They had not put anything in writing (as requested) so they are despatched to work together and prepare something. A few days later it came back.

school fair

my idea for a stall **sketch**

Our idea for our stall is to bring two reliable ponys to do pony rides, everyone who rides a pony. will wear a hard hat.

We have desided and are allowed to do our pony rides on the bottom of the playing fields near the new surface.

Everyone will be on and go for the same time, and the same distance at one speed.

One person will be leading and one person on each side for safety, and one with the money. 12p

by Sarah Debbie Vicky Della **class** 2L

It is certainly a convincing plan! *Reliable* ponies, everyone *will* wear a hard hat, we are *allowed* to do it (they had seen the head), *same* time and distance at *one* speed; one person each side for safety, one leading. When this came back to stalls committee it was received enthusiastically. However, Robert was not convinced. He was still worried about insurance, about the lack of adults and what happens if it is wet. The committee passed it nevertheless. I was *very* worried about it!

Nov 14: Stalls Committee

Following Kim's plea 'it's best to ask *them* where they want their stalls' the committee had sent out sheets to be filled in with details of where? and what size? With these collected, they felt ready to place the stalls.

Three of them, Steven, Michelle and Ian, work together occasionally remarking, questioning, proposing as they sort the 'where?' sheets. All the gym's over here. – Dining Hall here. – Others here. – Have you got the stairs and foyer? – What's this? – That other's over here? – No that's small hall. I've got the library here. – Hold on there's some more. – These are small hall. – Count them. – Not so sure about small hall and gym. – We've got small hall. – Not so sure . . . – Small hall's got sixteen. – Sure – Better count again. – Yes there's 16! Ian gets hold of them – there can't be. – Gym, gym, gym, these are all gym! – Somebody has mixed them all up! – Right . . . – That's small hall not dining room. – Seven for small hall. – Right . . . write it down. – Dining hall . . .

Nov 19: Stalls Committee

Three classes had put in to sell popcorn: 2H, 2P and 3V. Here the committee is debating 2P's application to sell fizzy drinks *and* popcorn.

Ian: They're not allowed popcorn; 3rd years have got it.
Steven: What if it gets demand for it – what if 3rd year popcorn runs out for some reason?
Ian: Yeah but not two lots.
Steven: Why?
Graham: There's two sweet things isn't there – there's two sweet stalls!
Steven: Yeah.
Ian: But if you think about it, that means that that class could have done something else when . . . when another class is losing money and someone else buying it why not . . .
Graham: If they are, then the popcorn runs out they'll go to you.
Steve: Yeah if yours runs out . . .
Ian: They should just stick to fizzy drinks.
Ainsley: No NO! Why should they?
Ian: Why . . . because it's two stalls in one, if you think about it.
Graham: But what if it runs out!
Ian: We'll make sure it doesn't.
Steven: OK so you buy a load and it doesn't sell – put it that way – because you buy too much then . . .
Ian: Well it's better than two classes wasting it if you think about it.
Graham: Theirs might taste a bit different than yours.
Michelle: Why don't we have a vote?
Ian: Right let's have a vote.

At the end of the meeting they returned to the arguments and there was some shouting and then some pushing and shoving as people got to their feet, and I had to ask for 'order' . . .

Nov 19: Minutes for the Stalls Committee
Today's meeting was a discussion to find out first details of where the stalls will go. None of these are finalised and so more details will follow in the next minutes. One of the problems that arose was popcorn. It appears that 2H have bought their popcorn over the weekend, but 3J do not want competition and third years get priority. After a vote by the stalls committee four wanted 2H to have their stall and four were against. The vote is now going to school council on 20 November.

When the minutes came out 2H were furious. Their teacher came to me to ask if they could have popcorn because they had already bought it and the class was so disappointed. Of course I explained it just wasn't up to me; it was school council's decision. I felt a great temptation to intervene to give my opinion to push things the 'right' way. Perhaps I should have done so – it certainly had caused a lot of aggravation and discontent. (Afterwards many of the stalls committee told me that this was the worst moment in planning the fair – 'it made me angry', 'I was furious', 'I didn't like all the arguments over popcorn'.) It certainly slowed the business down. But looking back now it was a most challenging part of the 'deciding' process. In these discussions children are making people re-think, they are challenging somebody's view, they are questioning, focusing attention to particular points, thinking aloud, sustaining a challenge and justifying their views, reinforcing the ideas of others in the group, convincing each other and

BY Kendra Haigh, Vicky
Helen Fountain, Zoe
1. Soda Stream.
2. Popcorn
3. Cash Box
4. Flavours.
5. Scoop Server.
6. Cups.
7. Soda Stream Bottles.
8. Popcorn Toppings.
TOPPING
Our stall sells Popcorn and
Soda Stream fizzy drinks.
We have a plan of the stall.
Popcorn costs 10p a cup.
Drinks cost 10p a cup as well.
Different toppings are available.

making changes in their stance. This mathematical thinking runs through the whole problem-solving experience.

Nov 20: School Council

I insisted from the start on a controlled and orderly debate (in the last two days there had been a stream of people to see me from 2H, 2D, 3W and I had passed them on to their class reps and to stalls committee) and I explained that I felt I needed to do this because of the controversy surrounding the decision! I believed that there would be too many negative feelings if I let it go its own way. I wonder if I was right? Perhaps I should have had more confidence in school council. Ian presented the argument for *one* stall and included a new persuasive viewpoint:

> Just think about the Houses of Parliament – what if they have said that we hang people – then just when someone is about to be hanged some of them ask if they can change it – there's no going back!

Steven replied and was supported by the 2H rep who had brought a written statement as well:

> About 1 month ago our class decided to have a stall which sold Popcorn and Fizzy Drinks (soda stream). Since then we have made lots of arrangements including Posters and also asking each person in 2H to bring in 15p. Last year 3W did popcorn and it sold out very quickly so it would be a good idea for both classes to sell popcorn.
>
> We have raised money to buy popcorn and also some members of the class are bringing it from home. Both Mrs Hunt and Mrs Carter agree that two stalls is a good idea.

After other speakers a vote was taken. No 2H stall allowed, by 13 votes to 6! How could they do it!

Nov 20: Stalls Committee visit the gym
We want to actually draw a plan now. – What's the measurements of the hall? – Let's look at Julian's maps.

Julian had drawn out each room on A4 graph paper.

– We need people to work out how much space there is. – What's the scale on this Julian? – I just drew it. – What's the use of that!

Unfortunately the dining-hall and gym are being used for a games lesson. Julian tries darting between the badminton players for a bit and I call him back!

– We've got to have the haunted house here (pointing just inside the entrance to the gym). They need to use the green poles. – Tarzan has to be over there with the ropes. – We want penalty shots down there (at the other end). – Basketball needs to be under the net. – Water fights could be here (by the entrance). – Don't be daft . . . everyone will be coming through here! – There are four others to fit in you know. – Do they have to be in the gym? – Not really. – They want them there though. – They could go anywhere really.

This was the strategy that they used in the other rooms, 'the go anywhere' and the 'must go here'. It had taken quite a time to make progress. It was the visit to the gym that had sparked it all off.

Julian: Won't take long to sort it tomorrow.

They were confident and jaunty. The standard 'scale drawing' had not worked out – somebody had said 'we don't need that'. Julian's maps had not been a success but he was to lead them to a new method that afternoon with the chalk.

As I passed through the dining hall at 1.30 the floor was awash with chalk. A dining table had been turned over and used as a template.

Julian: We left three tiles between each table so people can get through.
Barry: The food and drink stall said they wanted to be round the pillar.

I was given a guided tour of the marks. The whole 'plan' had been drawn life-size!

Nov 20 (2 more days to go)
Martin (deputy head) passed me in the main corridor. 'The teachers think we should put it off till next week,' he said. 'It doesn't seem to have been planned in time. Nobody seems to know what's happening.' I garbled something about it seems better than last year but I really felt quite hurt and disappointed. I talked to some teachers about it and began to understand. No wonder they were worried: they knew *nothing* about *anything*! I began to feel a whole lot better and in fact by the time stalls committee began at 10 am I was feeling quite heady – school council were really running the show this time! As I entered the meeting room I was met with cries of 'the teachers want us to put it off till next week!'

The stalls committee *still* felt they were nearly sorted and that at school council this afternoon they would get their plans 'passed'. By 3.30 all the classes should know exactly what they're doing and where they're going.

I insisted that they go to the staff meeting at lunchtime and that keeping staff in touch was something they needed to work at. Ian, Graham, Steven and Ainsley volunteered to attend.

– We were going anyway to see about pony rides and water games.

By lunchtime they had produced a complete list of stalls each with a number and three plans of the rooms indicating their positions.

Teachers' Meeting 12.20 pm

Steven introduced the plans and asked staff to look at the papers which Graham would pass round. Graham got out a magnificient looking attaché case, placed it calmly on the table top, opened it and passed around the four-page document. It looked amazingly efficient! The staff were thunder-struck and complimented school council on its organisation.

Ian then introduced the worries they had about pony rides. The teachers asked various things: Where are you having it? What if it rains? What about controlling the queue? Could you not charge more? Are you roping off the area? Have you got adults supervising? Are the animals placid?

This last one received a venomous reply: 'No they're bucking broncos!'

Underlying this was a pride that had been hurt – don't they realise we have thought through these things? – Don't they realise we've given this issue real care? If you look back at the questioning at school council it is almost identical and of course they spent much longer on it.

I have thought a lot about that meeting and that remark since and it seems to serve as a marker to show how far we *have* moved towards that 'problem-solving school'.

Nov 21 (9.30 am): The Stalls Committee: last minute jobs

A timetable for the day is completed by break and a 'message to stallholders' by the end of school. A leaflet for parents has been finished by 2 pm with a front cover design and this letter:

> Dear Parents,
> We are holding a Christmas Fair on Friday 23rd November at Shawfield School.
>
> Everything on the stalls will cost from 5p to 30p.
>
> Please could you provide your children with money, preferably in five pence pieces, but if these are not available, there will be a change machine.
>
> We are holding the Christmas Fair to raise money for school funds and the mini-bus. The money that is left we will use to buy things for school.
>
> We would be very grateful if your children would bring in bottles of drink, like orange or coke, for the drink stalls for they do not have enough.
>
> On Friday morning your children may come in any clothes they like but they do have to pay 10p. That money will also go into school funds.
>
> Thank you for your cooperation on behalf of Shawfield School.
>
> Yours sincerely,
>
> Kim Howarth
> Sarah Mills
>
> From School Council

It seemed quite ordinary at the time – but looking back now it is so fresh and succinct, quite unlike the turgid, formal letters schools generally send out. This seems closer to what is really required in a communication of this sort.

The fair itself went very well. Not everything went according to plan – the popcorn stall ran out after 20 minutes and there were terrible recriminations for weeks afterwards! However, nothing went seriously wrong. It had served as a focus for what *is* possible in the school. Yes you *can* take control of your own ideas, thoughts and decisions, and yes you *can* put them into practice.

Three years ago the stimulus came from teachers. Now it is beginning to be the problem-solving atmosphere within the school that is generating problems and it is this naturalness which is the hallmark of a problem-solving school.

Katie's message is important. It should be pinned to every staff room notice-board.

Part 2 Being Challenged by Tom

'I think it will turn out a bit funny.'
'Why do you say that?'
'Well average arms, average head and things.'

Tom and his class of 10-year-olds had been set the problem of designing and making a 'machine' to measure parts of the body so that together they could produce a model of the average child. At the end of one of the early discussions on 'What to do' Tom had suddenly turned to me and offered this 'worry'. He seemed to have a vision of some alien being that would never be representative of the class. He wasn't the only person who was worried, but although the class was very hesitant about how they would tackle things, at least they could make a start on designing a machine.

First sketches and then mock-ups using cardboard were tried out in the classroom and then taken down to the workshop where Derek Thomason helped each group with choice of material and assembly techniques. Katie and Susan had designed a machine to measure 'all parts of the body'. The actual machine proved to be based on a 2-metre stick with sliding markers and was eventually used only for height. Nicola and Kath, on the other hand, had concentrated purely on a machine 'to measure round the head'.

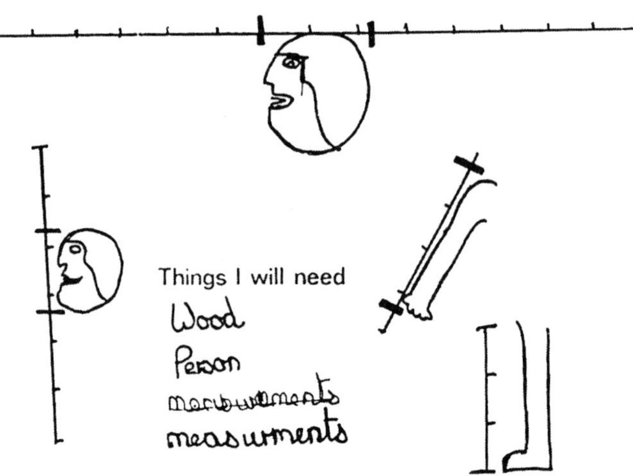

Oct 23: John Harris's class 1H
Three half-days of the constructional work are over. This was to be evaluation/discussion. Katie and Susan began by demonstrating their machine and John and I then asked the class to comment (see photographs). In particular we asked: what do you like about it? What don't you like about it? Have you any suggestions for making it better? Are there any faults?

This thing wobbles too much... you hold it and I'll read off the height... are you sure it's straight?...

... up a bit on your side... just a touch more...

... steady!... must concentrate on this... got it!

The group liked the machine – in particular they thought it would be excellent to measure height. Tom didn't agree: he thought there was something wrong.

'It won't give the right height.'
'Why not?' demanded Susan.
'It starts at 5.'
'So . . .'
'So it'll be 5 out!'

Tom showed us where the stick fitted into the hole. Yes it did start at 5! The rest of the class murmured agreement. The makers were furious. Katie grabbed the stick away.

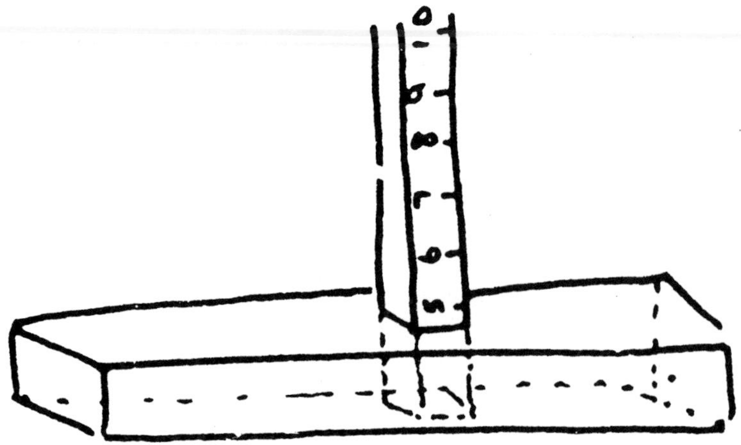

'Of course it will be right', she said. 'Look I'll take it out and measure you without the base – it'll be the same!' She did just that and the group could see the bottom of the stick was at zero.

'Yes but when the stick is in here . . .' and Tom grasped it back and put it in the hole . . . 'look it's at 5'.

'Yes but it's the same stick in or out!'

Tom was worried enough to sit down and the designers' reputations were intact. During all these 'challenges' John and I tried to remain quite impassive. Appealing looks were coming our way and we were being implored to take sides and 'umpire'. But there was such an intensity and vitality about the discussion that it proved easy to resist! Nicola then demonstrated her head machine on me. 'How big is it?' someone shouted. Actually that provoked some thought in the designers. 'We've left the other bit upstairs'. (The other bit turned out to be a 50 cm stick of wood marked out every centimetre.)

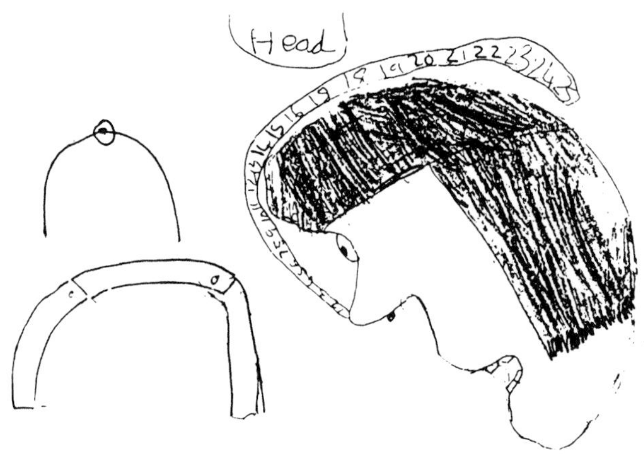

'I think it might slip,' said Tom. I asked him to try it out and he seemed quite satisfied with it. 'Mr. T. helped me tighten the screw up', offered Nicola. The machine was being passed round the circle and various comments were offered.

– 'I don't like the end bits!' (The ends were indeed a trifle odd.) – They don't meet when they come together. – The end bits are all crooked. – They're not at the same angle. – It would be better without them on.

In the rest of this short session two more machines were discussed. The last produced more comments: – Where do the measurements start? – They should stand on the floor. – You could put your feet either side. – Why is it in inches? (My ruler was in inches, was the reply.) – The plank keeps coming off the ground. – The scale starts at the bottom not at the start. – The shape of the slider is too difficult to get people under. (I designed it to keep the head in place and stop it wobbling.) – Put a new scale on. – Saw it in half. – It's too big.

Days later John and I suddenly realised that the evaluation had only gone halfway – no one had actually changed their machine at all as a result of the comments! Too late! They were past the point where we could pull them back.

Fortunately, Janet Clay's and Tony Rawlings' classes were slightly 'behind' and had only just begun their evaluation discussions. Janet was very disappointed at the destructive criticism of the saw-it-in-half type. I didn't feel this was *too* negative but certainly the atmosphere was not as supportive as with 1H. (I think this was to do with numbers really. Janet and Tony had their discussion with both classes together – fifty children.)

It was also taking too long – so we decided on a 'circus'. The machines were spread round the room and children encouraged to try out the machines and write a report on what they thought about them in answer to four questions. 1. Things I like. 2. Things I don't like. 3. How accurate is it? 4. What changes should be made? The comments on Zaffar's machine were rather critical:

Jane: It's not very accurate at all because the moving part wobbles so it could be in 3 numbers.

Andrea: When it gets to 40 it will not slide, it should be waxed. It is ½ cm off.

Mark: It could be changed by taking off one of those pieces of wood at the end because you can't see the number 1.

Claire: I think it is very accurate indeed in all ways except that it should start at one and it starts at 3.

Darren: After 40 it does not slide – but it's easy at the bottom – there is a ½ cm space. It is not accurate at beginning or at end because the number starts about 1 cm up.

The number-line on this machine was severely criticised. 'How can we measure anything with this?' was one comment.

Another machine though generally warmly welcomed, received these comments: – It is 9/10 accurate because it is measuring tape that is stuck on. It is not 10/10 because the tape is not straight. – It is accurate but he hasn't put the numbers on the centimetres and you have to count them and it takes quite long.

Many of the 'How accurate is it?' comments centred around what numbers should be at the start. Nicola, for instance:

I do not think it is accorate the thing at the biging should realy be nour nomber one

This is were it should be

1 2 3 4 5 6 7 8

Many of the evaluators argued that machines which began at '1' were correct and those which began at '0' (like this machine) were wrong. Another central problem was the width of the slider which often extended past zero. In Claire's report both these issues came together.

> If you put the block that moves next to the block that doesn't move you will see that it is on two and it should be on 1 because it is adding a centimetre on when you measure something.

All the reports were given to the designers to read and of course they caused a good deal of controversy – in particular there was much checking of rulers and metre sticks! Each designer then wrote out a list of improvements they would like to make and took this back down to the workshop. Nina wrote:

> I have to make the arms of my instrument longer and to make sure that they don't wobble and lose measurement of the person. I have to make the arms longer so that they'll get round at least half way on the waist or the head etc. . . . Also I've got to put a stopper at the end of my instrument.

Of course if the reports are too damning then it can be very destructive. One designer wrote:

Chnges

1. make it stable with 2 piece of wood
2. Mark of cms correctly
3. ~~Remake it.~~
~~4. First destroy then~~ find other design

That made me feel very guilty and I spent a long time talking with him. He crossed out 3 and 4 but in the end we agreed on 3 – using many of the bits of the old machine.

Oct 30: 2.20 – 2.50 pm
John: 'Now you've made your machines what are you going to do next?' There is a general discussion for five minutes and then John asks them to split up into groups and work something out. They are to report back in fifteen minutes.

3.00 – 3.20
Susan is the first to volunteer her group's idea: 'We're going to look at the labels on everyone's jumpers.' (General giggles and people begin to inspect their friends' necks.) 'You see, Mothercare and Marks and Spencers have age or size on them.'

There were some immediate objections: – My jumper is too big for me – you won't get it right. – My Mum made my jumper. – You could use the jumper to measure.

Then Sally reported: 'You find a few of the shortest and a few of the tallest . . . line them up and see who is the average . . . then do the same with heads to see who has the average head and so on . . .'

More objections: – That would take too long. – They might not want to be measured. – One person couldn't do it.

Another member of Sally's group went on, 'Well you could get two big, two small and two average and measure all the parts . . . that would make it easy.'

Nicholas's group said they wanted to measure all the class, add it all up and divide by the number of people. They wanted the big machines to measure height and the small ones to measure hands and things. Again there were some immediate responses: – Everyone will want to measure – There aren't enough machines, they would always be in use. – It will take a long time. – You could lend machines.

Sam began his report by saying: 'Don't blame me because it's Lisa's idea. Get all the very small and all the very tall – make a graph – see what the difference is.' And another group member added: 'See if people with long legs have long feet.'

John summed up: 'We're not ready to start yet so we'll continue these discussions tomorrow.'

Oct 31: 10.05 – 10.45
John: 'How can we sort the problem out?' There are eight offerings and as each is made John writes it down. At various stages he reads back the list acting as a kind of 'reporter' for the class.

1 'The people who made them use them . . . Katie measures height, Lee arms and legs, Simon hands and feet, Nicola's head and the rest for small things.'
2 'Make a list.'
3 'Get in a group and measure one thing for all.'
4 'Make a list of names and pick them out of a hat.'
5 'The person who made it joins with someone who didn't.'
6 'Each group uses different machines.'

7 'Write them all down and make a graph.'
8 'Draw up a chart like this' (Abda holds up rough book).

	parts of body
names	

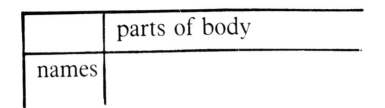

They then had a vote to decide between 1 and 5 and by 14 votes they go for 5.

John again: 'How are we going to choose the people?' – Out of a hat. – Sometimes two people made a machine and only one can do it. – It won't be fair. – You could have two hats. – You don't need two hats! (This was Tom.) – Yes you do ! (Shouts from group.) – 'You don't!' and Tom begins to argue for just one hat. 'All the people who made it go in one hat and the ones who didn't make it'. . . pause – it had just hit him that you did need two hats! He carried on . . . 'in one hat'. – 'In another hat you mean!'

There was a general chuckling and even Tom managed a wry laugh.

'You could make a mark M for maker and N for non-maker in one hat.' Tom had 'regrouped' successfully! 'You could write the maker's name on yellow paper and non-makers on white and fold them twice.' And that is what they did.

Nov 4: 1.30 – 2.30 Report back

Sammy and Katie had used Karen's machine on necks and had some difficulty deciding how best to use the machine. They had collected two sets of data which they called AC and FB.

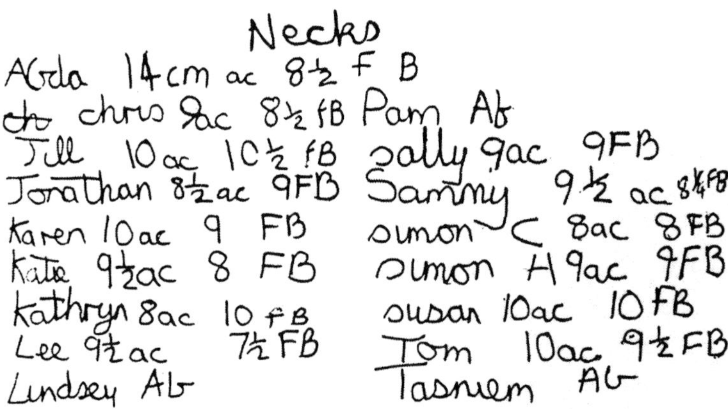

Necks
Abda 14cm ac 8½ F B
chris 9ac 8½ FB Pam Ab
Jill 10ac 10½ FB sally 9ac 9FB
Jonathan 8½ac 9FB Sammy 9½ ac 8¼FB
Karen 10ac 9 FB simon C 8ac 8FB
Katie 9½ac 8 FB simon H 9ac 9FB
Kathryn 8ac 10 FB susan 10ac 10FB
Lee 9½ac 7½FB Tom 10ac 9½FB
Lindsey Ab Tasniem Ab

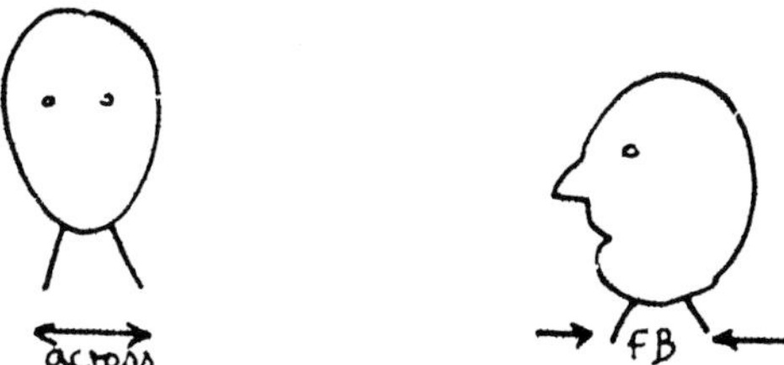

Lisa and Pam had been using Katie's height machine. Lisa reported that about 33 cm seemed to be common. No one challenged this at all.

I asked what the smallest and tallest measurements were so that it would dawn on her that something was a bit wrong. I also expected someone in the class to challenge it!

'The smallest is 23 cm and the tallest 45 cm.' Still no one said anything. I asked Lisa to measure somebody for us to show how she'd done it. Simon was chosen and Lisa measured him. '28 cm . . . 1 metre and 28 cm.'

'I'm not just that big,' said Simon using his hands to indicate the 28 cm distance. There were laughs all round.

Nicola and Tom had measured arms. Tom said that they had problems with the machine because it was very stiff and he demonstrated the problem.

The other problem had been where to measure it from: 'You can't keep it the same for everyone.'

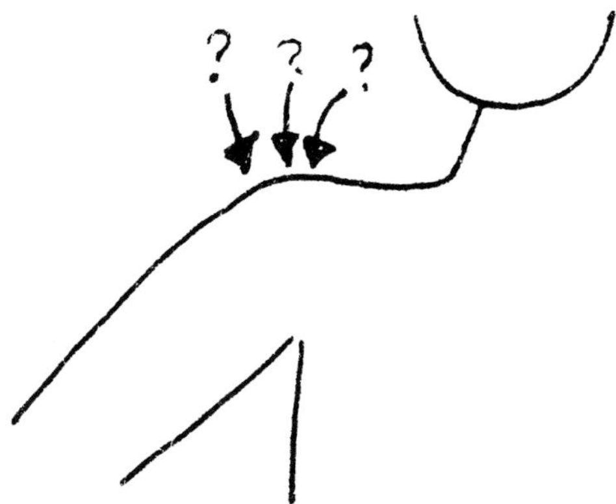

They had decided to measure it from the neck when the arm was held up. It was easier to be more 'accurate' then. Tom showed how you could put the measuring device right up to the neck. Then he showed the problems of deciding where the top of the arm was when it joined the shoulder.

Nov 25
John warned me that the class didn't seem in a good working mood. I tried to start the discussion by asking various people what parts of the body they had measured and how they were going to work out the average. They seemed to have forgotten everything! (In fact they had not followed up the project for 2½ weeks, which included one French week and one week's holiday, so on reflection it isn't surprising that this discussion went badly.)

I ditched the whole group idea and asked them to go back to their measuring groups, find out what they had done and try to work out their own ideas for the 'average'. This was pretty chaotic. Lots of people had to borrow my photocopies of their results because they had lost or not brought their rough books. Some couldn't even remember what they had done at all. Some hadn't been involved in measuring and I just tagged them on to the group of their choice.

The next fifteen minutes were terrible: everyone seemed to want either help or advice and most were confused and unsure. Then suddenly the atmosphere became much more purposeful.

Susan was working on the height data and soon produced this:

Hieght machine

The hieghest person is Sam = 1m 54cm

The lowest person is Nicky G = 1m 26cm

We found the hieghest and lowest and half them example

Nicky = 1m 26cm = 63 cm
Sam = 1m 54cm = 77 cm

63 cm
77cm
1m 40cm

Tom is the nearest to 1m 40cm

Katie and Sammy were looking at hands and feet like this:

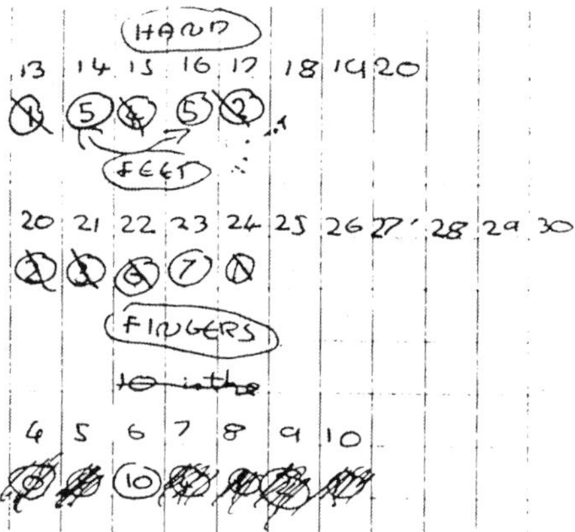

Tom was working on arms:

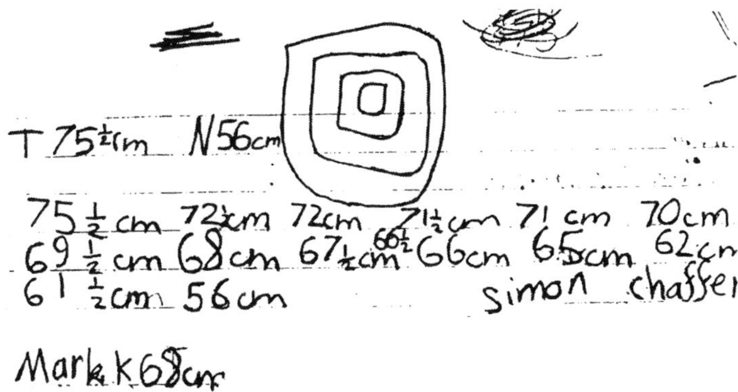

Having located T the tallest and N the smallest he had stopped. I came over and asked him how he was going to find the average. 'It's sharing,' he said. '75½ shared by 56.'

Tom wrote down this sum

$$\begin{array}{r} 56 \\ \overline{)\,75} \end{array}$$

– It's going to be thousands.– How many times will 56 go into 75? – Just once. – And immediately he scribbled all over. 'That's rubbish,' he said, and then after a pause, 'I'll find the middle instead.'

He came back to me with his rough book later – It's 67½. – Why's that? He began to count eight before 67½ and then 6 after – No, it's 68.

Pam was working on hand/feet measurement with Jill (where was Lisa?). She had written out her own version in four colours. It looked especially good. Of course this had taken about ¾ hr and it was only towards the end that she began to think about averages. I asked her about her hands and fingers 'workings out'.

Pam explained that she was looking for the one 'with the most'. For fingers she chose 6. For feet she chose 23. 'I'm not sure which one to choose for hands though.' 14 and 16 both had five people. I agreed that *was* a problem. 'What do you think?' – 14 – Why 14? – I think it's better to choose the lower one.

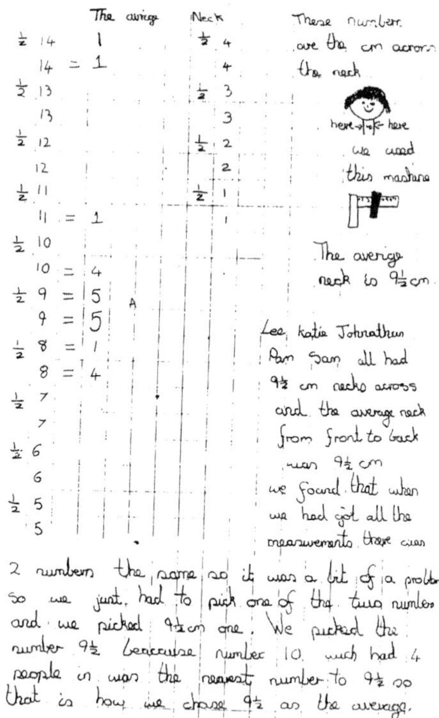

What next? The situation seemed ripe for a sharing of awareness of 'average'. We had some interesting and different ideas which could well be argued out. In particular John and I picked out four methods.

Katie and Sam (like Pam): Find out how many people have got each measurement. Work out the most. This is the average.

Susan: Find the largest and the smallest measurement. Take half the largest and half the smallest. Now add these together. This is the average.

Simon/Jonathan: Add up all the measurements. Divide this by the number of measurements taken. This is the average.

Tom: Put all the measurements in order smallest to largest. Pick the one exactly in the middle. This is the average.

Nov 26

Circle of children each having a summary of the four methods and a photocopy of Pam's data on hands, feet and fingers.

'Which method is best?' For the next hour-and-a-quarter there was a studious/frantic period of calculation and decision-making. Jonathan had

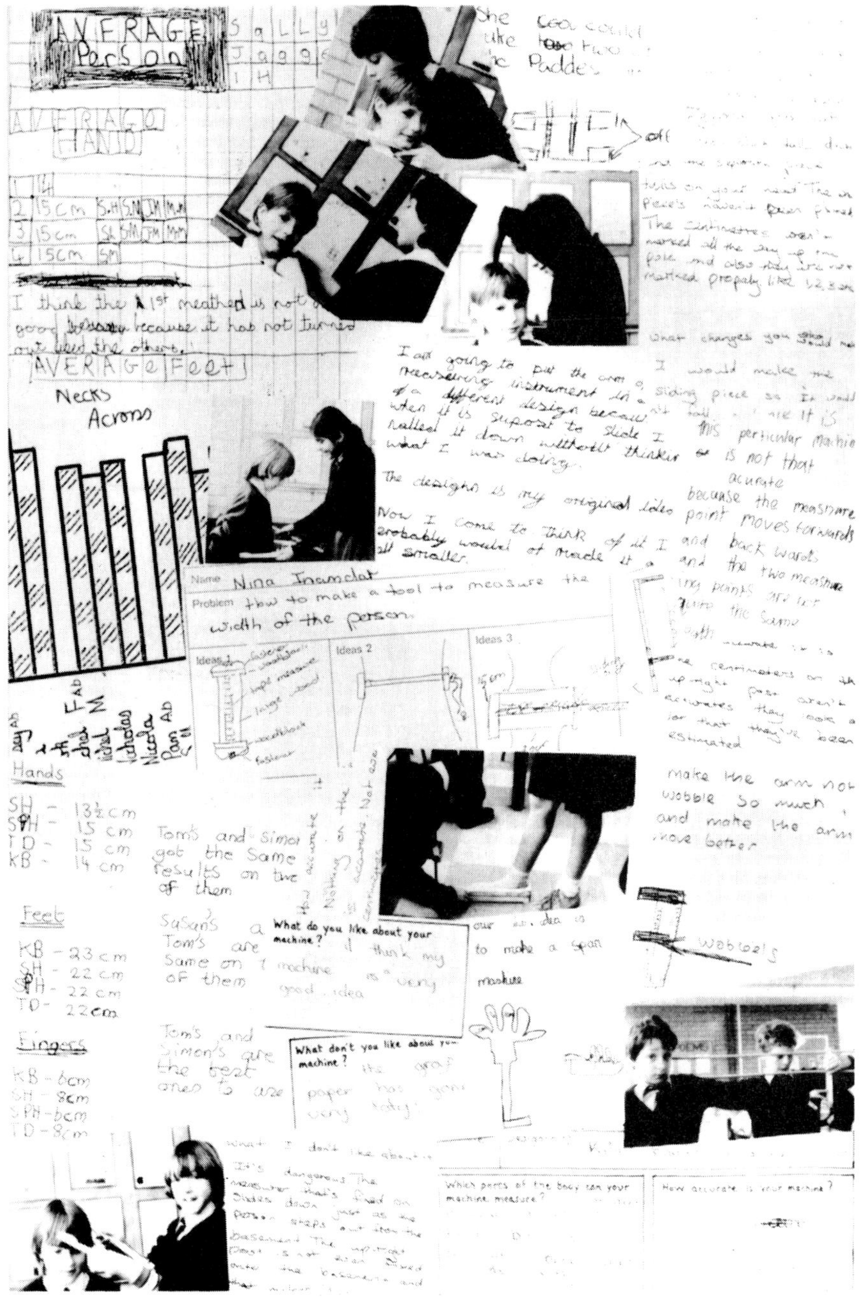
AVERAGE Person
AVERAGE HAND
1 14
2 15cm
3 15cm
4 15cm
I think the 1st meathed is not good because it has not turned out like the others.
AVERAGE Feet
Necks Across
Hands
SH - 13½cm
SPH - 15 cm
TD - 15 cm
KB - 14 cm
Feet
KB - 23cm
SH - 22cm
SPH - 22cm
TD - 22cm
Fingers
KB - 6cm
SH - 8cm
SPH - 6cm
TD - 8cm
Tom's and Simon got the Same results on the of them
Tom's and Simon's are the best ones to use
The centimetres aren't marked all the way up the pole
What changes you would make
I would make the sliding piece so it would not fall
this perticular machine is not that acurate because the measure point moves forwards and back words
make the arm not wobble so much and make the arm move better
Name Nina
Problem How to make a tool to measure the width of the person.
Ideas 2
Ideas 3
What do you like about your machine? I think my machine is a very good idea
What don't you like about your machine?
Wobbels
Which parts of the body can your machine measure?
How accurate is your machine?

recorded all his results on one page of his rough book. I believe this is the nearest thing to a work of art I can remember. The page is bursting with energy – all his strategies, concerns, mistakes, inventions.

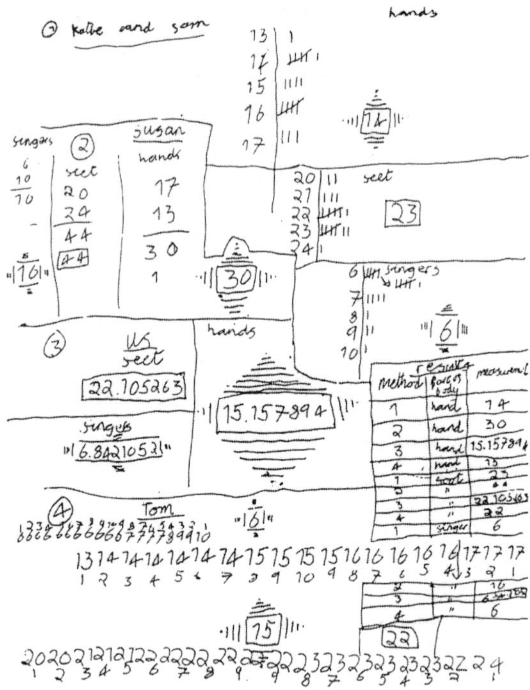

Everyone seemed 'tuned-in' and there was a buzz of discussion, argument and the sharing of information. Some groups went off to cut up some sugar paper to begin a model, but by the next week Christmas activities seemed to take over and a final class model was never produced.

Tom's initial conjecture 'I think it will turn out funny' had been the start of a series of challenges and questioning that had generated many more new 'problems' along the way. In discussion he had shared the awareness inside him and offered many possibilities and insights. The shared experience of the whole class had given each child the possibility of real 'know how'.

There were no worksheets.

There were no 'lessons'.

Bob Smith is the headteacher of a Yorkshire middle school.

5

A problem-solving approach to diagnostic assessment

Christine Shiu

Introduction

When I began to write this article, I envisaged a simple description of some procedures I carried out in my own classroom, which I found helpful to my teaching, and which others might find similarly useful. As I told the story of how I attempted to adapt researched techniques in diagnostic assessment to give me information about my own pupils' understanding of particular mathematical concepts, I began to see an analogy between their attempts to make sense of mathematics and my attempts to make sense of their needs. Thus I came to write up my investigation of their understanding in a format which I hope will reveal that similarity. As so often in the analogous mathematical problem solving, the unforeseen outcomes were frequently as absorbing as the hoped-for ones, and became the basis of the inevitable question 'What next?'

The context

In the autumn of 1982 I was faced with 140 'new' fourth formers, one third of my 14–18 Upper School's new intake. I started the year's mathematics with some problem solving around the theme of sequences. For some, it was quite a struggle to relate a geometric 'growing pattern' to a number sequence and predict the next term, though many could do this and were able both to graph their results and give verbal descriptions of how to obtain subsequent terms. Some could give general formulae for linear sequences, and spot the more obvious non-linear relationships such as squares or powers of two. A few were able to interpret and use a method for deriving a quadratic formula from number sequences with constant second difference, and even extend this to sequences of higher powers. Clearly there was quite a wide spread of attainment in mathematical terms!

A question

Although the work on sequences had given me much information about individuals' mathematical understanding and technical competence, there remained many questions about their understanding of the number system in general. Most had stuck almost exclusively to integer sequences, which had given me insight into their familiarity with square numbers, multiples, powers, etc. However, what was their appreciation of the decimal number system?

The findings of the mathematics team working on the project 'Concepts in Secondary Mathematics and Science' (CSMS) had been published the previous year (Hart, 1981). Reading these told me that it was quite likely that some of my students would have difficulty with place value, at least when dealing with digits to the right of the decimal point, whilst others might find their ability to approximate impaired by misapprehensions about the effects of multiplication and division.

Investigating

In order to probe these possibilities, I asked them to attempt a written test which used items suggested by Malcolm Swan (1982), based on the CSMS findings. I explained that their responses would help me plan the next phase of work which I offered them.

Unexpected results

I was not surprised to discover that sizeable groups of pupils had one or both of the two difficulties outlined, and I was able to use some of the activities suggested by Swan to work on these. There was, however, one item which left me unsure as to how to proceed. This was:

A story which goes with this sum is:

5 + 2 = 7	John had 5 records. His father gave him 2 more for his birthday. So now he has 7 records altogether.

Write your own story to go with this sum:
4.6 + 5.3 = 9.9

Although I was intrigued by the variety of responses the pupils gave to this, I was at a loss as to what use to make of them, and at this stage simply concentrated on using the information from the rest of the test.

Trying another example

The school worked on a two-year cycle so that pupils should have as far as possible the same set of teachers from 14 to 16. I was therefore faced with the equivalent situation two years later. I again administered the test, with the same purpose and offering the same explanation to the pupils, but this time I decided to analyse the responses to this item, and see if I could use what I found out in setting up my teaching. Sure enough, as with the previous group, most pupils had tried conscientiously to give an appropriate response, but had a variety of interpretations of what an appropriate response might be.

Results

It was perhaps to be expected that some pupils would try to use the offered story for whole number addition as a direct model, so I was not surprised when Richard wrote:

> *Richard's story*: John had 4.4 records for his birthday. His father gave him 5.3 more so now he has 9.9 records altogether.

Other pupils had seriously tried to find another context, though sometimes the measured object should have been the object of discrete counting, for example:

> *Stella's story*: Robert had a jigsaw. He had fitted together 4.6 pieces, then Stella fitted together 5.3 pieces so altogether 9.9 pieces were fitted together.

I recall that most of Stella's stories at that time involved a character called Robert. Gary, on the other hand, favoured a different variety of fantasy.

> *Gary's story*: Enoch had 4.6 dogs because one didn't have a tail. For Christmas his dad gave him 5.3 dogs because one dog had a tail so now he has 9.9 dogs.

Most pupils realised that such stories were properly integer stories, and that their efforts needed to take account of the fact that the quantities in the sum were represented by decimal numbers. For some, this seemed to imply that the context had to be a mathematics lesson. Hence:

> *David's story*: Simon typed in his calculator 4.6 then pressed the plus sign. Then typed in 5.3. He pressed the equals button and got the answer 9.9.

Others showed awareness of the meaning of the figure to the right of the decimal point as tenths, and constructed stories to demonstrate this, as in:

> *Ross's story*: John had 4 cakes, and 6/10 of another one. His friend gave him 5 cakes and 3 tenths of another one. When he put them together, he had 9 cakes and 9/10 of another one.

Others tried to use the same context but treated the decimal as a small but undefined part of a whole, thus:

> *Denise's story*: Jane ate 4 pieces of cake plus 6 remaining crumbs. She later came back and ate a further 5 pieces of cake and three remaining crumbs. Jane has now ate 9 pieces of cake and 9 remaining crumbs (9.9).

By the time I came to Lisa's paper I became convinced that at least one of our feeder schools must have a policy of introducing the idea of decimals through the cutting up of cakes!

> *Lisa's story*: Jack had 4.6 of the cake and Joe had 5.3. They put it together to make 9.9 of a cake.

It was not uncommon to find stories which used sums of money as the quantities involved. These were usually accurate and plausible, though a slight measure of dissatisfaction might have indicated awareness of a mismatch, since the notation was often amended to:

$$4.60 + 5.30 = 9.90$$

as in:

Debbie's story: Simon had £4.60 and his mum gave him £5.30 so he now has got £9.90.

In Ruth's story the dissatisfaction became more overt, when she offered an alternative story which did not need a change in notation for the numbers. However, her new story did not provide a context for addition.

Ruth's story: Joanne had to go shopping for her mum so her mum gave her £4.60, when her dad heard she was going shopping he gave her £5.30 to get something so she set off with £9.90 and went shopping. (This story could also be told as her dad wanted to get a piece of wood 4.6 by 5.3 therefore making its area 9.9.)

One story, which made very ingenious use of the money context by introducing the notion of rate of profit, fell down because again the use of the operation of addition was very contrived.

Robin's story: John had a paper round and each paper he delivered he got 4.6 pence profit and then he decided to get a morning round so he gets 5.3 pence for each paper he delivers in the morning so if you add them together each paper he delivers morning and night he gets 9.9 pence profit.

Some recognised that length was a context in which decimals were used to represent quantities which are continuously variable. However, the 'parts' offered were not always tenths.

Marie's story: Kerry was 4 ft 6 inches in height and Jane was 5 ft 3 inches in height. When their height was added up it equalled 9 ft 9 inches.

$4.6 + 5.3 = 9.9$

Others used lengths appropriately as the quantities, but the justification for adding as an operation modelling a situation was sometimes suspect, as in:

Daniel's story: Tim had a ruler which was 4.6 cm long and glued it to his friends who's ruler was 5.3 cm and it made the ruler 9.9 cm long.

and even more so in:

Vikki's story: Sally had a piece of string which was 4.6 cm long, she found a bit 5.3 cm long and tied both bits together so her string was 9.9 cm long.

Other measures which were recognised as lending themselves to decimal representation included weight and volume. In both of these, aggregation by addition seemed more easily plausible than was the case with length. Examples include:

Gary's story: John had 4.6 oz sherbet, his father gave him 5.3 oz of sherbet so now he has 9.9 oz of sherbet.

Mark's story: Fred's dad had 4.6 litres of petrol and Fred gave his dad 5.3 litres of petrol leaving Fred's dad with 9.9 litres of petrol.

A more unusual context for the use of decimals was provided by Joanne, though it appeared to be a familiar one within her own experience.

Joanne's story: Jane got 4.6 marks for her dancing exam and she got 5.3 so altogether she got 9.9.

Classification of results

I was now sufficiently intrigued to see if I could use this analysis suggested by the responses to classify all the pupil stories. As I read through them they seemed all to fall into one of the following categories.

1 No response.

2 Attempting to model discrete objects such as records by decimals.

Pupils in these categories appeared not to have perceived any useful reason for the extension of the number system from whole numbers to include decimals. Richard, the first pupil quoted, seemed to perceive mathematical tasks as fairly arbitrary and mysterious, and often seemed to indicate that his only hope of success lay in following a model answer or pattern.

3 Using objects which can be subdivided, such as chocolate bars or cake, to illustrate the number sentence.

Pupils who gave such responses were demonstrating awareness that the numerals to the right of the decimal point were indeed 'parts of a whole', but appeared to think that an invented model was needed to demonstrate these parts, rather than seeing decimals as a useful means of expressing quantities which arose of necessity. Their responses also raised the question of to what extent was the model chosen a reflection or reconstruction of the model used by a previous teacher to introduce the topic of decimals.

4 Describing the carrying out of the calculation as an exercise in a mathematics classroom.

These responses could be taken to mean that decimals were perceived as a completely arbitrary invention. However, such responses were often given by children who were high achievers mathematically. Perhaps such pupils were indicating that they were quite happy to see the real number system as sufficiently interesting as an object of study in its own right, and were not concerned about whether decimals could be used to model aspects of the physical or social world.

5 Stories which accurately interpreted the sentence in terms of money.

Category 5 responses were almost always completely acceptable in terms of the quantity measured and of the operation of addition. A very few pupils made the mistake of interpreting £4.6 as four pounds and six pence though most realised that it would in fact be four pounds and sixty pence. However, it has often been noted that even if children can handle money with confidence and competence, that does not necessarily transfer to equivalent but decontextualised problems. Money responses therefore left me with some unresolved questions.

- Were these pupils aware that they had greater confidence in the money context and were thus making a conscious choice?
- Did they therefore feel they had taken the 'easy way out' by giving a money story (see, for example, Ruth's response)?
- Were they aware of making the slight transformation in notation needed to make a money story 'look right'?

6 Stories which involved continuous quantities which are appropriately measured using decimal units, but where combination by addition is not appropriate.

7 Stories which involved continuous quantities which are appropriately measured using decimal units, and involving an operation appropriately modelled by addition.

I found responses in these last two categories the most encouraging. I believe that children making them were building bridges between their practical experience and their mathematics learning. However, even within these responses there were more and less successful stories.

Applying the conclusions

Having analysed these responses I decided to use them as a starting point for further work on decimals. The 140 pupils were divided into six mixed-ability teaching groups for mathematics. I met each group at a different point during the same week in order to set up the beginning of their work on the new theme.

As in this article, I collected a set of 'stories' illustrating the various kinds of response, and read them out (anonymously) to the class. In encouraging them to analyse which were the 'best' stories and why, I was hoping that they would begin to recognise the relevance of looking for links between purely numerical calculations and the kind of situations they might model. The 'stories' engaged their interest, and they seemed to recognise when stories did not fit the calculation, even if their explanations of why that was the case were less than articulate. In subsequent discussion, most revealed the possession of an implicit criterion for classifying 'good' stories which eventually one or two were able to link explicitly to the notion of measurement. Taking my cue from this I gave a follow-up task which was to make a note of any occasion when they measured a quantity involving decimals 'any time in the next week'.

One week later they reported that they had not needed to do any measuring in mathematics lessons (though for many of them the work I had given involved decimal quantities, often with the data obtained from other people's measurements). On the other hand, they had measured a variety of quantities in science lessons, in design lessons (whether working in fabric, metal, plastic, or wood), in home economics, in control technology and in a variety of situations at home. Perhaps this was the beginning of bridge building for more of the pupils.

However, what was possibly more important for my teaching in the long run was the extra light shed on the beliefs of individual pupils about the nature of decimal numbers, and indeed about mathematics in general, implicit in their responses to the tasks described. All teachers continually collect and mentally store information about their current pupils and this is often done unconsciously. This information affects teachers' judgements and decisions for those pupils and thus helps to determine the future mathematical experience and instruction provided. If all the information remains implicit, then the reasons for the decisions made cannot be recognised and judged by the teacher.

Although it is clearly impossible for a teacher to reflect on all the available information in the classroom, still less to record it, it was my experience that the specific information about pupils provided by their decimal stories was a useful check on the mental pictures I was building up of them. In some cases, the story they offered was not a surprise and confirmed overall impressions I already had, but in others I was startled by a hitherto unrevealed mismatch between my ideas and theirs, or delighted by a demonstration of insight I had not expected. These surprises alerted me to the opportunity for giving appropriate help or challenge in this topic area, and to look out for further information about these particular pupils.

Sharing the classification

Some time later I described my categorisation to a colleague, who agreed to try it out and see if she could apply it. She reported that she did not always find the categories well defined, with some blurring of boundaries between, for example, categories 2 and 3 where

Jane's story: Betty had 4.6 bars of chocolate. Her friend came round to see her and gave her 5.3 bars of chocolate, so she ended up with 9.9 bars of chocolate.

seemed to fall into category 3, whereas

Sally's story: Kate has 4.6 of a chocolate bar, Joanne has 5.3 of a chocolate bar so altogether they have 9.9.

though similar, was more properly classified as belonging to category 2.

Other categories might easily be subdivided: for example, the stories in category 7 could be divided into more and less plausible ones. However, accepting that seven categories were a reasonable amount to handle, she accepted the task as given and was able to classify almost all of the two batches of scripts. There was only one response in each year which could not be allocated to any of the categories. In both cases the decimal point was ignored and a story given to fit the integer calculation 46 + 53 = 99.

The complete classification is given in the table below:

Category	*1982 stories*	*1984 stories*
1 (blank)	18	15
2 (discrete)	45	29
3 (divisible)	18	15
4 ('maths')	11	18
5 (money)	16	18
6 (decimal quantities)	2	5
7 (addition modelled)	32	34
X (decimal point ignored)	1	1
Total	143	135

The classification revisited

In addition to applying the categorisation to all of the scripts, my colleague made two observations that I had missed. The first was that my use of the word 'story' seemed in some cases to have affected the form of response which I got, as in:

Kevin's story: There was a lonely piece of cake, it was only 4.6 big. Then a nice old man came and gave it a little bit more and that was 5.3 big. That equalled 9.9. The little piece of cake was very happy.

The second observation was that a few pupils seemed to be slightly uncomfortable with an answer of 9.9 and coped with this by 'rounding up' to 10, as in:

Mick's story: Tom ate 4.6 of the pie and his brother Alex ate 5.3 of the pie. That made 9.9. Where did the other 0.1 go? The cat ate it.

These comments prompted me to re-examine the task I had offered to see what other hidden messages it carried. I immediately noticed that the story used in setting the task involved a boy and his father. New questions then arose.

- How many girls used male characters?
- How many used female characters?
- How many used a gender-neutral context?
- What were the equivalent numbers for boys?

Secondly, I observed that the story involved consumer acquisitiveness.

- How many of the pupils' stories reflected this theme?
- What other recognisable themes might be identified?

Just as I had thought all possible information had been milked from responses to an apparently simple task, a whole range of new possibilities opened up. There is little point now, perhaps, in pursuing these questions for this set of pupils. Nevertheless, perhaps such thoughts help me to account for my own immediate response to what remains my personal favourite of the stories offered:

Claire's story: A caterpillar was 4.6 cm long. It grew another 5.3 cm. It is now fully grown at 9.9 cm long.

References

Hart, K. (ed.) (1981) *Children's Understanding of Mathematics 11–16.* London: John Murray.

Swan, M. (1982) *The Meaning and Use of Decimals* (pilot version). Shell Centre for Mathematical Education, University of Nottingham.

Christine Shiu was curriculum innovator for mathematics at a comprehensive school; she is now Lecturer in Mathematics Education at the Open University.

6

Modelling sunrise data with a graph plotter

Bob Ansell

The background

The modelling exercise described here took place with a group of fifth form pupils who were considering A level mathematics in the sixth form. My aim was to illustrate some of the differences between O level and A level using a modelling exercise.

Over the course of a week these pupils attended several 'tasters' designed to discuss different aspects of sixth form life and how subjects and methods change. My particular aim was to compare different approaches to graph work. Lower-school philosophy tends to emphasise plotting graphs while at sixth form level we expect pupils to come to grips with graph sketching and graph fitting.

I have always had doubts about the way we approach graphical methods. For example, consider the need to draw the graph of $y = 2x^2 - 5$. This type

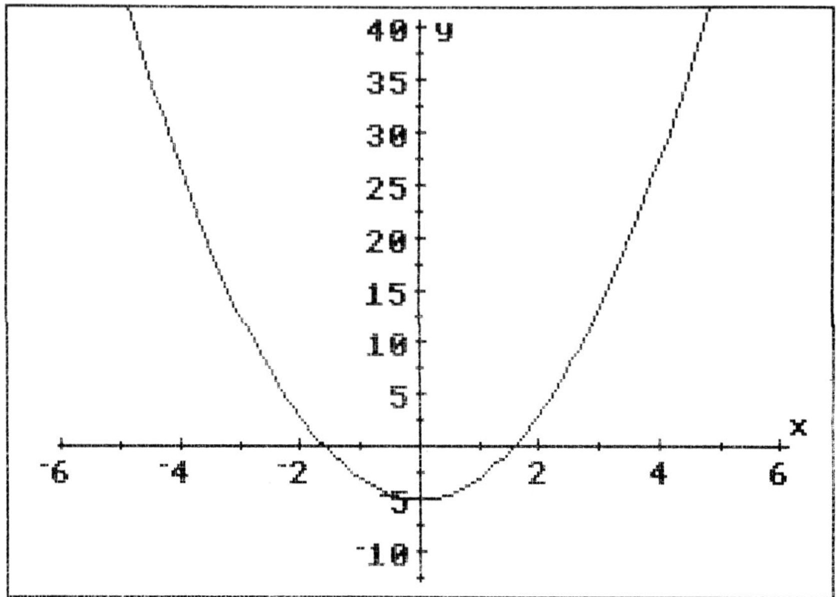

f(x)=2X^2-5

of question has always been a favourite with both examiners and teachers at O level (and to a lesser extent at CSE). It offers the well-*trained* pupil the chance to pick up some easy marks. Additionally, many girls, wrongly encouraged to be neat at the expense of mathematical depth, feel they could score well with a nicely presented, accurate graph.

In the long run, I feel graph-plotting questions to be destructive of real mathematical thinking. They encourage pupils to see the parts rather than the whole – to see functions as discrete rather than continuous – and encourage them to be too eager to fill in any missing bits with straight lines. But, most importantly, such methods encourage narrowness of thought, with pupils seeing the problem as a graph to be plotted, as an end in itself; whereas I want them to be able to construct functions as a *means* of problem solving.

We expect sixth formers to be able to view the graph $y = 2x^2 - 5$ as a stretch of the graph $y = x^2$, scale factor two in the y direction followed by a translation downwards of 5. However, we should not be surprised at their failure to comprehend this view if their diet hitherto has been one which portrayed such functions as a collection of individually calculated points joined together by straight-line segments.

I hope my teaching of graphs was never quite as bad as that outlined above. Nevertheless, I still succumbed to the need to 'train' fifth formers to pass an examination question, and in so doing missed many opportunities to provide long-term understanding.

Out of this thinking grew the following exercise.

The real problem

From common experience the time the sun rises varies throughout the year. But what causes the time to vary and what pattern (if any) there is in the variation is not easily grasped. My aim was to concentrate on the second aspect, that of investigating any pattern in the variation. One reason for not giving fuller consideration to the first aspect was that I did not have the physical models to hand. Also, I felt I could easily get out of my depth in attempting unsatisfactory explanations. I would much rather tell them I was unsure and invite someone else to offer an explanation.

I presented them with an outline of the problem and posed the question mentioned above. A discussion ensued during which some pupils attempted to explain to the others why the sunrise times vary. There was general agreement that the question is harder than it first appears. There was also general agreement that it has something to do with the position of the Earth relative to the sun. I invited them to leave the question unanswered for the moment and was relieved when they agreed.

This qualitative approach allowed many aspects of the problem to be discussed without the need to become involved in detailed mathematical analysis. But, for a more detailed look at the nature of the variation in sunrise times, I gathered data for each week of the year from a diary and plotted the results on graph paper. However, before showing any of this to the pupils I explained what I had done and asked them to discuss and decide for themselves what the general shape would be like and what sort of function might best fit the data. I did not want to offer them my data at this stage, because I felt it important they should do as much of the work as possible from 'first principles'.

Forming a model

Although most of those taking part were prospective A level candidates there was a very wide spread of ability. This was reflected in the level of analysis of the problem at this stage. Comments varied from 'Well, it will go down and then up again', to those from one or two pupils able to hazard a shrewd guess at the sort of periodic function involved. In fact, only a few realised the data would have a strong resemblance to a periodic function.

I invited them to form small groups and to try to sketch their ideas. Only when they had had a good deal of time to get a feel for what was happening did I offer the real data taken from a diary.

8.05	8.04	8.01	7.54	7.45	7.34	7.22	7.09	6.55	6.40
6.24	6.08	5.52	5.36	5.21	5.05	4.51	4.37	4.24	4.12
4.02	3.54	3.48	3.44	3.43	3.43	3.44	3.47	3.52	4.00
4.10	4.20	4.32	4.44	4.57	5.12	5.28	5.44	6.02	6.17
6.32	6.47	7.01	7.15	7.28	7.40	7.49	7.56	8.02	8.05
8.07	8.07								

The data represent the time the sun rises for each week of the year. The first entry is for the first week in January and the table is to be read across. British Summer Time has been ignored.

We discussed the way I had set out the data – by taking the first week of January as week zero and the last week of December as week 51. I was pleased when several mentioned the fact that I had not taken account of British Summer Time. This gave us the chance to talk about simplifying the model in order to make it amenable to mathematical treatment. The pupils readily accepted this.

Treating the model mathematically

We also discussed the fact that sunrise data is necessarily discrete, since there are a finite number of events. However, there was general agreement that it might be useful to know a continuous function which would be a good fit for the data.

Exploring functions which might be a good fit can be very tedious with pencil and paper. One reason for this is the 'trial-and-error' or iterative approach which many would adopt. This method involves them using intelligent guesswork to determine a possible function and then plotting it to see if it is a good fit. Their function would then be amended in the light of experience.

Such an approach cries out for a computer. And since this activity was taking place at the end of the summer term, demand on resources had eased, so I was able to secure about one computer between three.

I had a graph-plotting program which allowed me to enter my own data as a series of points. This I had done earlier and saved the data on disc. With the data available immediately to each pupil, they were able to get straight down to exploring which mathematical function might best fit the data on the screen.

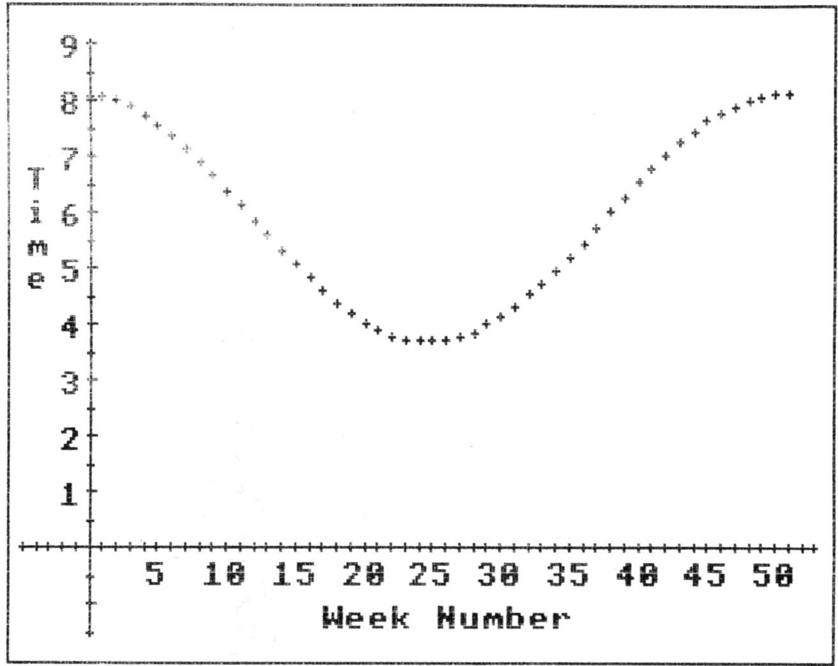

With the computer they could simply try to make a function fit over the data. There was instant visual feedback allowing corrections or conjectures to be tried out immediately.

The computer allowed almost any function to be tested. Depending on how good they considered the fit to be they could then either adjust the function slightly or try a totally different avenue to explore.

Is the problem open or closed?

I wanted to be wary of providing an activity which was so 'open' that pupils felt unable to progress. They had pursued several open-ended activities during their time in the lower school. From feedback it seems that these activities were well received but they often generated comments like 'Well it's interesting, but is it real maths?'

I also wanted to avoid the question of open-ended activities being regarded as directionless – pupils not knowing why they were doing a particular exercise. So, in planning the activity I was consciously looking for something which could be regarded as both 'open' and 'closed' at the same time.

The 'open' aspect was provided by the pupils' freedom to use the graph plotter in any way they chose – they were free to fit any type of curve to the data. But, since I had a result in mind and a curve which was going to provide a possible 'best fit', the activity could be regarded as closed – there was a sort of 'right answer'. However, since we did not have the time to examine the various meanings of 'best fit', any result was going to be subjective. I left them to interpret the term as they saw fit.

It was now their problem

What so excited me about this activity was the enthusiasm with which the pupils entered into it – it immediately became *their* problem. In maths education we hear a lot about the need to make mathematics 'real' or 'relevant'. I believe that *any* problem is real and relevant if pupils take it on board as their own. And provided that pupils can find something intrinsically interesting about a problem then we are three-quarters of the way there.

Even though many of the pupils had rarely used the computer before, after some initial hesitation they quickly became proficient. In fact, after a few moments I was able to wander round and observe the buzz of activity, and listen in to conversations. I was asked if I knew the answer. I said that I didn't, but had a good idea about the sort of function we were looking for. The fact that I did not know the answer to the problem I was setting them made no difference at all to their enthusiasm. As I have already said, this was now their problem.

Their involvement left me free to try to optimise the effort of each group so that everyone gained from the exercise. This included preventing 'know-alls' from shouting out answers or interfering with others, but at the same time not stifling genuine interaction between groups. In tackling the problem there was an element of competition between groups to 'find the mystery function'. But there was also a great deal of co-operation with information and ideas being exchanged freely.

The freedom to make mistakes . . .

What also excited me about the exercise was the high level of mathematical thought taking place. One sort of graph which closely fits the data is that of a cosine function. However, it needs to be stretched in both the x and y directions and then translated.

This sort of exercise would be way above most of the pupils without the use of the computer. But, since the computer allows instant changes, even relatively weak pupils were able to home in from a long way off and achieve success – they had the freedom to make and learn from mistakes. Learning from mistakes, seeing them as a positive force in the learning process, is something which I believe should be given greater consideration when designing courses.

. . . And to make progress

Progress took many forms. One group steadfastly believed they could fit a parabola to the data. They eventually got what was probably the 'best-fit parabola' possible and were very pleased. On the way they learnt a lot about transformations of functions. And when they finally abandoned their quest they had acquired sufficient skills to transfer their ideas to periodic functions. Having secured the principles they quickly caught up with others who had started immediately looking at periodic functions.

After about half an hour nearly all of them, either on their own or with some help, had managed to fit a curve that had a strong resemblance to the data on the screen. Most felt this was a respectable point to stop and to discuss their findings.

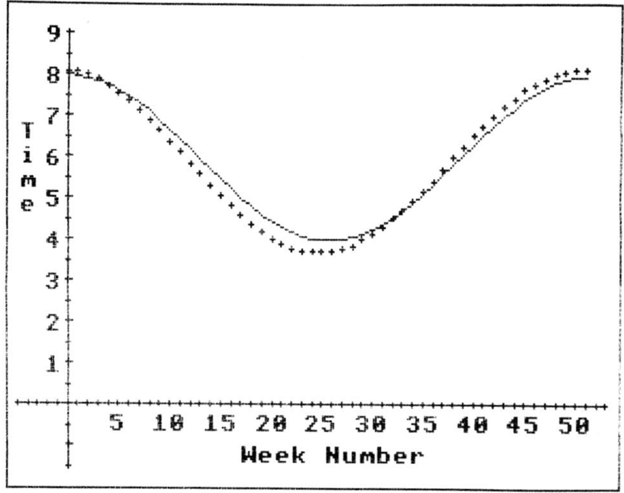

f(x)=2COS(7X)+6

I asked if they could see my point about the different approaches. They were used to taking a known function, given by a particular formula, calculating lots of points and joining them up. I was asking them to take lots of points (the real data) and try to fit a function to them. This second approach demands that they consider classes of functions and look at general principles underlying their shape. I am not sure they were entirely convinced about the differences, but the exercise was regarded by all as fun and worthwhile.

A summary of the activity

I do not want to claim that this exercise had everything. Because this was not a normal lesson but a one-off exercise lasting about 70 minutes, my aim was to give them a flavour of mathematical modelling in the short time allocated to us. We had taken a real problem – what affects the time at which the sun rises and what is the yearly pattern of events. We had concentrated on the part we felt confident of solving. We had looked for mathematical patterns in the data produced from the real problem. Some pupils had then gone on to use their findings to make predictions. They calculated from their function when particular sunrises would occur and checked the results against the original data. This proved very satisfactory for them as it meant they could check their own functions without reference to me.

I believe that modelling exercises should form a much larger part of a mathematical curriculum. Such exercises can take in many different aspects of content and provide a unifying theme so often lacking in current practice.

Modelling also allows pupils to come to terms with a very important point about mathematics. In the real world there are rarely right answers. Methods can vary and are chosen to suit the current problem. Solutions are usually a matter of intelligent guesswork and intuition (whatever that is) and rarely the result of following a predetermined method to a cut and dried conclusion.

Where do we go from here?

To achieve a change in philosophy and approach which might enable modelling to be a natural part of a pupil's mathematical life, the issue must be addressed by all teachers. They must be the driving force for curriculum change. This will no doubt challenge the demands of universities and their grip on the sixth form syllabus which I believe has, in the past, prevented a lot of genuine curriculum development.

Teacher-driven curriculum development would also be able to build on excellent progress made over the last decade towards process and modelling and away from content alone. This progress has allowed new life into lower-school mathematics. But, assuming we can prevent the constraints of a National Curriculum from setting back the clock, we need as a matter of urgency to make sure that the good work does not stop as soon as a pupil enters the sixth form or begins an examination course.

A similar shaped path is obtained by looking at the position of the sun over a 24 hour period. Where must these photos have been taken?

Bob Ansell is Head of Mathematics at a comprehensive school in Milton Keynes.

7

Computer modelling in a problem-solving environment

Dave Pratt

Queuing situations often provide opportunities for problem-solving activities which involve a modelling exercise. In the School Mathematics Project's *Advanced Mathematics Book 1* (p. 249) there is a question which I have used as a starter with fourth and fifth year pupils as well as sixth formers:

> As part of a large-scale construction process, a mechanical digger scoops up material and loads it into a series of lorries. These then transport it to the site of a new embankment and return to the digger. It has been observed that the times are fairly constant (as given in the diagram) except at the digger, where the following table was drawn up.

Time at digger (min)	2	3	4	5	6	7	8	9
Frequency	3	18	35	20	12	2	6	4

What is the best number of lorries to employ? What criterion are you adopting?

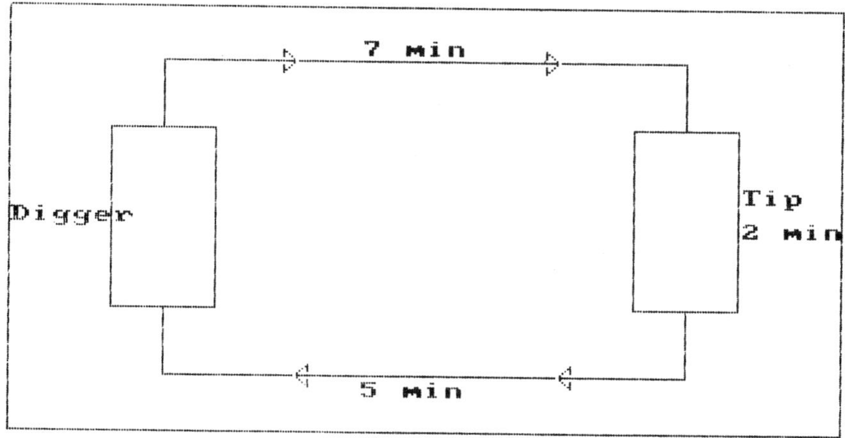

Often teachers would want to start a problem from a stage before this point, i.e. they would want their pupils to decide what data they need to collect and then to go through that process themselves. On this occasion I was not so concerned about those sorts of statistical questions. These pupils had not to my knowledge encountered 'simulation' as a technique for solving problems, and I could see that we might well be involved in that sort of activity. They had done some work on sketching graphs, but they had not really used this knowledge to any great extent to help them solve a problem. With these vague notions in mind, I hoped that the problem as set would generate discussion leading to a variety of problem-solving activities.

In fact, some of the modelling had already been done for us. The text suggests that we should be concerned about times, and the frequencies of those times. Indeed, it tells us that only the digger times vary significantly and quotes precise times for the other stages of the journey. The pupils began by querying these assumptions. We discussed under what circumstances it might be appropriate to assume that only the times at the digger would vary, and why did the digger times vary anyway? This sort of discussion culminated in us deciding that there were feasible conditions under which the modelling, which had already been done for us, might be valid.

I then asked the pupils to estimate how many lorries they would use. At this stage I denied any opportunity for discussion. I wanted them to commit themselves and in so doing each individual was forced to make assumptions. We then discussed their 'answers' and their assumptions. The pupils all chose between three and five lorries. They tended to feel that they should spread the lorries out equally around the track in such a way that the gap between lorries equalled the mean time at the digger. A few of the pupils thought that they had then finished and were ready to move onto another problem. Little did they know (nor I for that matter!) that there was going to be another two to three weeks' work yet. Others could see that variation in the digger times might be a problem, because you could get runs of long digger times, thus causing the lorries to wait, or indeed runs of short digger times, thus causing the digger to wait.

In practice, such runs were likely as they would coincide with a section of hard or soft ground. There was some discussion about these somehow cancelling out before it was accepted by all that both types of runs were disadvantageous because they would waste somebody's time, and so would not cancel out in that sense. There was now silence, because no one could see how you could possibly allow for all these factors, and yet, because there were conflicting ideas in the class, we needed a way forward.

Then David suggested 'Let's do it!' He proceeded to take over the class. Before long he had them organised in a rectangle, equally spaced. He explained that the OHP was the digger and that we were the lorries. I wondered whether this method of simulation had been borrowed from our 'play turtle' Logo activities from a few months before. We discussed how we could use random numbers, generated from a calculator, to determine our moves. The calculator produced a random number between 0 and 1, so we could read off the first two decimal places to get a random number between 0 and 99. This was then interpreted as a digger time using the following cumulative frequency table.

Random number on calculator							
00–02	03–20	21–55	56–75	76–87	88–89	90–95	96–99
Time at digger (min)							
2	3	4	5	6	7	8	9

Of course, not all good ideas lead to successful solutions, and it was not long before the class was in chaos. No one could remember where they should be, whose go was next and so on. Fortunately, the bell was imminent. I suggested that they sort this mess out for their homework. They had to try to find a way of simulating the process, perhaps using counters and dice, or cards or a spinner to get the random numbers.

Now I had to think hard because I knew that some of the pupils would find this quite difficult, and that none of them would have the time to generate the quantity of data that we required. I wrote a Logo program on an RM Nimbus in which the turtles were the lorries. The program generated random times at the digger in much the same way as the pupils had tried to do in class. However, the program kept a careful record of where each lorry was at any time; unlike our personal attempts, *it* did not get confused. The program would run either for a fixed length of time or for a certain number of transported loads.

In the next lesson, we first discussed their efforts to simulate the problem. We talked about what sort of things they had measured, and what the weakness might be of their experimental design. Generally, they had measured the amount of time wasted because the digger was waiting or because the lorries were waiting. However, it was agreed that some of them had failed to start the lorries off in a sensible way. For example, if all the lorries began at the digger, there would immediately be a large amount of lorry waiting time. In fact, another weakness in their simulations was that they were unable to run them for a long enough period in order to smooth out any early freakish results. Furthermore, they had failed to standardise their results. Was it fair to compare a simulation for four lorries which ran for 100 minutes with a simulation for three lorries which ran for 80 minutes? Indeed, would it be fair to standardise on total running time, when four lorries would transport more loads than three lorries in the same fixed time? Perhaps we should standardise on total loads transported, however long it took.

I then introduced them to the program. After a few dummy runs, they could see that the program was essentially the same as their own attempts in class and at home, but that the program overcame their design weaknesses. We set about using the program to collect the data.

I tried to involve the class during this process by getting them to predict what the total waiting times would be for the next number of lorries. They made noticeable improvements the longer we did this, and also they seemed to recognise that they should not expect to get the answer exactly right in an experiment subject to random fluctuation. By the end of the lesson we had collected this data.

No. of lorries used	*Digger's total waiting time (mins)*	*No. of loads transported*	*No. of minutes overall*	*Lorries' total waiting time*
4	53	50	252	86
5	11	50	250	313
3	89	50	349	34
2	231	50	477	12
6	13	50	260	589

The bell intervened at an opportune time once again. I was able to ask them to use these figures to predict the data for one lorry and for seven and eight lorries.

In the next lesson, we discussed their predictions and how they had reached their conclusions. Most of the pupils had drawn graphs of the number of lorries' waiting time. They had extended the trend forwards and backwards. Here came a salutary lesson for us all (including me since this was the method I had expected when setting up the homework). Nick pointed out that given the conditions of the problem, namely that it took each lorry precisely fourteen minutes to leave the digger and return, and that no lorry could be quicker than two minutes at the digger, the digger's waiting time had to be zero when using more than seven lorries! Furthermore, with one lorry there was obviously no lorry waiting time. This was a good example of the dangers of mindlessly assuming that trends continue beyond the observed data.

We spent the rest of that lesson discussing how the graphs could help us to decide how many lorries we should use. Their attention was drawn to the fact that one graph increased while the other decreased and so the graphs crossed. They interpreted this as an optimum point, in terms of minimising wasted time; if we moved away from that point then either the digger's waiting time would increase or the lorries' waiting time would increase. (In fact, because of the near symmetry of the picture containing the superimposed graphs about a vertical line through the cross-over point, this point is also close to the minimum total wasted time.)

However, we were making some pretty large assumptions in this decision. At first, the pupils were happy because the result we reached was in keeping with their original estimates. I tried to focus their minds on what assumptions they had made. With some leading, they began to appreciate that we were giving equal weighting to both the digger and the lorries, in terms of the time each was kept waiting. But the digger might be very expensive in comparison with the lorries, or vice versa. We discussed what contributes to these expenses and why there might be a discrepancy between their costs. Since we did not know how much they cost I declared that I wanted a general solution. I explained that I would only be satisfied if, given how many times more expensive the lorries were than the digger, I was able to find the number of lorries to be used. They agreed that this would be a considerable achievement, but, like me, they did not have much idea on how to proceed.

We discussed what would happen to its graph if the lorries were twice as expensive as assumed in the graphs already drawn. 'It would move up.' 'What do you mean?' 'A waiting time of say 50 would be worth 100.' 'Ah, so the graph would be stretched upwards.'

We had done some work earlier in the year on transforming graphs, and so the class knew that this would multiply the function by 2, or whatever the scale factor happened to be. Again the bell was approaching and it was clear to everyone that we were soon going to need some algebra. I asked them to try and find a graph that would roughly fit the points that they had plotted.

In the next lesson, I went armed with *Logoplotter*, a flexible graph plotter. I first plotted the data observed, and we then superimposed the various algebraic models that they had worked out for homework. One or two of the models were remarkably good. Clearly the pupils had been applying some of the knowledge gained earlier in the year to do with sketching graphs. From an initial recognition of the shape of the points plotted, they had made a guess at a possible curve. Then, through a process of trial and error and by applying their knowledge of transformations of graphs, they had reached a variety of conclusions. One came up with:

$$y = \frac{22.4}{x^{2.7}}$$

and Kevin found

$$y = \frac{600}{x} - 80,$$

where y was the digger waiting time and x was the number of lorries, whereas

$$y = (x - 0.5)^{3.7}$$

was found where y was the lorries' waiting time.

The picture overleaf shows two of these algebraic models superimposed together with the original data generated by the computer program. The x-axis shows the number of lorries while the y-axis shows the total waiting time of the digger in the one case and of the lorries in the other.

To choose the 'best' functions took an enormous amount of discussion about why one model was better than the other. It was generally agreed that we wanted the curves to be as 'near' as possible to the points.

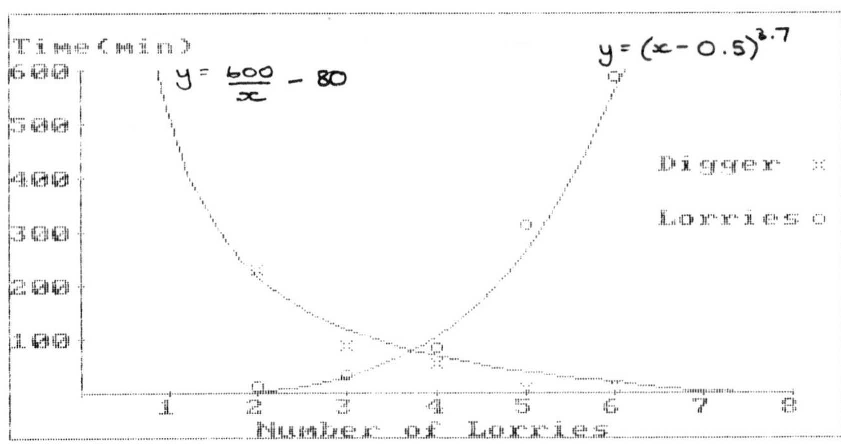

However, one graph might be very good over a specific range of x but not over the whole range, whereas another graph might have the opposite attribute. One graph might fit most points well but be disastrous on just a couple of points, whereas another graph might not fit any point well, but on the other hand it might not fit any points badly. We decided that the 3 to 5 range of x was crucial and this was where the curve must fit well. We also discussed how we should measure the error between the curve and the points. It was felt that the sum of the absolute perpendicular distances between the points and the curve was probably the best. I contrasted this with classical methods which tended to use the square of the vertical or horizontal distances.

We tinkered a great deal with these functions on the graph plotter, trying to move them around to improve the model. Again we were approaching the end of the lesson. I asked them to try to use these models to find the number of lorries that should be used, and how they would interpret their fractional answers.

In fact, solving these equations algebraically was well beyond their (and my) capabilities. Indeed, I am not even sure it is possible. They came to realise this in their homework, but at least some of them had used trial-and-error methods to get an approximation. I spent most of this lesson showing them other approximation methods, some of which worked and some of which did not. We used a spreadsheet to help us with the laborious calculations that were often involved. Fractional solutions were accepted as a measure of how much worse it would be to round the result either way. Thus 3.5 lorries would mean it did not matter whether you adopt 3 or 4 lorries. However, 3.7 lorries would mean 4 is best but 3 would not be too bad, if for some reason outside the confines of the problem you could not use 4 lorries: 3.9 lorries would mean that you really should use 4, and it had better be a good reason if you do not!

In the next lesson, I pointed out that the numerical methods were not much use when we wanted a general solution. If the lorries are k times more expensive than the digger, how many lorries should we employ in terms of k? We cannot put k into our spreadsheet, nor into our calculators! Are we stuck?

Here we have the classic modelling conflict, which traditional teaching methods rarely, if ever, generate. We have found models which fit the data very well, but they are so complicated that we cannot do the mathematics. What can we do? Compromise. We will have to simplify the models or accept that the problem is unsolvable, at least by us.

The pupils played around going back over their work trying to see how they could simplify their algebraic models to the point where they felt they might be able to solve the equation. Ideas were passed back and forward, and some were tried out again on *Logoplotter* to see how they fitted the data. Eventually we settled upon:

digger: $y = \dfrac{341}{x}$

and lorries: $y = \dfrac{341}{7-x}$

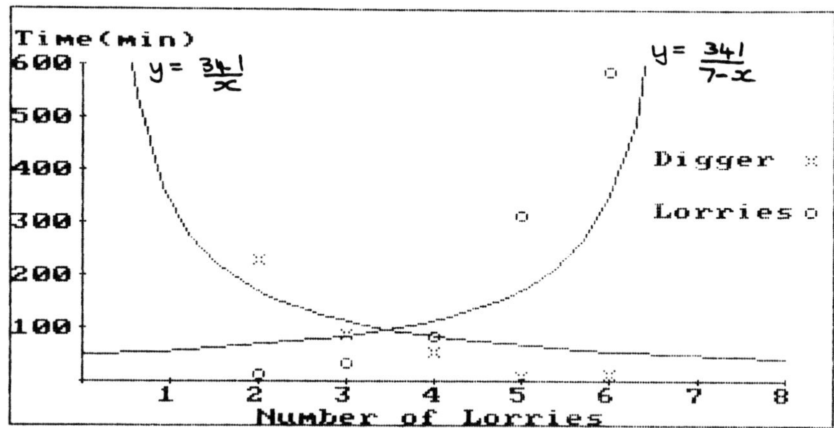

So we needed to solve the equation:

$$\frac{341}{x} = \frac{341k}{7-x}$$

where k was how many times more expensive the lorries were compared with the digger.

This gave us:

$$x = 7/(k+1)$$

Finally, we checked our solution against the known facts of the problem to see how well it fitted. With equal weighting to the cost of lorries and digger (i.e. $k = 1$) we have 3.5 lorries. This seemed a satisfactory answer and was roughly in order with the pupils' original estimates. As the lorries become relatively more costly (i.e. as k increases), we employ less of them. If $x = 0$, there is no solution and this seemed also to make sense. If $x = 7$, $k = 0$: i.e. with seven lorries, the lorries were free compared with the digger, i.e. the digger was infinitely expensive. We would perhaps have preferred to see this phenomenon occur with 8 lorries, but we were pleased to see it as a feature of the solution at all.

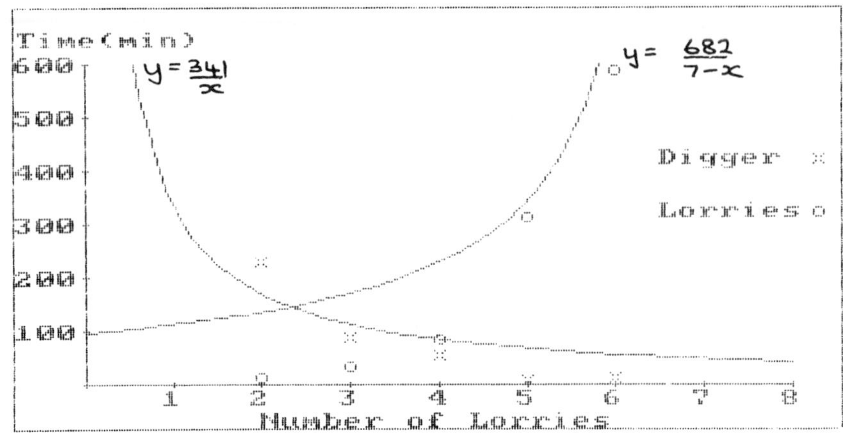

The solution for $k = 2$

Conclusion

It seems to me that the above is a description of what can happen if the teacher is prepared to enter into a problem-solving exercise with the pupils, even though the teacher may not know precisely where they might be going or how they will get there; or even whether they will ever get there. The series of lessons raised many interesting issues, which would probably not have arisen in a teacher-controlled situation.

1 The computer was used naturally as a tool to help with a problem which was posed without the computer. We would not have reached so far without its help.

2 Because we had a meaningful problem to start with, we were able to resolve conflicts and difficulties along the way by reference to that problem. When pupils are given activities in which they do not pose a problem, or in which a problem is not posed on their behalf, then they will look to the teacher to resolve issues as an authority which replaces the authority of the problem.

3 Open discussion was the mechanism through which those conflicts were resolved. Although this continued throughout the lessons, there were a few key moments.
   (a) Initially, when the pupils discussed the problem as set, and came to accept that there were conditions under which the problem could be valid. They began to understand the problem better and to make it their own problem.
   (b) The discussion that took place to force out their predetermined assumptions and thoughts, and established that there was a problem to solve.
   (c) The discussion about their experimental designs, which led them to an understanding of the superiority of the computer program.

(d) The discussion about how they had made their predictions of the outstanding results, and how this led to a realisation of the dangers of mindlessly following a trend.
(e) The discussion in which we recognised that if the lorries and the digger were not equally weighted then we had a whole new problem.
(f) The discussion about what 'best' meant when it came to fitting curves to points.
(g) The discussion in which we compared our eventual solution with the reality of the original problem.

4 The modelling activities were typical of so many problem-solving situations. We were required to set up a model, and discuss its value as against alternative models. We played around with the model until it seemed to fit the observed data to our satisfaction. Then we tried to use this model to solve our problem, using the sort of techniques that are the sole attention of traditional teaching methods. In fact, we had to simplify the model in order to make further progress. Finally, we checked out our solution against the known features of the problem, especially since our simplification of the model might have rendered the solution meaningless. These are all classic activities which you will find yourself in, when you embark upon pupil-driven problem solving.

Reference

School Mathematics Project (1979) *Advanced Mathematics Book 1*. Cambridge: Cambridge University Press.

Logoplotter is a Logo microworld developed by Dave Pratt and Bob Ansell and is available from GEM Software, 13 Trinity Close, Balsham, Cambs CB1 6DW.

Dave Pratt is Head of the Faculty of Mathematics and Science at a comprehensive school in Essex.

SECTION II

Social, Political and Personal Issues

'Children who need to be able to count and multiply are learning anti-racist mathematics – whatever that may be.' Mrs Thatcher quoted in *The Times Educational Supplement* 16.10.87

Row as maths CSE examines arms spending

By PAUL BROWN

An examinations board is to vet future mathematics papers for political content after complaints about a question on military spending in its CSE examination this year.

The London Regional Examination Board, which oversees the test which 6,000 children took this week, accepted that part of one question 'might be offensive to some people who stand on the right.'

Baroness Cox, a campaigner against political bias in education, described the paper as 'utterly unacceptable,' and said she would raise the matter with the Education Secretary, Mr Kenneth Baker.

The question, one of 20 on the paper, was complex and carried 15 per cent of the marks. It dealt with comparative spending of East and West on arms.

One part read: 'The money required to provide adequate food, water, education, health and housing for everyone in the world has been estimated at pounds 11,500 million. How many weeks of Nato plus Warsaw Pact military spending would be enough to pay for this?

The exam, Secondary MATHS Individual Learning (Smile) has questions set by Ilea teachers. About half the children who sit it come from inner London schools.

The exam is intended to relate mathematics to real situations, a concept praised by Sir Keith Joseph when he was education secretary.

Mr David Board, for the examination board, said they had always vetted the social science subjects to avoid any political bias, but it had never occurred to them to check mathematics. The questions were looked at only to see if they were appropriate to the syllabus.

'One part of one question in this exam, in my view, might be found offensive to some people who stand over to the right. The examination is expected to relate to life but I can see this might be a little tendentious, politically.

'The board will clearly want to avoid this in the future and I can see no alternative for them but to look at the questions for political content in the future.'

The Guardian 14.6.86

Revealing messages

The thought-provoking article by Jenny Maxwell (Hidden Messages, MT 111) on the politics of learning mathematics, has prompted me to offer two recent examples of the social and political context of education which – like air – is all around us yet passes so easily unnoticed. The first example is from the June 1985 Additional Maths (A/O) paper (London), in Pure Mathematics and Theoretical Mechanics. It was brought to my attention by a teacher colleague, who tells me that in her class of fifth-years, it is referred to as 'The Falklands Question':

> A pilot flying an aeroplane in a straight line at a constant speed of 196m/s and at a constant height of 2000m, drops a bomb on a stationary ship in the vertical plane through the line of flight of the aeroplane. Assuming that the bomb falls freely under gravity, calculate, (a) the time which elapses after release before the bomb hits the ship, (b) the horizontal distance between the aeroplane and the ship at the time of release of the bomb, and (c) the speed of the bomb just before it hits the ship.
> (15 marks)

Letter in *Mathematics Teaching*, September 1985

Anodyne report angers Minister

The Government's working group on maths teaching has aroused the wrath of the Education Secretary. Its interim report – along with a critical letter from Mr Baker and the announcement of its chairman's resignation – were published last week. Ian Nash Reports.

Some aspects of mathematics would be better taught in technology and art classes, according to the national curriculum maths working group report that has aroused the fury of the Education Secretary.

Among the few decisive statements in the otherwise woolly report are assertions that calculators should be more widely used in primary maths than the Cockcroft Report suggested, and "testing" of young children should be limited to classroom observation.

Neglect of mathematics by other subject teachers during project work has encouraged the pupils to think that maths is "boring" or "too difficult", it adds.

"Whole-school policies to mathematics education are needed to ensure that the whole curriculum contributes as appropriate to the development of positive attitudes to mathematics."

But beyond stating current practice and suggesting a few tentative curriculum reforms, the working party says little, asserting that time was too short to make any firm proposals.

Mr Baker responded the moment the report was published, saying he was "disappointed that the group has not made more progress in their thinking about attainment targets and programmes of study".

Article in *The Times Educational Supplement* 25.12.87

Introduction

Although class teachers have considerable personal autonomy over their classes with regard to both the mathematical content and the manner in which this is encountered, they are far from free of the social world which they, and, as importantly, their pupils inhabit. There are numerous pressures on them which manifest themselves in a variety of ways within the classroom setting. The majority of the articles in this section move on from accounts of what it can be like 'being there', to 'looking out' at some of the external issues which impinge on the teaching of mathematics in schools. The last four articles in this section reverse this direction of gaze, where the accounts are 'looking in' instead and describing some of the personal struggles with regard to teaching and change – change either imposed from outside or desired from within.

Helen Jenner looks at what might be meant by 'multicultural mathematics', as well as examining some of the issues arising from the cultural and ethnic diversity of the pupils in many of our schools. Her discussion is amplified by the account of Valerie Emblen of her visit to examine the traditions and practices of education in Bangladesh (the cultural origin of many of her pupils) and how this might inform and influence her community's educational practices (not least with regard to parental involvement). Zelda Isaacson examines some of the 'facts' about differential achievement between girls and boys in mathematics and takes a considered look at the types and depth of some of the varied explanations put forward to account for them. But hers is not a detached examination – she writes of her belief that 'action makes a difference' and outlines some of the possible practical steps that can be taken as a result of her (and others') analysis.

Liz Trickett and Frankie Sulke report on the effects of the LAMP (Low Attainers in Mathematics) and RAMP (Raising Achievement in Mathematics) projects on both the teachers and pupils who participated, providing a challenge to all teachers to examine their views about both what their pupils are capable of and what mathematics is and should be about. Jenny Maxwell and Dawn Gill both take up the challenge of the presumed cultural and political neutrality of mathematics and, by means of an examination of the common (and therefore frequently invisible) setting for mathematical problems, bring to light many (contentious) presumptions about acceptable, appropriate and valued uses for mathematics.

In **Looking for relevance: can we let them decide?** Barbara Edmonds and Derek Ball pose the question 'what is relevance?' from the point of view of the pupils themselves. Brenda Denvir takes up one of the most pressing contemporary issues, that of the multiple roles of assessment in schools, by looking at the intimately-related questions of 'what are we assessing?' and, 'what are we assessing for?' Eric Deeson explores ways in which the future, in the guise of developments in information technology, may shape the teaching of mathematics.

The last four articles (17–20) deal with teachers as individuals and look at the forces and pressures on them. Anne Watson offers experience and advice about some of the personal preparation a teacher may need to undertake when moving to a more 'investigative' style of teaching. Her title, **Opening-up**, can be seen as referring to teachers becoming more responsive and accessible to their pupils (but also hence more personally vulnerable). **Responding to change** by Rita Nolder gives a detailed account of three teachers undertaking personal change and some of the successes and stresses they encountered along the way. John Mason in **Tensions** vividly describes some of the (necessarily) conflicting forces on teachers and suggests ways in which they can be seen as productive. In the final article in this section, Rosemary Clarke compares the activities of teaching and Gestalt therapy, drawing parallels and pointing up interesting distinctions, as well as offering some of what she has learned in the course of being both a teacher and, subsequently, a therapist.

8

Mathematics for a multicultural society

Helen Jenner

Why do we need multicultural mathematics?

For many of us who work in urban schools, multicultural education has felt like the correct response to our growing awareness of the multiracial nature of our schools. There has also been an increased recognition of the need for a multicultural curriculum in all schools to enable pupils to recognise diversity in society and global issues more than a limited ethnocentric approach might permit. This is embodied in the Swann Report[1] principle of 'Education For All' to develop a fair and harmonious society. The range of books on this area of education has steadily grown and most local education authorities have some kind of equal opportunities policies which include a commitment to multicultural education. But there have been warnings against this – both from black parents[2] and from the conservative popular press – and these are helping teachers to re-evaluate multicultural education and to consider much more fully why it is of benefit for all children and should lead to increased achievement and awareness amongst our pupils.

Mathematics is a central aspect of the curriculum in our schools. It is essential, therefore, that a clear theoretical basis for multicultural mathematics be developed if we wish to demonstrate the value of a multicultural approach to education. If a sound basis cannot be found for multicultural mathematics, then we may need to reconsider the value of this approach in other areas of the curriculum. When considering why mathematics should reflect our multicultural society, a wide range of reasons can be identified. I have found it helpful to categorise these into two areas – those which relate to the nature of mathematics and those which relate to the nature of mathematics education. Of course, there is considerable overlap between these and both are intrinsically linked to the nature of society.

Reasons relating to the nature of mathematics

Some mathematics teachers express the view that there is no need to reconsider how we teach mathematics since, as it deals with universals, it is bound to be multicultural in that its abstract nature reaches across cultural divides. Mathematics is viewed as socially neutral and its content is held to be independent of the material world. This perspective puts mathematics educators in a very comfortable position, until we recognise that it is not uncontentious and, in any case, is rarely made explicit to children, which would involve them in a detailed consideration of how mathematics has developed and the relations between abstract mathematics and reality.

When examining the mathematics curriculum we need to keep in mind that any curriculum consists of choices and selections from what is available, based on decisions made about what is valuable. Paul Ernest[3] examines the ways in which societal values pervade the British mathematics curriculum and Munir Fasheh[4] explores the influence of four different authorities on the mathematics syllabus of the West Bank of Jordan. In her article 'Hidden Messages', Jenny Maxwell[5] demonstrates how problems set for children learning mathematics in different countries reflect the dominant political ideologies of those countries. Whilst the examples used avoid questioning the assumptions on which these ideologies are based, mathematics is said to be neutral and divorced from social issues. As soon as mathematics teachers address issues which are contentious, such as the 1986 CSE question related to arms spending,[6] the question is seen as political not mathematical; this reinforces an image of mathematics as having nothing to do with explaining society.

If we really want to help children develop an awareness of which aspects of mathematics are universal, then it is essential that we extend the range of examples we use to illustrate abstract points, demonstrating more clearly how generalisations have been formed from examining patterns across individual instances. These examples must be multicultural, if they are intended to show the universal nature of mathematics, and should also demonstrate how we move from reality to abstraction and back again. We could also extend to all pupils the advantage bilingual pupils have in recognising language as a symbolic system,[7] which helps with understanding mathematics as communication, by utilising the different languages in our society. For example, through examining number systems in a variety of languages, a much clearer vision of how place value works as a simple way to communicate information about large numbers can be developed. Martin Hughes discusses this in his book *Children and Number*.[8]

Part of our understanding of the nature of mathematics must also involve a recognition of the fact that the symbolic representation used in any society is simply a particular convention. Mathematics is a powerful tool for communication using culturally-defined conventions. The fine definitions used in mathematics may differ from the general use of particular words. The Cockcroft Report[9] uses the example of the word 'difference' to illustrate a particular convention in British mathematics teaching. As the language of mathematics is so tightly defined, the ability to use mathematics to communicate in a particular language may take longer to develop than we would expect, and this may lead us to underestimate pupils' grasp of ideas, particularly since language is so closely related to culture.

We also need to recognise that in our highly industrialised, extremely complex society, the dominant rationality is based on scientific determinism. This is the ideology which validates decisions on what is considered valuable knowledge, leading to assumptions which Keddie[10] sees as fostering the myth of cultural deprivation. Syer[11] discusses how deterministic thinking is one of the aspects of institutional racism, affecting all subject areas. Scientific rationality is reflected in the perception of mathematics in our society as being either right or wrong. We are beginning to recognise the limitations of this approach in encouraging pupils to think mathematically, recognising the value of considering different approaches as well as logical determinism. When mathematics is divorced from its social context, and becomes more abstract, the tendency to focus on scientific reasoning is increased. A more multicultural approach might help expand pupils' mathematical experiences beyond a simple deterministic approach to a more realistic exploration of mathematics in life, which would also promote a more positive attitude towards diversity.

Reasons relating to the nature of mathematics education

Fundamental to British education is the aim to help all children achieve their full potential, and this is generally seen as involving building on the strengths children bring with them to schools. As our society becomes more multicultural it is more essential for teachers to recognise the variety of skills children bring with them. Part of our role as mathematics educators is to ensure that children know that the skills and background they bring to school are valued. Valerie Emblen[12] describes how important a knowledge of the children's mathematical background is when planning the mathematics curriculum for Bangladeshi children in London. Success in mathematics is one of the critical filters in British society. As mathematics educators, we may need to face our responsibility in encouraging pupils to have high expectations of their ability to succeed in mathematics. Increasing the range and diversity of role models children meet in mathematical textbooks and building on the knowledge they have already acquired are two of the ways we can contribute to building the self-esteem shown in many Government reports to be crucial for success.

We also need to ensure that all children are educated beyond an assumption that mathematics has one correct form. The tendency to assume that there are only right and wrong answers in mathematics may be limiting children's ability to cope with the diversity of problems they meet. We have to help children to recognise the power of mathematics as a tool to solve problems, and that the tools are constantly evolving. An historical, multicultural perspective, such as that employed by Hughes,[13] may help children use and develop more versatile mathematical skills. All adults need to be able to cope with diversity and to expect variety as we live in a highly varied world. Ensuring a multicultural approach in schools is one way we can make sure children are aware of and respond positively to diversity.

Our society is multicultural and one particular group is undeniably underachieving – black children. Reasons for this seem to be many and varied, but certainly the implication that only white boys participate in mathematics, as shown in many materials, cannot help. Over recent years much work has been done to promote more positive images of women in mathematics, but this does not seem to have developed into a comparable awareness concerning race or class. Mathematics has become dehumanised, rather than developing as a means to explore patterns and relationships in the real world. Western society places the highest value on the most abstract, thus creating an elitism which means many people feel alienated from mathematics, and, apart from small groups, feel it has little to do with their lives. In mathematics education, we need to re-examine our approaches to ensure pupils see mathematics as for, and about, everyone, thus promoting recognition of mathematics as an activity we can all engage in.

As teacher expectation has been shown to influence achievement, we may also need to examine how teachers are socialised into expecting some groups to fail. Twenty years ago Estelle Fuchs[14] discussed the implications of the following statement made by an enthusiastic teacher in an urban school:

> You have to remember that in a school such as ours the children are not as ready and willing to learn as in schools in middle-class neighbourhoods.

Similar views are still expressed in many staffrooms. They are rarely challenged, nor are the implications of such statements examined, despite the effects they are likely to have on educational success.

It is also possible that as teachers we assess bilingual children's mathematical ability without reference to their first language, again creating lower expectations and failing to recognise the pupils' full abilities by confusing fluency in English with mathematical competence. John Hyland's research[15] suggests that teaching and testing in children's home languages reveals a much greater understanding than is shown when asking them to work in English only. Until we recognise the particular skills bilingual children bring to mathematics lessons, we are likely to continue to underestimate their abilities.

What can teachers do to promote mathematics for a multicultural society?

A first step is to try to raise our own awareness of the issues involved in multicultural education generally. Books such as *Multicultural Education: Towards Good Practice* by Arora and Duncan[16] or *Multicultural Education* by Twitchin and Demuth[17] are good starting points as they provide some theoretical background as well as practical suggestions.

Another invaluable resource is the ILEA book *Everyone Counts.*[18] This book is an excellent guide for ensuring that the materials you are using do not portray racist or sexist stereotypes, and do reflect the range of cultures in society. Reviewing current materials is a good first step for any re-evaluation of approaches to education.

If we are planning on providing quality education then we must build on what we know are good basic principles, as listed below.

- Multicultural mathematics should start from the children in our classes and the rich variety of cultures that they bring to our school with them.
- Mathematics for a multicultural society must recognise the skills children already have as well as those we want to enable them to develop. Valerie Emblen's article[19] explores this more fully.

- We know that children develop mathematical concepts through manipulating objects and talking about what they are doing. Any activities we introduce should build on these principles. A wide range of activities will stimulate wide-ranging discussion.
- We also need to ensure that we do not ignore the importance of talk for bilingual pupils because of our own inability to speak a particular language. It is crucial that we provide as many opportunities as possible for children to discuss what they are doing in the language with which they feel most comfortable. We need to provide a range of starting points which can be developed in any language, and to consider introducing some pupils' home languages.

If one of our aims is to increase pupils' understanding of the universal nature of mathematics, then we need to widen the range of examples from which generalisations are drawn.

- The range of bilingual materials available is gradually increasing. One example is the number stamps from Philip and Tacey.[20] Books and charts in a variety of languages provide good starting points for discussions.
- We need to take advantage of the books which are available which provide ideas from non-European countries, such as Claudia Zaslavsky's books *Africa Counts*,[21] *Count on your Fingers African Style*[22] and *Tic Tac Toe*.[23]
- Most schools have a selection of resources based upon a white, ethnocentric curriculum, and publishers and producers still feel there is little market for anything else. It is important that we ensure that the materials we use are a reflection of attitudes and expectations more suited to a diverse society, so many teachers may feel they need to collect a more multicultural range of resources. Several local education authorities have resource centres that may be able to help, e.g. ILEA, Brent, Bedford, Coventry.

If we are aiming to help children to be aware of the relationship between mathematics and society, several approaches are possible. We need to look more closely at the applications of mathematics and to consider using mathematics to challenge racist assumptions.

- We need to be more sensitive to the messages underlying what are seen as politically neutral questions. Dawn Gill's article[24] looks at examples of 'neutral' questions from secondary mathematics textbooks.
- We can re-examine the choices of data we make in demonstrating statistics as a tool. Howson and Mellin-Olsen[25] comment on this and the role of mathematics teachers:

> Can maths teachers be entrusted with drawing inferences, trends etc. from significant data, or must they automatically stick to anodyne data which will offend no one but will automatically remove true significance from their work and lead to many students being bereft of motivation?

There are many opportunities to use more socially relevant data and to employ statistics to challenge myths presented as facts.

- We can look at the history of how maths developed and the cultural presumptions of maths historians. George Joseph's article 'Foundations of Eurocentrism in Mathematics'[26] explores the weaknesses of the classical, eurocentric view of how mathematics developed.
- We can use mathematics to help us examine differences between countries using games such as The World Feast Game[27] or The Paper Bag Game.[28] By changing the context in which we use mathematics, we develop a more multicultural perspective and can help pupils to see how powerful mathematics can be as a tool for examining society.

Some issues to consider

Tokenism

Any initial work in multicultural mathematics may be seen to be tokenistic, especially if the only obvious reason for its inclusion is that it represents other cultures. Colouring a few faces brown and celebrating a couple of extra festivals does not constitute multicultural education. There are many teachers, however, who feel daunted by the possibility of the work they are doing being 'tokenistic' and therefore feel unable to do anything. Avoiding tokenism certainly is not easy, but any developments we make must improve the quality of mathematics education, as well as introducing different cultures. Detailed consideration of all aspects of multicultural mathematics can help ensure ideas are introduced from a theoretical rather than a random basis. A recognition that education is an area where racism has become institutionalised, and that this needs to be changed, is perhaps the starting point for this.

The status of knowledge

It is important that we recognise that not all knowledge carries the same status. As Kelly[29] says:

> Not only is the value element in education crucial, it is also highly problematic and it is this that creates particular problems for curriculum planning.

As the school curriculum is usually determined by the dominant ideology in society at present, a multicultural approach has low status. This means that we have to be doubly careful to ensure that multicultural mathematics does not become a second-class mathematics curriculum for multiracial urban schools. Maureen Stone's[30] arguments that multicultural education is based on a deprivation model of black children explain how multiracial education may actually be placing them at a disadvantage. It is crucial, therefore, that mathematics be recognised as being of less value if it is not based on a multicultural approach. Multicultural mathematics is unlikely to be tokenistic if it can be justified in terms of mathematical purposes, linguistic purposes and anti-racist purposes. If any of these criteria are not being met then there is a danger that the ideas being introduced are tokenistic.

A project-based approach

In some schools, there is a tendency for any work to be justified on the grounds that it is 'part of a project' rather than because of its educational value. It is crucial that this does not happen with aspects of multicultural mathematics. Learning to draw Islamic patterns at Eid, or Rangoli patterns at Diwali cannot be considered to be mathematics unless the mathematical ideas embedded in the patterns are fully explored – considering rotation, reflection and translation can turn this investigation into one where the place of mathematics in different cultures is clear rather than leaving one feeling that examples of important geometric ideas are somehow 'outside' the real world of mathematics. A project-based approach can provide interesting and meaningful links between mathematics and other subject areas, but only if the curriculum aspects are considered in sufficient depth, and the actual mathematics involved is made explicit.

The involvement of parents

It is very easy for those of us in schools to decide on what is 'good' multicultural education for the children we teach, without ever consulting their parents. This means that we deprive ourselves of their expertise and the valuable contributions they can make as well as failing to challenge the implications of statements such as Prime Minister Margaret Thatcher's claim, 'Children who need to be able to count and multiply are learning anti-racist mathematics – whatever that may be.'[31] All parents are rightly concerned about the quality of education their children receive, and an important aspect of multicultural education must be discussing its value with parents. An interesting introduction to this area can be found in A.G. Davey's article 'Giving Parents a Voice in Multicultural Education'.[32]

Bilingual pupils

Research into the progress of bilingual pupils has demonstrated that support for, and recognition of the value of pupils' first languages are crucial for achievement. If we consider the World Bank research,[33] which demonstrates the need for some pupils to be educated in their home language if they are to reach their full potential, we must face the implications of this for mathematics education. The SMILE (Secondary Mathematics Individualised Learning Experiment) team have addressed this issue and suggest ways in which their own materials may be amended to make them more appropriate for bilingual pupils.[34] These include content review, vocabulary explanations, pictorial support and checking for cultural assumptions. These steps are needed but do not actually take advantage of the skills of bilingual pupils. We should aim to build on bilingual pupils' increased potential for divergent thinking,[35] and their abilities for concept transferral between languages.[36] We should also consider how far our mathematics curriculum can respond to linguistic diversity, and whether, for some of our pupils, new concepts might be more appropriately introduced through their home languages. Dawe's[37] research demonstrating the importance of pupils' first language competence to mathematics, as well as the need for pupils to understand mathematics ideas in English, highlights the importance of both languages for children's progress. Considering the links between mathematical development and language should be an important aspect of any curriculum which recognises our multicultural society.

Whose culture is it anyway?

The children in our schools come from many cultures and as teachers we try to introduce materials into the classroom that reflect their backgrounds. We need to be aware that many of the ideas we introduce on an assumption that they are reflecting the children's backgrounds may have little or no meaning or relevance for the children. To assume that a study of Islamic pattern will have particular meaning for all Moslem children is imposing an idealised view of others' cultures, rather than starting from the children's real community. Mathematics materials need to offer images of a world which pupils recognise and feel part of, not unrealistic, ill-informed views of their pupils' cultures.

Moving forward

It should be clear from this article that a more multicultural approach would improve the quality of mathematics education, and that there is much that can be done to ensure that the mathematics we teach prepares children for our multicultural society. As with all curriculum development there are many questions to be raised and pitfalls to try to avoid. Many teachers will have already tried ideas presented here and there are many more to be worked on. An essential part of developing an effective multicultural curriculum will be the willingness of individuals to work within the field whilst being prepared to recognise that the mistakes they make will be the lessons for future teachers.

Notes

1 DES (1985) *Education For All* (The Report of the Committee of Inquiry into the Education of Children from Ethnic Minority Groups, under the Chairmanship of Lord Swann). London: HMSO.

2 M. Stone (1981) *The Education of the Black Child: the Myth of Multiracial Education*. London: Fontana.

3 Paul Ernest (1986) 'Social and Political Values', *Mathematics Teaching*, Volume 116, pp. 16–18.

4 Munir Fasheh (1982) 'Mathematics, Culture and Authority', *For the Learning of Mathematics*, Volume 3, Number 2, pp. 2–8.

5 Jenny Maxwell (1985) 'Hidden Messages', *Mathematics Teaching*, Volume 111, pp.18–19.

6 'Row as Maths CSE examines arms spending', *Guardian*, 14 June 1986.

7 L. S. Vygotsky (1962) *Thought and Language*. Cambridge, Mass.: MIT Press.

8 Martin Hughes (1986) *Children and Number: Difficulties in Learning Mathematics*. Oxford: Basil Blackwell.

9 DES (1982) *Mathematics Counts* (Report of the Committee of Inquiry into the Teaching of Mathematics in Schools, under the Chairmanship of Dr W. H. Cockcroft). London: HMSO.

10 N. Keddie (1973) *Tinker, Tailor . . . The Myth of Cultural Deprivation*. Harmondsworth: Penguin.

11 M. Syer (1982) 'Racism, Ways of Thinking and School' in J. Tierney (ed.) *Race, Migration and Schooling*. London: Holt, Rinehart and Winston.

12 V. Emblen (1986) 'Asian Children in Schools', *Mathematics in School*, November 1986, pp. 26–9, and January 1987, pp. 7–9.

13 M. Hughes (1986) op. cit.

14 E. Fuchs (1968) 'How Teachers Learn to Help Children Fail', *Transactions*, September 1968, pp. 45–9.

15 J. Hyland (1987) 'Mother Tongue Mathematics Teaching and Testing', *Multicultural Teaching*, Volume V, Number 3, pp. 31–2.

16 R. Arora and C. Duncan (eds) (1986) *Multicultural Education: Towards Good Practice*. London: Routledge & Kegan Paul.

17 J. Twitchin and C. Demuth (1985) *Multicultural Education: Views from the Classroom*. London: BBC Publications.

18 Inner London Education Authority (1985) *Everyone Counts: Looking for Bias and Insensitivity in Primary Mathematics Materials*. London: ILEA.

19 V. Emblen (1986) op. cit.

20 Philip and Tacey Number Stamps.

21 C. Zaslavsky (1973) *Africa Counts*. Boston: Prindle, Weber & Schmidt.

22 C. Zaslavsky (1980) *Count on your Fingers African Style*. New York: Thomas Y. Crowell.

23 C. Zaslavsky (1982) *Tic Tac Toe*. New York: Thomas Y. Crowell.

24 D. Gill (1986) 'Politics of Percent', *Mathematics Teaching*, Volume 114, pp. 12–13.

25 A. G. Howson and S. Mellin-Olsen (1986) 'Social Norms and External Evaluations' in B. Christiansen *et al.* (eds) *Perspectives on Mathematics Education*. Dordrecht: D. Reidel.

26 G. Joseph (1987) 'Foundations of Eurocentrism in Mathematics', *Race and Class*. vol. XXVIII, no. 3, pp. 13–28.

27 Christian Aid (1982) *The World Feast Game*. London: Christian Aid.

28 Christian Aid (1981) *The Paper Bag Game*. London: Christian Aid.

29 A. V. Kelly (1980) 'Ideological Constraints on Curriculum Planning' in A. V. Kelly (ed.) *Curriculum Context*. London: Harper & Row.

30 M. Stone (1981) op. cit.

31 Quoted in *Times Educational Supplement*, 15 October 1987.

32 A. G. Davey (1987) 'Giving Parents a Voice in Multicultural Education', *Multicultural Teaching*, Volume V, Number 3, pp. 20–4.

33 N. Dutcher (1982) *The Use of First and Second Languages in Primary Education: Selected Case Studies*. World Bank Staff Working Paper No. 504, Washington D.C.

34 S. Alladina (1985) 'Second Language Teaching Through Maths – Learning Maths Through a Second Language', *Educational Studies in Mathematics*, **16** (2), pp. 215–19. .

35 S. Ben-Zeev (1975) 'The effect of Spanish–English bilingualism in children from less privileged neighbourhoods on cognitive development and cognitive strategy', *Working Papers in Bilingualism*, Volume 4.

36 J. Keats, D. Keats and Liu Fan (1984) 'Language in Thought Processes in Bilingual Chinese Children', *Multicultural Children's Literature*, Volume 3, Number 1.

37 L. C. S. Dawe (1983) 'Bilingualism and Mathematical Reasoning in English as a Second Language', *Educational Studies in Mathematics*, **14** (3), pp. 325–53.

Helen Jenner is the headteacher of an ILEA primary school.

9

Asian Children in Schools

Valerie Emblen

Part One

This is the first of two articles written to discuss some aspects of the mathematical education of young children from the Indian sub-continent. It is written after a trip of some five months to Pakistan, Northern India and Bangladesh. The purpose of the trip was to study the education of young children in these countries. During my stay I visited schools, homes and families. My school, Thomas Buxton, is in the East End of London. 95 per cent of the children are from families of Asian origin, with more than 90 per cent from Bangladeshi backgrounds. The staff has worked for some years to create links with the community and has worked to develop the curriculum, giving special attention to the learning needs of bilingual children. The learning of mathematics has been a particular focus of attention.

Education and the family

These articles are written primarily to discuss the mathematical education of young children, but it is necessary, firstly, to see education in a wider social context. In many of the places that I visited, universal primary education is not yet established. A child's access to schooling varies greatly from place to place. For instance, in the relatively prosperous city of New Delhi, in India, the municipal council provides free school clothing and a midday meal for poor children. In Bangladesh, schooling is government organised and is free. A recent survey showed that in a rural area only two-fifths of the child population between the ages of 6 and 14 was enrolled in school.[1] The average literacy rate in India is about 34 per cent. This includes a 98 per cent literacy rate in the Southern Indian state of Kerala.[2] In Bangladesh the literacy rate is probably between 22 per cent and 25 per cent.[3] The 1981 census gives these figures: literacy amongst men 32.9 per cent; amongst women 14.8 per cent.

In all three countries the town child's access to schooling is better than that of the rural child. Boys' education is seen as likely to bring direct economic benefit to the family and so is given priority over girls' education.

The tables below show the number of children on the rolls of two schools in rural districts of Bangladesh. The tables show the relatively short school careers of some children. For many it is not long enough to become literate or numerate in any real sense. They also show that in all classes fewer girls attend than boys.

Number of pupils	*Boys*	*Girls*	*Number of teachers*	*Class*
252	152	100	2	1
165	100	65	2	2
143	80	63	2	3
120	75	45	1	4
88	48	40	1	5
768	455	313	8	total

Fatehabad Khadimul Primary School

Number of pupils	*Boys*	*Girls*	*Number of teachers*	*Class*
41	26	15	1	1
32	22	10	1	2
27	15	12	1	3
18	14	4	1	4
18	12	6	1	5
136	89	47	5	total

Shrenath Government Primary School

Schooling is sometimes seen as yet another burden on scarce family resources. A child in school is not a productive member of the family. A father explained to me that he would put one of his three sons through primary and secondary education. He explained, 'We need two boys to help in the fields. Shuel, the youngest, will be a doctor or an engineer, then we will all be better off'. Resources may be organised to support the family as a whole, rather than be geared to the needs of the individual.

The distinction between education and schooling becomes clear in a rural society. A child's education may consist largely of the mastery of traditional skills to be done in a traditional way. The authority for doing things this way lies in the fact that they have always been done this way and so questioning is not encouraged. The child is also subject to the authority of the joint family system, which puts the making of decisions in the hands of one or two senior male members of the family.

This authority is reflected both in the school teaching methods and the children's learning. Learning is almost entirely by rote. The child is required to memorise the next lesson in the centrally-prepared text-book, sufficiently to pass the next weekly, monthly or yearly test. The next passage is quoted from *Cenbose*, an education magazine published in New Delhi, India.

> Educators advocate a mental flexibility and independence, while teaching practice aims at transmission of knowledge and culture, traditions that are certified by authorities and not to be questioned . . . these factors result in a very great weakness of the exclusive reliance on text books and other such authoritative sources of information.[4]

The mathematics curriculum

In Pakistan and Bangladesh the curriculum for all subjects is created by government-appointed textbook boards. In India each state provides the curriculum. These are four reasons for a centrally-controlled curriculum given by officials of the textbook board in Islamabad (Pakistan).

1. Ideological reasons: the intention is that the curriculum will support the building of a united country and an Islamic society.
2. Economic reasons: textbooks produced on a large scale are cheaper.
3. Teachers, up till now, have lacked professional expertise and so need the support of a well structured teaching programme.
4. The middle classes, especially those in government service, have to move from place to place and so need continuity of curriculum.

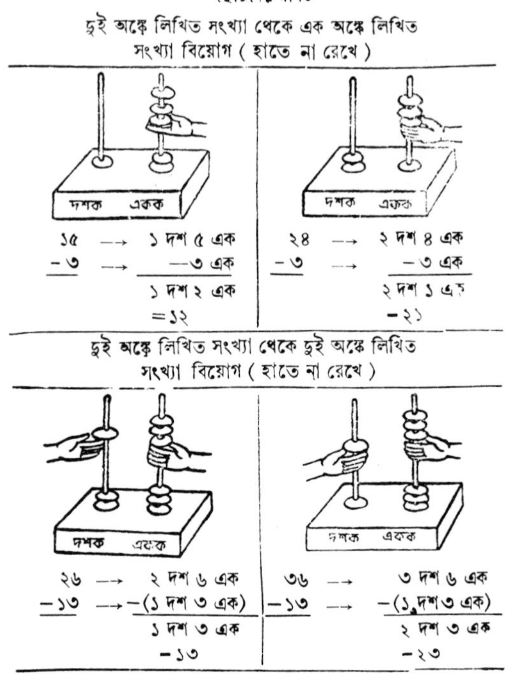

A page from the first book of the mathematics scheme in Bangladesh

The memorisation of the textbook is often seen as an end in itself. I rarely saw the learning supported by the practical work the textbooks themselves suggest. Yet the children show a great deal of ingenuity and imagination in finding objects for their play. They make boats from leaves and dolls from sticks and play games with stones. The teachers themselves sometimes feel untrained to cope with the syllabuses. This is particularly true of the mathematics syllabus. A teacher in Pakistan told me, confidentially, 'We miss out the chapter on sets'.

Because of economic and other pressures, schools in South Asia may place too great a reliance on a curriculum trapped between the covers of a book. This curriculum is learnt almost entirely by rote, and mathematical knowledge and skills are acquired by teacher exposition, followed by repetition and practice. The advantage of this is that teacher and child both know what the task is and what must be done to achieve success. However, the content is far removed from the children's lives. It also puts little stress on those problem-solving skills that are vital to the development of village life.

When Asian parents, particularly those from rural backgrounds, emigrate to Britain they enter a society with different expectations of schooling. Teachers should not be surprised that many such parents find difficulties in understanding the aims of the curriculum and the teaching methods used in United Kingdom schools. The onus is on each school to communicate its aims and justify its procedures to all parents.

Mathematics in Asian schools

There is growing pressure for schooling in many parts of South Asia. Schools are often bursting at the seams. Where the climate is dry a yard, a garden or the corner of a field can become a school. Mats are spread, a blackboard set up and a school is in session (see below). The smallest children bring a slate or a tathi. A tathi is a wooden board, whitened with a chalky substance on which the child writes with a wooden pen dipped in black ink. It is taken home every night to be re-whitened. In this way parents can see the lessons for the day. In one tiny school in rural Bangladesh I saw the children practising their numbers on cut pieces of banana leaf.

The little girl opposite is copying her numbers carefully from the blackboard onto her slate. She will learn to manipulate numbers through practice and repetition. Her first task will be to learn to write and say the numbers. She will move on to simple arithmetic, addition then subtraction. Later, she will tackle tens and units, multiplication and division. She will learn to chant addition and multiplication facts and her mathematics will be almost entirely 'sum' based. For instance, she will learn about weights and measures by tackling tasks in a work book (see diagram on p. 88), such as those Bangladeshi children use. I saw almost no practical work in school. The children, of course, use their fingers as a counting aid. The thumb on the right hand is used as a pointer to the other fingers on the same hand. By pointing to the three sections of each finger, plus the tip, sixteen can be counted on the right hand.

A lesson in Pakistan

I visited a government school in the Lahore district of Pakistan. The fourth class was tackling a problem to do with the Muslim Inheritance laws. This is in line with the Islamisation of the curriculum. The teacher copied the problem onto the blackboard.

> If a man who owns so much land dies and his sons are entitled to such a percentage, how much do his four sons each have, how much do three daughters each have, how much does the widow own?

The teacher went through each step and the children answered in unison. The children then copied it into their books. In this school mathematics and science were taught in English, social sciences in Punjabi. This is the pattern in many schools in Pakistan and India: science and mathematics taught in English, social sciences in the local language. In Bangladesh, Bengali is the teaching medium; English is taught as a subject from the first class.

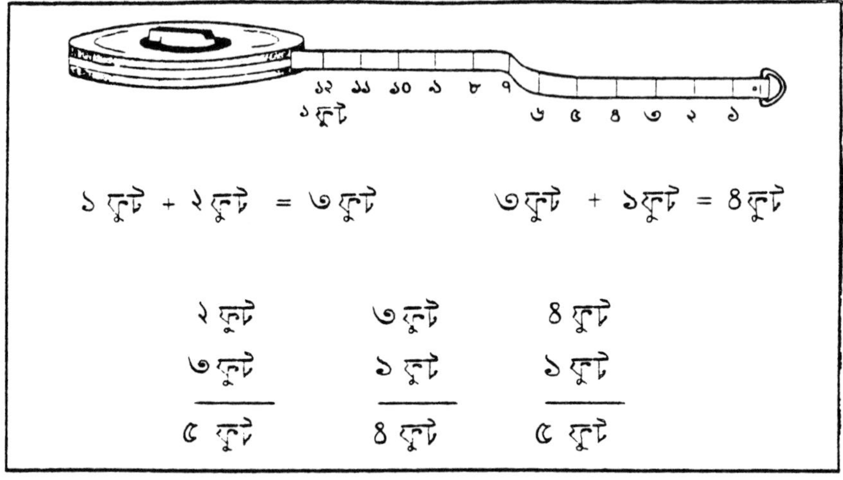

Learning about length from a Bangladeshi text book.

A village school in Sylhet

My school is in the Spitalfields area of East London. The community we serve is largely made up of families who have come to England from a rural district of Bangladesh called Sylhet. Some sub-divisions of Sylhet are areas in which nearly every family has relatives in London, and so my visit there was of special significance to me. I was invited to the school in the village of Atgor. From the main road I took a bicycle rickshaw along the banana and coconut fringed lanes. Before I saw the school I heard children's voices: one class was chanting its tables, another counting together, another reading out loud. The school is a long low building. It is 'semi-pacca'; that is with white-washed brick walls and a roof thatched with banana leaves. Inside, the headmaster's room is partitioned off at one end of the building. The rest of the building comprises one long room divided by woven screens. The youngest children sit on mats on the floor; older children sit on benches, balancing their books on their knees. I was taken to visit the classes. The first was tackling simple arithmetic. The teacher was demonstrating on the blackboard, the children copying onto slates. The second class was reading in unison from the reading book.

When I came to the third class, the head introduced me as the 'expert from London'. Would I show them how to teach today's lesson? Today's lesson proved to be $10 \times 10 = 100$. The headmaster handed me the chalk. To me, it seemed that those teachers were more likely to be experts in their own system than I would be. However, the head persisted and so I quickly racked my brains and said I would do the sort of thing I do in my classroom at home.

I looked round for some small objects to work with. The men produced matches from their pockets. I asked for some children to work with me. Six boys from the front bench were selected. Children are ranged in order of their performance in the last test. These were the most successful. I put a handful of matches on the floor. 'How many matches do you think there are?' I asked. I got no response. I asked for my question to be translated into Bengali. Still I got no response. I knew the children were not usually encouraged to guess so I asked one boy directly. He looked anxious, but answered, 'Thirty'. Another child counted them one-by-one and found twenty-one. More children joined the circle. I put a few more matches down. There were more guesses, e.g. fifteen, twenty. The first boy was obviously thinking hard. 'No, more. Thirty.' It was twenty-nine. Girls were at the back, looking on, but not joining in. I moved some girls into the middle and asked them for their guesses. Now the children were talking to their friends. Although I did not understand I could see that they were discussing the problem. The guesses became more realistic. They took into account whether I had put matches down or taken them away. Now I suggested that they might find a quicker way to count the sticks. After a moment a girl shyly took them and began counting in twos. The next time they were counted they were put in piles of four. This proved difficult as the children did not readily count in fours. A boy opposite me was obviously working something out in his head. Suddenly he announced, 'Forty-four.' 'How did you know?' I asked. He answered in Bengali. His teacher translated. 'Eleven piles and eleven times four is forty-four.' Now we got on apace. We tried grouping in different numbers and decided that ten was 'best', because as one little girl said 'Is counting easy, ten, twenty.'

I enjoyed working with the children. They were alert, and bright and co-operative. They were working in a foreign language with a teacher who was making far from usual demands. It interested me to note that, before the children understood the task they had trouble in understanding what I was saying. When they understood what was expected we had few communication problems. 'Understanding' depended at least as much on understanding the situation as on the words used in it. It also seemed that those who were successful were those who were confident and willing to take risks.

My particular interest has been in the learning of mathematics by children of Asian backgrounds in English schools. In the next part

I will discuss some of the ways my trip has helped to improve our teaching in London.

Part Two

This is the second of a set of two articles, written after a trip of some five months to Northern India, Pakistan and Bangladesh. In this article I will look at some of the ways we can support the mathematical learning of children from Asian backgrounds. Most children come to school speaking little or no English; many are recently arrived in the country. The discussion will focus on the youngest children, but I feel much will be relevant to the education of children of all ages.

Children of Asian families in English schools

It is said that 'travel broadens the mind'. Unfortunately, it can also be true that previously-held prejudices can be reinforced. Soon after arriving in Pakistan, I met a very wise woman. She was the headmistress of a girls' school. She warned me against noticing only the differences between life in the Indian sub-continent and in England and she warned me about being seduced by the apparent 'exoticness' of it all. 'After all,' she said to me, 'people here don't find themselves strange or exotic. They find their lives very ordinary.' A parallel can be drawn between this and the way we view the children in our care. We must see all our children as potential learners. Whether they have just arrived in this country, or speak little English or have difficult home circumstances, unless we see them as competent learners we will soon find reasons why they cannot learn.

In my first article I wrote of the ingenuity and imagination I saw in children's play in Asia. I also referred to the child's role as a productive member of the family; children often take on real responsibility at an early age. A child may work with father or mother; s/he may look after a younger brother or sister; s/he may be responsible for the family cow or goats or for selling the family produce in the market. In my own school, the nursery teacher drew attention to a four year old girl who showed remarkable judgement in handling quantities of water. We made enquiries and found that she had helped her mother to carry water every day in Bangladesh. If you want to carry the smallest possible quantity of water or get the best possible price in the market, the judgements you make are important in a way those made in a water tray or school shop can never be.

In any class the children will bring a wide variety of experience to school. Whether this has been in Bangladesh or Bradford or East London, the teacher must learn to accept the children as they are as the starting point of her teaching. Rather than seeing the children as 'deprived' she can identify each child's strengths and build on these.

I am fortunate to work in a school where all the children are seen as people with questions to ask, ideas to share and problems to solve. Under these circumstances, children are able to use all their skill to develop and share their thinking (see the picture opposite). I remember many instances of children finding ways to share their thinking. Abdul Shahid, a Bengali-speaking five year old and a beginner in English, wanted to show off his three sand pies lined up in order of size. He pointed and said proudly, 'Father Bear, Mother Bear, Baby Bear'.

At this time Syeduz was nearly six and in his second term in the infant school. He was tackling a problem, to find the heaviest of three parcels. He had used a balance to find the answer and declared: 'This one big one, this one little one, this one nothing.'

Factors affecting the teaching approach

Having acknowledged that all children need the intellectual stimulation provided by the school curriculum, the question is, how do we, as teachers, devise a teaching scheme which focuses on each child's strengths rather than on 'deficiencies'? This is, of course, not a question only for teachers of children from ethnic minority groups, and is particularly relevant when considering all aspects of underachievement.

At Thomas Buxton school developing our mathematics curriculum is a continuing process. The insights I gained from my trip to Asia have supported this process. We want to provide for the children's cognitive development, yet do not wish to assess them by something they are not fully competent in: the English language. This has forced us to look closely at what we want the children to achieve and our ways of teaching. These are some of the things we have considered.

1 **It seems important that children should not be confronted by unfamiliar ideas and unfamiliar language at the same time.** New mathematical ideas are set firmly in a known context. I am reminded of the lesson I took in a school in Sylhet which I described in my first article and the way the understanding of the task helped the children to understand the English I was using. Stories, outings and practical experience all provide starting points for mathematical exploration. In this way very soon every child can join in the work of the class. Mumith was, at the time I am thinking of, just six years old. He had come from Bangladesh about three months previously and had been in school about two months. We had been working on ideas of time and speed. The children had run races, pushed cars, made clocks, etc. Today we were talking about animals. 'Do you know an animal that moves quickly?' I asked Mumith. 'Tiger, Miss,' he answered. 'Why do you think tigers have to go quickly?' I asked him. There was a long pause. I began to get anxious. Had I asked too much of him? Then he stretched out his hands and made pouncing movements. 'Tiger hungry, Miss.' He had been able to join in mathematical discussion with the English he had at that time.

2 This anecdote also illustrates the next point I will make; **the importance of accepting the meaning and intention of a communication, without criticising the form it takes.** Communication is vital if we are to see the quality of a child's thinking and assess the support it needs. The children must feel confident to use any means they have to pass the message. A child who is new to using English will inevitably use more non-verbal means of communication than a native English speaker, in an English school. More time may be needed for the child to devise a way to make the meaning.

3 Our teachers have also found that the **mathematics curriculum provides many opportunities for the children to develop their language skills.** The learning context demands that the children express prediction and uncertainties; they must make and test guesses and share them with those they are working with. We have become aware of the interdependence of mathematical and language learning.

4 **Children whose families have come from other countries may have a whole range of skills that are not normally recognised in English schools.** In Asia, I became far more aware than I had been in London of the very rich tradition of songs, stories and games. Parents and children can share these skills with the school. Some of our children were writing the number symbols used in Pakistan and Bangladesh. This led us to wonder how many number names and symbols we could collect. Parents, friends and relations joined in and wrote, or counted onto a tape recorder, the numbers one to ten.

Aziz was, at that time, the only Arabic speaker in the school. He brought his uncle to write the Arabic numerals. Aziz became the 'expert' and enjoyed showing off 'his' numbers, Shahid, a Bengali speaker, and Javed, a Punjabi speaker, were seen comparing the Bengali and Urdu symbols. Shilpi, counting in Bengali, looked up and she said, 'We better 'an you,

Miss.' 'Oh, yes, Why?' I asked. 'Cos we know English and Bengali. You know English.'

Many benefits derive from involving parents and from giving value to home languages. This was on top of the mathematical work generated. It involved a great deal of counting, sorting, matching, etc. For example, Nobinul noticed that in all the notations we had collected, two digits were used to express ten. This lead to valuable work on the way the number system works and on 'tens and units'.

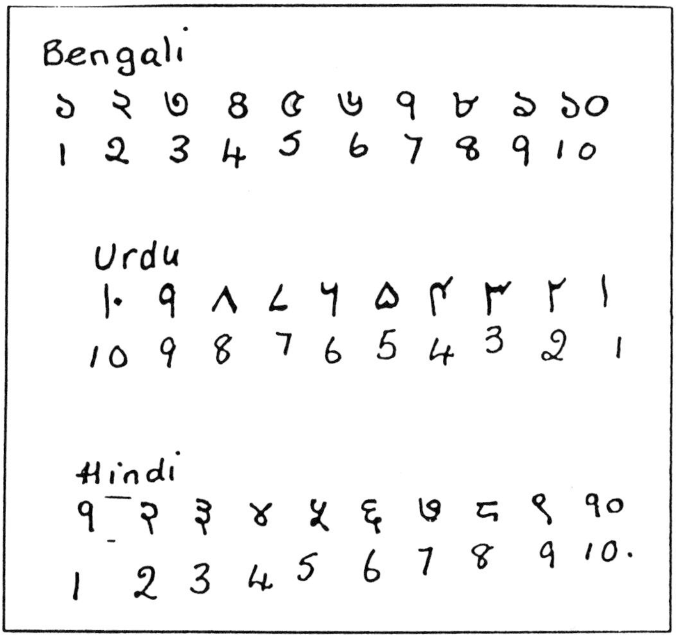

Bengali

১ ২ ৩ ৪ ৫ ৬ ৭ ৮ ৯ ১০

1 2 3 4 5 6 7 8 9 10

Urdu

۱۰ ۹ ۸ ۷ ۶ ۵ ۴ ۳ ۲ ۱

10 9 8 7 6 5 4 3 2 1

Hindi

१ २ ३ ४ ५ ६ ७ ८ ९ १०

1 2 3 4 5 6 7 8 9 10.

5 **Many parents find difficulty in understanding the aims and methods of mathematics teaching.** In my first article I explained why there might be special difficulties for parents educated in Asia, as expectations differ. It is the school's duty to articulate its practices in a way that parents can understand. Formal links, such as parents evenings, can be useful but more informal occasions often provide a relaxed atmosphere in which parents can ask their own questions. For this reason, parents are always welcome to see their children at work in our school. The school has various other ways to encourage parents to join in the work of the school. One of these is a regular weekly games afternoon in which parents are invited to share games and equipment with the children. Whenever possible, speakers of mother tongues are available so that questions can be asked and answered. This contact with parents has brought many benefits to the school; not least are the many new games we have learned.

6 **Teachers need to record the things that the child has learned; they need to see how thinking is developing and the best way to support it.** We feel that assessments should take place as part of the normal learning activity.

Our teachers try to be aware of what the children are saying and doing and to record significant instances which tell how thinking is developing. For instance, Parvin and Sabina had been given the task of measuring each other with bricks. The teacher had given them bricks of different widths. Parvin had measured her friend and was waiting to be measured. Her teacher noted that she said, 'I got big bricks. She got little ones. She want more 'an me.'

This told us a lot about Parvin's ability to predict outcomes, to make and express judgements and to engage with a task, as well as her knowledge of concepts of size and measuring. Also, we can often see that children can use concepts that they cannot yet express in English.

I have learned that there are no special practices or techniques we must learn in order to teach mathematics to our bilingual children. I feel that everything I have mentioned in this article is part of good mathematical teaching practice, e.g. that all young children should be allowed to formulate mathematical ideas in familiar language, that all children should be regarded as potential learners and that parents should be helped to understand what the school is trying to achieve. Asian children, like all the children in our schools, deserve the very best mathematical teaching that we can give.

Notes

1 Quoted from *Primary Education Network in Bangladesh, Capacity and Utilization*, National Foundation for Research in Human Resource Development. June 1979.
2 Figures given by the University of Delhi.
3 Quoted from *Universal Primary Education in Bangladesh* by Ellen Sattar, University Press Limited, Bangladesh. 1982.
4 From *Cenbose* Vol. XVI, No. 3. Published by the Central Board of Secondary Education, New Delhi. 1980.

Valerie Emblen was a teacher in the 'language of mathematics' post in a London infant school; she is now Senior Lecturer for the Early Years at the Polytechnic of North London.

10

The marginalisation of girls in mathematics: some causes and some remedies

Zelda Isaacson

Introduction

In the last few years the volume of literature concerned with gender and mathematics has grown apace, both at home and abroad. The same can be said of literature in the broader field of gender and science, where there is much which is of interest to mathematics educators. During this period there has also grown up an international community of people interested in gender in mathematics and/or science and/or technology. Organisations have been formed and conferences held.[1] This broad and international perspective is extremely valuable in enabling us to move forward – in knowledge, in interpretation, and in strategies for change. So, although the focus of my discussion here is the experiences of girls in mathematics in the UK, I shall also refer to other work where appropriate.

This article is organised into four main sections.

- What are the 'facts'?
- Why does it matter?
- What might some of the reasons be?
- What can we do about it?

As will become clear, I do not see these questions as independent of each other, but I think it is helpful to try and consider them separately as well as in interaction.

In the course of discussion, I shall also consider two further key questions.

(a) Can we identify processes which exclude or marginalise girls in mathematics?
(b) Can we place the marginalisation of girls in mathematics within a broader canvas and see it as a particular case of deeply-rooted social forces which affect many other groups in society?

What are the 'facts'?

What do we actually know about the achievements of girls in mathematics? How do these compare with the achievements of boys? What are the experiences of girls as learners of mathematics? Are girls treated equally with boys in mixed mathematics classrooms? These are the sorts of questions to which we have at least partial answers, and which I shall look at in this section.

Data which go toward answering the first two of these questions derive from a number of sources. One large-scale source is the public examination statistics for England and Wales, which are published each year. These show that there has been a gradual improvement in girls' performance in mathematics relative to that of boys. For the majority of pupils, it is probably the case that girls now do as well as boys. However, at the higher levels of attainment, boys are still achieving proportionally far better results than girls and are participating more. For example, in the old 16+ system, despite a gradual improvement in girls' achievements (see, for example, the table below), each year more boys than girls were entered for O level mathematics, and of those who entered, a higher proportion of boys than girls obtained grade A. At CSE, the entry (and pass) rate of girls has in recent years been higher than that of boys – but boys have obtained the most grade 1 passes. In GCSE, assuming the existing pattern continues, we can predict that more boys than girls will be entered at the top level, and proportionally more boys will gain grade A.

	1974	*1984*
Girls	36%	40%
Boys	64%	60%

Proportion of girls and boys obtaining an O level mathematics pass

At A level, nearly three times as many boys as girls enter, and as at 16+, a greater proportion of the boys who enter gain the top grades. In 1975 the A level pass rate was two girls to every seven boys and in 1985 it was two to every five – undoubtedly an improvement, but still far from approximate equity. If one presumes that girls are innately as capable as boys of learning mathematics, then these figures suggest that girls are underachieving relative to boys, for whatever reason (or that boys are overachieving). Alternatively, girls would have to be presumed to have a lower ability to learn mathematics than boys. These possibilities are discussed in the section entitled 'What might some of the reasons be?'.

The work of the Assessment of Performance Unit (APU, 1985) provides another large-scale source of data in this country. The APU surveys, carried out over the five-year period 1978–1982, monitored the attainment and attitudes of large numbers of 11 and 15 year old pupils. Writing about gender differences in their data, Lynn Joffe and Derek Foxman of the APU mathematics team concluded that their findings show deteriorating confidence of girls compared with boys. (That is, comparing the results of the 11 year old pupils' surveys with those of the 15 year olds.) They also found that at age 15:

> The differences in performance are minimal – except in the top attainment bands.

and that

> The proportion of boys to girls among 15-year-old pupils obtaining the highest 10 per cent of scores on APU concepts and skills tests is 61 per cent to 39 per cent. (Joffe and Foxman, 1984)

There is an interesting parallel between these figures and the O level pass rate statistics of 60% to 40% in 1984. (See the table above.) To add to this gloomy picture of girls lagging behind boys at the top attainment levels in this country are the results of national mathematics competitions, where year after year boys overwhelmingly gain the top scores.

Internationally, the situation is less clear-cut. At an IOWME (International Organisation of Women and Mathematics Education) discussion group in 1986 (see Isaacson, Rogers and Dekker, 1986), Gila Hanna reported on a gender analysis she and Erika Kuendiger had carried out on data from the Second International Mathematics Study (SIMS). The SIMS data, gathered during 1982 in twenty countries, provide information on the mathematics achievement of pupils aged 13 and 17.[2] Hanna and Kuendiger found that differences in mathematics achievement *between countries* are much greater than differences *between girls and boys*. There were five countries (of the twenty involved in the study) where there was no difference between girls and boys, five where girls did better and ten where boys did better. However, these are global figures. I do not know whether the pattern which we see in this country – of significant differences between girls and boys appearing only at the higher levels of achievement – would also apply to the SIMS data.

But at what stage does this difference appear, and why?

In the article on the APU data cited above, Joffe and Foxman claim that 'the main differences in performance are already established by age 11'. This statement is in direct contradiction to the view of other researchers that at least up to age eleven, girls do as well as boys in mathematics. Indeed, this is an area of heated debate and it is quite difficult to tease out what is actually going on. I shall refer to those who believe that differences in attainment appear during adolescence as the A group, and those who argue that these differences are evident during (or at least by the end of) the primary years as the P group. The argument goes something like this:

As: When the 11+ tests were widely held, every year girls as a group did better than boys as a group on all three tests, including the one for arithmetic.

Ps: That may be true, but the 11+ arithmetic test was very limited in scope. It only really tested computational ability.

As: The primary mathematics curriculum *was* arithmetic. The 11+ examination tested what teachers believed it was important for children to know before going on to secondary school. Girls learned these crucially important skills extremely well – and continue to do so!

Ps: That's so, but these are only computational skills.

As: You're saying girls failed because they did well at what was taught and tested!

Ps: No, we're saying that once pupils get into the secondary school, additional skills are needed for learning mathematics. The 11+ didn't test for those, and as they become more important – spatial skills and problem-solving ability, for instance – so girls' performance in mathematics tends to deteriorate.

The argument then divides up. One lot of As holds that not only do girls succeed in primary school, they continue to succeed in secondary school. What goes wrong for girls, they claim, is that teachers do not appropriately value the good work which girls do in mathematics. This point of view is exemplified by the work of Rosie Walden and Valerie Walkerdine (1985). Another A group perspective is that girls do succeed at *what primary schools ask them to do,* but that primary schools and teachers fail to prepare them adequately for more advanced mathematics. The mathematics curriculum is much broader now than it was at the time of the 11+. Primary teachers, however, often continue to restrict the curriculum they offer to one which is mainly arithmetic. One group of Ps ends up at a very similar position to this. The differences are there at primary school, they would say, but this is largely because of the educational experiences of the children (in and out of the classroom). More extreme Ps would hold that the differences are necessarily there.

Most people do not make their position explicit, partly at least because this is still one of the many questions to which we have uncertain answers. All we can say is that girls do as well as boys at the mathematical skills which primary teachers value, such as computation, but that the APU surveys, and the analysis of other researchers such as Hilary Shuard (1986), have picked up differences in the performance of girls and boys which mathematics educators regard as significant. In the main, Shuard focuses on differences in achievement in specific areas of the curriculum – boys doing better in questions involving understanding of place value, spatial visualisation and problem solving, for example, while girls, as ever, do better on straight computational questions. The APU surveys confirm these findings with the added perspective that such differences are only apparent at the top attainment levels. Whether these differences would remain if primary teachers emphasised different aspects of mathematics and different ways of approaching mathematics is unknown. Shuard comments that:

> It would be mischievous to suggest that pupils who pay attention to the teacher's traditional emphases in primary mathematics give themselves a positive *dis*advantage for future success in mathematics, but the evidence seems to point in this direction. (Shuard, 1986)

This debate is important because it points up that 'the facts' are not necessarily as simple and straightforward as they might at first sight seem. And how one interprets 'facts' has a significant effect on the actions one might then take in response to them. Interpretation of the facts is very closely bound up with the question raised in the third section – 'what might some of the reasons be?' – and I consider this further there. Also in that section, I examine the possible answers to the other questions posed previously – that is, 'what are the experiences of girls as learners of mathematics?' and 'are girls treated fairly in mixed-sex mathematics classrooms?'. First, however, I diverge from these to address the question 'why does it matter?'. If differential achievement is of no importance after all, then subtleties of interpretation need not be seriously debated and girls' experiences would hardly be worth exploring.

Why does it matter?

There are several different kinds of answer to this question, to some extent bound up with one's understanding of the reasons for and interpretation of 'the facts'. One has to do with justice. If the reason girls achieve less than boys is because of remediable educational or social conditions which disadvantage them, then it is clearly unjust that girls should get a less fair deal than boys. Attainment and confidence in mathematics are crucially important for many further and higher education courses, and for jobs in the future. Even if only part of the reason for the discrepancy we see is because of factors under our control, natural justice would demand that we strive to put these right. Schools, at least, should not discriminate against any group of pupils and should strive to counter discriminatory 'social' factors. The parallel with anti-racist education is clear.

Leaving justice aside, however, there are good pragmatic reasons for concern. These can be summed up in the words of the Royal Society's working party on Girls and Mathematics:

> . . . without a much increased output of mathematics graduates moving into a range of jobs, the UK faces considerable problems. . . . (The Royal Society, 1986)

And these problems, of course, are not confined to the UK. The shortage of people with adequate training in mathematics is world-wide. Presently, the talents of large numbers of girls and women who might have the potential to work in jobs which require mathematics, are being lost. After all, amongst the girls who do not obtain the top 16+ grades, or who do not go on to do A level mathematics, are some very able pupils. The examination statistics as a whole show girls ahead of boys in numbers of subjects taken and passed, and grades obtained at 16+, and almost on a par at A level. It is only in certain subjects – notably mathematics, technical subjects and physics – that boys do better than girls. In other areas of the curriculum, such as in early language work and later in modern languages, history and biology, girls are ahead of boys.

However, there are significant differences in the way the education system responds to discrepancies in achievement. When boys have difficulty learning to read in the primary school, people do not say 'Oh, well, never mind, boys just aren't very good at reading'. Instead, great efforts are made to ensure that boys do keep up, through, for example, remedial classes which continue into secondary schooling. It has often struck me that remedial classes everywhere in the school system are heavily populated with boys needing help with their language development, yet when able girls slide down in mathematics, that is generally considered as something 'natural' about which no active steps need be taken. Similarly, to revert to the question of the 11+, the fact that girls as a group consistently did better than boys did not result in more grammar school places for girls. Instead, the pass mark was set higher for girls! It was argued, and firmly believed, that boys were 'really' intellectually more able than girls and therefore more likely to benefit from a grammar school education. The reason girls appeared to do better than boys at age eleven was due to the earlier onset of puberty in females, with its accompanying accelerated maturation. 'Positive discrimination' in favour of boys was operated in that context for many years, yet such 'discrimination' in favour of girls – such as by providing them with extra help in their mathematics, or the opportunity to make up lost ground in CDT – is generally frowned upon.

I would therefore argue that even if the discrepancy between girls' and boys' performance at the top levels of achievement in mathematics was entirely due to differences in ability (which I do not believe, but nevertheless should stay as a possible hypothesis), there is a strong case for saying that we should act to try to alter the situation. As stated above, there are close parallels here with anti-racist work in education. In both cases, regardless of the reasons for measured differences in attainment between groups of pupils, both justice and need demand that we act to alter an inequitable status quo.

It matters that girls are getting a less fair deal than boys if, as is the case, fewer of them leave school with qualifications which are useful for employment. Some years ago Lucy Sells (1978) talked about mathematics as 'the critical filter' that determined which careers people might enter. This is still very much the case today. It also matters that society is losing out on a great deal of badly-needed potential mathematical talent. But how best to direct our efforts for improvement is bound up with our perceptions of the reasons for the differences.

What might some of the reasons be?

Over the years, many types of explanation have been put forward to account for 'the facts'. These range widely, encompassing such disparate hypotheses as: genetic differences in mathematics ability; parental expectations; the mathematics curriculum and methods of classroom organisation; and girls' 'fear of success' in mathematics. There are so many 'explanations' that I find it helpful to subdivide them into categories. There are different ways of doing this. One set of categories I have used is: (a) cognitive, (b) educational, and (c) a group which I call the affective/attitudinal/social category. According to this grouping, genetic or innate differences in ability would go into the 'cognitive' basket, as would another hypothesis, namely, that the reason for girls' lower achievement in mathematics is their poorer spatial visualisation ability. Parental expectations and girls' 'fear of success' would go into the affective/attitudinal/social group together with such factors as lack of confidence, differences in the perceived importance of mathematics, peer group pressures and so on. Classroom organisation, teacher behaviour, and the influence of single-sex vs mixed-sex teaching of mathematics would be classed as 'educational', and so would sexism in the curriculum or in classroom materials. There are far too many for me to examine them all properly in this article. I shall select just a few for analysis, and readers are directed to the reading list for additional sources of information.

There is, however, a different way of analysing these many hypotheses. That is, by asking about each one where its proponents place the responsibility for the relative lack of success in *mathematics* of females who are, in a general educational sense, able pupils. In other words, by asking about each how it answers the question – 'do girls fail, or do we fail them?' In many instances, the same 'explanation' can fall into either of these camps. Reverting again to the 11+, it would have been possible to respond to the results of the tests by saying, 'boys are less able at age 11 – they are failing to make proper use of their primary school education' or, as in fact happened, by removing the responsibility from individual boys and situating it elsewhere, in this instance in biology.

A paradigm example of this is the vexed question of spatial visualisation. It has been argued, for a long time now, that the reason girls do not do so well at mathematics is that females, from at least adolescence onwards, have poorer spatial visualisation ability than males. Tests of spatial visualisation have indeed seemed to confirm that this is the case. (See, for example, Maccoby and Jacklin, 1974.) Now, there are a number of ways of responding to this 'fact'. The simple one is to say, 'here we have our answer, and we need look no further – males just are naturally better at spatial visualisation, and hence at mathematics'. Another is to say, 'yes, females are lacking in this respect', but then deny that spatial visualisation is an important factor in the learning of mathematics. A third response is to agree that *as things are presently constituted* females do end up with poorer spatial visualisation skills by adolescence (which may or may not affect the learning of mathematics), but then claim that the *reason* for this outcome is differential male–female learning experiences. (See, for example, Fennema, 1979.) These differential learning experiences (and/or social influences which discriminate against girls in this respect), it may then be argued, also independently affect the learning of mathematics. Often cited in this context is the fact that young boys, far more often than girls, play with Lego and other constructional toys, thus building up their spatial concepts and skills gradually over time. (See, for example, Taylor, 1986.) Differences in spatial visualisation ability and mathematics attainment may thus be different outcomes of the same basic cause or may themselves be cause and effect.

The difficulty is that we do not have enough evidence to come to a sure conclusion. We do know that *at present* males perform better than females at spatial visualisation tests. We also have some evidence (see, for example, Whyte, 1986) that this may be a learned difference which can be altered through appropriate educational experiences. The extent to which this can be done, and, further, whether or not attainment in mathematics is significantly affected by this difference, is unknown. We are forced to conclude that our present knowledge is too limited to cope with these complexities. Individual teachers and researchers will, of course, form their own conclusions from the available evidence, backed up by their own experience; conclusions which could put this particular 'explanation' into either of the two groups I described above.

Similar problems arise if we look at 'the facts' about girls' experiences as learners of mathematics, where the single/mixed-sex debate, the question of teacher behaviour and the debate on classroom organisation and curriculum materials must be considered. Here, too, there are great areas of uncertainty. There is some evidence that in mixed-sex classrooms teachers give more attention to boys, to the detriment of girls' learning. There is also some evidence, but very limited indeed, that girls may prefer a less competitive and more collaborative style of working, so that classrooms which are resource based and organised for group working tend to be classrooms where girls thrive.

To take the single/mixed-sex question: there is some evidence, mainly based on one school (Smith, 1986) that when pupils in a mixed school are taught in single-sex classes for mathematics for some years, girls' performance improves. It is essential, however, to be very cautious about all such evidence. For one thing, conclusions drawn from a very limited sample may not be reliable. For another, there may be other factors at work giving rise to the outcome noted. In this instance, the very fact that a school cares enough about the success of its female pupils to try an experiment in single-sex teaching may be sufficient to account for their improved performance. Many significant messages will have been conveyed to both teachers and pupils. For instance, teachers involved in this scheme would know that the success of their female pupils would be very carefully monitored, and that senior people in the school would be looking at the girls' test results. In those circumstances, teachers would be likely to offer girls a great deal of encouragement, perhaps more than they previously had done. Similarly, the girls in the scheme could hardly fail to be aware of eyes on them, and of their success in mathematics being of importance to significant others. In other words, it could be these unspoken messages which altered the classroom climate sufficiently for girls to do better, rather than the simple fact of them being in a single-sex environment.

Another kind of explanation is offered by Rosalinde Scott-Hodgetts (1986). She applies Pask's notion of two distinct learning strategies – serialist and holist – to the gender and mathematics issue and suggests that girls may tend towards serialist strategies, which are also emphasised by primary teachers and thus reinforced. Boys, on the other hand, tend towards holist strategies, and get training in serialist strategies from their teachers, thus providing the opportunity for them to become versatile learners. As 'the most successful mathematics students will generally be versatile learners', this, if it is true, could make a significant contribution to our understanding of the processes by which girls are gradually marginalised in mathematics. As this is quite a difficult idea, which I have no space to elaborate here, readers are recommended to read Scott-Hodgetts' paper cited above. She offers a persuasive and very interesting hypothesis, as yet unsubstantiated, to which classroom research could usefully be directed.

And, indeed, if we look closely at any of the explanations which have been offered, we are forced to admit that we actually *know* very little beyond the bare statistics of attainment in public examinations or national surveys. Where does this uncertainty leave us? How can we act when so much is unknown? It is in this context of agnosticism that I shall look at my fourth question, 'what can we do about it?'

What can we do about it?

For a start, I begin with the premise that action makes a difference. My second premise is that in such a complex area, where social, cognitive, pedagogic, affective, inter-personal and indeed ethical factors interact – as they do in all aspects of education – there is unlikely to be a simple or single answer.

From my perspective, then, our lack of certainty should lead, not to inaction but to action on a multitude of fronts simultaneously. Where changing something *could* make a difference, and seems unlikely to do harm, we should go ahead and do it. Into this category I put such obvious improvements as eliminating sexism from textbooks, other curriculum materials and examinations. For instance, if examples in which females play an active role appear as often as those in which the active person is male, this may help counteract the prevailing view in society that mathematics is primarily an activity for males.

Similarly, where changing something seems commendable anyway, for ethical or social reasons, for example, and may incidentally benefit girls, we should do that. Changing classrooms from solely competitive places to ones where all pupils can learn the vital skills of co-operation and collaboration is such an instance. The ability to work well as a member of a team is a life skill and one which is increasingly valued in the world of work. If this also makes mathematics classrooms places where girls feel more comfortable and therefore encourages them to stay with mathematics longer, that is all to the good. Extending the curriculum to include a range of applications which more adequately than at present represents the kinds of human endeavour where mathematics is used would be another such change, with fewer examples involving ballistics and war, for instance, and more involving such activities as working with fabrics, designing appliances for the disabled or looking at the school canteen's queuing problems. Also, examples which reflect everyday human interests – e.g. going on holiday, buying household goods, holding a raffle – rather than ones which focus on male-dominated activities such as football and motor car racing, may help girls (and boys) become aware of the *general* usefulness of mathematical skills in everyday life. This would be good in itself as well as helping to decrease sexism in mathematics classroom materials.

Into this category of changes which are good in themselves also fall such strategies as encouraging girls as well as boys to play with constructional toys and engage in CDT activities as they move through the education system from nursery to secondary school. This could have the effect of improving girls' spatial visualisation skills – and may also, directly or indirectly, favourably affect their learning of mathematics. It could also have the effect of suggesting to girls that activities society regards as 'male' are pleasurable and rewarding, and therefore encourage them to stay with the male-dominated subjects – science, technology and mathematics – throughout secondary schooling. If, alongside this, boys are allowed to develop e.g. their caring faculties and to contemplate traditionally female careers such as nursing and social work, we might also see fewer boys taking A level mathematics and finding it unsatisfying for them, as Sheila Russell's research (1983) indicated is all too frequently the case. Russell interviewed sixth form pupils in the Bradford area during 1982, and amongst other things commented that 'it was disturbing to discover the number of boys who were reluctantly studying the subject mathematics at A level, and were not enjoying it'.

Other changes, such as experimenting with the creation of single-sex mathematics classes in a mixed school, are less straightforward and would depend for their success on the particular context of each individual school, and especially the reasons for employing this strategy. As a way of focusing the attention of school staff on the importance of encouraging girls to work at their mathematics, it is an excellent strategy. It also, by the simple fact of providing a space in the school day where girls are separated from boys, can relieve the stresses for girls who may be suffering harassment from their male peers – in or out of the classroom. (See, for example, Mahony, 1985.) Some mature women who had returned to study mathematics and science described their memories of learning mathematics at school.[3] Many commented on the effect on their learning of having boys in their class. For example:

> Especially in maths I couldn't stand the competitiveness of seeing the 'clever boy' (there's always one in every class!) do the exercises miles before everyone else and understanding things quicker than everybody which just reinforced the idea that I didn't have a 'mathematical brain'.

> I was encouraged to do A level maths at school, but didn't fancy being in a group full of nasty adolescent boys (as I then saw it) and so opted for English and languages.

Single-sex setting can, however, backfire. If the staff of a school are required to 'do something about equal opportunities' and have read that a single-sex environment improves girls' performance in mathematics and science, there may well be the belief that once they have reorganised their classes in this way, they have done all that is necessary. And in a social context of too few well-trained and experienced mathematics teachers, where the parents of boys are more likely to complain if their children are badly taught, the girls' classes may well be assigned the less competent or less experienced teachers. The justification given could be that it is easier to control girls than boys, and therefore the 'stronger' teachers should be given the more difficult classes, i.e. the boys' classes. If this happens, the simple fact of shifting to single-sex classes is unlikely to benefit girls.

Conclusions and future directions

The previous section starts with a premise – that action makes a difference. This section too starts with a premise, which is that individual pupils are active participants in their own education. This may seem so obvious as not to need stating, but I believe that it can be overlooked. It is easy to fall into the trap of looking for causal relations between what we (the education community) do and what pupils achieve, and forget to take into account our pupils' own efforts, perceptions and experiences. I believe that there is a very complex social dynamic operating in this (and other) areas of education and that therefore simple cause-and-effect hypotheses are unlikely to be adequate.

The title of this article may suggest that I am claiming that *all* girls are marginalised in mathematics, but I hope that I have indicated that the situation we actually see is far more complicated than this. The examination statistics, for example, depressing though they are, do not convey a uniform picture of low achievement in or exclusion from mathematics learning for girls. There are indeed significant differences in the achievements of boys and girls, but nonetheless, many girls do succeed. Further, there is such a large overlap between girls' and boys' test or examination results that it is true to say that a great many girls do better at mathematics than the majority of boys.

Another way to put this is to point out that it is interesting and significant that many females are *not* alienated from mathematics. Further, many females who are alienated or marginalised at one stage of their lives are included at another, and vice versa. The statements written by two of the women on the HITECC course cited above are illustrative of the latter claim. I therefore see the *processes* by which these shifts come about as crucially important to our understanding of the interrelationship of gender and mathematics. In a recent paper (Isaacson, 1988) I put forward two theoretical constructs, *coercive inducements* and *double conformity*, which 'individually and even more so together offer powerful explanations and far-reaching insights'. Coercive inducements are inducements which are so powerful, and so difficult to refuse, that they come to act as a kind of coercion. The rewards and approval granted girls for appropriately 'feminine' behaviour – dates, pretty clothes, marriage and children – are an example, as are the rewards for appropriately 'masculine' behaviour, such as money and power, offered to boys. Double conformity describes a situation where a person has to conform, at the same time, to two, mutually-inconsistent sets of standards. Women in 'male' occupations often experience just this – there is conflict between, for example, 'behaving like a proper woman' and behaving in a manner appropriate to an engineer or scientist.

There is, regretfully, no space in this article to spell out in greater detail just what I mean by these dynamic explanatory constructs. I can do no more here than say that I believe that they illuminate some of the processes whereby females come to *wish* to disassociate themselves from mathematics and other scientific and/or technical activities. Males, also, can especially be affected by coercive inducements, usually in the opposite direction. That is, boys can be coercively induced into careers which are traditionally male, while girls are being coercively induced into adopting traditionally female choices and modes of behaviour.

Further, the operation of these processes is not restricted to the male–female dimension. I believe that these (and not only these) deeply-rooted social-dynamic forces act on other groups in society in such a way as to make it relatively more difficult for some groups than others to enter particular occupations. Here, yet again, there is a parallel with anti-racist education. An understanding of the processes involved in 'choice' and participation is essential if we are to include more girls, and members of other disadvantaged groups, and alienate fewer. The marginalisation of girls in mathematics is an exemplar of many parallel trends and I believe that the way forward here, as in others, is through a study of the dynamic processes involved.

Notes

1 Examples of organisations:
   (a) IOWME (International Organisation of Women and Mathematics Education) was formed in 1976, has met at the ICME (International Congress on Mathematical Education) conferences in 1980 and 1984, and since 1985 has produced a bi-annual newsletter. In 1986 and 1987 an IOWME discussion group took place within the PME (Psychology of Mathematics Education) annual conferences. At ICME-6, held in Hungary in 1988, IOWME was recognised as an International Study Group and was allocated four sessions on the international programme.
   (b) GASAT (Girls and Science and Technology) has held international conferences biennially since 1981. At the last conference (1987) informal international networks were set up, including one for mathematics. The next conference is likely to be held in Israel in 1989.
   (c) GAMMA (Gender and Mathematics Association) is a national association in the UK and has produced a newsletter since it was founded in 1981. A national conference has been held each year in different parts of the country, and local GAMMA groups put on occasional day and half-day conferences in their own areas. GAMMA, in conjunction with academic institutions, has also collaborated in putting on conferences for schoolgirls, such as MAYF (Maths and Your Future), a residential conference for sixth form girls held at Goldsmiths' College, and 'Be a Sumbody' day conferences for 13 to 14 year old girls at Avery Hill College. To get more information about GAMMA (and through GAMMA about IOWME and GASAT), write to: GAMMA, c/o Marion Kimberley, Department of Mathematical Sciences, Goldsmiths' College, New Cross, London SE14 6NW.

2 The data from the Second International Mathematics Study relating to England and Wales have recently been published (Cresswell and Gubb, 1987). The international data have not yet (at time of writing) been published, but draft results have been available for research purposes.

3 These are women on a HITECC (Higher Introductory Technology and Engineering Conversion Course) at the Polytechnic of North London, 1987–1988. The course is designed for people who have A levels in subjects other than mathematics and physics and wish to enter a degree course, such as Electronic Engineering, which requires these. The author teaches these students and is also gathering data on them for research purposes.

References and further reading

Assessment of Performance Unit (1985) *Mathematical Development: A Review of Monitoring in Mathematics 1978–1982*. Windsor: NFER.

Brown, S. I. (1986) 'The Logic of Problem Generation: from Morality and Solving to De-Posing and Rebellion', in Burton, L. (ed.) *Girls Into Maths Can Go*. London: Holt, Rinehart and Winston.

Burton, L. (ed.) (1986) *Girls Into Maths Can Go*. London: Holt, Rinehart and Winston. (A collection of UK papers on research initiatives and analysis.)

Chipman, S. F., Brush, L. R. and Wilson, D. M. (eds) (1985) *Women and Mathematics: Balancing the Equation*. New Jersey: Lawrence Erlbaum. (A collection of papers on research initiatives and analysis from the USA.)

Cresswell, M. and Gubb, J. (1987) *The Second International Mathematics Study in England and Wales*. Windsor: NFER/Nelson.

DES (1985) *Statistics of Education 1984*. London: HMSO.

Easlea, B. (1981) *Science and Sexual Oppression*. London: Weidenfeld and Nicolson.

The Fawcett Society (1987) *Exams for the Boys*. The Fawcett Society.

Fennema, E. (1979) 'Women and Girls in Mathematics – Equity in Mathematics Education', *Educational Studies in Mathematics*, **10**(4), pp. 389–401.

Gilligan, C. (1982) *In a Different Voice*. Cambridge, Mass: Harvard University Press.

Grant, M. (1983) 'Mathematics Counts in Craft, Design and Technology – but not for some', in *GAMMA Newsletter*, 4.

Inner London Education Authority/Open University (1987) *Girls Into Mathematics*. London: ILEA/OU. (A resource pack for teachers.)

Isaacson, Z. (1982) 'Gender and Mathematics in England and Wales: a Review' in *An International Review of Gender and Mathematics*. ERIC, Ohio State University.

Isaacson, Z. (1986) 'Freedom and Girls' Education: a Philosophical Discussion with Particular Reference to Mathematics', in Burton, L. (ed.) *Girls Into Maths Can Go*. London: Holt, Rinehart and Winston.

Isaacson, Z. (1988) 'Of course you *could* be an engineer, dear, but wouldn't you *rather* be a nurse or teacher or secretary?', in Ernest, P. (ed.) *The Social Context of Mathematics Teaching (Perspectives 38)*. School of Education, University of Exeter.

Isaacson, Z., Rogers, P. and Dekker, T. (1986) 'Report on IOWME Discussion Group at PME 10' in *IOWME Newsletter*, **2**(2), 3–6.

Joffe, L. and Foxman, D. (1984) 'Assessing Mathematics: 5. Attitudes and Sex Differences', *Mathematics in School*, **13**(4), pp. 22–6, (Also published as 'Attitudes and Sex Differences: some APU findings', in Burton, L. (ed.) *Girls Into Maths Can Go*. London: Holt, Rinehart and Winston.)

Keller, E. F. (1985) *Reflections on Gender and Science*. New Haven, CT: Yale University Press.

Kelly, A. (ed.) (1987) *Science for Girls?* Milton Keynes: Open University Press.

Maccoby, E. E. and Jacklin, C. N. (1974) *The Psychology of Sex Differences*. Stanford, California: Stanford University Press.

Mahony, P. (1985) *Schools for the Boys?: Co-education reassessed.* London: Hutchinson.

The Royal Society (1986) *Girls and Mathematics.* A report by the Joint Mathematical Education Committee of the Royal Society and the Institute of Mathematics and its Applications, The Royal Society.

Russell, S. (1983) *Factors Influencing the Choice of Advanced Level Mathematics by Boys and Girls.* Centre for Studies in Science Education, University of Leeds.

Scott-Hodgetts, R. (1986) 'Girls and Mathematics: the Negative Implications of Success', in Burton, L. (ed.) *Girls Into Maths Can Go*. London: Holt, Rinehart and Winston.

Sells, L. (1978) 'Mathematics – A Critical Filter', *The Science Teacher*, **45**, pp. 28–9.

Sharma, S. and Meighan, R. (1980) 'Schooling and Sex Roles: the Case of GCE 'O' level Mathematics', *British Journal of Sociology of Education,* **1** (2) pp. 193–205.

Shuard, H. (1986) 'The Relative Attainment of Girls and Boys in Mathematics in the Primary Years', in Burton, L. (ed.) *Girls Into Maths Can Go*. London: Holt, Rinehart and Winston.

Smith, S. (1986) *Separate Tables?* London: HMSO (for the Equal Opportunities Commission).

Smith, S. (1987) *Separate Beginnings?* London: Equal Opportunities Commission.

Taylor, H. (1986) 'Experience with a Primary School Implementing an Equal Opportunities Policy', in Burton, L. (ed.) *Girls Into Maths Can Go*. London: Holt, Rinehart and Winston. (Also published as 'Girls and Boys and Lego', *Mathematics Teaching*, **115**, June 1986.)

Walden, R. and Walkerdine, V. (1982) *Girls and Mathematics: the Early Years.* Bedford Way Paper 8, Institute of Education, London.

Walden, R. and Walkerdine, V. (1985) *Girls and Mathematics: from Primary to Secondary Schooling.* Bedford Way Paper 24, Institute of Education, London.

Whyte, J. (1986) *Girls Into Science and Technology: the Story of a Project.* London: Routledge & Kegan Paul.

Zelda Isaacson is a Senior Lecturer in Mathematics Education at the Polytechnic of North London.

11

Low attainers *can* do mathematics[1]

Liz Trickett and Frankie Sulke

> Why can children handle money situations in town on Saturday and fail to do the 'sums' in school on Monday?
>
> I don't know, I just put the title 'Division' on the board and they immediately wail that they can't do it.
>
> But they've got to know 'the basics' so they can survive.
>
> How can I get them doing any more interesting work if they can't concentrate for more than ten minutes at a time?

Such comments are familiar in any school environment. The Low Attainers in Mathematics Project (LAMP, 1983–6) was concerned about the issues underlying comments like these. The Project set out to develop and encourage 'good practice' in the teaching of mathematics to low-attaining pupils, but it became clear at an early stage that low attainment was not limited to pupils in the 'bottom 40 per cent' attainment range. Many teachers express concern that even their more able pupils do not fulfil their potential in the subject. Teachers involved in LAMP found the changes they were making in their teaching approaches were encouraging *all* their pupils to become more involved in their mathematics and to surpass traditional expectations at every level. The problem became one of underachievement across the whole age and ability range. This general concern of underachievement became the focus for LAMP's successor, the Raising Achievement in Mathematics Project (RAMP, 1986–9) which involves teachers from 34 LEAs nationally. This article reflects the ongoing, personal classroom-based research of teachers involved in the projects. It is an invitation to all those concerned with raising achievement in mathematics to experiment, discuss and debate as a result of their *own* experiences.

Mathematics seems to be viewed by most people as a body of established knowledge and procedures – facts and rules. This describes the forms in which we observe mathematics in calculations, proofs and standard methods. However, most mathematicians would see this as a very narrow view of their subject. It denies the value of mathematics as an activity in which to engage. Decision making, experimenting hypothesising, generalising, modelling, communicating, interpreting, proving, symbolising and pattern finding are all integral parts of that activity. Without engaging in processes such as these, nobody would have been able to create the procedures and systems mentioned above in the first place. When teachers involved with LAMP began to allow their pupils to engage in mathematics in this broader way they found their pupils better able and more willing to question, to transfer and apply their mathematics and to sort out even quite difficult problems. They found their pupils thriving on a kind of learning which requires a minimum of factual knowledge, a large element of challenge and a great deal of experience in dealing with situations using particular kinds of thinking and practical skills.

Although children of all ages and abilities, including those in MLD schools, were benefiting from such experiences and teaching approaches, there has been a resistance within the special needs sector to allow pupils to engage in a broader-based mathematics curriculum. It is often the case that the mathematical diet for these lower attaining pupils consists of little more than basic arithmetic, presented in simple step-by-step learning sequences, and repeated frequently. This is usually because it is felt that they cannot cope with anything at a higher level or with more demanding work – they 'cannot concentrate', 'cannot transfer knowledge from one situation to another', 'cannot remember from one day to the next', 'cannot cope with sequential tasks', 'get confused by experiencing more than one way of doing something', and most definitely 'cannot do fractions'. These beliefs about what low attainers *cannot* do dictate and reflect the kind of learning experience these pupils have. If teachers do not believe that their pupils are able to be more responsible for their own mathematical learning, then they are not likely to give them the opportunity to be so. Such teacher perceptions about how children learn have enormous implications for actions taken in classrooms.

Consider the contrasting lists opposite. The caricature of teacher beliefs in List A would give rise to a correspondingly narrow set of teacher actions, whereas a teacher characterised by List B may well have a wider, more enabling, range of teaching strategies available.

The commonly-held view that good teachers are ones who can pass on their expertise through clear explanations so as to avoid confusing their pupils has some interesting implications. The view implies that the teacher is the holder of answers in a classroom, one who knows the answers to all of the pupils' questions. In a classroom where such an answer-orientated atmosphere exists, it is difficult to imagine much exploration into unknown territory taking place, as pupils will find it difficult to believe that there are areas where their teacher does not know 'the answer'. This leads to a marked lack of independence on behalf of pupils as is evidenced by their constant cries of 'Is this right, Miss?' This atmosphere also helps to perpetuate the view of mathematics where the only problems are those with a right or wrong answer, or a right or wrong method. Teachers have found that the more solutions and strategies pupils see and discuss, the more likely they are to develop a real appreciation of mathematics at their own level.

The view also implies that the teacher is seen by pupils as having total responsibility for leading and controlling the work that is going on in the classroom. LAMP and RAMP have found that because pupils rarely get the chance to use their own initiative, they become even more dependent on their teacher for direction. Staffroom complaints about fifth years still having to be 'spoon fed' are therefore not really surprising. This 'teacher authority' can lead to pupils being stifled by their teachers' expectations.

LIST A	**LIST B**
Pupils dislike mathematics and will avoid it if they can.	Children freely engage in activities that are essentially mathematical. Away from the classroom they make up complex games, work on puzzle books and generally succeed in finding their way around their environment.
Pupils want to be told what to do and be directed towards appropriate tasks.	Pupils are able to identify and direct themselves towards appropriate tasks.
Pupils are mainly motivated by teacher approval, or a desire to succeed at examinations or achieve 'tokens of merit'.	Pupils can become fascinated by mathematical contradictions and absurdities and are motivated by mathematical activity itself.
Most pupils have little creativity or imagination, except when it comes to thinking of excuses for not having done their homework.	Creativity and ingenuity are widely distributed and evident in the natural activities of children outside school.
There are identifiable skills which the teacher knows and which need to be explained to the children and practised so that they are well equipped for life.	The mastery of skills is of little use if they cannot be applied. The skills pupils need are the strategies of problem solving; interpreting mathematical forms and statements; representing situations mathematically. These must be developed in context, through experiences.
Pupils need clear step-by-step explanations in order to avoid confusion.	A state of temporary confusion or puzzlement is at the heart of all learning.
Pupils are empty vessels waiting to be filled from the teacher's stock of expert knowledge.	Pupils bring their own knowledge and experience and need to be actively involved in their mathematical development.

This teacher highlights the problem:

> In developing work in the classroom one's own expectations and experiences often interfere with a child's progress and it is important to be aware of this and exercise self control.
>
> My main aim is to direct their work as little as possible, letting them find their own system and choose their own path to follow. I am not advocating no guidance though, since a teacher's role in this respect is a vital one, but it can easily be overdone and destroy a sense of personal achievement.
>
> This requires cutting the instructions to a bare minimum, so that you are, in effect, just providing them with the seed of an idea, and allowing them to culture it.

In a climate of teacher expertise, teachers frequently pre-empt pupils' decisions because they do not want them to 'get into a mess'. However, this enthusiasm to convey solutions to pupils often ends up by precluding the pupils' own ideas and can not only be inhibiting but also take away the pupils' enjoyment of getting there themselves.

In our efforts to make things easier for our pupils we often act in other inhibiting ways. Four common classroom actions that restrict pupils' mathematical development are outlined below.

1 The subject is broken down into 'easily digestible topics'. Teachers often lament that pupils do not see and use links between different areas of the subject. When it is considered that in the 'real world' mathematics does not come in the small, fragmented packages that so frequently exist on our syllabuses (e.g. 'Fractions' and 'Decimals', 'Addition' and 'Multiplication', 'Perimeter' and 'Area'), it is not surprising that pupils are unable to get a useful overview, or see relationships.

2 There is an over-concern to simplify, by breaking general ideas into seemingly unrelated stages. The point of the overall task in hand is often obscured when step-by-step instructions are provided: for example, when a pupil neatly sets out a multiplication sum in order to multiply by 10. The development of flexible mental mathematical skills is also inhibited by such an approach.

3 Difficulties are smoothed out for pupils by, for example, ensuring that awkward cases do not occur or that the numbers cancel or that the answer is not a fraction. This presents a false view of the subject and can lead to the situation where unusual extensions of these easier cases are not recognised. It also restricts opportunities for pupils' own interesting mathematical questions like:

> 'Is 0 a number?'
> 'What does this '–' mean on my calculator?'

4 It is often assumed that techniques must be learned and practised before problems are mentioned. This can lead to a lack of motivation, as well as to a lack of understanding and meaning. When pupils complain that they 'don't see the point of doing all these', they are often given a remote justification – 'you'll need it when you buy a carpet'.

Remarkable results have been achieved with children from mainstream and special schools when the teaching of mathematics has been opened up in order to allow pupils to find their own strategies and solutions to problems. Teachers have found their pupils well able to cope with the frustrations and floundering inherent in mathematical challenge provided it is in a supportive atmosphere or environment, where the process of struggle is viewed as successful in itself.

The following teacher's writing illustrates how his pupils have gained in confidence and initiative. The group is a non-examination class who have become used to engaging in mathematics in an enquiring way. The teacher had been sent some worksheets to try out.

> The idea was that the pupils would just work through the sheets, working out the answers. They had a sheet showing a car park and also cars to cut out. They had to fit the cars in the car park in such a way that each car could get in and out. The cars (four of them) were all different dimensions. Well, we started off as expected but then the pupils started asking:
>
> How did we know it would be those four particular cars? (I thought I had got out of this by saying it was a firm's car park so it would be the same four drivers.)
>
> Ah yes! But what if one or more changed their cars?
>
> They thought the entrance to the car park on the sheet was not in the best place, so they changed it.
>
> Some decided they would have an entrance and an exit. I tried to say perhaps this was not possible as we did not know what was outside the car park, walls, buildings, etc. They decided that as there was nothing shown on the sheet, there was nothing there and if there was, it should have been shown.
>
> They were no longer happy to accept worksheets at their face value and we had two whole lessons with them querying and rearranging. It made me suddenly realise how much they had changed. I had never known low-ability children to question worksheets. They had always been fed a diet of worksheets which led them along step by step – now they were thinking and making decisions for themselves.
>
> I have to say that my approach to teaching mathematics has changed beyond all my expectations and I now see my pupils enquiring and searching for answers themselves. It certainly keeps the teacher on the ball when the pupils are not prepared to accept everything you say or do without questioning.

Teachers have also found their pupils more able and willing to apply 'routine skills' to a level exceeding previous expectations. Children have shown themselves able to take ideas further than ever before. The pupils' work shown overleaf illustrates this. Their teacher had played a 'think of a number' game with them, using starters like: 'I think of a number. I divide it by two. The answer is five. What was my number?' The children responded by making up their own problems for each other. Their problems were far more complex than any the teacher might have set them.

These changes in teaching approach have developed through teachers coming together to question and challenge their own and each others' assumptions about mathematics learning and teaching. Through reflecting on and discussing their experiences in the classroom, both successful and unsuccessful, teachers involved in LAMP and RAMP have found themselves better equipped to facilitate the mathematical development of their pupils. This ongoing professional development is based on the

Norman's work:

I think of a number double it, minus 4 minus 5: plus 3, plus 6, minus 1, plus 2, split into 3rds plus 1. the answer is 10

I think of a number I plus 5, minus 10, plus 5 and the answer is douple what you come up with

Youre Got the number 10 your plus 2 X it by three -26 and your answer is -

Take a number double it +2 what do you need. to get 10.

I think of a number I plus it with double 2 and your answer is 10

Terry's work:

I think of a number .. add 3 Take-away 2 The answer is 11 - number was..

I think of a number Take away 10 - add 25 double it - answer is 60. number was..

I think of a number - Take away 10 - add 3 half it - double the answer is 66 number was..

fundamental premise that solutions and strategies lie in teachers' own expertise and experience. The process of intensely examining one's own practice is not an easy one. This teacher wrote of his experiences:

> I have been enabled to think seriously and deeply about my approach to the subject. It has made me question every aspect of my teaching, including things that I though I was doing well! Psychologically this has been quite traumatic; but essential. Towards the end of this 'shake down' period it has enabled me to experiment confidently, often using the experience and success of other teachers as encouragement.

The Project provides a focus and catalyst for a large and continuously growing network of working groups whose emphasis is always on the development of professionalism and improved practice. A group of teachers involved in one such group attempted to draw up a list describing necessary ingredients for a rich mathematical activity.

WHAT MAKES A RICH MATHEMATICAL ACTIVITY

- It must be accessible to everyone at the start.
- It needs to allow further challenges and be extendable.
- It should invite children to make decisions.
- It should involve children in speculating, hypothesis making and testing, proving or explaining, reflecting, interpreting.
- It should not restrict pupils from searching in other directions.
- It should promote discussion and communication.
- It should encourage originality/invention.
- It should encourage 'what if' and 'what if not' questions.
- It should have an element of surprise.
- It should be enjoyable.

They then went on to pool ideas on strategies for generating mathematical enquiry in the classroom.

START WITH EXPLORATORY TYPE QUESTIONS LIKE:

HOW MANY DIFFERENT............ways to work out 21 + 13?
............ways to draw an equilateral triangle?

WHAT HAPPENS WHEN............? CAN YOU FIND A BETTER WAY............?

IS IT TRUE THAT............14 − 13 is the same as 13 − 14?

GET PUPILS TO SET THEIR OWN QUESTIONS.........pass them around.

ASK THEM TO FIND OUT HOW TO DO SOMETHING............find the area of a triangle.
............construct a 30 degree angle.

START WITH A PROBLEM OR DILEMMA............explore.
............sort out the contradictions or confusions.

START WITH AN ANSWER............explore.
............how did they get it?
............what was the question/problem?
............what's gone wrong?

USE AN OUTSIDE STIMULUS............radio/TV/newspaper puzzles.
............advertisements.
............familiar everyday anomalies.

GET PUPILS TO MAKE OR INVENT SOMETHING............to measure turn.
............to measure time.
............to carry a certain weight.

USE GAMES............can they make them harder?
............can they understand each other's rules?

All these strategies have the potential to involve *all* pupils in mathematical challenge, enabling them to engage in a broader curriculum.

The following list is taken from *Gifted Children and their Education* (Hoyle and Wilks, 1977). It is part of 'a teacher's checklist' designed to help identify the gifted child in the classroom. The gifted child will:

- have great intellectual curiosity;
- learn easily and readily;
- have a wide range of interests;
- have a broad attention span that enables them to concentrate on, and persevere in solving problems and pursuing interests;
- have ability to do effective work independently;
- exhibit keen powers of observation;
- show initiative and originality in intellectual work;
- show alertness and quick responses to new ideas;
- possess unusual imagination.

Teachers involved in LAMP and RAMP have found that their so-called 'low attaining' pupils are continually showing themselves to have these learning characteristics and more. This should make all those involved with mathematics education question what it is that we can do to enhance and develop these talents. Our pupils' mathematical attainment and experience must not be limited by our restricted expectations.

Note

1 This article is based on evidence from the Low Attainers in Mathematics Project (1983–6) and the Raising Achievement in Mathematics Project (1986–9). RAMP is directed by Afzal Ahmed.

References and further reading

Ahmed, A. G. *et al.* (1985) *Mathematics for Low Attainers.* WSIHE/West Sussex County Council.

Beers, S. (1975) *Platform for Change*. Chichester: Wiley.

Bird, M. (1983) *Generating Mathematical Activity in the Classroom.* Mathematical Association.

Department of Education and Science (1982) *Mathematics Counts* (The Cockcroft Report). London: HMSO.

Dickson, L., Brown, M. and Gibson, O. (1984) *Children Learning Mathematics*. London: Holt, Rinehart and Winston.

Donaldson, M. (1978) *Children's Minds*. London: Fontana.

Hart, K. (ed.) (1981) *Children's Understanding of Mathematics 11–16*. London: John Murray.

Holt, J. (1969) *How Children Fail*. London: Penguin.

Hoyle, E. and Wilks, J. (1977) *Gifted Children and their Education*. London: HMSO.

Low Attainers in Mathematics Project (1978) *Better Mathematics*. London: HMSO.

Macnab, D. S. and Cummine, J. A. (1986) *Teaching Mathematics 11–16*. Oxford: Basil Blackwell.

Liz Trickett is a peripatetic remedial teacher in Surrey.

Frankie Sulke is Senior Lecturer in Mathematics Education at the Mathematics Centre, West Sussex Institute of Higher Education, Bognor Regis.

12

Hidden messages

Jenny Maxwell

There is an almost unchallenged assumption that mathematics education, for both teacher and taught, occurs in a political vacuum. This I cannot accept: it seems impossible that such a central part, mathematics, of such a political institution, education, should really be politically neutral.

It is easier to be objective about, and therefore to recognise, the social bias of mathematics questions from abroad. Chinese examples stress agricultural and military applications; a Cuban textbook asks children to find 'the average monthly number of violations of Cuban air-space by North American airplanes'; Russian children are asked about collective farms; East German children have a similarity problem about a tower in Berlin and a bigger one in Moscow. All the following problems contain assumptions, some explicit and some implicit, about the society from which they (or in some cases their enemies) come.

> Twenty-three peasants are working in a field. At midday six guerrilla fighters arrive to help them from a military base near to their village. How many people are working in the field? (Mozambique)[1]

> Once upon a time a ship was caught in a storm. In order to save it and its crew the captain decided that half of the passengers would have to be thrown overboard. There were fifteen Christians and fifteen Turks aboard the ship and the Captain was a Christian. He announced that he would count the passengers and that every ninth one would be thrown overboard. How could the passengers be placed in the circle so that all the Turks would be thrown overboard and all the Christians saved? (USA)

> A Freedom Fighter fires a bullet to an enemy group consisting of twelve soldiers and three civilians all equally exposed to the bullet. Assuming one person is hit by the bullet, find the probability that the person is (a) a soldier, and (b) a civilian. (Tanzania)

> When worker Tung was six years old his family was poverty-stricken and starving. They were compelled to borrow five dou of maize from a landlord. The wolfish landlord used this chance to demand the usurious compound interest of 50% for three years. Please calculate how much grain the landlord demanded from the Tung family at the end of the third year. (China)[3]

These examples coming from foreign cultures strike most of us as blatantly political, a part of the indoctrination of the young into the currently dominant values in these societies. But I feel that we are less aware of this same process when it occurs in British schools.

To find out more about this I recently made up a small collection of questions on percentages. They were based on textbook questions, some almost as printed, but slightly altered to make political points. I then asked some twenty-five teachers (in schools and FE) for their reactions to these questions.

One question concerned Mr Jones who owned a factory employing 100 people. He drew a salary of £15000 pa, paid each of the 20 supervisory staff £10000 pa and the other 80 employees £6000 pa. The question asked for the total wage bill and went on:

> The company has done well in the last year so Mr Jones decides to give himself a 15% rise, the supervisory staff a 10% rise and the non-supervisory staff a 5% rise.

There were then questions about the new wage bill. Only ten out of my twenty-five teachers found the social and political assumptions here worth commenting on:

- There's a bit to talk about there . . . we might have a little talk about industrial justice.
- This is the shocking one . . . I'd have to have a laugh about it . . . I couldn't resist a comment.

It was surprising that there was divided opinion even amongst teachers from the same institution, about whether or not the student would notice the inequalities of this industrial situation.

Another question was ridiculous, about a spider's weight which increased to 500 g. Sixteen teachers commented on this absurd situation, six more than had mentioned the social context of the previous question. Was this because the first consolidated their own view of the world?

One question was about a man who won £2000 in a competition and the way in which he shared the prize money, his wife getting nothing and each of his sons more than their (older) sister. No one mentioned the latter point and only four teachers the former. Again, did they notice or was it that this is how they know things are? One teacher made a different point: I don't believe in competition . . . I usually say so.

It was alarming that only about half the teachers responded adversely to the use of the word 'alien' in this question:

> Assuming that the number of aliens in the UK is $\frac{1}{3}$% of the population and that a football crowd is a random sample of the population, how many aliens would you expect to find in a crowd of 60000?

- I would avoid [it] . . . [It is] likely to cause embarrassment to certain people and give rise to the nastier feelings of one or two members of our society.
- Calling people 'aliens' smacks of racialism.
- We'd be on very dangerous ground . . . to use words like 'alien' or even draw to children's attention that our society is a racial mix. We've got quite a few pupils in our school who will seize on anything like this as a means of causing friction between the various groups.

But what of the half who did not comment? They came from a variety of schools and backgrounds and it is difficult to believe that their pupils are more immune to racial prejudice than those mentioned above, or that such wording does not encourage prejudice, albeit subconsciously. Indeed on two occasions a teacher accepted the question without comment while another in the same school mentioned the extreme dangers of its use. (One of the teachers whom I interviewed, and who did not comment on this question, has since told me that she used it with a class. A Greek boy strongly objected to the use of the word 'alien'.)

Just under half the teachers I spoke to broadly agreed with the two who said of this collection of questions: 'very establishment' and 'obviously class-biased, sex-biased and race-biased'. But the rest either did not find them so, or did not consider it relevant to their teaching of mathematics. It would have been interesting to see the teachers' reactions to questions about profits from burglary or tax evasion rather than investment. Even more revealing, had I been asking the questions now (the year of the miners' strike), would have been the reaction to this one, suggested by Griffiths and Howson.[2]

> A coal-mine employs 1000 men and loses £N per year. If it were closed down suppose 750 of the men would not expect to find another job and would have to live off social security payments. What value of N makes it cheaper to the state to keep the mine open? Is this a good way of thinking about the problem?

Would *you* use this question? Why? Or why not?

Swetz[3] found a problem in a Tanzanian textbook about canned peaches and 'is concerned about asking a poor man to struggle through the problems of the rich'. Likewise British textbooks use questions about mortgages, investment and interest for those whose families, or who themselves, are on social security. In fact, the time has perhaps already come when some people would find questions about wages offensive. Few questions ask the rich to struggle through the problems of the poor.

After further discussions with the teachers, covering attitudes, methods and topics ('If a few more people had understood what inflation meant, they might not have won the election'), about a quarter of the teachers remained clearly of the view that mathematics education is, and should be, politically neutral. It was interesting to see the pervasive and unanimous attitude of guilt and apology whenever a teacher felt she was questioning the norms of society. Four teachers expressed fear of being thought 'leftist'. Yet none was anxious about upholding the values of the right.

For some, discussions, and particularly the examples, caused a shift of position:

- Just looking at these questions . . . one can . . . have an influence even through mathematics which I see as being unlike many other subjects . . .
- You've exposed to me that it is quite easy to subconsciously . . . accidentally, inadvertently . . . put forward views which . . . you may not believe in. But . . . through a degree of thoughtlessness and ill-considered preparation you may end up putting forward social views that you disagree with.

But no one went as far as the teacher quoted by Len Masterman.[4]

> For over twenty years I worked under the delusion that I was teaching maths. The social pressures I put upon the kids were designed to make my maths teaching more effective. I now realise that I was really teaching social passivity and conformity, academic snobbery and the naturalness of

> good healthy competition, and that I was using maths as an instrument for achieving these things.

For me, the final proof that mathematics education is by no means neutral came in answer to the question 'Has mathematics a role to play in furthering social causes and political understanding?'

Two teachers, from the same institution, replied: 'Yes, definitely' and 'Oh, I shouldn't think so'.

How can anything which can elicit two such opposing but adamant replies be neutral? Politics is about conflict and there was conflict here.

Notes

1 Paulus Gerdes: 'Changing Mathematics Education in Mozambique', *Educational Studies in Mathematics*, 1981, **12** (4), pp. 455–77.
2 H. B. Griffiths and A. G. Howson: *Mathematics, Society and Curricula,* CUP, 1974.
3 Frank J. Swetz: *Socialist Mathematics Education*, Burgundy Press, 1978.
4 Len Masterman: *Teaching About Television,* Macmillan, 1980.

At the time of writing this article, **Jenny Maxwell** taught adult basic literacy and mathematics classes for a community education project in Birmingham.

13

Politics of percent[1]

Dawn Gill

The declared objectives of the curriculum focus on traditional mathematical topics – things like area, ratio, percentage, simple and compound interest rates, algebra, measurement and the manipulation of statistics. However, the content through which these mathematical skills are taught has a set of messages all of its own and because we live in a capitalist society we can easily be unaware of these messages – about the exploitation of labour, the sexism, the inequalities based on racism and social class – that are all a part of the ideology of capitalism. The point was well illustrated by Jenny Maxwell in her article 'Hidden Messages'. Here I want to focus on some examples from recent textbooks for O level and CSE courses.

I have taken those of Greer as a basis for discussion, not because his books are more sexist or pro-capitalist than other textbooks used in 16+ examination preparation, but because they are typical of such textbooks. Another reason for selecting Greer's books is that they are used in almost all of the ILEA schools which do not use the Authority's SMILE project and in many secondary schools nationally.

Greer's *CSE Mathematics Book 1* was first published in 1978 – it is now into its fifth reprint; *Book 2* was first published in 1979 and has been reprinted twice. *Comprehensive Mathematics for O-level* was first published in 1983 and it has been reprinted twice to date. This book is the successor to Greer's previous O level book, which is still, according to the publisher, one of the leading O level texts in this country and abroad. The books are sold in Africa, Singapore, Hong Kong – almost everywhere that British O levels are taught, except for the Caribbean for which there are special editions.

In both O level and CSE texts, Greer defines simple interest as follows:

> Interest is the *profit return on investment.* If money is invested, then interest is paid to the investor. If money is borrowed, then the person who borrows the money will have to pay interest to the lender. The money which is invested or lent is called the *principal*. The percentage return is called the *rate per cent.*

The example is used, like those in other mathematical textbooks, to present 'interest' outside the political and ideological context within which investment takes place. Interest seems to be a concept which is entirely theoretical and context-free. It is a phenomenon which occurs in a social and economic vacuum. It is presented as a neutral and value-free mathematical construct. The idea of interest seems to have a clean and rational image.

Mathematics textbooks present the notion of profit in a way which can only confuse students in their quest for an understanding of the term. To distort the notion of profit in the way that these examples do is likely to blinker perceptions and prevent a critical awareness of contemporary social reality.

Greer writes:

> When a dealer buys or sells goods, the cost price is the price at which he buys the goods and the selling price is the price at which he sells the goods. If the selling price is greater than the cost price, then a profit is made. The amount of profit is the difference between the selling price and the cost price.

The definition of profit implicit in this description is an entrepreneurial one. The mathematical exercises which follow are mainly to do with shopkeepers and car dealers making profit or loss. On the other hand, other exercises on the concept of ratio use the term 'profit' in quite a different way. The entrepreneurial definition is clearly inappropriate here. What, then, is a useful way of conceptualising profit in relation to such examples?

For Marx, the value of a commodity is determined by the total amount of labour that has been put into it and this labour 'constitutes exactly the fund out of which surplus value, or profit is formed'. If a profit is equivalent to surplus labour, then the capitalist, in keeping a larger share of the surplus than is given to the workers, is in effect 'stealing' from them, although what amounts to theft is written into an agreement and therefore not recognised as such. The capitalist becomes rich *because* the workers become poor. Thus poverty is related directly to the accumulation of wealth. This argument oversimplifies the relationships between people today; the idea of 'the capitalist' and 'the worker' is an unreal abstraction in a world where GLC pension funds are invested in Rio Tinto Zinc. However, in presenting *profit* as ultimately *unpaid labour*, Marx suggests that if the total of goods or capital in a social system is unequally divided between people at different levels in the social-industrial hierarchy, exploitation is necessarily taking place.

When removed from the toy-town world of textbooks, information about investment and calculations based on an understanding of interest rates can be illuminating for the young mathematician who may also be studying geography, business studies or economics at school. It can also be taken seriously as part of an education which is about the real world.

The following 'sums' (from Greer's *CSE Mathematics Book 1)* involve working out average wages:

- In an office, 5 people earn a wage of £36 each, 3 earn a wage of £40 each and 2 earn a wage of £42 each. Calculate the average wage.
- A business employs 125 people. The wage bill for a certain week was £3537.50. What was the average wage?
- In three weeks a man earns £60, £50 and £58. His average weekly earnings for four weeks is £54. How much did he earn in the fourth week?

Incidentally, these examples illustrate how quickly textbooks date and the above three questions illustrate that mathematics which attempts to be relevant can quickly become ridiculous. The wages quoted are low by today's standards; the examples can be dismissed as irrelevant in real life, and seen only as the means by which averages are learned – in which case they are what Cockcroft would describe as 'about nothing at all'.

However, the main point of interest is the unintended learning outcomes of such questions as these. The first example describes, and because it does not comment, appears to legitimise the hierarchical organisation of labour in offices, with the majority of workers on lower pay than the minority. Similarly, the third example can be seen to legitimise systems of employment in which people's weekly income is uncertain and variable – as in fact it is in certain trades and industries, building being a notable example.

The hardships associated with uncertain wage levels include difficulty in obtaining a mortgage, difficulty with HP purchase, or uncertainty about whether the rent – or the food bill – will be paid. Uncertain and variable wages are a great problem for the people who receive them; it is not necessarily desirable to appear to legitimise such methods of payment. This unquestioning acceptance of the established conditions of work is a form of indoctrination (even if unintended) of the students, many of whom will end up in jobs where wages are variable and income uncertain.

Here is another exercise:

> A man is paid at the rate of £1.50 per hour for normal working. His overtime rate is double time for Saturday and all weekday time over 8 hours and treble time for Sunday working. His deductions for a particular week were £5.50 plus 6% of his wage for the pension scheme. If during that week he works the following number of hours, how much should his take home pay be?

Sat	*Sun*	*Mon*	*Tue*	*Wed*	*Thu*	*Fri*
4	*3*	*8*	*7*	*9*	*8*	*9*

This example is an interesting one. A man . . . (most of the examples in mathematics textbooks refer to men: women are invisible – a point not picked up in the Cockcroft Report which devotes a whole chapter to why girls perform less well in mathematics than boys do) . . . earns £74.50 for a 48 hour week. Another example of out-of-date statistics, and therefore irrelevant content. However, the hidden messages in such a question may be of some importance in terms of conditioning the consciousness of the – largely working class – students for whom CSE mathematics courses are intended. Does the example implicitly condone overtime working as a means by which a living wage is earned? Does it also present as natural and inevitable the fact that for many working people the concept of a 'weekend' is nothing to do with ideas of rest and leisure with family or friends?

Like other textbook writers, Greer seems to have a clear understanding of the ways in which the examination system services a class-ridden society: *CSE Mathematics Book 2* has a whole section on overtime and piecework, with a briefer section on salaries paid to 'people like teachers, civil servants, secretaries and company managers'. The four examples provided list hypothetical annual salaries from which the students are expected to calculate average monthly earnings – the salaries range from £3,144 per year to £10,152 per year.

There are perhaps two main conclusions to be drawn from the above discussion:

- examples like these cannot possibly be politically neutral if they are rooted in an economic system and the ideology which supports it;
- textbook examples like these, which strive for relevance, need updating at least annually.

The second of these conclusions is important if teachers and syllabuses are to meet the objectives of mathematics education which are outlined by Cockcroft in relation to relevance. The first, however, is even more important if we are to avoid the kind of education which merely confirms – and therefore helps to perpetuate – an unequal status quo. As teachers, we need to be aware of the extent to which inequalities are enshrined within the status quo and the fact that many of the students with whom we work are the products of an unequal social system. Perhaps one of our tasks should be to examine the extent to which we are complicit in reproducing structural inequalities through the very nature of the work we do. A further task which could become the focus of co-operative endeavour in mathematics departments and curriculum development groups is to engage in the preparation of learning materials which do not simply support the status quo, but which enable our students to question and challenge it. This should certainly include some detailed attention to how mathematics might be used to expose the racist, sexist and class-ridden nature of the society in which we live.

Note

1 This article is an abbreviation of a longer version published in *Anti-racist Education through Mathematics*, D. Gill and E. Singh (eds), ACD, 1988.

Dawn Gill was an advisory teacher seconded to the ILEA anti-racist strategy team at the time of writing. She is currently Head of Geography at an ILEA comprehensive school.

14

Looking for relevance: can we let them decide?

Barbara Edmonds and Derek Ball

It is fashionable at present to suggest that the school curriculum should be relevant. The HMI document *The Curriculum from 5 to 16* suggests that 'all that pupils learn should be practical, and therefore relevant, in ways which enable them to build on it or use it for their own purposes in everyday life'.

Mathematics, more than almost any other subject on the school curriculum, has long been perceived as useful (and relevant?) by pupils themselves, their parents, their teachers, industrialists and Government. Unfortunately, the ways in which these groups define relevance may vary widely.

Pupils not infrequently ask teachers what is the use (or relevance) of what they are currently struggling to learn. We believe that pupils ask this question when they are finding the work they are doing boring or difficult. For pupils, work is relevant if it is enjoyable.

Most teachers, too, want their pupils to enjoy their learning. More importantly, however, teachers want to enjoy their own teaching. Because teachers are, on the whole, expected to have quiet, orderly classrooms they will be most likely to regard mathematics as relevant if it leads to good behaviour.

Parents are likely to want children to do well in life. Some parents, who as children may have been afraid of school or bored by it, may only see education as relevant if their children are finding education unthreatening. Other parents equate education with the passing of examinations. To them mathematics will be relevant if it helps their children gain a qualification which, in turn, will enable them to obtain a good job. The content of the mathematics qualification to them is immaterial. It is hardly surprising that many children eventually acquire a similar attitude towards the relevance of mathematics.

Politicians are likely to have different goals. They frequently have to deal with awkward and unpleasant problems which may or may not be of their own making. Frequently it is useful to have someone else to blame for such problems. If the problems involve young people it is convenient to blame school teachers. One way of doing this is to accuse teachers of failing to teach relevant skills and attitudes. Because mathematical skills are perceived as being easy to define and to recognise, and because such skills are perceived to be relevant, schools may be attacked if it is believed that they are not teaching such skills effectively.

It is against this background that we turn to the mathematics curriculum and ask what mathematics is relevant to real life.

Skills learned as part of the school arithmetic syllabus are perceived by almost everybody to be relevant mathematics. To what are such mathematical skills relevant? It is undoubtedly true that without a certain facility with money and with other arithmetical skills, people are handicapped in going about their daily business. It is also true that many of the comments made about the usefulness of arithmetic do not address this central theme.

A teacher was doing some mental arithmetic, including estimation, with a group of 15 year olds. One girl objected that practising getting the 'wrong answer' to the questions posed was rather silly. When it was suggested that estimation might be a useful skill when shopping in the supermarket, she replied, 'Yes, but we are not in the supermarket now'. She was suggesting that 'relevant' skills are best learned in the context in which they are relevant, and that teachers can never be certain that their pupils are acquiring the ability to cope in any particular context unless they see them operating in that context.

Arithmetical skills are often considered to be 'basic skills', and the implication is drawn that such skills are relevant to everyday life. Pupils in most schools spend a considerable amount of time practising the manipulation of fractions, perhaps because of the mistaken belief that such skills are useful. It seems clear to us, however, that such skills are not useful in adult life. Indeed it is a very good thing that this is so, because research shows that very few pupils leave school with any competence at these skills. We consider it strange that adults (teachers, parents, publishers of textbooks and examiners) behave as if they believe both that manipulating fractions is a useful skill and that most children can acquire this skill.

Calculators, on the other hand, are still not entirely approved of by some parents and teachers, even though our experience would suggest that an ability to use a calculator is a far more relevant skill for everyday life than almost any of the pencil-and-paper arithmetic taught in schools.

Geometry is a part of the mathematics syllabus which has been in decline in recent years. This is partly because teachers have acknowledged that mathematical proof, as it was taught in O level Euclidean geometry, is too difficult for the vast majority of pupils. The teaching of geometry has also declined because it has become increasingly fashionable to focus on 'achievable objectives': children work steadily through textbooks and workcards.

Geometry is not a subject which lends itself to such treatment. The facts and skills in geometry, such as calculating the third angle of a triangle, are relatively trivial and appear to have little practical relevance. But geometry is about spatial relationships, and an appreciation of space and form is of considerable practical value. This cannot be taught by means of a sequence of graded exercises.

It is significant that some parts of the mathematics curriculum (notably arithmetic and algebra) are seen by many people both inside and outside education to be relevant, whereas other parts (topology and, perhaps, geometry) are not. When there is general agreement that a subject is relevant it appears that no justification is required to maintain its position in the school curriculum. Arguments that some of the skills practised by pupils are obsolete fall on deaf ears, or are heeded only very slowly. There is still widespread popular belief in the efficacy of practising such 'relevant' skills, even though research clearly indicates that such practice is largely futile: if pupils are unable to master a skill fairly quickly they do not appear to improve subsequently. Perhaps some teachers and others believe that, nevertheless, such practice is good for the soul!

During the next few years children are likely to be engaging in more sustained projects as part of their learning of mathematics. In several primary schools children are working together at 'turtle geometry' projects in which they set their own goals and spend several days or weeks achieving them. GCSE mathematics includes a coursework element which will become compulsory in 1991. This development has its opponents, but it does provide a way in which mathematics can become more meaningful to some of the children studying it. It would be sad if teachers and others were seduced into believing that the most useful projects are those which involve 'real-life' problems. One reason why this will not always be the case is that 'real-life' problems are frequently adapted to make them more 'mathematically respectable' when they are studied in schools.

The value of projects lies less in the subject matter than in the fact that topics are chosen and worked on by the pupils themselves. The 'relevant' skills learned concern the ability to plan projects, to apply mathematics as and when appropriate, to sustain work on them until some conclusion is reached and to communicate what has been learned to other people.

The National Criteria for GCSE mathematics make it clear that the curriculum must be differentiated. In other words, different pupils will follow different curricula so that what they learn is 'appropriate to their individual levels of ability'. On the face of it this seems to be a good idea: one frequently voiced criticism of comprehensive education is that all pupils have been forced to follow a grammar-school curriculum. On the other hand, who is going to decide what is appropriate for a particular pupil?

As we have already indicated, there is lack of agreement about what is relevant or appropriate because different groups of people use different sets of criteria. It is not easy to achieve the recommendation of the HMI document *The Curriculum from 5 to 16*, that pupils should be able to use what they learn for their own purposes, because each of us has different purposes in life, and what is relevant to one pupil will not be relevant to another. The only way to make mathematics relevant to pupils who study it is to involve them in deciding what they want to learn and how they want to learn it. To accomplish this, children must be treated more like adults. This may seem a revolutionary step, but it is surely the most significant step we can take to ensure that, in the words of *The Curriculum from 5 to 16*, education 'is seen by pupils to meet their present and prospective needs'.

Barbara Edmonds is Head of Mathematics at a Leicestershire comprehensive school.
Derek Ball is Senior Lecturer in Mathematics Education at the University of Leicester.

15

What are we assessing in mathematics and what are we assessing for?

Brenda Denvir

Introduction: some examples of assessment in school mathematics

Example A

Staff in infant school A have listed the concepts that they hope children will learn. These were chosen by examining the mathematics scheme, deciding what the children were most likely to grasp and determining what is important, in terms of relevance and application to their present world and to their future mathematical learning. The list of concepts includes:

- one to one correspondence

and suggests, as ways of assessing this concept:

- can set out cups and saucers so that there is one cup for each saucer;
- when counting, says one number word for each object counted.

Example B

Junior school B is in an LEA which has developed a primary mathematics record card. Teachers are asked to complete this for each child to show their attainment. In discussion, members of staff became aware that they had different interpretations of some objectives, such as:

- in a reasoned argument has shown evidence of being able to argue 'it can't be . . . because . . .'
- can describe a movement in terms of: left and right, . . . reference points, . . . rotations.

As a consequence of their different interpretations, they had different criteria for judging attainment. They decided to discuss each group of objectives to clarify the meaning and find suitable assessments and organised occasional teaching in pairs to agree criteria. The school is building up 'case lore' for each objective, by keeping a written record of their agreements.

Example C

School C sets NFER Basic Mathematics Tests (NFER, 1969–80) for every junior school pupil. Papers are administered and marked by class teachers in March. Scores (the total of correct answers) are given to the headteacher who makes year-by-year comparisons for classes and individual children. The majority of teachers also examine the results by looking at:

- performances of individuals, to see who did badly and which questions they got wrong;
- overall numbers of correct and incorrect responses on each question for each class.

Example D

School D, a secondary mixed comprehensive, uses the Graded Assessment in Mathematics system of assessment (GAIM, 1988). Some of the regular work, including investigations and problem solving, is examined carefully by teacher and pupil together, in relation to GAIM criteria which describe objectives in learning mathematics. These are listed by mathematical topic, and grouped together into levels according to their difficulty. For investigative work, an overall grade which reflects an holistic assessment of the pupil's work is also given by the teacher. The objectives attained are recorded on pupils' profiles, which are useful for:

- planning learning activities;
- reporting to parents or informing discussions where there are enquiries or causes for concern;
- reporting to future employers, or further or higher education institutions at the end of secondary schooling.

Example E

School E is a secondary (11–18) boys' comprehensive. New entrants do written tests in mathematics and English in their first week. Scores are used to allocate pupils to one of eight streamed classes. Results of end-of-year tests in mathematics, English, science and the first foreign language are used to reallocate some pupils to a new stream at the beginning of the new school year.

Example F

One local education authority, which gives all children a written test in the final year of junior school (10+), offers help from advisory teachers to those schools where many pupils achieve only low scores in the test.

These examples of assessment illustrate a variety of purposes, including:

- to inform the teacher's task of selecting appropriate learning experiences;
- to inform pupils about their progress;
- to report to parents, employers or the next stage of education;
- to organise teaching groups;
- to assist in the evaluation of a school's overall performance.

There are other purposes, not exemplified here, including:

- to motivate pupils and teachers;
- to influence or control the curriculum.

Sometimes assessments are carried out simply as a classroom routine.

The term *formative assessment* refers to assessment which looks forward to pupils' future learning, as opposed to *summative assessment* which looks back at what pupils have already achieved. Assessment for selection and evaluation is summative; assessment to inform the teaching is formative. At a first glance, the information collected for summative assessment for one stage would appear identical to that of formative assessment for the next. However, summative assessment seeks, for each pupil, to classify mathematical knowledge into what is 'known' and what is 'not known', whereas good formative assessment attempts to focus on precisely the 'grey areas in between' that summative assessment sets out to avoid. Thus, the content of summative assessment is very different from that of formative assessment, and the crude distinctions usually employed in summative assessment are insufficiently precise to be useful in planning activities.

Subsequent sections of this article explore, in turn, assessment for teaching, selection, evaluation and curriculum control.

Assessment for teaching

Assessment for teaching involves collecting information which helps the teacher teach effectively. It may involve one or more of a range of assessment activities from informal observation to oral, practical, or written procedures. In some instances, it may be impossible for the teacher to select appropriate learning activities for a particular pupil without collecting more detailed information. This deliberate gathering of detailed information for teaching is termed *diagnostic* assessment. It is a type of formative assessment, insofar as it looks ahead to future learning activities, but differs in that it usually involves the use of more specific procedures or protocols. There is, however, no clear-cut distinction, rather a continuum exists between the specific procedures and general information gathering. Towards one end of this lies, for example, brief verbal questioning of the whole class about their ideas in a particular topic; towards the other lie perceptual discrimination tasks designed by psychologists. Diagnostic assessment will not be necessary for all pupils, at all times, but appropriate techniques should be used when more general formative assessments fail to indicate activities from which the pupil can learn. At times, diagnostic assessment is necessary not only for 'low attainers', but also for 'high' or 'average' attainers.

Diagnostic assessment

An older term than 'formative assessment', diagnostic assessment is a metaphor derived from the medical world. It originally referred to special treatment for remedial pupils in an analogy with 'the sick'. The remedy was more practice in identified areas of weakness. This now appears inadequate in its view of mathematics and of the learner. In Example C, information was collected about which questions were answered incorrectly by each child, from items ranging across the whole primary mathematics curriculum. The teaching which followed aimed to show children through exposition and practice how to answer correctly those types of questions which they got wrong. This both reflects and promotes a view of mathematics as a collection of arbitrary, fixed procedures in which learning comes through repetition, and teaching is by telling. This is an inadequate view of mathematics; it is also unhelpful in educating pupils who are required to make decisions and to adapt to change in a complex technological society. The learner is seen as passive. This 'analogy with the sick' adopted by Rees and Barr (1984) is rightly criticised (Shiu, 1986), because it fails to take into account research results which indicate that pupils are active in their learning and logical in tackling tasks.

Pupils' responses in individual interviews (quoted, for example, in Dickson *et al.*, 1984, pp. 262–3) support this perception of learners actively and logically seeking solutions. These show how pupils' mathematical thinking may be inferred from what they do and say. In one large-scale study, the secondary mathematics project 'CSMS' (Hart, 1981), extensive interviewing was carried out on a range of mathematical topics, and the strategies that pupils used were identified. In many instances, the same incomplete or inappropriate strategy was frequently used, producing the same incorrect answer. Often, these strategies were invented by the pupils rather than taught by the teacher. They are referred to as 'child methods' and give correct answers for easy questions, but not for more complex items. Insight gained in the interviews allowed an informed interpretation of results in the large-scale written assessment. The 'Chelsea Diagnostic Mathematics Tests' (Hart *et al.*, 1984), which are based on this research, were designed to measure pupils' levels of understanding and identify particular errors which each of them make. 'Levels' are described for each test, and these refer to both the mathematical ideas and the strategies which pupils use. In a similar way, the study carried out by Christine Shiu (this volume) revealed pupils' mathematical thinking within a topic, which was of considerable value in planning the teaching. The research projects 'Strategies and Errors in Secondary Mathematics' (for example Booth, 1984) and 'Diagnostic Teaching' (Bell *et al.*, 1985) both focus on developing teaching approaches to help pupils develop appropriate strategies and avoid common errors.

Using only a small sample of children, we (Denvir and Brown, 1986) developed an oral and practical diagnostic assessment to assess 'low attaining' 7–9 year olds' understanding of number. Again, the technique was to attempt to identify children's available strategies. The assessment was based on a framework which described the orders of acquisition of number concepts. We identified 'hierarchical strands', in which, for the children interviewed, the acquisition of one ability depended on the development of an earlier ability, allowing assessment of each child's understanding of number concepts. The results indicated that this progressed in several broad stages. However, results of the teaching studies did not support a step-by-step approach to teaching the 'next skill' in the hierarchy, but gave a useful indication of a range of strategies that each child might soon acquire, which was valuable in planning the teaching.

Assessment of pupils' understanding of certain concepts is more validly based on their use of strategies than listing which items in a written test they answer correctly or incorrectly. However, there are difficulties in using pupils' strategies to measure mathematical attainment. These relate to context, mode of presentation and response, and pupils' interpretations of the task.

First, the mathematical thinking that is prompted in an individual depends on context as well as underlying mathematical structure. For example, a highly motivating task, or a familiar and easily recognised context, might prompt a 'common sense', pragmatic solution; a mathematical context might stimulate recall of a standard procedure, and a threatening context might be avoided. Response to any task, then, may not provide a valid description of mathematical knowledge. Moreover, individuals will be affected in different ways by different contexts. To minimise this difficulty pupils might be assessed in a range of contexts and the contexts in which pupils are most likely to succeed might be sought. If one context has been presented as an exemplar, however, evidence for the pupils' grasp of the idea should be sought in a different context.

Secondly, the mode of presentation and response is likely to influence pupils' thinking. One reason for the widespread use of written tests is the ease of administration and collection of data. Oral and practical assessments take more time, yet yield richer, but more ambiguous, information. In order to examine the feasibility of assessing children's understanding of number in a class, rather than an individual setting, we (Denvir and Brown, 1987) carried out a small-scale study with 8–11 year olds. Individual responses in a class test were compared with responses to the same items presented in an interview: many were found to differ. For example, in the class test, Neelam responded to the verbally-presented problem '52 take away 36' by writing the standard decomposition algorithm and producing the correct answer. In the interview she replied:

. . . eighteen.
B: How did you decide it was eighteen?
Neelam: Well first I thought it was twenty something, but then I realised it was six; two take away six, can't do that . . . so . . . um . . . it went down to ten. And there was the six . . . sixteen. And then there's the two left over from the fifty-two.

In contrast, Simon wrote '52−36=24', but said:

> Sixteen. I took thirty from fifty, that gives twenty, then took two from the six and took away four from the twenty.

Different modes of presentation and response, then, may provoke different strategies. In the study, about one-quarter of the children performed markedly less well in the class test than they did in the interview.

The third difficulty is related to both those already outlined. In order to reflect accurately the pupil's mathematical thinking, it is vital to assess the response in terms of the problem as the pupil perceives it. There is, in most assessment activities, an assumption that once a question has been stated, then the problem perceived by the teacher becomes the pupil's problem. In fact, inability to 'see' from the teacher's viewpoint may result in an 'inappropriate' response, which may be regarded as creative or worthless. The pupil may be labelled genius or idiot, and the mathematical thinking not credited for what is is. A possible way of minimising this difficulty is outlined in the following section on more general formative assessment.

General formative assessment

Teachers do carry out formative assessment, sometimes deliberately, but often unconsciously selecting activities because they 'feel right'. Frequently based on sound experience, these criteria are often implicit or not clearly articulated. Consequently, these judgements are underrated, labelled 'subjective' and accorded less status than the numerically-quantifiable results of standard written tests, although they are capable of reflecting attainment with greater subtlety.

Shiu's assessment (this volume), the 'Chelsea Diagnostic Mathematics Tests' and the written test used in the Denvir and Brown study (1987) which were discussed under the heading 'Diagnostic assessment' are all, when used without individual interviews, examples of formative assessment and carried out before teaching, because they indicate suitable starting points.

The difficulty of interpreting results of written tests, the time-consuming nature of individual interviews, and uncertainty about the task which the pupil is actually attempting to solve, have also been discussed under the heading 'Diagnostic assessment'. To avoid these difficulties in making formative assessments, our current curriculum development initiative, 'Learning Mathematics and Science through Investigative Work' (Murphy and Denvir, in preparation), which focuses on assessment only insofar as it assists the teaching and learning process, aims to establish a rich meaning in the learning activities which are selected. This is done by embedding activities within a theme in which the pupils have 'expert' knowledge and by 'negotiating the meaning' of the tasks through discussion. This work aims to help teachers provide challenging tasks, at an appropriate level, which are rich in mathematical and scientific concepts and procedures, will motivate pupils and will thus enhance learning.

In this work, formative assessment is seen to involve collecting a range of different types of information about the children, including an awareness of:

- the mathematical and scientific concepts and procedures that they have grasped;
- the contexts in which these have been experienced and understood;
- the children's interests, knowledge and expertise in their everyday world, as well as in their school work.

For example, in a sequence of activities on the theme 'Packing', children spent time discussing occasions when they packed and problems encountered in particular packing activities. Both discussion and the way that activities were tackled gave some indication of children's understanding of the ideas. Subsequently, they carried out the investigation 'Maxbox', which involved deciding which of the open boxes that can be made from a 12 cm × 12 cm square of paper by cutting squares from the corners and folding into a lidless cuboid 'held the most'. Various materials were provided and children's strategies were noted and listed (Denvir, Brown and Eve, 1987). Like other forms of assessment, this approach has some limitations: a child's strategy may not represent the most sophisticated available. However, much is revealed about children's thinking in incidents as well as in the general strategies used. For example:

> One child looked in surprise whilst members of her group zeroed the pointer on the balance before weighing the sand filling one of the boxes. Then she asked 'Why are we doing this?', revealing much about her understanding of measurement.

This type of assessment is demanding for teachers, who need to observe pupils' strategies carefully. However, primary school teachers attending an INSET course were able to determine what strategies were adopted by most of the children in their classes.

Formative assessment seeks to serve pupils' interests by helping teachers teach more effectively. It seeks to answer three questions.

- What do pupils know within this topic?
- What are they likely to learn next?
- What activities should be provided to foster this learning?

Assessment for selection

Within school, pupils may be selected for a teaching group according to particular aspects of their school performance. This may be done in a rigid way, as in setting or streaming, where allocation to a different group occurs infrequently, as in Example E. By contrast, there may be flexible groupings for particular activities within the classroom.

Selection also takes place for purposes which go beyond the school. Some local education authorities assess children at the end of primary school in order to make allocations to secondary schools. Public examinations, employers', schools' and colleges' own assessments and profiles, such as that described in Example D, are used to decide whether a pupil will or will not be accepted for a job, vocational training or higher education.

What selectors desire is good predictive information. The question they wish to answer is 'Which pupils will excel in this area, will make useful contributions or will benefit most from the opportunities which are in our power to grant?' They need information about what constitutes and causes success or failure within a particular domain, as well as strategies for detecting this at the time of the selection. However, there are considerable difficulties associated with assessment for selection. First, the state of knowledge about what, precisely, we mean by 'mathematical attainment', and what particular aspects are needed for certain jobs or courses of study, are unclear. Secondly, even where there is some clarity about the required attributes, there is difficulty in measuring their attainment. Thirdly, there are insurmountable difficulties in ensuring equal opportunities for all pupils, regardless of gender, or socio-economic and cultural background, because all assessment tasks are bound within a particular context and culture which will inevitably favour some pupils to the detriment of others. Finally, pupils who perceive that they are unlikely to be selected for anything which is valued may become disheartened and fail to fulfil their potential.

Assessments for selection primarily serve the interests of the selectors, who, in turn, represent concerns within society such as industrial and economic achievement, or academic excellence. However, selection for opportunities outside affects what happens at school. Choices about the mathematics syllabus at secondary level for *all* pupils may, for example, be dominated by the needs of a small minority who wish to study mathematics at university, and this can result in an inappropriate syllabus for many.

Selection for teaching groups within the school may also affect pupils. For example, many schools organise pupils into groups according to 'mathematical ability'. This may reflect teachers' beliefs that mathematics by its nature is learned most effectively in groups of homogeneous ability. Alternatively, it may be the strategy with which teachers feel most able to cope with the wide range of pupil attainment. In either case, it encourages the perception of pupils' attainments as being at one of a number of discrete 'levels'. There is little evidence for the existence of meaningful 'levels', as constants across the whole of the mathematics curriculum. This oversimplification is likely to lead to inappropriate curricula for many, and also to affect attitudes adversely through the labelling associated with allocation to a particular group, especially to a bottom set or stream.

For any selection procedure, there are three questions to consider.

- Is it fair to pupils in allowing equality of opportunity to all who might benefit from what is offered?
- Is it effective in selecting employees who can do the job or pupils who can learn from the course?
- Does it have a negative and disproportionately large influence on those who are not selected, especially those who do not wish to be considered for selection?

Assessment for evaluation

The purpose of evaluation is to allow pupils, parents and society as a whole to question the educational system. For evaluation to be carried out constructively, it is vital that evaluators, teachers and pupils have some shared understanding of what they are trying to achieve. The intention is to determine whether pupils are being offered appropriate experiences and the school is adequately fulfilling its task. Results of assessments are sometimes used to evaluate the progress of pupils, classes, schools or local education authorities. Their use is also envisaged to evaluate a particular teaching approach, or even for the appraisal of individual teachers. There are a number of caveats which concern the validity of using the results of assessment in this way.

Evaluation such as that carried out in Example F is likely to misrepresent what has been achieved in the teaching unless it takes into account pupils' initial performances and the relative difficulty of what they are learning. The question which should be addressed in evaluation is whether the *progress* is satisfactory and, if not, where it falls short and could be improved.

Drawing the distinction between what is satisfactory and what is not raises three substantial educational issues. First, there is no point in labelling children, progress, teacher or school as 'unsatisfactory' unless this goes hand in hand with the means to bring about improvement.

Secondly, the notion of 'satisfactory' implies some sort of 'norm', but this is difficult to define. Rates of progress are erratic: the transition from one idea to another may be accomplished by one pupil in a matter of minutes, whilst another will take months apparently covering the same ground. The question of how, and if, one might define a 'unit of progress' would probably be answered best empirically. Since pupils' performances vary across different mathematical topics, profiling, such as that described in Examples C and D, will provide a fairer description of pupil progress than will a single grade. It is not clear, however, how profiles might be compared for the purpose of evaluation. Background variables which affect learning are difficult to quantify, making the idea of a 'fair' comparison still more elusive.

Thirdly, while evaluation intends to assess outcomes such as progress or performance, inevitably it is people who are labelled. This labelling of some learners and teachers as 'unsatisfactory' is likely to lead to poor motivation and disengagement from the proper tasks of learning and teaching.

What pupils and parents require is some notion of progress in relation to other people, that is *norm-referenced* data; in relation to mathematical objectives, that is *criterion-referenced* data; and in relation to pupils' own earlier performances. This information can assist individuals in developing an awareness of the areas of strength on which they can build, and areas of relative weakness which need to be developed. For pupils themselves, good evaluative assessment might aim to provide both summative data, describing what has been achieved, and formative data, suggesting current priorities in learning. For this to be effective, it is best done together with pupils making their own self-evaluation, so that teacher and pupil may agree what has been achieved. In mathematics, there is considerable difficulty in clarifying for pupils what it is hoped they will achieve in the future, since mathematics, in the way that it is commonly described in the school syllabus, is very heavily concept-laden and learning is almost synonymous with forming new concepts. In modern languages, for example, the student can be asked to work towards ordering a meal in a German resturant, with the reasonable expectation that what this involves will be meaningful. However, in mathematics, the pupil who does not have a meaning for vectors, say, will hardly be motivated by knowing that this is the 'next topic to be learned'.

Assessment for evaluation is justified on the basis that it serves the interests of the consumers of education: pupils, parents and society. However, since evaluation gives prestige and rewards to those who are judged to be doing well, and condemns those who are not, it is very important that any evaluation should be fair and linked to positive suggestions for improvement. Two major questions emerge in relation to assessment for evaluation.

- Does the assessment and the way that results are reported accurately reflect what progress has been made?
- Are there adequate and appropriate resources to remedy any deficiencies which are exposed?

Assessment for curriculum control

Many people and institutions, not just the pupils themselves, are likely to be judged by pupils' performance in assessment tasks. Consequently, teachers, wishing their pupils, their institutions and themselves to perform well, will prepare carefully for the assessments. Thus, imposed assessments, either incidentally, when assessments are carried out for selection or evaluation, or deliberately, if they are so designed, can have the effect of controlling the curriculum. For the majority of the population, 'mathematics' is synonymous with what has been selected from the vast field of mathematics for inclusion in the exam syllabus. For secondary school teachers of mathematics who have been eager to respond to the call for investigative work, the introduction of GCSE coursework assessment may have come as a rational consequence of what they see as timely changes in the curriculum. But for the majority of teachers, the converse is true and changes in assessment are forcing changes in the curriculum. In a similar, but more localised manner, some education authorities which carry out 'blanket' testing, or testing a sizeable sample of the junior school population, have introduced items which must be carried out using a calculator. In some cases, this has been done deliberately to encourage use of calculators, and also in order to change the emphasis in the aspects of number which are taught and learned.

The perceived advantages and disadvantages of using assessment to control the curriculum hinge on one main and two linked subsidiary issues. First:

- Who should have control of the curriculum; do those who have control have the education of *all* pupils as their first priority?

and, secondly:

- Is the envisaged change in the curriculum seen as educationally valuable, and are the assessments effective in producing the change?

Summary and discussion

I have addressed two major issues in assessment in mathematics education (what is being assessed? and what is the purpose of the assessment?) in this article. Different answers to these will suggest different practices. Failure to address and resolve these issues will lead to conflict.

What is being assessed?

I raised several different ideas of what is being assessed. The intention may be to assess or evaluate:

- pupils' attainment;
- pupils' progress;
- teachers;
- schools;
- teaching approaches.

There is a fundamental issue which is concerned with the nature of mathematics and mathematical learning. The public view of mathematics as a system of fixed rules and absolute truths ignores perceptions of mathematics as a creative human activity for children who are 'learning' it, as well as mathematicians who are 'inventing' it. It also ignores the reality that school mathematics, both what is studied and the way that it is taught, is selected by groups within society from a vast range of possible topics and approaches.

Before we can agree about how to assess or evaluate mathematical attainment or progress in learning, we must clarify what we mean by 'doing mathematics'. Does it, for example, refer to the marks made on paper, or is it the whole of the thinking process involved in solving mathematical problems? In the current political climate in which the government seeks to establish a national curriculum and associated assessments, many concerns are voiced about assessment in mathematics (for example Schwarzenberger, 1987; Denvir, Brown and Eve, 1987). These reflect many basic conflicts about the nature of mathematics and its role within education and society (see, for example, Gill, this volume).

What is the purpose of the assessment?

I have underlined four major purposes of assessment. This categorisation could have been carried out in other ways, and other purposes seen here as secondary could have been given greater prominence. Nevertheless, whatever the grouping, one major distinction will remain and this will give rise to a fundamental conflict for the teacher. In response to imposed assessment for selection and evaluation, the teacher will prepare children to perform well. For many, this preparation consists of rehearsed responses to boost pupils' scores. It has, then, the deliberate aim of covering up weaknesses and encouraging pupils to adopt behaviour which apes understanding.

In contrast, formative assessment will encourage a very different teaching approach, one in which pupils will be encouraged to find their own solutions instead of having to learn ready-made rules. Since these two purposes are in fundamental conflict, one will, inevitably, dominate. It is vitally important, if we are to improve the mathematical attainment of our society, that the educational purposes of formative and diagnostic assessment, which seek to improve the teaching, take precedence over the monitoring and evaluative purposes, which at best merely seek to describe.

References

Bell, A. W. *et al.* (1985) *Diagnostic Teaching*. Shell Centre for Mathematical Education, University of Nottingham.

Booth, L. R. (1984) *Algebra: Children's Strategies and Errors. A Report on the Strategies and Errors in Secondary Mathematics Project.*, Windsor: NFER/Nelson.

Denvir, B. and Brown, M. (1986) 'Understanding of Number Concepts in Low Attaining 7–9 Year Olds: Part I', *Educational Studies in Mathematics,* **17**(1), pp. 15–36.

Denvir, B. and Brown, M. (1987) 'The Feasibility of Class Administered Diagnostic Assessment in Primary Mathematics', *Educational Research,* **29**, pp. 95–107.

Denvir, B., Brown, M. and Eve, P. (1987) *Attainment Targets and Assessment in the Primary Phase: Report of the Mathematics Feasibility Study*. London: HMSO.

Dickson, L., Brown, M. and Gibson, O. (1984) *Children Learning Mathematics*. London: Holt, Rinehart and Winston.

GAIM (1988) *Graded Assessment in Mathematics: Mathematics Development Pack*. London: Macmillan.

Hart, K. M. (ed.) (1981) *Children's Understanding of Mathematics: 11–16*. London: John Murray.

Hart, K. M., Brown, M., Kerslake, D., Küchemann, D. and Ruddock, G. (1984) *Chelsea Diagnostic Mathematics Tests*. Windsor: NFER/Nelson.

Murphy, P. and Denvir, B. (in preparation) *Learning Mathematics and Science through Investigative Work*. Centre for Educational Studies, King's College, London.

NFER (1969–1980) *Basic Mathematics Tests*. Windsor: NFER/Nelson.

Rees, R. and Barr, G. (1984) *Diagnosis and Prescription in the Classroom: Some Common Maths Problems*. London: Harper & Row.

Schwarzenberger, R. L. E. (1987) *Targets for Mathematics in Primary Education*. Stoke-on-Trent: Trentham Books.

Shiu, C. (1986) 'Medications', *Mathematics Teaching,* **115**, p. 61.

Brenda Denvir is Lecturer in Mathematics Education at King's College, London.

16

School applications of IT

Eric Deeson

Some people expect that in a few decades' time youngsters will learn from their home tutor computers and rarely, if ever, have contact with a human teacher. Such views (for example, Stonier and Conlin, 1985) imply that information technology (IT) will lead to the dismantling of schools as learning centres. In that scenario, children will then go to school only to gain social skills and join in curricular and other group activities.

To most of us, this may be a revolutionary picture. Yet IT will certainly be able to allow such an approach, should we decide to go that way. It is, after all, the case that open learning is growing fast in all phases of school and college work as well as for adult study. Open learning involves an individualised approach to meeting the needs of the learner; he or she need not then be part of a larger formal group treated as one unit. This important predecessor of computer-based study at home is exemplified by the style of the Open University, though there are many other cases in Britain and elsewhere, for work with adults or with younger learners.

My preferred vision of the future is what I call *computer-aided freedom* (caf) (Deeson, 1983). Here semi-formal learning still takes place in semi-formal learning centres, heavily intermediated by each learner's powerful, portable, personal micro, a machine no more costly than a calculator is now. The 'freedom' in the name has all kinds of implications. The most important, perhaps, is freedom from the restrictive grasp of the 'all together now' class teaching system that goes back to Victorian times. There are also connotations, however, of freedom from fear, freedom from the boredom of having to deal with work for which the learner has no motivation, freedom to move from activity to activity as desired.

Such a system would be able to help learners in almost any context including, of course, the study of mathematics at most levels. In its way, caf is just as revolutionary a picture as computer-based home learning; the roads to take are very different, though. Roads have beginnings as well as ends, so where are we now?

Where are we now?

First, perhaps I should explain what I mean by information technology.

Information technology (IT) is the application of modern ideas and techniques in the fields of computing, telecommunications, microelectronics and video to the handling (storage, access, processing, transfer) of information. As with any technology its prime concern should be the betterment of the lives of the individuals in society. Megarry (1985) provides a particularly readable introduction. IT is not just computing, but that is the aspect I spend most time on here.

Mathematics differs from a number of other parts of the formal curriculum in needing an investigatory component for successful delivery. Useful investigation can take place in an individualised environment (as many Open University students know); however, it is often best to approach it as a co-operative endeavour.

From the definition of IT above, it should be clear that IT ought to be able to offer a lot to mathematics learning in schools and colleges – but how much, in fact, has IT affected it?

The answer is – 'not a lot'. While there are a few changes in detail, most British school and college mathematics classrooms do not differ much from those of a hundred years ago. The subject matter taught is much the same; the approaches are much the same; the anticipated outcomes are much the same; and the teachers' and learners' attitudes are much the same.

There *is*, however, somewhat more investigation now than in the past, and occasionally the teachers may wheel in a micro or a video player to provide a degree of reinforcement of learning in a given field. Yet even at university, it may well still be a minority of departments that expect all mathematics students to use computers as a matter of course; indeed, some people fear that higher education will be the phase most resistant to new IT, rather than the one that provides a strong lead.

A recent British Government report (DES, 1987) made this clear. It noted that most headteachers feel that IT has as yet made little impact on formal education.

We should not really expect otherwise. Most secondary schools have now reached double figures in their stocks of micros – but only a few years ago the authors of a book (Howe and Ross, 1981) could gently suggest that 'we can readily envisage the time when every educational institution in the country will have access to at least one microcomputer'. Such a short period is hardly enough to allow the development of mature and coherent styles of usage.

It is only in the last few years, then, that new IT, mainly in the form of the microcomputer, has started to play a part in formal education. The change will go on. By the mid-1990s, powerful compact machines will exist at prices that should allow at least a couple in each classroom and workshop plus plenty in staff and student work areas. By that time, the patterns of usage – still being developed as far as mathematics is concerned – will have become fairly clear. People have been struggling to explore and clarify those patterns in recent years. What, then, are they?

Learning mathematics with computers

Most current and currently potential uses of micros for mathematics learning apply to other subject areas too, at least broadly. The general outcomes of research and development in educational computing apply in this context, therefore. Here is a list of the current main types of use:

- awareness – allowing the learners to gain familiarity with the IT systems they are likely to meet in the outside world;
- computer studies – the computer (and its uses) as a subject of study in its own right, rather than as a tool in other curricular areas;
- management and administration – the computer as a tool for background departmental work;
- using office software – word processing and so on;
- computer-aided learning – where systems add to the other resources learners can call on;
- control – using a computer to capture data from its environment and to control other equipment.

When computers first reached secondary schools and colleges, many mathematics specialists, like colleagues in physics, welcomed the new horizon and set up computing/IT departments. The first two types of educational computing in the list above are at the moment basically the province of such departments – but it is good to know that in many schools and colleges there are strong links with mathematics. This is despite the fact that the problems of mathematics staffing have increased as a result of the 'brain drain' to educational IT. (In primary schools, there has been a similar move, but by no means to the same extent; primary IT has not suffered so much, as a result, from a leaning toward mathematics and science.)

The next two areas in the list of uses – management and administration, and using office programs – come together in that both involve much the same hardware and software. The difference is that in the former case it is the teachers and support staff who use the systems, while in the latter it is the learners.

Computer-aided learning (cal) is, for me, a portmanteau term for all cases in which computers help along the learning process. Here we view the micro and its software (including program languages like LOGO) as a learning resource – in the same way as an overhead projector and *its* associated software, a video player and *its* pile of cassettes, a library and *its* contents, are all learning resources.

Defined in this way, most cal programs tend to be very restricted; however, people have long seen in them much potential as resources. They mainly include what most commonly carry the name of educational software, packages such as:

- revision drills and objective test programs – like some of the ideas in *132 Short Programs* (Mathematical Association, 1985);
- so-called page-turning – barely interactive – routines that present screen after screen of text, maybe with a few simple diagrams and/or questions;
- simple games based, perhaps, on co-ordinates (like *Pirates* – ITMA, 1972) or building up intersecting sets;
- more advanced games, including adventures like *L* (ATM, 1984);
- graphic introductions to certain areas, maybe with animation and maybe with interaction (for example, *Graphic Calculus* – Tall, 1986);
- teaching-machine-style programs with perhaps a certain degree of branching, and leading to interactive video;
- simulations of, for instance, loaded structures and situations to analyse;

- exploration of specially relevant computer program languages such as LOGO.

The final area in my list of mathematics education IT uses is control, in essence the first step to robotics. Microprocessor-controlled rows of lamps can help learners with number work (for example, in binary), while using a computer to collect temperature data, for instance, and present it ready for a graph is also of value. Using LOGO or similar to help a real floor turtle draw a pattern is a well-known use of IT at all levels. All the same, mathematics learners do not always seem to gain as much from this kind of work as one might expect; maybe present syllabuses provide a barrier?

Down to business

Office (or business) software is now fast coming to be recognised as able to offer as much to education as to training. In comparison with, say, a suite of games and teaching programs in the field of 2D figure areas (which would cost much the same), a business program has several advantages.

First, it is content-free, so can offer much to other subject teachers. This has implications for curriculum integration, finance and staff training.

Second, it *is* office software, so that the college, school, or department office may use it too – with the same implications.

Third, more and more educational establishments are starting business studies (or at least enterprise schemes). To the same implications we may now add the advantages of having high-level staff expertise to call on. It is also good for business students to see office software used in very different contexts – the concept of its near infinite flexibility is a crucial one. In other words, no one working with a computer should be forced into a straightjacket of usage: IT should liberate rather than restrict, and the best applications are those in which the uses are almost boundless.

The potential of office software as a factor in the integration of the curriculum must not be ignored, therefore. This is because each program in the category *is* content-free, highly versatile, limited in practice only by the user's imagination.

It is useful to divide office software into two groups – the first division and the rest (Deeson, 1987). The main types of business program – those in the first division – are word processor, business graphics system, data base management system (data base for short), communications package and spreadsheet. (There is often a degree of integration between these; this aims for the use of the same key-presses for the same effects and allows the transfer of data between functions.)

There is insufficient space in this article to explore the other types of office software. They include such things as stock control, critical path analysis, and organiser programs – and may well have a major role to play in mathematics learning in the future. Indeed, all these are coming to be used as powerful tools for tutors and learners in some schools and colleges already.

There are many possible uses for staff and learners of each of the main types of office software. After a quick outline of what each type of program lets you do, I list some uses to whet your appetite. In each case, I do so for both the tutors and the learners, even though their needs do not really differ so much. Note that each list gives just a few of the very many uses of the techniques concerned in mathematics learning. However, I do not provide references: in each case there are many books and articles that report background theory and teachers' views in practice.

Word processing

A word processor is much better than a typewriter in letting you enter and edit your text more easily; print it out as required with much more flexibility; save it on disc for future work; and transfer it through an IT link (see, for instance, below, under communications) to a colleague elsewhere.

Staff:
- handouts
- notes
- notices
- question banks
- stock lists
- test papers
- worksheets

Learners:
- essays and other assignments
- investigation reports
- projects
- text for displays

Many tutors now accept word processed output from their learners. The main barrier seems to be fear of getting non-original work – but we get that anyway. Word processing can be such a liberation from what most young people would call the drudgery of pen and paper that it is as bad to ban it as to ban calculators. The word processor is a very powerful tool for the transfer of thought from brain to paper; probably most IT teachers would use it as the first introduction to practical computing, at least with literate students.

A really effective technique for tutors with access to many keyboards is to expect the learners to complete word processed task sheets on screen, and store them on disc for later study, marking and collation. It may or may not be a disadvantage to use word processors with an in-built calculator feature! Better is a programmable word processor; though a sadly rare beast, this allows some very exciting interactive work with learners (Deeson and Megarry, 1987).

There are several other newer forms of word processing software that have exciting implications for work with learners. I deal with two of them – desktop publishing and hypertext – after graphics. Predictive typing is of particular value with disabled learners; the software guesses the word or phrase you are currently typing, and offers you its guesses to save you key presses.

Graphics

Business graphics programs are picture processors – they can produce a range of histograms, line graphs and pie charts from data sets; they also often offer statistical analysis features. More specialised graphics software includes computer-aided design (cad) programs; the so-called art software that can give you displays and printouts of diagrams (freehand or line, for example those of structures, flowcharts, geometrical situations); and special programs for work with shapes and patterns. The last type comes under the cal umbrella, but it should be clear which application in the lists below apply to which of the others.

Staff:
- drawing geometric and trigonometric figures
- plotting many types of relationship in the contexts of theoretical and practical concepts
- producing quality illustrations for overhead projection, for notices or for distribution to others
- showing expenditure and assessment breakdowns clearly

Learners:
- drawing sets, geometric and trigonometric figures
- graph drawing activities of all types in all contexts
- plotting investigation results
- producing quality illustrations for projects, assignments and reports

It was mentioned above that many people find word processing to be the best way in to practical computing for learners. For the less literate this is less true, and graphics, especially in mathematics, is an excellent way to start learners getting their hands on the equipment.

However, in practice, processed pictures and processed words mostly support each other; use of *desktop publishing* (dtp) software can make achieving this support easier than it is otherwise. With dtp, the user can process pages of material as wholes, as well as the individual text and graphic items that make up the pages. An advanced form of word processor, a dtp program is perhaps better called page layout software.

Another advanced form of processor is *hypertext*. View this as a system for setting up three-dimensional banks of text and graphics, between which the 'reader' can jump at will by pressing a special key when a highlight on screen shows there's a link to material on another layer. Such links within pure text may lead to illustrations, definitions, references or further notes, for instance.

Data base management

Data base management is structured information processing – the software offers the electronic equivalent of card and paper files. Applications depend greatly on the flexibility of the program used. Searching and sorting and some further degree of processing are allowed.

Staff:
- glossaries
- learner records (but do not forget data protection laws)
- orders, suppliers, and stock records
- practical class registers and profiles
- question banks
- reference files

Learners:
- glossaries
- a huge range of information processing needs
- reference and revision notes

Communications

Here, under message processing, I exclude local area communications, for example, computers in adjoining teaching areas sharing data and printers, or departmental work stations being part of a network. Rather, I am thinking of access to public data bases (such as Prestel, the Times Network System, and NERIS, this last being a data base of worksheets and such); here too come electronic mail and other forms of electronic communication, such as computer conferring, between departments in different areas or even different countries.

None of these are as yet much used in mathematics education (except for the dissemination of papers and electronic conferring in higher education). However, if we are to go much further along the road to open learning mentioned earlier, we need to explore and extend the potential of electronic information transfer. There are also a few experiments in Earth geometry that gain from the rapid transfer of data between distant schools.

Staff:
- consulting with others elsewhere during new course planning, development, and dissemination
- more rapid ordering of stock
- obtaining up-to-date data to make problems closer to real life
- sharing text files and other resources

Learners:
- finding out material for projects
- getting help and reinforcement, especially in open and distance learning situations

Spreadsheets

A spreadsheet – a table processor – is a 2D (normally) grid of cells; each can hold text, a numeric value, or a formula that relates the values in other cells.

Staff:
- analysis of assessments and examination results
- budgeting, stock control and accounting
- processing and analysis of experimental results

Learners:
- linear programming
- vast ranges of problem solving
- tuck shop accounts and planning
- tabulation and analysis of investigations
- work with matrices

To close

The educational computing euphoria of the early 1980s has gone for ever. While we are not far off the figure of a micro to every teaching room, we do not have the masses of high-quality, subject-specific learning software everybody thought there would be. Indeed, we could not afford it if it were published. Using business software can make a great deal of difference to learning mathematics, because of its flexible open-ended nature as described above. Other possible approaches that may come to the rescue include interactive video, expert systems (a form of 'machine intelligence'), and the use by tutors of authoring systems to produce at speed specific, computer-based 'lessons' made up of text, graphics, and self-assessment questions.

However, in practice often the micros are not to be found near the chalkface: rather they tend to live on trolleys and inhabit locked cupboards in primary schools, and cluster in specialist departments at secondary and FE levels. There are other problems teachers have to face up to in practice; getting to learn how to use the programs and how to fit them into their schemes, for instance: both require much thought and time.

At the start of this account, computer-aided freedom, caf, was proposed as the future way forward many tutors and learners would like to tread. We have seen that caf can have several roles; to move toward it we must break away from keeping our learners straightjacketed in systems that do not allow them to express their individual needs and ideas. Office software, interactive video and expert systems offer a great deal more hope in that regard than does 'traditional' cal.

The following points seem clear.

- IT is of growing importance in all areas of life, including all those which affect our pupils and students now and when they leave us; it would be artificial not to use IT in learning mathematics.
- IT offers the tutor more effective methods than before of helping learners explore concepts and carry out investigations, and of organising the department.
- IT is no use on its own: the attitudes and energy of tutors and learners are very relevant to making it a valued and effective resource.

However, the most important question that follows the introduction of new technology into mathematics education concerns how much the curriculum should change. I have implied that the curriculum is Victorian; even if you do not agree with that, ask yourself if the current approach to school/college mathematics is what the citizens of the early twenty-first century need. *Will* society want them to be literate and numerate in the senses we now use the words?

We are long overdue for a complete overhaul of the mathematics curriculum at all levels. And I mean *complete*. It is ironic that IT makes fundamental change both essential and possible, but – to repeat – we need the change anyway. Computer-aided freedom is worth working for!

References

ATM (1984) *L: a Mathemagical Adventure*. Derby: Association of Teachers of Mathematics.

Deeson, E. (1983) *BBC Micro in Education*. Chapter 9. Nantwich: Shiva.

Deeson, E. (1987) *Managing with IT*. Chapters 3 and 4. London: Kogan Page.

Deeson, E. and Megarry, J. (1987) *WordPlus Software Across the Curriculum*. Glasgow: Jordanhill College.

DES (1987) *Aspects of the Work of MEP*. London: HMSO.

Howe, J. and Ross, P. (1981) *Microcomputers in Secondary Education*. London: Kogan Page.

ITMA (1972) *Pirates*. Harlow: Longman.

Mathematical Association (1985) *132 Short Programs for the Mathematics Classroom*. Cheltenham: Thornes.

Megarry, J. (1985) *Inside Information*. London: BBC.

Stonier, T. and Conlin, C. (1985) *The Three Cs*. Chichester: Wiley.

Tall, D. (1986) *Graphic Calculus*. Barnet: Glentop.

Further reading

(a) General

Hammond, R. (1985) *Forward 100*. Harmondsworth: Penguin.

O'Shea, T. and Self, J. (1983) *Learning and Teaching with Computers*. Brighton: Harvester Press.

Scanlon, E. and O'Shea, T. (1987) *Educational Computing*. Chichester: Wiley.

(b) Periodicals

Here are the most useful magazines published in Britain at the time of writing. Many other papers and journals (for example NCET's *British Journal of Educational Technology*) publish occasional relevant material, and the *Times Educational Supplement* publishes many reviews and articles, and often carries a special supplement on educational IT.

Computer Education (termly, CEG, Polytechnic Computer Centre, Blackheath Lane, Stafford)

IT and Learning (twice termly, MUSE, PO Box 43, Houghton, Leics., LE7 9GX)

Micromath (termly, Basil Blackwell or Association of Teachers of Mathematics)

MicroScope (for primary teachers, termly, MAPE, Newman College, Birmingham B32 3NT)

School Computer User (twice termly, 141 Drury Lane, London WC2B 5TF)

(c) Specific

Burton, N. (1986) *Exploring Mathematics with Microcomputers*. London: CET.

Kelman, P. *et al.* (1983) *Computers in Teaching Mathematics*. Cambridge, Mass.: Addison-Wesley.

Oldknow, A. (1987) *Microcomputers in Geometry*. Chichester: Ellis Horwood.

Oldknow, A. and Smith, D. (1983) *Learning Mathematics with Micros*. Chichester: Ellis Horwood.

Eric Deeson is Director of Resources and Information Technology, Joseph Chamberlain Sixth Form College, Birmingham.

17

Opening-up

Anne Watson

How often have you read articles about open-ended investigative work in the classroom and thought: 'This is all very well but I wouldn't have a clue where to start'? Courses do not always help to get rid of this feeling and can even make it worse. The tutor extols the virtues of this approach and you, of course, agree. She sets you some work to do in groups and you enjoy it. Every other group produces more sophisticated results than yours, your own results seem to vanish in the general feedback, and to cap it all she then shows you work which is more sophisticated than any of yours, probably containing a result which is on the A level further mathematics syllabus, and declares that it is work from mixed-ability 13 year olds! All your enthusiasm vanishes; not only have you not been able to 'do' it, but you are now convinced you are not cut out for mathematics teaching at all and none of your pupils could produce anything like that.

Strangely enough, I think self-doubt is an ideal state of mind in which to start thinking about working investigatively. The teacher who knows all the answers and expects pupils to produce a fixed sequence of arguments leading to some final conclusion is not the best person to draw creative thought from a class. The teacher who sometimes admits ignorance, is prepared to accept hunches and half-truths, and generates a feeling of shared problems, is more likely to enjoy and encourage their own thought-processes.

Let us suppose that your department is keen to try investigative work; some have been on courses; there is access to a few ideas from books and journals; and the main concern is how people will cope personally and pedagogically in the classroom. I offer a few ideas which have worked for me in this situation.

Planning to listen

It helps to listen to what pupils are trying to say in order to see the direction of their thought. A cunning little exercise to help you test your listening skills is to ask a class to think about a rectangle and then describe it one-by-one. They think it is a geometry exercise and some of them will produce accurate classical descriptions which you can acknowledge with a nod. One also gets a selection of more unusual descriptions such as: 'stretched square', 'an endless shape with corners', 'it looks like this

. . .'. So long as these descriptions are more or less correct they should be praised, and everyone's attention drawn to the most unusual ones. This exercise does several things which will be of use to investigative work later on.

- You learn to listen because you know what a rectangle is and you can measure your idea of it against theirs.
- You encourage the creative approach and the unusual ideas. Those who produced classical responses might have been slightly shocked at what you found praiseworthy.
- You encourage less-able pupils and publicly acknowledge the value of their contribution.
- You enable pupils to verbalise concepts which are apparently easy to understand. This is good practice for verbalising more difficult ideas later on.

This exercise can be extended to answer questions like: 'What is a circle?' 'What is adding?', 'What can you use a line for?' and so on.

Planning for mess

If a long time is spent teaching pupils how to present work and arguments neatly, insisting on underlined headings, dates, and sharp pencils, there are going to be problems convincing them that rough work is valuable and that you are prepared to spend some time looking at it. Perhaps you have to convince yourself first! Next time you work something out in rough keep the paper for a week and then look at it again. Can you follow the train of thought you had then? Are all the arguments written down? Probably not, but that does not invalidate the work. How often do you write up something neatly when you have worked it out in rough? Probably not very often, or only in special circumstances.

This is not an argument against neat presentation of work, but you may need to prepare pupils to find ways of recording their work at the speed of their thought. There will be times during a good investigative session when they need to draw several quick diagrams perhaps, or they may suddenly see connections between things which they cannot yet explain but need to indicate immediately. The use of circling or underlining parts of their work, arrows to show how pieces of work connect, brainstorming, asterisks to show things which may be worth returning to, parts of diagrams abandoned as a result becomes clear, and other messy ways of working may need to be encouraged if people are used to hiding their rough work or throwing it away. I have shown pupils examples of my rough work and neat finished products. I often ask to see rough work from other areas of the mathematics curriculum. I sometimes start an investigation by doing a bit of 'working-out' on the board and using intentionally 'messy' techniques to illustrate how useful they can be, always emphasising that they will, at some stage, have to look back at their work to write it up neatly in some form or other. If people are working in groups, anyone who spends too long recording or drawing will either be hurried up by the others or excluded from the group's progress.

Planning for sharing

Working in groups can yield a wide range of benefits. It can help to speed up the work where an investigation involves the results from several different cases. It can help pupils appreciate each other's contribution to the work and develop their own. It can help some to keep track of what is going on if they have others to help them. On the other hand it can isolate quiet pupils from the action, and very quick pupils can ignore slower ones without intentional cruelty. Individuals can resent their own ideas being absorbed or submerged by other people's, just as some of us do when we work in a group.

Classes already used to working in groups for mathematics have no problem. Otherwise perhaps there is some other curriculum area in which groupwork is used and the experience of other teachers can help get things started. If you have to start from scratch you need to think quite carefully about the ability-grouping and gender-groupings. This is a big topic which I do not intend to tackle here, but in my experience groups of like ability do not produce the best or most imaginative work. The more able pupils often produce stereotypical work which may generate the 'right' answer but may not stimulate them to ask further questions. On the other hand, groups of mixed ability may not be able to conclude their work in the form of a generalised theorem or similar conclusion, if there is one to be found. Having decided on groupings, a straightforward topic might be tried at first; I suggest tangrams, or the building of solid models, as a suitable exercise. One task while this is going on is to observe how the groups are working, who is too dominant, who is too isolated, and what adjustments to the groups might have to be made.

Planning to get started

It is worth considering how to start the investigation: whether to do a bit yourself first to get them going, or work with the whole class as a large group, or just state the problem and let them do it all. Sometimes an investigation can grind to a halt after five minutes because there is a flaw in the statement of the problem. This is not your fault or theirs. You can congratulate them on getting into the problem so quickly, discuss the flaw, come to a mutual agreement about definitions or regulations, or dictate further instructions as needed. The types of questions which can arise are varied; for instance, 'Can we turn the paper over?', 'Does line mean straight line?', 'What are we supposed to be counting?', 'Can we used dotted paper?' and so on. The more of these questions you can anticipate the better, but there will always be surprises.

Planning to avoid collapse

Possibly the greatest fear one might have is that, because the lesson is relatively unstructured, it could grind to a halt.

It may seem obvious to try the investigation yourself first, but this can have hidden dangers. If you discover some wonderful patterns or general algebraic relationships hidden in the structure of the problem it can be very tempting to steer pupils towards them and generate a feeling of disappointment if they do not get there. It is often better to bite your lip and let pupils charge off in the 'wrong' direction, because the more of this kind of work you do the less you will be able to define 'wrong'. In the first investigative session I ever ran I expected pupils to produce a quadratic relationship, or at least a verbal description of one, from a problem involving lines and their intersections. Instead one group produced an entire family of curves 'stitched' from straight lines and some rather neat sequences of numbers to describe each one. So anything is acceptable within reason, but what if instead of 'anything' you get 'nothing'? As in any mathematics teaching, clever use of questions can nudge people along. Three of the most useful are 'Can you guess . . .?', 'Why?' and 'What if . . .?'.

'Can you guess . . .?' can be used to help those who are stuck but feel they understand where they are going. It can also be used when several results have already been found but people are unable to proceed further to a generalisation; for instance, they may have failed to spot a linear relationship or a well-known number-sequence in their results. After guessing comes testing, followed by more confident predicting and a verbal or symbolic statement of the pattern they have found occurring. Very many investigations can follow this kind of pattern and you can always encourage pupils to take this approach if they are stuck or you are unable to see where else they might go.

'Why?' is a useful question when someone has made an error but you want them to diagnose it. It is even more useful if people have produced verbal statements without explanation, or have given you a formula but missed the underlying structure. For instance, in the well-known 'frogs' puzzle, it is one step to say the puzzle can be solved in 15 moves, a further step to produce a general formula for different numbers of frogs, but an even greater step to say why the relationship is quadratic in terms of how the frogs move. Pupils can often fall back on a circular argument such as: Why is the relationship linear? Because it makes a straight line.

'What if . . .?' is the queen of questions in investigative work. It is worth having a store of them up your sleeve until confidence has grown to the state where they can be produced off the top of the head. Here are some examples: What if you . . . used triangular paper? tried it in three dimensions? plotted a graph? tried a simple case first? shared your results with someone else? tried fractions or decimals or negative numbers?

Planning for next time

I have a notebook near me throughout a session and I jot down any questions I could not answer. I think them through after the session or consult with colleagues. I also jot down the questions I did answer and ask myself if my answers were open or closed. I give myself a pat on the back for every question which I answered in a way which led the pupils deeper into the problem. I give myself two pats on the back for every answer which started with 'I don't know but what if . . .' because these answers show that I regard the investigation as a shared experience.

Self-doubt probably still lurks somewhere so I write down very quickly all the things which went wrong and get them out of the way by incorporating my ideas on them into my plans for the next investigative session right away. I sit back and feel good about the things which went right. How many pupils obviously enjoyed it? Did I enjoy it? How much enthusiasm was there? I think of what each group produced, not in terms of how far from a conclusion they were, but in terms of how much they had achieved. Perhaps I can remember what each individual achieved without looking at any written work. How many had ideas of their own during the session? How can I build on these achievements next time? Now what would be a suitable investigation to do next? . . .

Anne Watson is Coordinator for Mathematics at a comprehensive school in Oxford.

18

Responding to change

Rita Nolder

The experience of changing one's classroom practice may not be a comfortable one. It can be fraught with problems which all too often only surface once change is underway. This article contains three case studies of teachers, all of whom were involved with innovations designed to incorporate mathematical activities of an investigative and practical nature into their classrooms. The contexts in which they work vary, as do their personal and professional backgrounds. In each case a number of issues arose, some of which were resolved, as they attempted to modify their classroom practice. My focus here will be upon those issues which have arisen because of the challenges being made to pre-existing ideas about:

(a) what constitutes mathematics;
(b) how children learn;
(c) who controls access to mathematical knowledge.

Rick has been teaching for twelve years and is Head of Mathematics in a boys' secondary modern school in a small town, with an intake mainly from middle-class homes. His experience of mathematics teaching in his first post was SMILE in its early days. He did not enjoy it and this has coloured his attitude to individualised schemes ever since. When he moved to his present school, he abandoned individualised learning and lessons fell very much into the mode of 'exposition by the teacher, pupils do the exercise'.

Personal boredom with the formal way in which he was working, coupled with an awareness of the lack of relevance to the pupils of much of the mathematics he was teaching, led Rick to begin making changes to his classroom practice. Initially, he experimented with his second and third year lower sets, basing his syllabus on the Cockcroft Foundation list (DES, 1982) and using games and other activities to try to make lessons more enjoyable. However, he kept the 'traditional' way of working with exam classes because of external pressures.

> I wasn't prepared to totally drop things from the various courses (because they still came up every year) but over the years less and less emphasis was placed on the more mundane work. Many parents still expected their sons to have a 'sound' mathematics education and I'm sure the idea of playing with bits of coloured paper and Sellotape instead of doing 'proper' maths like they had to, would have horrified some of our parents.

Rick felt that he knew very little about practical mathematics apart from 'making a scale drawing of the minibus and taking kids out to measure the rugby pitch' and even less about investigations and problem-solving. He signed up for a ten-week 'twilight' course in order to 'remedy this deficiency'. It served a dual purpose; it provided him with lots of material for the classroom and enabled him to discuss his ideas with colleagues from a wide variety of schools.

> I personally needed to know that these ideas were not wrong. I needed reassurance from many colleagues that they too were thinking along the same lines. The idea of investigations or, more importantly, an investigative approach, had to have the backing of my peers within the profession to give it respectability.

A combination of peer support and the 'legitimising' effect of the GCSE upon the new ways of working encouraged Rick to contemplate making radical changes to his mathematics curriculum for the intake year.

The idea of changing from a syllabus-dominated to an activity-based curriculum was not welcomed by the headteacher. He was concerned that parents would want to see their children doing 'real' maths, and advised injecting investigations into the existing syllabus instead. In the event, an activity-based curriculum went ahead, albeit somewhat clandestinely. The other teachers in the department were prepared to support Rick in this, partly because of their personal and professional regard for him, but also because they too knew things had to change because of the GCSE. Rick tried to ensure their involvement by inviting each of them to contribute one unit of activities to the year's scheme of work. Everyone took up the invitation.

One major issue for Rick was parental concern. Complaints from parents took some time to appear. More precisely, one complaint from a parent actually appeared, but this was enough to set alarm bells ringing. It pointed out that:

> Everything seems to be done by trial and error. When will it be consolidated into 'proper' mathematical theory?

and

> Pupils are tempted not to do the job properly because they do not see the work as 'proper' maths.

A concluding remark was that their son was 'enjoying the work immensely' but he was not sure that he was doing maths.

Behind what was often voiced as concern for 'what parents want' is the fundamental issue of what constitutes mathematics. Whilst Rick's aim in changing the curriculum was to focus on mathematical thinking, this was at odds not only with many parents' perceptions of mathematics, but also those of one member of his department and the headteacher. Their ideas were based on what one might describe as 'school mathematics' – a set of facts and techniques – in which questions have one right answer and prescribed methods of solution. Hand-in-hand with this notion of what constitutes mathematics goes the perception of how it is to be learned. Mathematical knowledge is transmitted from teacher to pupil; telling, showing and explaining are the order of the day.

Rick's method of dealing with these conflicting images was to hold an evening parents' workshop in which he outlined the rationale and aims of the new mathematics curriculum for the intake year. By undertaking mathematical activities themselves, and through discussion with members of staff, parents began to see that there was an alternative, and viable, view of mathematics. Additionally, they were given the opportunity to experience other ways of learning mathematics than those which they knew about from their own schooldays.

The evening was a great success, evidenced both by parents' reactions during the course of the evening and by the positive comments made by parents on a questionnaire Rick had devised.

> Maths is much more interesting these days.
>
> I now understand what my son has as maths homework. I now see the light – many thanks.
>
> A helpful workshop to better understand the system being used to teach maths.

From this point onwards the headteacher was completely won over. The issue of parental concern had been resolved, at least for the time being, and Rick and his department could proceed with their curriculum development without the spectre of parental complaint haunting them.

To the outside observer, there has been considerable change in classroom practice within this maths department. Children work in groups rather than sitting in rows facing the blackboard. All the elements of paragraph 243 of the Cockcroft Report are in evidence rather than simply exposition and practice. Yet with this one major issue resolved, Rick is now questioning whether what goes on in his classroom has really changed so much.

> I come in. I control the class. However little time I spend at the front they don't come in and get on with something, they come in and wait for me. Whatever the activity, I still see this as the old style . . . it's teacher-led from that point of view in that they rely on me to start them off and I mean it's almost as if I stand there with a gun and say 'Go!' So I start the lesson, I tick it over half way through and I finish the lesson and my discipline and control is there all the time overriding everything.

A concern with pupil autonomy manifested itself in two ways. The first, and the easiest for him to deal with, involved classroom organisation. Instead of retaining exclusive control over classroom resources, Rick showed pupils where equipment, etc. was kept and expected them to help themselves to whatever they needed. The second, and the one with which he is still struggling, required him to search for a means of making the pupils less dependent on him for their mathematics. By setting more open-ended tasks he is encouraging pupils to do 'their maths', although he is aware that he still controls the selection of these tasks. Rick is unsure as to what his next move in this direction will be. Older pupils, who are still being taught in a more 'traditional' way, demonstrate a much higher degree of dependency upon Rick in their maths lessons than do younger pupils who are involved in the new curriculum. The former frequently ask 'Is this right?' or 'What do I do next?', whilst younger pupils seem to spend more time showing him what they have found out. Rick hopes this attitude will spread up the school as these pupils grow older. This aspect of his practice is only just beginning to change, but he intends to persevere with it, spurred on by the personal satisfaction he has derived from 'seeing them do *their* maths'.

For Betty, pupil autonomy is also an issue, though not in the same way as it is for Rick. She teaches in a middle school where she has worked for many years. The school's mathematics syllabus reflects its more 'academic' past, still containing references to logarithms although no one teaches them any more. In an effort to make the mathematics curriculum more practically-based, the new headteacher introduced a commercial maths scheme which he thought would improve teachers' classroom practice by shifting the emphasis away from whole-class 'chalk and talk' lessons and towards more individual and group work.

Betty uses the scheme once a week, although she is unhappy about the fact that she has to spend so much time getting the equipment ready. Her room is not equipped for easy pupil access to equipment and she has to store apparatus on a trolley elsewhere. Betty's other criticism of the scheme is that she has been told to use it for individualised learning and she does not believe that the children learn properly this way. She would prefer to be spending her time on planning for a teacher-led lesson, rather than on organising equipment and administering a scheme:

> There's no time to do detailed work any more.

In addition, her long-established methods of classroom organisation are better suited to whole-class teaching. When she uses the scheme she stays at her desk whilst pupils queue for help, for marking or to find out what they should do next.

Practical tasks do feature in Betty's mathematics lessons outside of the commercial scheme. Her normal pattern of working with this type of activity is for everyone to undertake the same task. Betty demonstrates the way they are to tackle the task and the pupils carry it out in unison, at least initially. A technique she often uses after such an activity is to ask the pupils to write about what they have learned.

A member of the mathematics advisory team was invited by the headteacher to work in the school and while it was not compulsory, it was assumed that every teacher would work with him at some stage. In the course of this involvement, he undertook a series of once-weekly sessions with Betty and her class. A variety of practical and investigative activities was tried out, largely with the children working in groups and occasionally with the groups engaged in different tasks. The latter was reluctantly agreed to by Betty who thought that 'when one group sees another doing something more exciting they'll be discontented'. In the event, each group was so involved in its own task that this did not happen.

After some initial scepticism, Betty gave enthusiastic support to the venture. She was involved in planning the activities with the advisory teacher and took on full responsibility for organising the equipment for each session. She supplemented the once-weekly group sessions by finishing activities begun in the session with her class and she sometimes initiated a task for the whole class to do to reinforce what had been done with the advisory teacher.

The advisory teacher and Betty disagreed in their views about how a task might be presented. This difference could be described as a conflict between 'discovery' on the one hand and 'showing' on the other. Betty acknowledged:

> I'm scared to let the children try things out for themselves. I'm happier showing them everything.

The reason she gave for this was that she felt that experiencing repeated failure was bad for pupils. She referred to one pupil's piece of writing which described what he thought he had learned in the first session with the advisory teacher:

> I lern not much at all.

However, she was prepared to go along with the advisory teacher's point of view in the sessions and reassured herself concerning her own fears by using whole-class lessons to reinforce what she felt pupils should have discovered.

When the series of sessions with the advisory teacher came to an end, Betty said that she thought that the work had gone well and that the children had enjoyed it, although she had noticed that the response of the 'difficult' children, whom she also described as 'poorly motivated', was much the same as usual. Her concern now was how she was going to cover the syllabus since she had used up so much time on these practical activities. One thing the advisory teacher had failed to convey was that the syllabus *was* being covered via these activities.

Betty's stated guiding principle, that every child should experience success, was not at variance with the philosophy behind the school-imposed innovation with which she had been virtually obliged to become involved. Where a major difference arose was the means by which this might be ensured. Betty's technique was to set all her pupils the same task and then to teach them to accomplish it. One possible reason for the lack of motivation within her class could be attributed to tasks not being sufficiently challenging for some pupils, whilst being beyond the intellectual grasp of others. She did not accept that within a more open-ended task, all children could experience success by setting themselves goals which they would work towards accomplishing. These goals, and the methods of achieving them, would not be the same for all pupils, and hence the criteria for judging success would need to cater for this.

Embedded in the teaching method employed by Betty is the transmission model of learning referred to earlier. She believes that the most efficient way for pupils to learn mathematics is by being told what to do, and preferably by a teacher, rather than a textbook. This was at odds with the view of mathematics and the theory of learning underpinning the innovation with which she was involved. In this, the pupil was seen as being very much an active participant in the learning process rather than as a passive recipient of someone else's mathematical knowledge. Betty's classroom practice changed whilst she worked with the advisory teacher, but the lack of congruence between her beliefs about mathematics and about how children learn and those behind the innovation, made it unlikely that such changes would be sustained once he left. This was evidenced by the continuation of her long-established teaching methods and forms of classroom organisation between sessions with the advisory teacher.

For Rick, the motivation to change his classroom practice came from within himself, whereas for Betty the pressures were primarily external. It could be suggested that this is one determining factor in whether teachers are able to effect and sustain change. The concluding case study concerns a teacher whose decision to change was strongly influenced by external factors but whose personal enthusiasm and commitment sustained the change in classroom practice.

Joanne works at a grammar school and almost all her teaching experience has been at this school. She describes herself as an 'old-fashioned' teacher in referring to what might be considered rather traditional teaching methods. These consist largely of exposition and practice with the occasional excursion into recreational mathematics 'to spice it up a bit'. Joanne was quite happy with the way she was teaching until the GCSE began to be talked about, particularly in relation to its emphasis on investigative work and school-based assessment.

It was clear that the department would need to move with the times if its pupils were to continue to get good results, and, encouraged by her new Head of Department, Joanne found herself entrusted with the management of a curriculum innovation for the intake year. She began by rewriting the syllabus to bring it in line with GCSE, which involved some reduction in content. Then, in conjunction with her Head of Department, she grouped the remaining content into broad areas and added a list of process objectives, for example, 'to specialise, think systematically, hypothesise, generalise, etc.' Other teachers involved in the intake year were invited to take responsibility for preparing materials for some areas of the new curriculum. These were to incorporate practical and investigative mathematics.

Joanne and the other members of the team of teachers working with the intake year embarked on the new curriculum with a good deal of enthusiasm and more than a little apprehension. Without exception they had liked the role they played within the classroom and a remark by Joanne sums up how they felt about the more pupil-centred approach:

> The idea of kids finding things out for themselves appeals to me, but I enjoy explaining.

In addition, Joanne felt that the new approach exposed her weaknesses as a teacher. By this she was referring to her perceived poor organisation and her lack of knowledge about other approaches to teaching, learning and assessment. She felt that

> It's lack of confidence in your ability to use a new approach that stops you changing. You've been doing things the same way for years and you know you can get things across, but . . .

Once the new curriculum was underway, the predominant concern of the department was the time it was taking to cover the syllabus. This concern was voiced by Joanne within the first month of the new way of working:

> Inside I was screaming, 'I'm never going to get this done!'

Joanne often felt that she could have taught a topic to the whole class in a fraction of the time it was taking them to find it out for themselves. The issue of coverage did not dissipate during the year and with the exception of the Head of Maths, everyone was worried that they were not able to complete even this much-reduced syllabus, and that the knock-on effect could lead to serious repercussions in later years. When the syllabus was referred to, it was the content objectives to which everyone referred; the process objectives were for the most part ignored.

In the past, Joanne and the other teachers had been able to measure how well they were doing by 'ticking off' sections of the syllabus as they completed them. The end-of-year panic on discovering that other teachers had covered more had led to a general feeling that the quicker topics were completed the better. There was also the belief that traditional methods ensure that everyone in the class gets the same information and that you therefore know what pupils have learned. Joanne sensed that this was not quite true as she was aware that there were children within her classes who had not learned what she thought she had taught them.

'Rounding off' was a preoccupation of all teachers implementing the new curriculum. When Joanne worked on more open-ended work, she liked to have a whole class session to ensure that everyone had 'got the basic idea'. She described a strategy she had developed to deal with this:

> The thing that worked best when we were going through an investigation was to get individual kids to come and explain it . . . mind you they made such a racket applauding them when they'd finished etc., but I felt they were listening more carefully to them than they were to me!

Joanne began to focus on what she could see as the positive aspects of the new approach, and while she did not specifically identify them as such, they were related to the process objectives within the scheme of work. An example which was particularly significant for her arose in some work on graphs. The pupils were asked to plot pairs of points and to try to find a rule for working out the coordinates of the midpoints of the lines joining these pairs of points. The vast majority of her class was able to state a rule in words and then to generate an algebraic formula. In the past, her pupils would have been shown the way to work this out, given the formula to memorise, and in many cases they would have forgotten it. Joanne was impressed with their ability to formulate the rule for themselves and felt that since they understood what they were doing there was a better chance of retention.

On other occasions, teachers commented that tasks without an obvious method of solution which were set to the intake year and also to other years were tackled better by the intake year in spite of the fact that they were younger. It was felt that they were prepared to 'have a go' whereas the others foundered in the absence of a well-defined and pre-specified method. A feeling began to emerge that the advantages of the new approach might be long- rather than short-term, but the dichotomy between wanting to work in the new way because of its potential advantages and 'Are we ever going to get the syllabus done?' continued to be problematic. It did not, however, stop them continuing with the innovation in the next school year, after making some modifications to the scheme of work.

The major underlying issues for Joanne and for the department in which she works concerned teaching methods and the distinction between content and process in mathematics. As regards method, most teachers were concerned with 'getting things across', the transmission mode of teaching again. Because they had taught a topic, it followed that the children had learned it. When test results did not confirm this, they could still console themselves with the fact that every child had been given the same opportunity to learn. This method of teaching was effective in that it produced good results in an examination which focused on mathematical content. The teachers understood that what they were doing would have to change if they were to foster skills of mathematical thinking, but it was still difficult for them to change well-established habits for others of unproven value.

When Joanne had first contemplated changing her classroom practice, the GCSE had been her prime motivation. She had included process objectives in the syllabus because these featured in GCSE. She was aware that these could be developed by investigative work, but once she became immersed in the new curriculum, struggling on occasions to keep her head above water, she began to lose sight of these objectives, focusing instead on the more familiar content objectives. For other members of the department, some of whom were less aware than Joanne of what they were trying to achieve via the new approach, this was even more the case. As Joanne herself commented:

> It's just that you've been doing things the same way for ten plus years and it's second nature.

Change in classroom practice is often talked about as if it were easy to effect and impatience expressed towards teachers who are unable to accomplish it overnight. As these case studies show, even when the willingness to change is there, whether the initial impetus comes from within or without, actually bringing about change is hard for the individual. It requires teachers to look critically at their own present practice as well as being able to conceive of alternatives. This needs time and it needs support and encouragement, from within the school, from other colleagues, and from the Advisory Service.

Reference

DES (1982) *Mathematics Counts* (The Cockcroft Report). London: HMSO.

Rita Nolder was a mathematics advisory teacher; she is now Lecturer in Mathematics Education at Loughborough University.

19

Tensions

John Mason

Have you ever had the experience, in the middle of a lesson, of suddenly wishing you were not there? Like a wave washing over you, you realise that things are not going well. Perhaps you 'take control' and conduct things from the blackboard; perhaps you 'let them keep working', waiting for the bell to ring. The feeling of inadequacy, but of having to cope, is an example of a tension.

Have you ever found yourself talking, telling pupils things, and wished that somehow things were different, that *they* were doing the work? Or have you ever got a group of pupils talking, and having heard how inarticulate they are, how little they understand, wished that you had never embarked in this direction? This is an example of a tension.

Like elastic bands wound up, feelings of inadequacy or guilt, or just knots in the stomach, are indications that you have touched a basic tension. Another way to detect tensions is to notice 'if onlys'.

- If only pupils wanted to learn . . .
- If only they would pay attention . . .
- If only the class were smaller . . .

These too are indicators of underlying tensions. Despite the fact that 'if only' implies that things could be different, they do not actually go away when the ideal conditions are achieved, they just surface in a new guise. Yet each day these tensions *are* coped with in some fashion by each and every teacher. Some stance, some action is taken, which often obscures the underlying dilemma.

The resultant of all the many forces on teachers is often, not surprisingly, inaction and numbness. In this article, I want to acknowledge openly a number of tensions that I experience, and which I suspect others may recognise. I do this in the belief that by admitting them publicly we will discover that others share them. The history of education in general, and mathematics education in particular, is riddled with attempts to nullify basic tensions. Yet I suspect most tensions are endemic and inescapable. Getting them out into the open means that they can be robbed of their numbing effect, and turned instead into potent sources of energy.

Consider the following quotes from pupils and teachers.

- The pupils asked me if this was 'on the exam'. I said, 'Well, no, not exactly . . .' and they switched off immediately.
- I want to get them enjoying mathematics. They just want to get through the day.

- Don't make me think about it, just tell me how to do it!
- I've read the card, Miss, but is it an add or a multiply?

These are the sorts of remarks that are heard quite often, signalling the presence of a basic tension of teaching and learning. In what follows I have tried to be explicit and specific about experiences which are by their nature woolly and indeterminate, resisting expression. Looking back over them, I see that in many cases the same underlying tension is addressed in different ways.

Keeping control

I must keep my class under control, both to permit individuals to work, and so as not to disturb other classes.

- With a new class I want the pupils to feel that I am in control and that I know what I'm doing. I tend to keep a tight rein at first, and gradually relax as I get to know them.

The stronger my control, the less opportunity for individuals to explore, to express their own ideas. Yet inevitably there are one or two pupils who do not seem to respond to my way of working, who are hard to control.

- The only question is how to survive to the end of the lesson. If I turn my back, then some of them immediately start break-dancing round the room!

Do other teachers have similar difficulties? New teachers on probation may be afraid to admit to difficulties, for fear of being branded inadequate, and even losing their job. An experienced teacher may be wary of revealing uncertainties for fear of losing status in the eyes of colleagues, or perhaps the chance of promotion.

- If I work the way I want to, what will the teacher think who takes them next year?

A head of department may be too concerned with gaining or keeping the respect of colleagues to admit to having problems.

Time

The syllabus is packed, the examination looms, there is too little time to cover all the material. If I stop and get the pupils discussing, or investigating, I will lose valuable time, and some topic will be missed.

The tension of time is unresolvable, no matter how it is approached, due to the pressures of society to 'get on'. If I take the time necessary for pupils to really understand a topic, then I will certainly have trouble exposing them to everything that is expected. On the other hand, I might be able to demonstrate, even inculcate, ways of thinking that will enable them to take on new topics much more quickly.

Notice how discussion of lack of sufficient time brings up some standard primitives and metaphors:

- I was afraid we wouldn't get there/reach the topic.
- I felt I had to push a bit harder to get to the answer in the lesson.

The metaphors of 'knowledge as place', and of 'teaching as movement' are quite common. Are they appropriate? A related metaphor is revealed in expressions such as

- There isn't time to cover the syllabus.
- I haven't covered inequalities yet.

Painting seems to be a popular pastime – but is it an appropriate image? What images might be more accurate or more precise?

Shortage of time is a common complaint in every walk of life, but perhaps it is only a perception. If I really want to do something, I will find the time. Put another way, perhaps the things I do with my time *are* really what I want to do.

Confidence vs challenge

It has been said over and over again that pupils need to gain confidence, and that confidence comes from success. Unfortunately, success is associated only with jumping hurdles, like tests and examinations, and not also with seeing a generality, or capturing it in words and symbols, or explaining it to someone else. The result is that we try to 'give pupils confidence' by providing simple tasks with little or no challenge.

For example, the current concern about 'low attainers' stems directly from the requirement that all pupils study mathematics every year, but indirectly from the age-old observation that 'standards are falling'. (Cicero complained bitterly of this, and was by no means the first!) The confidence–challenge tension leads educators to simplify the tasks given to low-attaining pupils, to break things down into tiny, anodyne steps. Any intellectual challenge is removed on the grounds that they cannot handle it, and so all edge, all interest, is gone.

Product vs process

I want my pupils to participate in mathematical thinking, and to take the initiative. I know that *their* actual task is to pass the examinations they meet. *Their* attention is on learning what they are told they have to learn, on being able to do the questions. *My* wish is to emphasise thinking skills so that they will be able to deal with unexpected questions on an examination, and more importantly, continue thinking and questioning throughout their lives. As soon as I start 'teaching' mathematical processes, there is a real danger that they will simply become products, words to be memorised.

For example, I want my pupils to realise deeply within themselves that it often helps to specialise – to try simple cases, systematically as well as randomly – and then to generalise – to look for a general pattern. But how long do I let them struggle with a complicated example before intervening? If I come in too quickly, specialising will become a superficial behaviour, and it will not be available as a potent force when they really need it. If I give no clues, they may never become aware of the power of specialising.

- Pupils will quickly learn to say the 'right' words back to you, but do they really appreciate their real meaning?

This dilemma is endemic. The way we cope depends on many factors, such as whether the particular answer really matters or whether it is being used as a vehicle to introduce, or work on, 'specialising'. Frustration is important in mathematics, for you cannot really experience release, that beautiful sense of things falling into place, if you have not previously been confused, feeling that things were out of place.

Analogously, you cannot guide trainee teachers past the fundamental teaching tensions. They have to experience the dilemmas themselves before they can even 'hear' the advice. It is an old story; but there is no royal road to learning (or teaching).

Autonomy

Pupils need standards against which to measure their own performance. The more the standards are imposed by the teacher, the more the pupils are 'working for their teacher', rather than for themselves. In primary and early secondary school there may appear to be no harm done, but when pupils get older and dissaffected with school, their teachers become part of 'the system'. Pupils may lose their reason for working unless they have learned to work for themselves, to value the pleasure that comes with seeing, and with being able to explain to others.

What then do I do with a capable but unproductive pupil? Some forceful pushing may help get through a barrier, but it may also produce dependency on me to keep pushing. If the teacher imposes all the discipline, then will the pupils learn to access their own will, or do they simply bide their time until they leave school? If a teacher leaves it up to the pupils to work on their own initiative, will they miss out on essential skills while coming to grips with being responsible for their own learning? When they are stuck, it is so much more attractive to tell them what I think than to encourage and cajole them to tell me what they think. It also gives me pleasure to rehearse a story clearly that I have thought about. It reinforces my 'seeing'. Unfortunately, it also reduces their opportunity to 'see'. For me, Gattegno's memorable expression 'the subordination of teaching to learning' sums up this tension. To teach, to take the initiative, to impose what shall be attended to, puts the student in the position of reacting to external pressure. Military disciplinarians believe that by imposing very strong discipline you break through barriers and train people to be highly self-disciplined. Some pupils take to it, others reject it as soon as possible. At the other extreme, I can elect to work with and respond to those who give evidence of wishing to work mathematically, and simply keep some semblance of order amongst the rest. Some may 'take advantage' of this way of acting, and not discover until too late what they were missing.

There is no answer to this tension, no way to relieve it. I can decide how I am going to act, stick to my guns, and ignore the consequences. I can also keep alive inside me an awareness of the delicate balance, looking out for an opportunity to support independent initiative within whatever restrictions are imposed. What *is* important is being alive to the tension, rather than trying to avoid it.

Intervening

The tensions mentioned so far are fairly global. There are also many more specific ones felt moment to moment in the classroom. For example, a group of pupils are 'working' at a table. Should I intervene? How? Why? Shall I let them carry on and see for themselves; shall I 'guide' or 'direct' them? Must I be present for something worthwhile to happen?

Must I check that everything is correct? What if they go away with a misunderstanding? (When don't they?!) In any group there are liable to be passengers. Does it matter? What should I do? How can I tell if someone is working, or just copying?

A standard way to intervene with one or more pupils is to ask them something along the lines of 'tell me what you're doing'. Another way to intervene is silently, simply listening to what they are saying, and watching what they are writing. Some pupils don't like being watched, however.

Sometimes an intervention provides a useful impetus to try to articulate what they are doing, and in the process, see things more clearly for themselves. Sometimes an intervention blocks progress. Just when the struggle is most important, my intervention may draw pupils back to earlier parts of their investigation, perhaps even exposing unsuspected or overlooked difficulties, and leave them feeling that they are getting nowhere.

If I am working on pupil autonomy, then I have to find some way to remind pupils that it often helps to talk out loud to someone, and to establish an atmosphere in which they readily approach each other and me for this purpose.

Didactic contract

The didactic contract is between teacher and pupil although it may never be made explicit. The teacher's task is to foster learning, but it is the pupil who must do the learning. The pupil's task is to learn, or at least to get through the system. They wish to be told what they need to know, and often they wish to invest a minimum of energy in order to succeed. Guy Brousseau, who coined the expression 'didactic contract', points out that it contains a paradoxical dilemma. Acceding to the pupil's perspective reduces the potential for the pupil to learn, yet the teacher's task is to establish conditions to help the pupil learn. But what does it mean to learn, and how is it best assisted? The teacher looks for certain tell-tale behaviour, as does the examiner. The pupil seeks to provide that behaviour. Soon the focus is on the behaviour, not on the inner state which gives rise to behaviour. The dilemma is then that everything the teacher does to make the pupil produce the behaviour the teacher expects, tends to deprive the pupil of the conditions necessary for producing the behaviour as a byproduct of learning; the behaviour sought and the behaviour produced become the focus of attention.

Put another way, the more the teacher is explicit about what behaviour is wanted, the less opportunity the pupils have to come to it for themselves and make the underlying knowledge or understanding their own. Thus for example, if I want pupils to understand subtraction, the more *I* rehearse the different details of the algorithm publicly, the less likely the pupil is to do anything other than pick up the outer show. If I want pupils to become aware of a generality, the more I guide them, the less chance they have of really appreciating it for themselves.

The dilemma is not even as simple as this, because under certain conditions, exactly what I need is to see someone else going through the steps, or to have my behaviour confirmed, or to hear the generality articulated.

Pupils have many different views as to the nature of learning and the role of teachers, and part of the work with a new class is in some cases to get them to modify their perspective. William Perry (1970) has brilliantly charted the development of different perspectives amongst college students; he has described a number of 'positions', which vary from

- my teacher knows the truth, and is responsible for telling it to me clearly, *to*
- in some areas there is certainty, and in some, only opinion backed up by reasoning; my job is to learn how to justify my opinions, and to examine critically those of others.

Certainly many of the 'Perry positions' are visible in staffrooms as well as playgrounds. To stay alive as a teacher, it is necessary to be aware of the variety of perspectives and the fact that they are very deep rooted.

In the midst of a lesson we have to cope, so we respond to the pressures of the moment. But I have also caught myself locking up energy in resentment or guilt or 'if onlys'. I experience a struggle between

- what I can do, *and*
- what I think I ought to do, what I think others do, what I want to do.

I believe that it is important to be open to these sorts of dilemmas, to take opportunities to talk about them with colleagues, to try to become precise in our articulations, because then it is possible to unlock the blocked energy and exploit it positively.

Reference

Perry, W. G. (1970) *Forms of Intellectual Development in the College Years: a Scheme*. New York: Holt, Rinehart and Winston.

John Mason is Director of the Centre for Mathematics Education at the Open University.

20

Gestalt therapy, educational processes and personal development

Rosemary Clarke

I am a Gestalt psychotherapist in a private practice in the Midlands. I moved into this work five years ago from having been in education since I started my working life. In that time, I have taught children aged from seven to fifteen in schools; I also set up a museum education department; I provided in-service training of teachers, and then worked with teenage school refusers and others in a special off-site unit. Looking back, I think that I was always more interested in the process, rather than the content, of education, if the two can be separated. And it seems, again in retrospect, a natural progression to move from teaching subjects to pupils, to standing back a little and considering what the purpose of all this education was (as distinct, I mean, from the social function of schools), to moving in closer to work with those who could not make use of the education system, and now to being with people who cannot deal effectively with much of their environment.

(For the purposes of this article only, unless specified, the therapist and teacher are presumed to be female and the client and pupil to be male.)

The context of education and therapy

There are some striking similarities between therapy and education and also some significant differences.

First of all, the leaders: ideally, the teacher and the therapist are both intimately and easily familiar with their subject and can therefore be free to pay attention to their pupils or clients. This is most true, in each case, of the experienced specialist, the 35 year old teacher who trained in maths and has been teaching for some years all through the age range: mathematical concepts are second nature to her, she does not feel caught out by the questions of bright pupils and her energy is not unduly taken up with lesson preparation. Of course, she needs to continue her own development and she participates in courses from time to time to keep in touch and lively. Similarly the therapist – age is less predictable here, as few people choose therapy as their first career – who has undergone a thorough training and has been in practice for some years, working with clients presenting a range of symptoms and, most importantly, who has the confidence that comes from knowing, from experience, that she is effective. Both these people can relax in the certainty that all will probably be well; they are familiar with the *content* of their lessons or therapy sessions, and they therefore have plenty of attention for the *processes* going on in the room, within individuals and between them. Thus they can concentrate on being a teacher or a therapist.

The young and inexperienced teacher, who has probably not specialised in mathematics, will be much more akin to the beginning therapist. For the former, the content of each mathematics lesson is a main concern; in the same way, the material presented by a client will be in the foreground of the beginning therapist's attention. Both people will have less attention available for the processes going on. I do not want to seem to suggest that content is unimportant. The subject matter of a maths lesson or a therapy session is vital to the pupil or the client. But it is the processes by which this subject matter becomes troublesome or intolerable that is the domain of the teacher and therapist.

Next, the subject: whether it be a school subject such as mathematics or history, or therapy, each of these disciplines comprises a series of recurring, overlapping and interconnected processes, though each one is coloured with a specific content, such as dynamic equilibrium (filling a bath with water), the fall of empires (the Roman Empire), or projection (matrimonial difficulties).

Then, the people: the pupils in education are aged between 4 and 18 mostly, whereas my clients are nearly all aged between 18 and 60. At first glance, a big difference might seem to be that your pupils are there under compulsion and my clients come voluntarily. But let us look more closely. Your pupils do have in them, well hidden perhaps, great curiosity and a need to learn; this is coupled with external necessity. My clients have also a need to be at peace and they have external realities of jobs, families, etc. to cope with; also they all possess a great determination to stay the same, not to change but to attempt to alter their environment to fit their personalities. The challenge facing both the educator and the therapist is to find ways of reaching that part in people that is *wanting* (to find out, to be loved, or whatever).

Another important similarity is that many of the modes of being in the world which in the adult necessitate therapeutic intervention are well established in children by the age of five, certainly by 18 or so. People go on behaving, all through their lives, and in all their relationships, in ways they have learned during their babyhood and in their school years. It is only when the behaviour is not chosen because of its suitability to the present context that it may be called 'neutotic'.

In fact, all of us have had our theoretically pure and unalloyed wants and ways of being in the world altered, shaped, directed, distorted and stopped. So all of us go around, if we could look beneath the surface, dealing with our environment, and particularly with other people, in ways which are hung over from our upbringing and which do not fully take into account the changed environments now. We are all neurotic to some extent! It is what makes us the individuals we are.

The format of the meetings in which education and therapy take place is not so different, either. In both cases, there are regular, timetabled sessions with clear time boundaries. Reviews take the place of school reports or assessment records. The end date of therapy is not known, whereas a particular school course will run a predetermined length. But in practice, the period of the relationship between therapist and client is likely to be similar to that between a teacher and a child or class – anything from about eighteen months to four or five years. I meet my clients, most of them, for one hour a week for, on average, 40 weeks in the year. An important difference, in my case at least, is that I work with individuals and you work mostly with groups. And even when therapists choose to do group work, which many do, they work with small or medium-sized groups, not large groups as you do much of the time.

The work of the teacher and the therapist

The task in which the teacher and the therapist is each engaged could be said to be the same in outline. Children need to be able (to understand and handle information and concepts) in order to be able to function effectively (for themselves, as well as others) in the world as it is. They need, for example, to be able to read, to express themselves in speech and other modes, to handle numbers, to have some grasp of the geography, politics and the past of the world, and so on: the reasons are to do with personal satisfaction but also with managing themselves in the type of culture in which they live. A client in therapy needs to be able (to be comfortable and easy in himself) in order to be able to function effectively (for himself, as well as others) in his environment as it is. He needs, for example, to be able to be free from anxiety in the presence of another person, because he lives with them or at least passes them in the street. In both cases, therefore, the task of the facilitator, we could say, is to enable or help the pupils and the client to do things which at the moment they cannot do.

The way in which the teacher and the therapist will attempt to enable their pupils/clients to achieve these aims is also similar: in each case they will provide a carefully chosen and new learning environment and will use all the skills at their disposal, as teachers (not mathematicians) or therapists (not experts on depression), to help the pupils or clients to work their way through the difficulties they encounter in this new learning environment. In Gestalt theory we use the term 'creative adjustment' to describe the result of the person having dealt with any difficulties in encountering the new situation and having arrived at a successful completion. This could be seen in something as simple as reaching out and touching the therapist, or, in a reception class at a primary school, in discovering and knowing for oneself that two and two make four (with all that that means).

The things that make children (and adults) into pupils, and people into clients, is lack of ability in certain areas. Both in education and in therapy the lack is in ability to do, to think, to understand, to create, etc. – all activities. And what, therefore, the teacher and the therapist must provide is the opportunity to experiment, practise and learn how to do (whatever is needed). This is where the content of education and therapy fit – as means whereby learning can take place.

In the case of therapy, the therapist sets out to discover what the client is not able to do that he wants to do, then to provide opportunities to practise these activities and to help him be aware of the difficulties he experiences and to overcome them. Then the client's success can be integrated into his personality which begins to change. A simple example: Mary comes into therapy because she is very depressed. I and she discover that she is *not able* to be excited in any way (to get angry, to be sexy, to laugh and so on). I create situations which might excite her (in some way). Gradually, by helping her to become aware of what she tells herself about getting excited (which her father used to tell her) and of what she does with her musculature to control any rising excitement (which is, of course, a physical activity), the automatic stopping of the excitement breaks down. She laughs. She has made a creative adjustment to her present actual environment. It is only when she becomes aware of (as distinct from 'knowing') what she does, that she can begin to act otherwise; indeed that real awareness is, in itself, change.

In the case of mathematics education, if the teacher knows that a pupil has a weak concept of ratio, a good teacher will not simply repeat the definition and explain it and tell it. She will provide material for the pupil to work on which is chosen for its relevance precisely to developing an awareness of ratio. And she will be alongside that pupil noting the points of difficulty and helping the pupil to discover the difficulties he is having so *he* can pinpoint them, unravel them and move on.

One difference between these two processes is the agenda – largely pre-set in schools and frequently seen in content rather than process terms, completely tailor-made in therapy, although there is in both a limited range of possibilities. An effective Gestalt therapist takes seriously the content, i.e. the story, presented by the client. However, for her, it is the vehicle by which she and the client can discover the processes the client is engaged in, diagnose the points of greatest interruption in the normal flow (and this will be a changing diagnosis as the therapy proceeds), and therefore guide her in how she promotes contact with her client. In other words, the client is enabled to work on his material (his difficulties in his work, his shame, his depression or whatever), while and because the therapist is focusing primarily on his process, by paying attention to his content!

This ability of the therapist – to listen and attend to several things 'simultaneously' (the client's verbal information, physical behaviour, the processes she understands to be happening, her own feelings and ease or lack of it) – is possible only if certain conditions are met. She will have fully integrated her learning of the processes, she has enough experience of the sorts of information clients are likely to come up with not to be unduly interested in that, and, perhaps most importantly, she is free enough of her own history not to have her attention (awarely or not) called to herself too often by the client's behaviour.

Similarly, in mathematics education, the best teacher has fully integrated her own learning about the processes which are the stuff of mathematics. Equally importantly, as a person she is sufficiently free of worries about herself not to be prey to comments her pupils might make, or concerns about 'not knowing' or making mistakes. With these conditions prevailing, her attention can be free to see and understand what is actually going on in and between her pupils.

Another difference between education and therapy is that, probably, the expectation in education is that the pupil *will* make a creative adjustment to each new situation and the teacher may be puzzled, irritated, etc. if the pupil does not, at least after a few tries. Such judgements as 'lazy', 'unmotivated' or 'stupid' suggest assumptions about motivation and intention and also suggest expectations as to the norm. Whereas in therapy, the therapist *knows* that the client will *not* make the creative adjustment, over and over again, because of the powerful fear felt at the possibility of letting go pieces of one's personality – who and what one is.

It is in this area – of the client's failure to adjust creatively – that most of the work of therapy is done. So that the successes scored over a four-year period will be vital but very few. Whereas the norm in education is the expectation that there will be many achievements with little time spent on 'failure', e.g. counselling, remedial lessons, active tutorial work. I think that this does not reflect the reality of the pupils. But as the system does assume the norm to be creative adjustment to new academic material, perhaps pupils learn to conceal or mask their failure or to 'adjust creatively' in other ways, all of which enhance or create neurotic patterns which may later be brought to therapy. One common way of masking academic failure is to be pleasing to the teacher, helpful and co-operative (perhaps most usual in younger children). Thus the good attention that would come from the teacher recognising academic success comes instead from her recognising 'a good girl'. A boy of fourteen is perhaps more likely to substitute peer approval, or at least attention, and will become the class clown. And so on.

All of my present clients' neuroses derive from their home circumstances as little children but nearly all of them talk also of incidents and regular events at school which filled them with fear they felt they had to conceal. And remember I was once a teacher, too, as well as once a little girl at school.

Modifications to the process

What I want to do next, therefore, is to describe the ways in which people (children in school, clients in therapy) do *not* manage to make creative adjustments to new situations, how it is that they are not excited by the new environmental stimulus, do not mobilise all their resources to master, destroy and integrate the new situation, and thus do not develop their personalities as they could. In order to do this, I shall first outline the process by which a person functions healthily in contact with his or her environment. And this is, perhaps surprisingly, a simple sequence of activity which is in broad outline the same for every normally neurotic person in any situation.

The sequence begins with the person at rest, in relaxation, 'suspended animation' – call it what you will: nothing is happening. Then an interest emerges: in a school, this may be stimulated by a remark of the teacher but in order that we may dignify it by the title of 'interest', it must call out some need, curiosity etc. in the pupil. Together the pupil's – let us call it hunger – for information and the teacher's remark coalesce into an interest, something which as the saying goes has 'caught her attention'. If the pupil, whom we will call Sarah, continues this process with no impediment, she will use whatever resources she needs – intellectual, motor, emotional – to grapple with this interest until she has reached a conclusion which is satisfactory for her. In this process she will have manipulated the interesting object 'out there' until she has fully 'made it her own' and returned to her previous equilibrium (relaxation). And in this process she will have added to her personality another so-called completed gestalt and filled out her personality (as 'intelligent' or 'successful' or 'energetic', etc.) by which Sarah knows herself and is known.

So far so good. Our energetic, intelligent, successful (and probably pretty, too) 14 year old Sarah has completed that gestalt. On to the next for her. Such a sequence may last a few seconds or less, or, as in the writing of an essay (or this article), many hours, comprising many smaller tiny sequences each complete in itself.

However, many times over, your pupils and my clients do not flow easily from a clear initial interest to a satisfying completed integration. At every step they seem to themselves or others hesitant, wilfully stupid, anxious, silly, fearful, frantic or in others ways disabled. Just as the process of gestalt formation and completion follows a simple and regular sequence, there are corresponding ways in which the flow can be blocked, diverted or destroyed.

At the outset, the child who is very troubled has little possibility of the type of relaxation possible for Sarah. Rather he, Christopher, may be permanently in a state of low-key anxiety, agitation or fear: and this is not the arena from which a clear interest of his own can emerge. He has, perhaps, relatively few satisfactorily completed events behind him in his life and is therefore permanently clogged with 'unfinished business', to use the increasingly common jargon.

But let us suppose that his friend, Mark, is much less encumbered by worries, and has, therefore, free attention for what is actually going on around him. Something occurs which could interest him; it has elicited an enthusiastic response from several others. But Mark's own impulses – the drives and needs and urges which inhabit his body – have been markedly repressed by a well-intentioned but smothering mother; and at the moment he is in the charge of a female mathematics teacher of a similar age to his mother, let us say. His mother has told him, often enough for him to know this now to be true, that 'he doesn't really think that' and that 'he shouldn't *want* Christmas presents', and she has always fed him healthily, knowing exactly what is good for him. And she has, of course, told him precisely what to write in his Christmas thank-you letters (since he did, anyway, get some presents), and so on. His mother would also be likely to deny his assertion of his feelings; thus anger would be greeted with 'that's nonsense – you have no reason to be angry'.

In these and other ways, Mark's natural impulses to go out to the world *wanting* from it have been subdued to a point where he seems to have little interest, curiosity, excitement. Most of the energy has to be supplied by the other, in this case Ms Shuttleworth, the mathematics teacher, who therefore finds him rather uninteresting and rather tiring. He is not sullen, that would be much more active, nor bolshie, but just rather passive. He really is not aware of wanting a lot, you see. And his way of approaching his maths lessons is to have several diffuse, hazy foci – her question to him about how he might find the area of the oddly-shaped hexagonal figure ranks equally with the Star-Trek-badge-shaped polygon in the book and Ms Shuttleworth's necklace and probably with inked-in graffiti on his table, in his hierarchy of emerging interests. So his energy and his competences are divided and weak.

It is important to know that these 'interruptions' in the pupil's flow are thoroughly commonplace and in various degrees at different times and in different situations belong to all of us. It is only when they are present in such a marked degree as to be very disabling or causing organic disease that they can be called neurotic.

The next, in order of its place in the sequence, is very common in our culture and is a result of our systems of education and upbringing of children. It is the process of gobbling down – food, information, someone else's suggestion – without knowing therefore whether one wants it for oneself and without assimilating it and making it one's own. So that it lies, undigested, within us. And this is instead of meeting the object from the environment with some interest of our own. I suppose small fledglings in a nest do this: they do have the urge of hunger and they gobble down the offerings from the parent bird without discriminating whether they fancy worms just now or not. This, of course, is a very necessary gobbling down, necessary to survival.

Similarly, it is necessary for the survival of a small child in our care to swallow down the command 'Stand still!' and thus to deny his own impulse to fetch the ball from the other side of the road. But in the days before I was a Gestalt therapist, and, instead, a teacher of history, I knew I was not happy with the ways the so-called top set dealt with our material and was much more satisfied by the non-exam group. This latter small group would struggle with some unwieldy ideas and events from the past, coming to a real understanding by way of 'That's stupid, why on earth did they do that?' and 'Yes, people still behave like that now' and 'I don't believe that would have worked, let's try it ourselves' and so on. The 'C' group, by contrast, all headed for O levels ('C' stood for GCE, not very subtle), seemed really to want to swallow it all and keep it close to them in their beautifully neatly written and drawn exercise books. And the sad thing was that they were the worldly-wise ones, they knew that, *then* at least, swallowing wholesale, without understanding – I mean knowing what made Henry VIII tick – was what would get them qualifications and jobs. And in some times and places still, I'm sure, the plaudits of their teacher.

We reinforce that mechanism – replacing our pupils' energy (to be interested, to choose, to reject) with our own – by not allowing little children to reject the food they dislike, by overriding their natural disgust. I can still remember, from my primary school with its mostly nice food, mashed swede with lumps in, because I had to swallow it. And this behaviour is reinforced by threatening to withdraw love. It is when the child has been controlled with fear so that he learns to take in whatever is

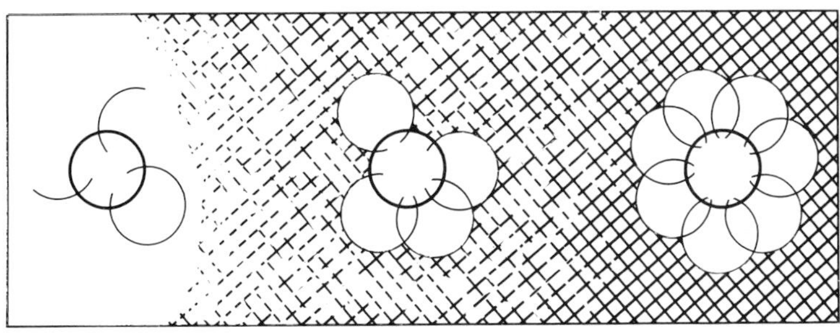

set in front of him in *spite* of his own wants that the co-operative, pleasing (desperately sometimes), untroublesome pupil is created. And don't we all love to have – and need to have – a few of these in each group.

And it is of course necessary to 'swallow' many things we might not choose, because we live in social groupings. Each of the 14 year olds in Sarah's mathematics set may genuinely have a different time of the day when they are at their most mathematical, but they have to accept – in most educational institutions – that maths happens at a time set by someone else – take it or leave it. So they take it.

And suppose another pupil, Rajinder, an Asian girl aged 15, has not met any of these obstacles in the course of her mounting interest in the control of infinity possible by algebraic means. She is not burdened by other worries. Her excitement has been called out and she is now fascinated by this remarkable phenomenon. Her intellect and emotion are at work. Motor activity comes into play as she goes to say something, but she stops almost as soon. She senses that there are people in her environment who would in some way be critical of her if she opened her mouth. We have only to remember some of the things she may have learned and which she now, in this moment, imagines are in the minds and hearts of those around her whom she sees as her critics and judges.

If she has very recently arrived here, she may know she must not initiate conversation with a man (her maths teacher, by the way, is 23 and all male); if she is second or third generation in this country by contrast she may know all too well that girls are not attractive to some boys if they seem too clever and she may be more in touch with the apparent cynicism and shoulder-shrugging 'boredom' of her girl friends. (Or she may have learned, perhaps from her parents, that she is clever and should always get it right and only speak if she is sure of that.) Of course, some of the ways she imagines others judge her are not without foundation, although Mr Jones is unlikely to reprimand her for speaking to him and probably no one will laugh if she 'gets it wrong'. The point here is that she, like all of us, brings all her life experiences to that moment in the maths lesson and she may allow fear about the attitude of others to cause her to stop her excitement, which thus sinks back into her.

Or maybe she will not be able to let it disappear and instead debates internally with herself about the pros and cons of making her statement. By then she is out of touch with her present environment, that moment has passed and she is only concerned with herself and her inner world – 'shall I, shan't I?' Her impulse to reach out, in this case in excitement, to another person, to part of her environment, has been stopped. She has not completed that gestalt, she has not made a successful creative adjustment and her personality is shaped accordingly. She knows herself to be a timid and disappointed person, perhaps, or she may know herself actually to be a superior person, self-controlled and better, astute and wisely cautious. She knows which, and she will be known as that by others.

So all the way from before the emergence of interest to the final moment of completion, there are hurdles to overcome, hurdles which your pupils unawarely carry around in their baggage and set up, unawarely, with the help of you and others. What they *are* likely to be aware of as they encounter their hurdles are feelings such as anxiety, fear, embarrassment, shame, unease, suspicion, contempt and so on. And whether they can get over those hurdles reasonably well or whether they come through limping and damaged, or whether they fall and retire feeling humiliated, or decide not to attempt them, are the factors which affect their learning and development as persons.

The teacher as a human being

It may have occurred to you, as you read about the behaviour of your pupils, that those descriptions could equally apply to your colleagues and friends, your families and you. They are, after all, how people are. Can you imagine the confusion and problems produced if we add the teacher and his or her difficulties to the pupils and all their difficulties. For example, Rajinder's maths teacher, Mr Jones, may have 'learned' (by gobbling down) on a race awareness course that it could be offensive to recently arrived teenage girls of Asian origin to approach them too directly. And he assumes this to be true of Rajinder. This could be stated as an 'equation', thus:

Mr Jones + Rajinder Kaur = non-communication/silence.

One of the features of my own training in Gestalt, which I have valued enormously is that we started with self-experience; we then went on to do work with one another, as client and therapist, and were supervised; and finally we learned the theory. This means that priority was given to awareness of self, including self in relation to others, of course, and to unlearning, unpicking, discovering and letting go of, where appropriate, precisely the sorts of behaviours we will expect to meet in our clients. So that in my dealings with a client I am relatively free and clear of self-absorption and I can attend to the other without putting clutter in his or my way.

Another thing that is significant about my training is that it did not claim to be a training for psychotherapy. It set out to train me in basic Gestalt, i.e. a basic understanding of the processes within and between people. The assumption of the trainers had been that those who wish to be Gestalt psychotherapists must have done or do additional study in psychology and human development, and get supervised experience of working with particular personality types and presenting problems. So what they are asserting, I believe rightly, is that the prerequisite is personal self-awareness, the next step is understanding the processes further, and that theoretical content is last and additional, but necessary.

My own experience of training as a teacher was the reverse; I did a postgraduate course. Hence, three years of content, then one year, afterwards, of more content and some little self-awareness and (more) attention to process. This reversal seems akin to the opposite norms I referred to earlier: I expect people to 'fail' for as long as they need to, you expect them to 'succeed' rapidly.

There is another factor, too, which is the question of whose responsibility it is for success or failure. I take the view that I will do the very best job I am able with every client in every session: that I will not be perfect – I will be more tired sometimes, less clear sometimes, slower to see what is happening sometimes. But at the end of the day my client must be, and is, responsible for his own changes or lack of them. If it is simply too difficult for him to take a desired step then that is not my responsibility – it belongs to him and ultimately to those who made him as he is. And that is nothing to do with blame, it is simply how things are.

However, I have a strong suspicion that the assumption amongst teachers is nearer the reverse: that they are responsible for 'getting the pupils through' the syllabus, for 'covering the ground' and probably, too, feel largely responsible for the quality of the exam results at the end.

If I am right, then these factors seem to be a recipe for being burdened and, of necessity, frustrated. You are not trained to understand in detail your pupils' process, you are not trained in ways which will minimise your own difficulties and reduce problems between yourselves and your pupils, from your own side. So at best you can only be sympathetic and kind, not truly 'understanding'. That may not be enough. You are taught to expect success and that it is your responsibility to ensure it.

Perhaps I am unduly pessimistic; certainly I am describing things in black and white, to make a point. But when I was a teacher I did find that as a person I was squeezed. And if this is inherent in the system as it is, then at least it will be important to face this reality and devise ways of supporting oneself and one's colleagues in that context. It is for this reason that I offer you some suggestions I have learned in the course of my work which I believe are just as relevant and liberating in the classroom as in therapy.

- Don't offer anything that you are not willing to have rejected.

For example, you may offer a recalcitrant pupil six chances to make amends because you really want him to have the chance, would like to be at peace with him, want to offer him a way out and so on. Up to and including the sixth time you feel well-disposed, generous. He still refuses. If that is your limit, stop there. If you offer a seventh chance which you *demand* he take, and he still rejects you, you will punish him somehow or other. More mundanely, but just as important, don't tell a joke to a group of pupils if you will be offended if they find it unfunny. And don't disclose information about yourself – how you are feeling, some details about your family – if you will feel hurt if the pupils do anything other than take you seriously. As sure as anything you will get your own back at some time.

- The other person can resist only if *you* are pushing.

If my client seems to me to be a doormat in relation to some other person, and if *I* try to make *him* more assertive – different from the way he is – he may resist me. Or, of course, give in to me, becoming a doormat to me! He will have many good and unaware reasons for having been a doormat. It is precisely only when I accept him as he is, when he becomes aware of how he is and he accepts himself as he is (a doormat) that he *can* change, and he will, if he wants to. Similarly, you might be working with first years in a secondary school on the concept of prime numbers (B) and Tony is stuck on factors (A) which is a prerequisite understanding, or indeed on something he saw last night on TV which really grabbed him. If you try to push Tony from A, where he is, to B where you are, he *must* resist. If, however, you go to A and be there with him and accept his worries or his excitement (whichever it is), he is then free to come to B of his own accord.

- How about getting some supervision of your work?

In my work as a psychotherapist, it is a basic assumption that my work will be supervised – overseen, literally. I imagine you feel defensive. I am sometimes defensive when being overseen. I, too, was brought up in a culture which is private and demands that people keep their problems to themselves, cope without help, put it right by themselves, etc. etc. But I also know that I cannot be aware of what I am not aware of, by definition. So, if no one else oversees what I have done, I will continue to do things less well than I could because I cannot see how I am doing them badly. One of the nice things also about well-organised supervision is that it is a properly constituted opportunity to tell others about encouraging results of work and interesting and exciting sessions. In our practice we have supervision in a group which means we can also hear about work with other clients and pool ideas and experience about specific problems (anorexia, sexual disfunction, etc.).

I suppose the nearest parallel in teaching is team teaching, in the primary school usually, where one teacher actually sees other teachers at work. If you can only suspend for long enough your fear of the word 'criticism', it can be very liberating to discover, for example, how in some ways you are so like that fourth-year boy who irritates you so much! Embarrassing too, at first, but then amusing and enabling of common ground in place of the previous polarisation. After all, if it has to be a choice, it is surely preferable to be at ease than 'right'. And it is very nice, too, to have validation from others of perhaps quite small but important things you do which make a difference. Some form of supervision could also be a very useful way in to dealing with the difficulty of a class with a particularly bad reputation; at the beginning of a year and with new teachers would be a good time to pay attention to the ways the patterns get established.

- Paradox is at the heart of therapy and, perhaps, teaching.

One example: the therapist and the teacher need to be able to be very close to other people – their clients or pupils – and at the same time quite separate and distinct. My clients would not appreciate me trying or pretending to be 'in their shoes'; I can remember the contempt (unspoken, of course) of the 15 year olds in the special education unit for the adults (social workers or others) who tried to 'be one of them'; and your pupils know how different you and they are. But they also need you, and me, to be able on occasion to be very accessible.

I have happened upon Gestalt almost entirely by chance, and found it to be a quite remarkably apt framework for understanding what goes on in people and an effective means of assisting them to be more content and realised. However, I do not think it matters so much which mode of therapy is used: a good practitioner is a good practitioner. What I do think is important is that those of us who work with people and who can reasonably expect to encounter difficulties should have some means of understanding and dealing with what is happening. The alternatives may be to resort to controlling, to be frustrated or to become cynical. And the young people in your care deserve better.

At the very least, there could perhaps be posts of special responsibility for educational process in each school, as there are for mathematics, science, etc. in some primary schools. Such a person could, on the same basis, take a lead in suggesting in-service training needs, could be available for consultation on particular difficulties and suggest ways round them. This is different from pastoral or remedial responsibility with their connotations, perhaps, of dealing with a difficult minority. Every one of us has real difficulties getting in the way of achieving our potential as people, and the schoolchildren in our society are no exception.

Further reading

One difficulty in suggesting further reading is that most of what has been written about Gestalt is American, which can be off-putting to English readers.

Axline, V. (1971) *Dibs: in Search of Self.* Harmondsworth: Penguin/Pelican. This has been a very formative book for many people who work with children: not Gestalt, but entirely consonant with it. About a therapist being lovingly and patiently with a disturbed boy and letting him be.

Oaklander, V. (1978) *Windows to Our Children.* Utah: Real People Press. American woman Gestaltist working with children and young people. Ideas for working, examples, brief case studies. I enjoyed it very much.

Stevens, B. (1985) *Don't Push the River.* Berkeley: Celestial Arts. Recommended by a colleague who was also previously a teacher. Gives an idea of (American) Gestalt.

Rosemary Clarke is a Gestalt Psychotherapist in the West Midlands.

SECTION III

Mathematical Issues

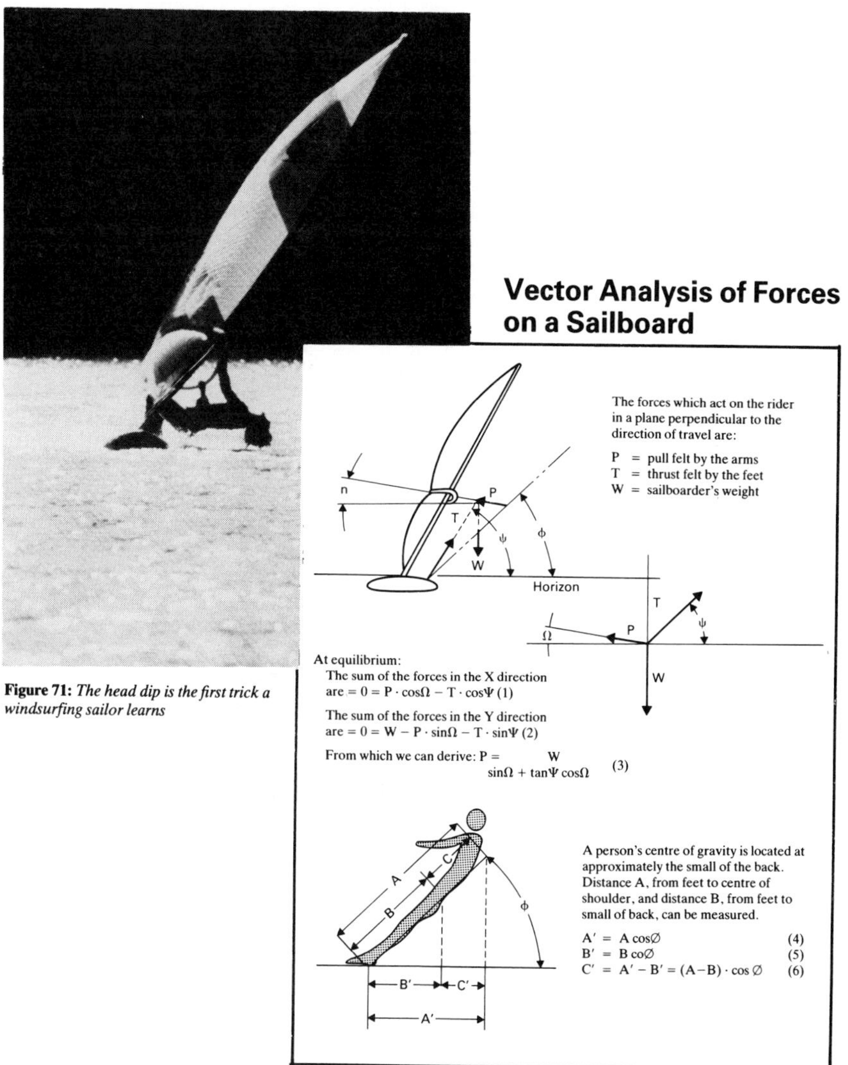

Vector Analysis of Forces on a Sailboard
The forces which act on the rider in a plane perpendicular to the direction of travel are:
P = pull felt by the arms
T = thrust felt by the feet
W = sailboarder's weight
n
P
T
W
ψ
φ
Horizon
T
P
Ω
ψ
W
At equilibrium:
The sum of the forces in the X direction are = 0 = P · cosΩ − T · cosΨ (1)
The sum of the forces in the Y direction are = 0 = W − P · sinΩ − T · sinΨ (2)
From which we can derive: P = W / (sinΩ + tanΨ cosΩ) (3)
A person's centre of gravity is located at approximately the small of the back. Distance A, from feet to centre of shoulder, and distance B, from feet to small of back, can be measured.
A′ = A cos∅ (4)
B′ = B co∅ (5)
C′ = A′ − B′ = (A−B) · cos ∅ (6)
A
B
C
φ
B′
C′
A′

Figure 71: *The head dip is the first trick a windsurfing sailor learns*

Introduction

The nature and structure of the discipline of mathematics also directly influences attempts to teach it. The nature of mathematical objects and the very concept of proof in all its guises is one important issue, while interrelations between mathematical ideas on the one hand and objects and processes in the real world on the other provides another. Uri Leron writes about what he sees as being mathematical in the activity of programming the turtle in LOGO (a question that can be usefully asked of many purportedly mathematical activities). Marion Walter explores techniques by which mathematical questions can be posed by anyone, offering systematic advice and assistance.

In **Modelling: what do we really want pupils to learn?**, John Mason looks at the crucial distinction between modelling as an activity, and mathematical models as the thing to be taught and learned. He concludes that pupils attempt to learn the models wholesale and that pupils' own modelling is the centrally mathematical activity. Finally, Nicolas Balacheff reports on work he has done with 13 year old pupils on what they consider proofs to be in response to a mathematical investigation. His work elicits a variety of strategies and understandings of what makes something convincing, and he codifies different approaches to the justification of mathematical generalities.

21

On the mathematical nature of turtle programming

Uri Leron

The invitation to write this short article gave me an opportunity to reflect once more on what I think is the fundamentally mathematical nature of programming with the turtle. My emphasis will thus be on fundamental processes of mathematical thinking, rather than specific subject matter.

What's in a rectangle?

Let me start by considering a procedure that 11 year olds can typically write on their own after a few weeks (or months) of learning LOGO:

```
TO RECTANGLE "SIDE1 "SIDE2
   REPEAT 2[FD :SIDE1 RT 90 FD : SIDE2 RT 90]
END
```

In my view the most important observation about this procedure is that it is *a definition of the concept 'rectangle', spontaneously written by a child in a formal language*. I shall return to the 'formal language' part later. For now, note that in writing this definition on her own, the child demonstrates a certain level of knowledge of all the following facts pertaining to any rectangle: it has four sides; the two pairs of alternate ('opposite') sides have equal lengths; all the angles measure 90 degrees; it is composed of two congruent parts, namely, the parts drawn by the REPEATed list.

In contrast, recall how hard it is for children just to repeat correctly – let alone create on their own – formal definitions in their regular geometry classes. Why the difference? Briefly I mention two sources. First, the LOGO style is mostly *procedural (how to do* a rectangle), whereas the standard mathematical style is mostly *declarative (what is* a rectangle). The children can 'act out' the LOGO procedure in reality or in their minds, thus rendering it more intuitive and meaningful. (This activity is usually referred to as 'playing turtle'.) Secondly, due to the nature of the interaction with the computer and feedback given by it, children can arrive at the definition by successive approximations, and do not have to 'get it right' the first time around.

Intuition and formalism

But the point is not learning geometry, and even the formal definition is only part of the story. The real drama (and the real mathematics) lies in the interaction between intuition and formalism. Children know what a rectangle is before programming it in LOGO – after all, they can easily imagine it or draw one on a piece of paper. By writing the RECTANGLE procedure, therefore, they do not *learn* the concept rectangle. Rather, the significance of their programming activity is that they start with an intuitive representation of a concept, and create a formal representation for it. What is truly important about the children's creation is not the formal presentation *per se*, but the *link* they have formed between the intuitive and the formal representations. This link is important both ways. Formalising intuitions helps where rigour and communication are necessary. Making the formalism more intuitive, on the other hand, is necessary for any meaningful and creative involvement in mathematics, such as problem solving.[1]

Change and constancy

I have not done yet squeezing mathematical and philosophical insights out of our innocent-looking RECTANGLE procedure. Looking at it in the standard way, this procedure defines the concept 'rectangle' by giving detailed and explicit instructions for drawing any rectangle. There is, however, a slightly different but revealing way of looking at the situation. The shift is from thinking of 'any rectangle' – a sort of 'generic object' representing the whole family of rectangles – to thinking of the family itself. The point here is that the use of variables enables the procedure's definition to capture neatly and concisely both the *invariance* across this family and the *variability* within it.[2] Thus, consider the parts emphasised in the following:

TO RECTANGLE "SIDE1 "SIDE2
REPEAT 2[FD :SIDE 1 **RT 90 FD** :SIDE2 **RT 90]**
END

These are the invariants. They describe what is the same across all rectangles in the family, hence what distinguishes members of the family from non-members. The rest of the procedure's definition is emphasised next:

TO RECTANGLE "SIDE1 "SIDE 2
REPEAT 2[FD **:SIDE 1** RT 90 FD **:SIDE2** RT 90]
END

These parts, naturally called 'variables', stand for the variability within the family; they describe how members of the family differ from each other.

To summarise, the first part serves to give the family its identity, i.e. to distinguish it from the outside world; the second part serves to give individual members their identity, i.e. to distinguish them from each other.

Controlling change and constancy

We have seen that LOGO enables us to capture pre-existing concepts (like 'rectangle') in a formal definition, by specifying what is the same and what is different about all rectangles, thus delineating the boundaries of the concept. But the real power of this method does not become apparent until we realise that LOGO further permits us to play freely with these boundaries, turning invariants into variables and vice versa. Thus, suppose we start with the concept 'house', and formalise it in LOGO as:

```
TO HOUSE "SIZE
   SQUARE :SIZE
   FD :SIZE RT 30
   TRIANGLE :SIZE
END
```

This definition reflects a certain decision as to the identity of houses, both as a family and as individuals within the family. In particular, according to this definition, only the size of the house matters, and not, say, its colour. Thus, two houses with the same size are considered equal regardless of their colour. However, we are totally free to decide otherwise by modifying our procedure's definition:

```
TO HOUSE "SIZE "COLOUR
   SETPC :COLOUR
   SQUARE :SIZE
   FD :SIZE RT 30
   TRIANGLE :SIZE
END
```

Here, finer distinctions are made. For two houses to be considered equal they must share both size *and* colour. Needless to say, we could go on making finer and finer distinctions by bringing in the house's position on the screen, the number of windows, etc.

Now suppose we are interested in tiny houses, say of size 20. We could view them as special cases of the general house procedure, or we could dignify them with the status of an independent procedure:

```
TO TINY.HOUSE "COLOUR
   HOUSE 20 :COLOUR
END
```

Similarly, we could play with the other variable and define:

```
TO BLUE.HOUSE "SIZE
   HOUSE :SIZE 5
END
```

It is noteworthy that while it is not uncommon to see teenagers spontaneously doing such transformations in their LOGO programming, the analogous situation in standard mathematical formalism causes difficulties even to mathematics undergraduates. I am referring to situations, often arising in calculus, in which one starts with a function of two variables $f(x,y)$, then proceeds to view it as a function of x alone by looking at y as fixed. This function, which depends on the y we fixed, is commonly denoted $g_y(x)$ – a striking similarity to our notation TINY.HOUSE :COLOUR and BLUE.HOUSE :SIZE.

Theorems-in-action

The phenomena described in this section also fall under the heading of 'formalising intuitions', except that what is being formalised is not the definition of a concept, but relationships between concepts, initially captured as theorems-in-action. Again, we start with a procedure, typically written by young teenagers:

```
TO SUN
  REPEAT 10 [ARC LT 90 RAY RT 90]
END
```

```
TO ARC
  REPEAT 18 [FD 1 RT 2]
END
```

```
TO RAY
  FD 20 BK 20
END
```

What is mathematically remarkable about this procedure is the choice of a 90-degree turn before RAY. When you ask children 'why 90?' they are likely to answer something like 'to make the turtle face away from the circle'. On the other hand, when the turtle is actually drawing the circle, it is clearly facing 'along' the circle. Thus the children are demonstrating in their programming the knowledge that 'if you are facing along the circle, you need to turn 90 degrees to face away from (the centre of) the circle'. This is in fact a turtle version of the well-known theorem, 'the tangent at each point on the circle is perpendicular to the radius at that point'.

Seeing a child writing on her own a procedure like SUN above, what can we infer about the state of her knowledge regarding the theorem? It would be a bit far-fetched to claim that she actually *knows* the theorem. Not only does she lack the terminology to *formulate* the theorem, but there is no evidence that she is aware of the *generality* of the inherent relationship. Nevertheless, as her programming demonstrates, she does know in some sense the fundamental relationship between the two directions, even if it is not yet elevated to the generality and formality of a theorem. Educationally, this seems a very good entry point to learning the more formal and general theorem – if and when the latter is appropriate.

Conclusion

The focus of this article has been the fundamental mathematical process of *formalising intuitions*, or, more precisely, creating links between intuitive and formal representations of concepts. This process is inherent to meaningful mathematical activity and should be central in any programme of mathematics education. We have seen that children working on LOGO projects naturally engage in this process. While formalisation is never easy, it seems to occur much more naturally in the procedural formalism of LOGO than in the standard declarative mathematical formalism. The merit of the LOGO turtle language in this respect is that while being a formal language, it does not force this aspect on the programmer too abruptly. One can pretend to be working wholly intuitively, only gradually coming to grips with the formal nature of the language, as bugs in one's mental models are brought to the surface by bugs in the program.

All this is not to suggest that the LOGO formalism should replace the standard mathematical formalism. Quite to the contrary! I believe the former could help learners eventually feel more at home with the latter. There are many aspects of mathematical activity for which the standard mathematical formalism is irreplaceable, e.g. proving theorems. The challenge to the LOGO community is thus to build more and better bridges between the two types of formalism, to help the learner move more easily between them.

Notes

1 That such links between intuition and formalism are indeed formed, is evidenced by the many instances of children pointing to a piece of LOGO *text* and saying things like, 'I want to put *this window* there . . .'.

2 This observation has been triggered by a remark of Joel Hillel's.

Uri Leron is Associate Professor of Mathematics and Computer Science at the Department of Science Education, the Technion (Israel Institute of Technology), Haifa, Israel.

22

Some roles of problem posing in the learning of mathematics[1]

Marion Walter

This article deals with some aspects of problem *posing* – not just with questions concerning new material given by the teacher or with questions related to the following of instructions given to pupils via a test or by a teacher. Instead, I shall discuss different levels of question asking or problem posing. The activities suggested encourage teachers and pupils to create their own problems so they can increase their understanding of the given material, and even extend it to new or more sophisticated content. In the process, both teachers and pupils can be encouraged to pose their own problems, not only to help in understanding mathematics but also to provide exercises for practice as well. Problem *posing* is intimately related to problem *solving*.

Professor George Polya, whose celebrated *How to Solve It* was published in 1944, was the 'father' of problem solving which now, in the 1980s, has come to the forefront of mathematics education. Many of his examples regarding problem solving suggest useful problem posing strategies. One of his heuristic pieces of advice (if you cannot solve the given problem, try to solve a related one) is really one of *posing*, for yourself, a related problem (and usually a simpler one, or one that is a more special or general case). Trying to think of a similar or related problem is a very powerful problem-posing technique. In this article I discuss some other problem-posing techniques. Posing problems is useful not only in order to help you to solve given problems, it can also help to generate new ones. Some of these new problems may turn out to be interesting in themselves. Some new problems may help you to understand pieces of mathematics or to see why certain methods for solving problems 'work'; often the posed problems may help you to find, for yourself, various methods taught in schools or explained in texts.

What often happens now

Think back to your own mathematics classes in school (or college for that matter). The chances are that they consisted to a large extent of three types of activities:

- the teacher telling the class how to do something – the material is usually also explained in the text;

- the pupils doing assigned problems that usually come from the section of the text just being studied;
- the teacher checking or working out the assigned problems after the pupils have attempted them.

Let us look at an imaginary class. In this class, the teacher might be explaining how to solve linear equations of the type $4x - 3 = 24 - 2x$ (although the techniques of problem posing work no matter what topic you are teaching). The homework might consist of ten problems of the same kind. For example

$$\text{Solve for } x\text{: } 5x - 8 = 42 - 3x$$

The pupils will, perhaps, be required or encouraged to check their answers by substituting each value of x found, to see whether a true statement results.

During class some question asking will be taking place. Below are some examples of the type of questions that are often heard in school.

$4x - 3 = 24 - 2x$	Pupil:	Did you say you first have to add the 3 to both sides or the $2x$?
	Pupil:	How do you know what to do first?
	Pupil:	Why don't you get $4x = 21 - 2x$?

Note the questions are often phrased in the 'you' form.

Posing problems

How can we broaden and extend the kind of questions pupils pose so that the questions become useful and powerful, and how can we encourage pupils to engage in such activities?

Problem posing is a bit like exercising; it may feel uncomfortable at first because you are not used to it. After a while you get to feel comfortable. You will be able to pose problems almost without being conscious of it (just as you can go up and down on your toes while waiting for a bus without being aware that you are doing this exercise!).

What are some ways of getting better at problem posing?

1 Accepting the given

One method, which Stephen Brown and I have called 'Accepting the given' (Brown and Walter, 1983), is to take the situation at hand without changing anything and just by brute force try to think of some questions. At first this may seem hard for you or your pupils, but after some practice with different starting points you will gain some facility.

Let us look again at the starting point, 'Solve $4x - 3 = 24 - 2x$'. What questions might a class of pupils or teachers produce? Pupils may be surprised that you are asking them to think up questions rather than answers! You may also find that some of the pupils who are not the best 'answer givers' are among the best 'problem posers'. Here are some questions that might be raised.

(a) Why do I want to know the root or solution of the equation?
(b) What is meant by 'solve' an equation?
(c) What is meant by the 'solution' of an equation?
(d) What is meant by an equation?
(e) Do we have to find an exact answer?
(f) What type of easier-looking equations can I already solve?
(g) Why is this equation more difficult to solve (than one like $4x = 24$ that pupils have already seen)?
(h) Can I change the form of the equation without changing its root?
(i) How can I change it to an equation that has the same solution?
(j) How many solutions does such an equation have?
(k) Does this equation have a root?
(l) Can two equations have the same root and yet not be the 'same'?
(m) What do we mean by two equations 'being the same'?
(n) Can I make up an equation that I do know how to solve, and 'disguise' it so that it looks 'difficult' (like the one above), but still has the same root?
(o) Where did the equation come from?

Note that the questions raised are not all independent of each other and are not in any particular order. Of course, the type of question raised will depend in part on previous knowledge, work and experience on the part of the pupils. Here questions at various levels of sophistication are given. A question by one pupil will often be triggered by a prior question or by another – as is shown by questions l and m, for example. Add some questions of your own now!

A look at our first list of questions

Note again that this list was obtained by what I called 'brute force' question asking. Pupils looked at their starting point and, without using any special techniques, posed questions that came to mind. Note also that 'the given' was not tampered with – that is, the pupils accepted as given 'Solve for x: $4x - 3 = 24 - 2x$'. After engaging in such a phase of question asking several times with different starting points, pupils become better and better at it. (See *The Art of Problem Posing* for many other starting points.)

What type of questions have been asked here? Some of the questions deal with the meaning of the terms; some deal with the origin or purpose of doing the work. Some questions deal with the techniques of finding answers – in this case, finding a solution of the given equation. Other questions deal with what you have gained when you have solved the given problem – what benefit might there be in knowing a solution of an equation? Others deal with how the given work relates to the work already understood by the pupils. With different starting points – as with different pupils – we obtain, of course, different questions.

How can we use any of these questions to help pupils understand equations better and to help them find a way to solve the given and other equations? *One* way of helping pupils find a way to obtain a solution is to work with one of the last questions on our list. You could start by asking pupils to give one or two equations they *do* know how to solve – suppose they suggest $5x = 30$ or $x - 3 = 10$. (We are assuming that for the first equation they already know how they can divide both sides by 5 to obtain $x = 6$). Ask them to disguise this equation to make it look more difficult! They probably know they can add, subtract and multiply both sides of the equation without changing its solution set, so they may 'disguise' it as $5x - 8 = 22$ by subtracting 8 from both sides.

How can they further 'disguise' it to make it look more like our starting equation $4x - 3 = 24 - 2x$, which has an x term on both sides? They may think of adding, let us say, $2x$ to both sides giving $7x - 8 = 22 + 2x$ Now they can ask 'How can this new equation be solved?' They can more readily see that they could undo their 'disguise' to return to $5x = 30$ which they know how to solve. How can they do this? By undoing what they did to create the disguise: subtract $2x$ from both sides and then add 8 to both sides giving first $5x = 30$ and then $x = 6$. This is one possible approach to learning to solve linear equations.

It is, of course, also one way in which the pupils themselves can make up equations that have a solution that is a whole number (if that is what is needed at the time) or any other type of solution (e.g. positive fraction, negative integer) for that matter. In other words, pupils find a technique that lets them control the nature of the solution. For example, if they wish to make up equations that have fractional roots, they could start with $3x = 8$ and proceed as above and disguise it.

This activity of asking pupils to make up problems is a powerful way for them to come to understand the material at hand. The teacher can thus use this technique as a teaching tool. The method is one that teachers themselves can also find useful when they want to create particular examples as exercises for their pupils.

Teachers of older children may wish to pursue the first question (or a related one such as why or when do we need equations) by giving just one problem where writing down an equation can be helpful. If the teacher wants to bring in some history she may wish to pose the following Ancient Greek problem and ask pupils to solve it without writing down any equation.

> Demochares has lived a fourth of his life as a boy, a fifth as a youth, a third as a man, and has spent thirteen years in his dotage. How old is he? (Eves, 1964, p. 174)

The pupils can then compare how they tried to do it, for example doing it by trial and error or by creating an equation.

2 The What-If-Not? technique

Another very rich and useful technique for generating a host of new questions related to any given situation is to employ what Stephen Brown and I have called the 'What-If-Not?' technique (see Brown and Walter,

1983). Let us see what it involves by returning to the first example and employing it to help pupils learn to understand how to solve *general* first-degree equations once they know how to solve simple ones. The 'What-If-Not?' technique consists of four stages, which I now describe.

First stage: choose a starting point

Our starting point is now the exercise:

Solve the equations $4x = 12$ and $x + 3 = 10$

Let us assume that these are ones that they already know how to solve. What do we want pupils to learn? Though we want to lead them to understand how to solve a general first-degree equation, it is easy to get trapped into this 'obvious' and somewhat narrow point of view. Perhaps pupils will be led to other questions such as 'What would a more general equation look like?' or 'What are other equations of this type?' or 'What is meant by "of this type"?' Or perhaps to a question dealing with whether the two equations given above can ever be satisfied at the same time or even whether they can have practical interpretations. Though we will pursue the *solving* of general first-degree equations here, it is worth noting that this is only one possibility for a direction to follow.

Second stage: listing attributes

The second step of the 'What-If-Not?' technique is to list some things that are noticed about the given starting point. We call these *attributes* of the 'starting point' or 'given'. The list of attributes will, of course, depend on the experience and background of the pupils and will also depend on their experience with this technique.[2] The list (for the first equation $4x = 12$) might include the following:

(a) $4x = 12$ is an equation.
(b) $x = 3$ makes the statement true.
(c) The right-hand side is a number.
(d) The right-hand side is a whole number (or positive integer).
(e) The left-hand side is an x term with a coefficient. (This may lead to a nice discussion of whether a 'plain' x has a coefficient!)
(f) The coefficient of the x term is a whole number.
(g) The number on the right is a positive whole number.
(h) The number on the right is a (positive) multiple of the number on the left.
(i) 4 goes into 12 exactly.
(j) The solution 3 is an odd number.
(k) There is one term on the left side.
(l) There is one term on the right side.
(m) The right term is a constant.
(n) There is no x^2 term.
(o) The x term appears only to the first power.
(p) There is just one variable: x.
(q) The two sides are connected by an equals sign.
(r) You are asked to solve something.
(s) You are asked to solve an equation.[3]

Note that the attributes listed are not independent of each other and some may be identical but expressed differently. Do not rule out any – rather use them for sources of discussion. Listing attributes by itself does not produce new problems. Before discussing how such an activity can lead to new problems, note that pupils can, in this way, become aware of how special the given equation is and that they themselves can generate equations that have the properties listed. When pupils list $3x = 15$ and $7x = 14$ (whose solutions are whole numbers) but not $3x = 16$, they are practising their multiplication facts. Even weak pupils can contribute and in general there is more involvement and discussion.

Stage three: asking 'What-if-Not?'

The next step, after attribute listing, is to pick one or two of the attributes and ask 'What-If-Not?' If we pick the attribute 'the two sides are connected by an equals sign', and ask what if that were *not* so, two obvious alternatives would be $4x < 12$ and $4x > 12$. Before examining where such 'What-If-Not?'-ing can lead, let us pick another attribute and ask 'What-If-Not?' Consider the attribute 'there is one term on the left side'. What if there were not one term on the left of the equation? There could be two or three . . . Let us be modest and say there are two. What then – what could the second term be? It could be an x term or a constant, for example. (Some pupils may also suggest a y term, which can lead to a discussion of two variables in an equation such as $3x + 4y = 15$, or an x^2 term, which can introduce second-degree equations.) Let us look at some possible examples of there being two terms on the left-hand side: $6x \square 2x = 24$ and $6x \square 4 = 24$. The pupils now are faced with deciding what sign to place in the box between the two terms. They may suggest:

$6x + 2x = 24$	$6x + 4 = 24$
$6x - 2x = 24$	$6x - 4 = 24$
$6x \times 2x = 24$	$6x \times 4 = 24$
$6x \div 2x = 24$	$6x \div 4 = 24$

Stage four: question asking on changed attributes

As we mentioned, asking 'What-If-Not?' and listing alternatives, by themselves, do not generate anything new; we must still ask a mathematical question. Consider now $4x < 12$. Even if we now ask the same original starting question as before – namely, 'what value of x makes the statement true?' – we have a new problem. Note also that since we now find more than one value of x that makes the statement true, we should say 'what valu*es* of x make the statement true?'. This makes you realise that when we ask for *the* value of x that makes the statement $4x = 12$ true, as we often do, we are depriving pupils of the chance to think about how many possible values of x there are. *We* know there is only one, but it is better to say 'find value(s) of x, if they exist, that make the statement true' than merely to say 'find the value of x'.

Returning to $4x < 12$ we may get such answers as $x = 0, 1, 2$, or such answers as $x = 0, 1, 2, -1, -2, -3, \ldots\ldots$ or $x = \sqrt{2}, 2.5$, etc. depending on the mathematical level of the pupils. There can then be a useful discussion about which of these numbers are (or should be) counted as permissible solutions. Could it be that, for example, -5 satisfies the equation but makes no sense for the problem? Pupils can thus see the need for specifying the set of permissible numbers from which x can be chosen (the domain).

Now let us consider some of the possible answers to 'What-If-Not?'s for the attribute 'there is one term on the left side'. Let us look at the alternatives chosen above where the second term was an x term or a constant.

$6x + 2x = 24$	$6x + 4 = 24$
$6x - 2x = 24$	$6x - 4 = 24$
$6x \times 2x = 24$	$6x \times 4 = 24$
$6x \div 2x = 24$	$6x \div 4 = 24$

Before even asking any questions, pupils may notice that all the numbers are even – an attribute that they had not noticed at first when considering $4x = 12$ – and so they could add the attribute 'all the numbers are even' to their list of attributes. They may then ask if and when there is anything different about choosing odd numbers as well as even ones:

$$4x = 15 \quad \text{or} \quad 8x - 3x = 20$$

We usually deprive pupils of the opportunity of exploring or even noticing cases that differ slightly from the given one. Some may also notice that in each case so far the first coefficient is larger than the second and explore what happens if this is not so for the cases of the type $6x - 2x = 24$. Pupils who are familiar with negative number (or fractions) may wish to make up equations with roots that are positive integers, negative integers, or positive fractions, etc. You may be thinking at this point 'why be so fussy?' This gives them a chance to see that varying an attribute (one as 'simple' as 'there is one term on the left side') has an effect. We *do* want them to realise, when they vary the attribute 'the x term appears only to the first power' that things are really different then. If pupils consider equations of the type $4x^2 = \square$ they can ask 'what numbers, if any, can I choose for $\square$ so that x is an integer?'

What if pupils decide to explore 'what if there is not just one variable?' ('What-If-Not?' attribute p)? What if there were two variables, for example $4x + 2y = 15$? What questions can be raised now? Here one of our 'old questions', for what value(s) of the variables is the equation true, surfaces of course, but new ones are brought to the fore as well – perhaps questions that we did not ask for the simpler case. For example, how can we represent possible solutions graphically? We did not ask this for the case $4x - 3 = 24 - 2x$. If we consider it and plot the solution on an x-axis the result is not too interesting. However, it is worthwhile to do this. The problem of how to represent inequalities such as $4x - 3 < 24 - 2x$ would be more interesting. (It is also worthwhile to consider graphing such equations as $x^2 = 16$, and more advanced pupils can consider how to represent complex roots for $x^2 = -4$ or $x^2 = -8$.) Returning to the case of two variables, asking how $4x + 2y = 15$ may be represented graphically could be used as an alternative entry to co-ordinate geometry.

Considering what if there were not an equals sign but an inequality sign can lead to graphing inequalities in the plane. In each case, the domain once again has to be considered and agreed upon. How does the solution set (graph) differ for various different domains? Pupils often have a hard time *not* connecting points, if the domain is only the set of integers and not the real numbers.

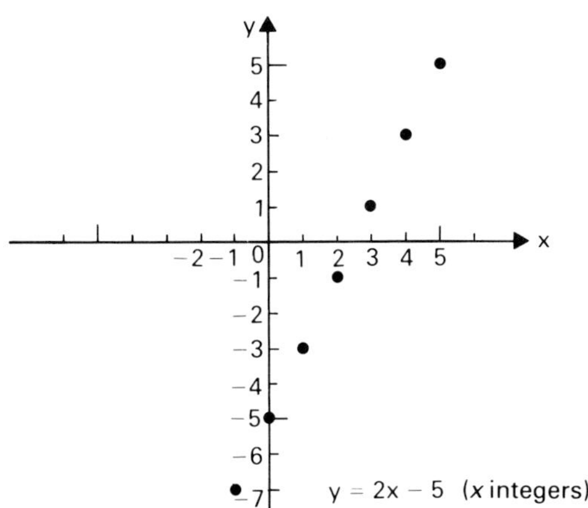

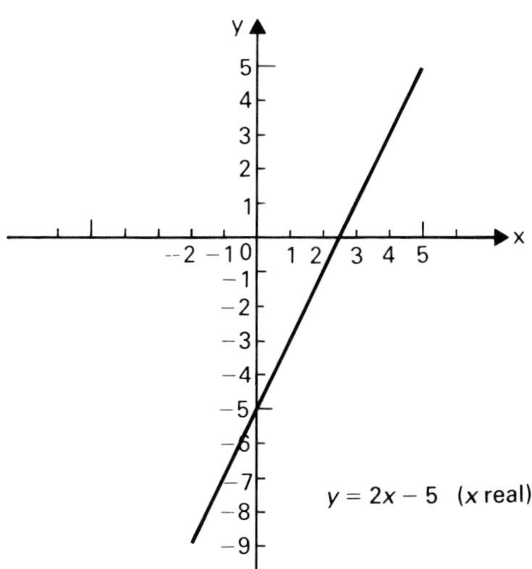

If we restrict solutions to integers, pupils may wish to explore what solutions, if any, are possible for equations such as $4x + 3y = 15$ and $4x + 2y = 15$, $4x + 3y = 12$ and $7 = 35x + 14y$. It is also a worthwhile activity to consider whether and how the graph of $x^2 = 4$ on a line relates to $x^2 = 4 + y$ in the plane.

Comments on some problems posed

The above problem 'What numbers can one write for □ to make $4x^2 = \square$ have an integer solution?' is a new problem for the pupils and one that gives possibilities for learning and insight *before* quadratic equations in general are studied by them. In this way pupils can be led naturally (by considering equations such as $3x^2 = 300$ or $3x^2 = 48$ or $3x^2 = 75$) to an awareness of the fact that here the choice of numbers in making up an equations makes a crucial difference if we want the solutions to be integers or fractions. Finding 'suitable' numbers to make $3x^2 = \square$ or $4x^2 = \square$ have integer solutions involves more thinking than asking pupils to solve 10 equation of the same type. The fact that the pupils can be led naturally to exploring equations such as $3x^2 = \square$ long before the formula for a quadratic equation is studied enables them to see that they are progressing along a path – the teacher shining a torch along the path a little ahead of the pupils so that they can see that there is a path (and not just isolated bits of work). It is a path that pupils will be more eager to travel along and explore than if the quadratic equation is just pulled out of a hat later during their studies.

A look back at the 'What-If-Not?' technique

In this short article it is not possible to spell out the stages of the what-if-not? technique in great detail. The four stages are:

1 Choose a starting point.
2 List some attributes of the starting point.
3 Pick a few attributes and ask 'What-If-Not?' of each of these attributes.
4 Take one or two alternatives of one or two attributes and ask the original questions (if the starting point was a question), or ask the same questions developed for the original starting point using the 'accepting the given' technique, or use that technique on the changed situation.

You will find all these stages interact (see *The Art of Problem Posing*, Brown and Walter, 1983, where we describe the interaction as *cycling*) and you will think of new attributes and new questions for the original starting point. Though the description of these stages sounds strict and perhaps rigid, you will find that you will engage in them naturally and flexibly and with some selection after you have practised the technique for some time.

3 Looking at each word in a sentence

There are other problem-posing techniques and I now mention only one more – one which is very closely related to the 'What-If-Not?' technique. This technique (*The Art of Problem Posing*, p. 81) is easy to apply and can be very rich. Take once again, for example, the problem 'Find the solution to the equation $4x - 3 = 24 - 2x$' as the starting point. Emphasise each word in turn starting with *find*. What could we do if we did not *find* the solution? We could sketch the solution or we could estimate the solution. What if it was not *the* solution? We could ask how could we create an equation that has more than one solution or no solution? Focusing next on *solution*, we might want to ask 'find an interpretation, rather than a solution, for the equation'. Or we might even ask find values of x so that the left-hand side differs from the right-hand side by no more than 2 say. And skipping to the word *equation* (and we do not always want to skip words like *to* and *the*), we might want to consider the two sides connected by an inequality sign $4x - 3 < 24 - 2x$ rather than by an equality sign. And obviously, of course, we can consider other equations – we might want to consider ones that look different but have the same root – or ones that have a different look and different root.

Concluding remarks

The example chosen here – solving linear equations – was purposely chosen because it is a 'routine' curriculum topic that is often considered 'boring' to teach, and is definitely not a very rich one with which to illustrate the few problem-posing techniques that have been discussed. It was also chosen because one can adapt some of the ideas to make them suitable for younger children and to older ones.

Teachers of older children may try 'solve a quadratic equation' as a starting point. A richer starting point would be to start with an equation without asking for a solution. We would then be forced to realise that $4x - 3 = 24 - 2x$, for example, asks no question at all and is merely an open sentence which is neither true nor false! However, here we did start with a more narrow starting point namely: solve the equation $4x - 3 = 24 - 2x$. In *The Art of Problem Posing* we take $x^2 + y^2 = z^2$ as a starting point and discuss the problems that can arise from it when we do not make the unwarranted assumption that *the* question is 'find a solution to the given equation'. However, the few techniques of problem posing – 'accepting the given', using the – 'What-If-Not?' technique and 'stressing each item in a starting point' – that we have discussed here, have the advantage of getting pupils involved and thinking about their work. They will see that sometimes they can explore and answer their own problems, sometimes they need help, and that sometimes not all the questions they pose can be answered either by them or by their teacher. Sometimes you, the teacher, could answer them for them but sometimes it would be difficult to make the answer meaningful to the pupils; sometimes the teacher will not know the answer, but will be able to work it out in class – in front of the pupils – or after class or will be able to look up some information or ask a colleague. No one might be able to answer some of the questions the teacher is unable to answer. All these situations will help pupils see that mathematics is not an 'all or nothing and all worked out already' subject.

Teaching depends very heavily on being able to ask the pupils those questions that will help them to understand. It often means asking questions that step back from or side-step the exact difficulty at hand in order to locate related material that the pupil *does* understand. Once such a position is reached it is easier to help guide the pupil forward to an understanding of the issue at hand. For this, too, problem posing is useful. Ideally, we want to try and help the pupils to learn to pose their own questions, not only for the sake of problem solving, but so that they can help themselves to move ahead in learning mathematics.

Notes

1 I want to thank Stephen Brown, the co-author of *The Art of Problem Posing*, who made many helpful suggestions as this article was being written.

2 Attribute listing takes practice. You might want to begin by asking pupils to list attributes of such things as a table, a library, a meal, . . .

3 Note that I did start with 'solve the equation $4x = 12$' here and 'solve $4x - 3 = 24 - 2x$' at the outset. If the starting point had been just an equation, without the request to solve it, it is easy to fall into the trap of thinking that there was a question asked and that the question was indeed 'find the solution'.

References

Brown, S. I. and Walter, M. I. (1983) *The Art of Problem Posing*. Hillsdale, NJ: Lawrence Erlbaum Associates.

Eves, H. (1964) *An Introduction to the History of Mathematics* (3rd edn). New York: Holt, Rinehart and Winston.

Marion Walter is a Professor in the Mathematics Department at the University of Oregon, USA.

23

Modelling: what do we really want pupils to learn?

John Mason

Introduction

[To start with] perhaps I should follow a framework and begin by Recognising a Problem:

> In the last six years or so there has been a spate of books on mathematical modelling, presenting polished models which answer a wide variety of questions. What is the pupil to make of it all? What do we really want pupils to learn?

I shall approach this question from three mutually supporting directions. In brief, the three claims which I shall develop are as follows.

1 There is a fundamental error in believing that relevance (i.e. modelling) is the complete answer to getting pupils engaged and participating in mathematics. Involvement and relevance are opposite sides of the same coin, and they require an action inside the pupil. I shall argue that such an action is most clearly manifested in asking questions, and one of the most important things we can do for ourselves and for our pupils is to foster questioning. A necessary condition for real questioning seems to be seeing and recognising generality when looking at particularities.

2 Demonstrating completed or well-begun models is a useful component in teaching modelling, but it is only relevant once the inner action of point 1 has already begun. We might learn a great deal from using and studying the quintessential modelling process, namely metaphor. The particular lesson to be learned from metaphor is a glimpse of the inner activities that give rise to the outer events of modelling, shedding light on 'entering a question and making it my own'.

3 Modelling is a complex process. Even when the initial 'getting-started' hurdle has been surmounted, producing effective and useful models is very much an art. The expert may feel no need for an overview, but the novice is very often lost in detail, unable to appreciate the modelling process as a whole – particularly if the modelling has been done by someone else! Why then are people so reluctant to employ a framework to structure their activity? Some people fear a straitjacket, others fear that pupils will use it as a crutch to avoid thinking. But frameworks (possibly fragmentary) are present whether they

are acknowledged or not. I claim that they can and should be used positively, with suitable weaning where necessary.

Before treating these three claims in detail, it is necessary to set the scene by examining typical responses to the question

> What do we really want pupils to learn?

Typical responses are usually along the lines of

> to apply mathematical techniques and skills to obtain useful answers to practical questions;
>
> to see mathematics in action, explaining and predicting;
>
> to become more interested and involved in mathematics, and so to pursue it further;
>
> to become better at using mathematics to help resolve questions.

These are the sorts of reasons that are listed in modelling books, and in those brief introductory chapters that talk sparingly about the act of modelling and about why it is worth doing with pupils, before getting down to the case studies. As justifications, these are really very superficial. They may be a delayed response to students of the 1960s who cried out for relevance, but they remain at the same level of vagueness. They may express a utilitarian philosophy, but they are not the result of looking closely at the question in the manner that utilitarians espouse. When pupils ask

> Why are we doing this?

they are rarely satisfied by a reply of the form

> It is important in the steel industry.

In fact, they are usually not asking a question at all, but rather making a plea for help, because they have lost contact with the content of the class. It is not 'relevance' in the utilitarian sense that is sought, but rather a statement that they are no longer coping. I claim that most attempts to 'make mathematics relevant to pupils' are misconceived and doomed to failure, because relevance is not a property of mathematics, nor of its application to a particular physical context. Relevance is a property of an appropriate correspondence between qualities of some mathematical topic and qualities of the perceiver. Relevance is a relative notion: it describes a 'ratio' between aspects of the content and the pupil.

Relevance is often used as a buzz word to signal that pupils will become involved, as if all or even most pupils will become involved when presented with certain material. Involvement, like relevance, is descriptive of a relationship between content and pupil, and does not reside in the content itself. I suggest that if pupils become involved in some topic or question, then they see what they are doing as relevant to them at the time, and conversely, if something seems relevant, that the way is open for involvement. In other words, relevance and involvement are different ways of describing the same experience. I cannot by my efforts alone involve a pupil, I can only work for conditions which facilitate involvement for pupils who wish it. I can, for example, make it easier for pupils to become involved by reducing pressures to get correct answers and listening to what pupils have to say in a conjecturing atmosphere . . .

Whatever approach is taken, it is bound to be more successful if attention is placed on the relationship between pupil and content, and not on the content alone. Care must be taken not to confuse mathematical involvement with physical activity. It is easy to get pupils 'doing' something, but often they are actively involved only in accumulating grades, and avoiding real thinking. Often physical activity actually precludes mathematical thinking!

The belief that 'I can involve my pupils' is rather like picturing pupils as pianos, as passive instruments waiting for me as pianist to strike a chord. It does great injustice to them, and wastes a great deal of our own time and energy. Pupils of all ages are active. When we present a fully developed model or our own version of a case study taken from a book, what fragments of our careful exposition can we truly expect pupils to pick up? For example, the following extract is taken from a comparatively sensitive and carefully constructed book on modelling by Saaty and Alexander (1981):

> Strategy for a Mailman
>
> A mailman must deliver mail to each house on both sides of a straight street of length L and width W. Suppose that all N houses have the same street frontage of length D. The houses on both sides may be considered as points in the plane and start precisely at the beginning of the street, and end at its end. The houses on one side are a mirror of those on the other. If the mailman crosses the street he does so on a perpendicular to its length. Compare the strategy of delivering mail to all houses on one side, crossing the street, and returning to his starting point by delivering to all houses on the other side with the strategy of crossing the street from one house to that opposite it on the other side, walking to its next door neighbor and crossing the street again.
>
> Note that $$\frac{N}{2} - 1 = \frac{L}{D}.$$

And so it continues for 6 more lines of packed algebra. The exposition of the model *is* the content. The modelling is totally obscured, as is the original question. Only exceptional pupils are likely to construe modelling as something that 'they' do, and mathematical models as just another source of awkward assessment questions on mathematical theory which has to be learned.

This cannot be what we really want pupils to learn.

The next section develops my first claim, that relevance and involvement are intimately connected with being aware of generality when focusing on particularities.

Seeing the general in the particular

There is a fallacy being promulgated currently that questions to do with the 'real world', the world of material objects, are by their very nature relevant and hence involving. As I argued in the last section, I maintain that questions themselves are simply questions. When they become *my* questions in the sense that they are a part of me and I of them, then relevance and involvement are non-issues, because the question-tension is inside me, and the only response apart from intentional avoidance is involvement.

Relevance/involvement begins when a person experiences an inner tension of surprise at something unexpected or curious, and then tries to make use of that tension rather than avoid it. It may begin with a question posed by someone else, but the question itself is not the source of tension. The question is more like a catalyst or seed crystal. It does not matter whether the question is practical:

> What is the most efficient route for a postman on foot delivering letters in a street?

or abstract:

> Which integers can be written as the sum of consecutive integers and in how many different ways?

Once a tension appears, and providing that the emotional context is supportive, mathematical thinking can begin. In order that the tension arises, the pupil must do some work, so that some sort of action, some bed of energy is essential in a pupil before a question can spark off activity.

It is true that an energetic and emotive teacher can carry a large number of pupils along, sweeping them into at least a partial appreciation of a question and its resolution, but even then pupils must supply something, must experience in themselves some of the tension. Teachers who have a charismatic quality in their style of presenting questions or in the way they conduct themselves mathematically have an energy or absorbing interest which can be infectious. Even so, the pupil must bring something to the event, and it is the nature of that something which I would like to understand. When that 'something' is present, mere 'questions' can become involving and relevant. The image which comes to my mind is of waves on a pond – their size depends on the depth of the pond as well as the strength of the wind. Perhaps a more apposite image is of people asleep. No matter what you say (without shouting!), little will come of talking to them. Even shouting will only rouse them from slumber, not equip them to take in what you have to say. So too a certain energy level is necessary in pupils.

To test the hypothesis that power does not reside in the question, one need only try recording oneself posing a question to a class (preferably one that takes off), transcribing it, and then presenting the written version to various people under various conditions. The result will be that 'interest' in the question will be unpredictable. It will be taken up most readily by colleagues who are already mathematically active (modulo time available), who have an attitude of mathematical (if not broader) questioning.

We now have a new (and possibly self-referent) question:

> How does a question become involvingly mine?

What to me is most surprising about this question is that it should need to be asked at all. As purveyors of models and modelling are aware, there is a plethora of potential problems around us all the time. Perhaps the best explanation for failure to question is as a defence against the overwhelming quantity of difficult questions. One of the most comprehensive collections of questions I know is Walker's *The Flying Circus of Physics* (1977) and it illustrates my point perfectly. Walker has assembled a vast array of questions about everyday events from thunder to vacuum cleaners. Despite my predilection for seeking questions, there is for me something initially exciting but ultimately debilitating about the 'Flying Circus'. His questions are not my questions, and furthermore I know that he has (mostly) resolved his questions at the back of the book. A book full of questions seems to me to run entirely opposite to a classroom atmosphere of enquiry, of asking questions, since much of the force of a question lies in the asking. This is why Burkhardt (1981) recommends eliciting pupils' concerns and massaging them into questions, though the chance of getting something mathematically meaty is small. A supply of seed questions can be helpful to get going, but they must be used very sparingly because a whole catalogue of them can be off-putting. The gap between a question being someone else's and being mine seems to widen when I know that there is a profusion of questions already written down, waiting to be set.

We wish to stimulate enquiry, because that can be followed by investigation and modelling. Usually the question source will be from someone else, but to stimulate appreciation of, and adoption of externally provided questions, it may be (and I claim it is) essential to help pupils develop their ability to recognise and pose questions for themselves. This brings us to a third set of questions.

> How can we foster an atmosphere of enquiry, investigation and modelling?
> How can we reawaken questioning in ourselves and our pupils?

Having pondered these questions for a long time myself, it has recently come to me that there is one feature about the noticing of (to me) interesting questions which is fundamental to mathematical thinking. To show you what I mean, have a look at the pictures on p. 205. Several of them evoke in me questions whose resolution could easily be aided by mathematical modelling. I would like to draw your attention to what you do when you look at these pictures. I am interested at this point not in *the questions*, but in *how the questions arise*. Please look back at them now before reading on.

Each of the pictures is either a particular object or a particular scene. Yet in order to make sense of them, to construe some sort of meaning, we each must surely relate what we see to things or scenes we have seen before. When we see the particular, we relate it to other similar instances. We automatically and subconsciously stress some features and ignore others. Without contrast there are no distinctions, and so no tension. With the awareness of contrast between what is seen and what is not, between the scene as it is and as it might be, tension arises. When our eyes are open and we look at a particular scene, we can only *see* what we can generalise or fit into a broad schema. For example, most of us simply cannot see distinctions in snow which are important to an Eskimo.

The noticing of a question requires the focus of our attention to be *seen as* a specific instance of a general phenomenon. It seems to me that awareness of generality is essential. Only then does it make sense to ask a general question such as

> What is happening?
> Does that always happen?
> What is the maximum/minimum . . .?

Many if not most mathematical questions are to do with explaining or predicting a repeating phenomenon, and so are inherently general. Do they make sense if there is little or no prior experience of particular instances, or if the pupil's attention is totally absorbed by the particular to the exclusion of the generality?

These observations suggest to me that we can be of direct benefit to ourselves and our pupils by taking every opportunity to indicate when we are 'seeing the general in the particular', because it is highly likely that our pupils are engrossed in the particular. Certainly this is true at the macro level of modelling when we present specific models. To the presenter, the model is only a specific instance of a general process called modelling. To the pupil, the model is the content to be made sense of and learned. Case studies become content, and not particular cases of anything more general like the process of modelling.

The same discrepancy between a teacher's perception of generality when talking about a particular example, and a pupil's perception of the particular as the totality takes place at all levels of mathematical presentation. (See Mason and Pimm (1984) for elaboration.)

Having developed the notion of 'seeing the general in the particular' by pursuing the theme of relevance and involvement into the realm of recognising and posing questions, and thus learning to make questions my own as well as making my own questions, the next section invokes metaphor as an aid to distinguishing between

> 'entering a problem and making it your own'

and the more usual pupil activity:

> 'Keeping a problem at arm's length, failing to make contact with it'.

Metaphor is closely akin to modelling, and appreciation of the richness of a metaphor is closely connected with being involved.

Metaphor

The previous section has indicated that it is important to distinguish between

> learning A model

and

> learning TO model.

I invite you to reflect on that difference a moment before rushing on.

STOP NOW AND REFLECT

As I was contemplating the distinction between the noun 'model' and the verb 'to model', and the import of the word 'learning', an image of pots and pottery classes came to me:

> I wouldn't attempt to teach someone to throw pots simply by showing them a lot of pots on a shelf.

Similarly, no one would attempt to teach modelling simply by showing pupils lots of mathematical models. Or would they? I recently approached some twenty or more books on modelling to find out what they had to say, and found very little in the way of comment on the process of modelling. (One notable exception was Burkhardt (1981).) They consist largely of worked out models, and exposition of techniques needed to solve the mathematical problems posed in the models. Perhaps this is not surprising, since books are often seen as the repository of knowledge, and models are often confused with knowledge in the same way that pots are often confused with pottery. [. . .]

Textbooks may correspond to books about pottery and completed models to pots on the shelf, but it is still possible to let pupils in on the really significant choices and awarenesses at the beginning of the modelling, which get the whole thing going.

Frameworks and straitjackets

According to the experts, teaching modelling is difficult:

> The only way we have so far to train an individual in modelling is to expose him to a wide variety of problems and to a corresponding variety of models which provide representations of those problems. This establishes a need for a methodological framework for problem formulation. (Saaty and Alexander, 1981)

> Once the significant features have been identified, the next stage is to translate these into mathematical entities. This is generally the most difficult stage, and one in which it is impossible to give formal instruction! (Andrews and McLone, 1976)

Behind all the discussions and case studies it is not hard to detect fragments of models and metaphors for the process of mathematical modelling. Occasionally these are made explicit – for example, many books refer to the two-state diagram:

REAL WORLD   MATHEMATICAL WORLD

It draws attention to a separation, but it gives little assistance as to how to go about modelling. A more detailed seven-box diagram is used in some courses at the Open University (1981) which expands the two states and tries to indicate what to do at each stage.

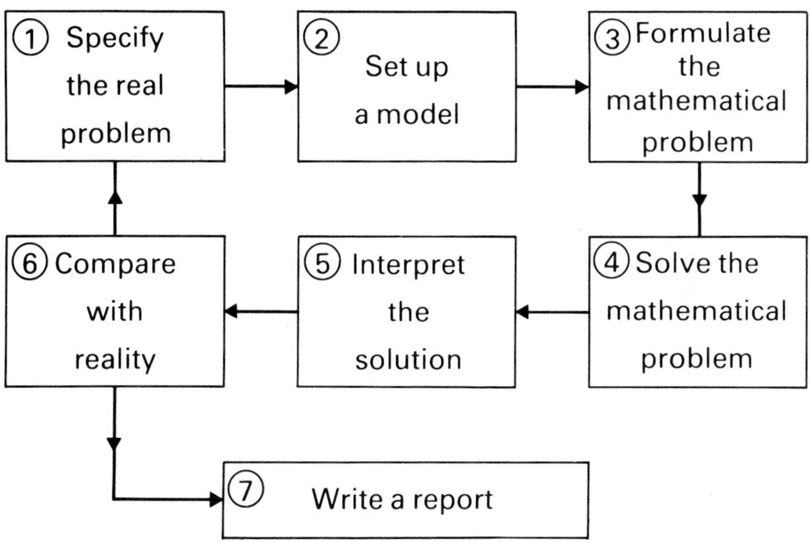

It is a refinement of the first diagram, the left column belonging to the real-world domain, the right column to the mathematical world, and the centre column offers a hint of the metaphoric quality of modelling which is cognitive by nature and belongs neither to the real world nor to the mathematical. The conceptualising is often not easy to talk about because it involves mental imagery, modeller-predilections, resonance with past experience and sensitivity to the purpose of the exercise. Rather than following most books and abandoning all attempts to try to communicate the metaphoric aspects of modelling because it is not easy to talk about, it seems to me sensible to grasp the nettle and invoke metaphors when ever possible. Describe what you are doing when modelling by using several different metaphors. Show that there *are* ways of talking about mathematical activities that we perform in our heads – they may be partial and idiosyncratic, but at least acknowledge that they exist!

James and McDonald (1981) offer nine stages in list form:

Recognition	Analysing
Familiarity	Interpreting
Formulating	Implementing
Constructing model	Monitoring
Validating	

which correspond closely to the seven boxes but have the disadvantage of profusion (nine is too many to remember) and lack of any supporting mental images. The only way that a pupil could try to make use of them would be as a flowchart/algorithm. Burkhardt (1981) offers both a complex flowchart and a list of modelling skills:

Generating variables or features
Selecting variables or pruning features
Formulating questions
Generating relations between variables
Selecting relations

Frameworks such as these arise as a result of reflection, in response to a wish to be able to encompass the whole and to be able to offer advice when the going gets sticky. They are of no use to pupils if they are mistaken for content, for another layer of things to be learned. In the words of St Paul, they are to be

> read, marked, learned, and inwardly digested

or as Halmos (1960) said in his beautiful book on set theory,

> read it, absorb it, forget it

by which he meant, let it descend so deeply into your awareness that it lies below the surface, subconsciously structuring what you are doing. We all have bits and pieces of frameworks operating subconsciously. By making them explicit we can actually modify them in the light of experience.

A teacher of mathematical modelling who refuses to expose a framework explicitly to pupils is like the potter who throws magnificent pots and expects pupils to discover the inner activities of mental imagery connected with aesthetic sense which guide the hands in the outer tasks of fashioning a pot, simply by watching and occasionally trying. Pupils under such circumstances naturally focus on technical details, and soon lose sight of the overall purpose.

Pupils need help to keep the wood in mind as well as the trees, and even some experts might just be able to improve their own performance a little bit here and there by adopting some structure or framework. Even the 'doers' that Halmos (1981) distinguishes from 'reflectors' could learn by a little reflecting.

One frequently-offered justification for concentrating on case studies of mathematical models without talking about the modelling process is that it seems so artificial to try to force what I want to say into someone else's framework. The clue lies in the 'someone else's', which suggests that Halmos' advice has not been taken. When a framework becomes one of my ways of perceiving the world, there is no sense of trying to force things, because the framework determines what is perceived. This positive feature is often turned around and used as a reason for dispensing with frameworks, because people are afraid that they will be trapped or controlled.

Many people claim they reject frameworks because they feel strait-jacketed, that it banishes creativity, and does not accurately reflect what really happens. It seems curious that people who claim to be experts at modelling and who espouse

> making a simple model to start
> then modify it as necessary

are unwilling to do the same thing consciously at a meta-level. By being explicit, the framework can be modified. A framework is only dangerous when it is implicit and fragmentary. Multiple frameworks, like multiple metaphors, add richness and flexibility, neither of which are available when the whole process takes place subconsciously.

The most substantial objection to promulgating frameworks to pupils is that process, when talked about and dwelt upon, can easily turn into a combination of content and empty ritual. The seven boxes or nine stages, when perceived as further content to be learned, get memorised and trotted out when a suitable stimulus (examination question) is applied. Once classified as 'learnable content', a framework is consigned to its own compartment and has no impact on pupil behaviour. Pupils can also latch onto a framework as a crutch to avoid thinking. By treating it as an algorithm, they can avoid contact with the problem, hoping that by going through the motions the answer will emerge. In this way, frameworks can turn into empty ritual.

Frameworks can certainly be misused, or rather fail to be used, but this is not a valid reason for ignoring them altogether. On the contrary, the real challenge, if either of the previous two sections has made any sense, is to exploit frameworks for helping pupils to become involved and to appreciate what it is like to construct mathematical models. Even in the modelling books which I sampled and which do offer some framework, the framework is most often used mechanically, even superficially by the authors, thus giving pupils an impression that it is only frill. The framework is usually used only to label stages, rather than to afford entry into the experience. No wonder pupils come away with an algorithmic, mechanical approach to mathematics.

So what could be done? The main thing, building on the observations of the previous sections, must be to develop and become imbued with some coherent way of going about modelling, and sharing that explicitly in detail with pupils. For example, take the seven-box approach.

Specify the real problem

The initial stages of coming to grips with a problem – called variously Recognition and Specify the Problem – are represented in most case studies simply by a statement of the question, but with no remarks about how that formulation of the question was reached, of what was considered and rejected and why.

Set up a model

This is a particularly subtle stage because it is by nature conceptual and metaphoric, and so pupils need most help. The phase of Setting up a Model (Constructing a Model) is usually presented by stating certain equations or inequalities. Even if the model is being studied as content to be learned, a pupil wants to know where these came from, and if the pupil is intended to be studying the model as a particular example of the modelling process, then it is vital to make process remarks. Even where detailed exercises are offered which indicate how to go about setting up a model by writing down all the features that seem relevant, and then discarding complex ones, the case studies rarely indicate *why* certain features were considered and rejected. Nowhere have I seen assistance given on the conceptual aspects of modelling, which involve forming and entering some sort of mental image of the situation being modelled, trying to experience it mentally. We all do this in some form or other, but we give pupils the impression that one simply 'thinks' and then writes down beautiful feature lists or completed models.

Formulate the mathematical problem

Translation of verbal relationship into symbols is not as easy as it seems, particularly when the relationships are someone else's. It is much easier when I have struggled to articulate the relationships myself. One author, Aris (1978), dismisses formulation as

> rational accounting for the various factors that enter the picture in accordance with the hypotheses that have been laid down.

If only pupils could 'enter the picture', perhaps then they could confidently and competently undertake 'rational accounting'!

Careful attention to what is known – to which symbols stand for parameters or data – and to what is wanted, will assist pupils to formulate the mathematical problem.

Solve the mathematical problem

This is frequently the domain of assessment, so naturally attention is focused on it, beyond its importance. Frequently, in practice, the problem cannot be solved exactly, so further assumptions or approximations are required. Unfortunately many case studies present the work of experienced modellers who have anticipated mathematical difficulties and so built in simplifying assumptions at an early stage. These mystify pupils who lack experience. Many modelling books focus on models built around a particular mathematical technique or theory (and usually this is the pupils' first introduction to the theory!). Tackling a question when you know what the technique is going to be is more like doing exercises at the end of the chapter than it is like modelling. Modelling should not be confused with theory and techniques. It is a separate and difficult art to learn. Pupils will only too happily focus on techniques which can be memorised and mastered, and avoid the conceptual challenge, the metaphoric thinking required by modelling.

Interpret the solution

Interpreting the mathematical solution involves retracing the conceptual-metaphoric leap, and can only be done by someone who appreciates what was in the modeller's mind to begin with. Routine mechanical exercises at this stage do nothing to help pupils appreciate the model.

Compare with reality

Comparing with Reality (Implementing) is usually barely even mentioned. Never have I found discussion about the difficulties of measuring quantities whose values are required in the model. Each measurement will introduce error, and may cancel out mathematical refinements in the model.

Off-hand remarks are often made about the cyclical, refining, multi-pass aspect of modelling in which the first model is almost guaranteed to be too simplistic and too rough, but rarely does the exposition actually traverse the cycle more than once. I suspect this is because the author presents the best, most refined model found to date, and omits the early versions. Pupils construe from the paradigm that it may be necessary to make several passes, but that one ought to get a pretty good one the first or second time.

Write a report

The natural assumption is that the case study itself constitutes the report, but it is very rare to find any mention of difficulties in writing a report. It is important for the modeller to pretend to be the user so that the report speaks in the user's language. Many of the comments suggested for previous stages would actually help the user to understand what the modeller set out to model, and how the model is meant to operate.

A framework is only a straitjacket if it is employed as a ritual algorithm in order to avoid thinking. Remember the Euclidean geometry classes in school? All proofs had to begin with Given, To Prove, Proof. These were meant to help get into the question, to feel it internally and to get inside the tension between Given and To Prove, the proof being a bridge constructed between them. And how did most students respond? By quickly writing down the rubric, then asking themselves

> What do I do now?

or in the language of schools,

> I've read the workcard, Miss, but is it add or multiply?

The framework was treated as empty ritual. Why? I submit that it was because the teacher *never* spoke about or acknowledged the inner work when writing down what was Given and To Prove. Most pupils never even realised that there was more to be done than writing down some words. (I can assert 'never realised' because clearly they never real-ised or made real for themselves.) You can avoid this by Being a Modeller in front of, and with your pupils, by voicing your inner thoughts as you metaphorically sit at the wheel and throw a pot, and by joining with your pupils, facing a problem together, listening to what they say, trying to enter their perceptions and helping them build on those rather than rushing along in your own direction. After all, what we really want pupils to learn, is to *become modellers*, do we not?

Some suggestions, by way of summary

1 Stimulate pupils to ask their own questions.
2 Practise exploring and developing metaphors, both mathematical and non-mathematical.
3 Work *with* pupils, genuinely. Suppress your own ideas and focus on helping pupils articulate and modify their own ideas. Do not push your own model. Give pupils time to express their thoughts and images in a mathematical conjecturing atmosphere – everything that is said is intended to be modified.
4 Present completed models, but stress the generic aspects and modelling process, and play down technical details. Dwell on the choices and decisions made in the early stages. Give voice to the mental imagery (the implicit metaphors) which accompanies the written statements.
5 Present incomplete models and invite development and criticism. For example, pupils could role-play a panel who have to select one proposal to be 'funded', and justify their choice.
6 Become aware of how often you use a particular example to illustrate a general point, and make sure that your pupils are aware of what you are doing. Take opportunities to draw explicit attention to the movement from particular to general and vice versa, at all levels, from modelling as a process to specific mathematical techniques.

References

Modelling processes

Andrews, J. F. and McLone, R. R. (1976) *Mathematical Modelling*. London: Butterworth.

Burkhardt, H. (1981) *The Real World and Mathematics*. Glasgow: Blackie.

Halmos, P. R. (1960) *Naive Set Theory*. Princeton: Van Nostrand.

Halmos, P. R. (1981) 'Applied Mathematics is Bad Mathematics', in *Mathematics Tomorrow*, ed. L. Steen. New York: Springer-Verlag.

James, D. J. and McDonald, J. J. (1981) *Case Studies in Mathematical Modelling*. Cheltenham: Stanley Thornes.

Leatherdale, W. H. (1974) *The Role of Analogy, Model and Metaphor in Science*. Oxford: North-Holland.

Mason, J. and Pimm, D. (1984) 'Generic Examples: Seeing the General in the Particular', *Educational Studies in Mathematics*, **15**(3), pp. 277–89.

Spanier, J. (1980) 'Thoughts about the essentials of modelling', *Math. Modelling*, **1**, pp. 98–108.

Open University (1981) *MST204 Project Guide for Mathematical Modelling and Methods*. Milton Keynes: Open University.

Case Studies

Aris, R. (1978) 'Mathematical Modelling Techniques', Research Notes in Maths 24. London: Pitman.

Saaty, S. L. and Alexander, J. M. (1981) *Mathematical Models and Applications*. Oxford: Pergamon.

Walker, J. (1977) *The Flying Circus of Physics*. New York: Wiley.

John Mason is Director of the Centre for Mathematics Education at the Open University.

24

Aspects of proof in pupils' practice of school mathematics

Nicolas Balacheff

(translated by David Pimm)

Introduction

This study is of the notion of proof from the point of view of the mathematical practices of pupils and not that of the logician. It relies upon an experimental approach which allows the processes of proof used in solving a problem to be seen more easily, in particular examining how the pupils arrive at their conviction of the validity of the proposed solution. In order to do this, we have used a social setting which requires spoken interaction (while minimising the intervention of the observer) which, by means of the discussion which occur, allows the processes which underly the decisions taken by the pupils to become visible.

Levels and types of proof

Pragmatic versus conceptual proofs

The most elementary form of expression of a proof is one of direct showing. The operations and the concepts used are acts, neither differentiated nor articulated. This does not mean the complete absence of language, but it is not used as the fundamental means of transmitting knowledge. A classical example of a direct proof by showing is that of the result that the sum of the first n odd numbers is n^2.

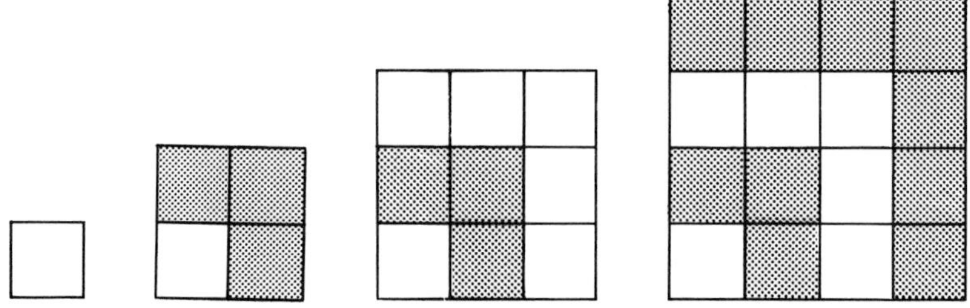

These proofs rely on the ability of whoever sees the diagram to reconstruct the reasons that the prover has implicitly in mind but does not know how to explain otherwise (Sémadéni, 1984). In this type of proof, a central role is played by theorems-in-action (Vergnaud, 1981) which consist of those properties used by the solver in a problem, ones which she could not actually specify.

In this article, *pragmatic* proofs are those having recourse to actual action or showings, and by contrast, *conceptual* proofs are those which do not involve action and rest on formulations of the properties in question and relations between them. This detachment from action, from the here-and-now, does not happen by itself. It gets expressed in the language of the everyday. The action made explicit by this language carries traces of time order and duration, the person who acts and the context of her action. Nevertheless, use of such language already requires a certain distance so that the action can be described and made explicit. As Sémadéni suggests (thinking of an extension of action proofs), the movement to conceptual proofs lies essentially in taking account of the generic quality of those situations previously envisaged. The example below provides an illustration.

4/ $2 + 10 = 12$ $\quad 10 - 2 = 8$

$12 + 8 = 20$

Therefore $(2 + 10) + (10 - 2) = 20$

$(10 + 10) + (2 - 2) = 20$

It will always be 10 + 10

I've chosen 2 and it cancels out so if I choose another number between 1 and 10 it will always cancel out and will always be equal.

The move into conceptual proofs requires an altered position: the speaker must distance herself from the action and the processes of solution of the problem (recall that pupils when posed the question 'why' often reply by repeating the operations they have used to solve the problem). Knowledge, up until now acted out, becomes the object of reflection, discourse and indeed disagreements. The language of the everyday, whose main support is natural language, allows some movement in this direction. But there must be more than this to produce 'formal' proofs. Language must become a tool for logical deductions and not just a means of communication. The elaboration of this functional language requires in particular:

- a *decontextualisation,* giving up the actual object for the class of objects, independent of their particular circumstances;

- a *depersonalisation,* detaching the action from the one who acted and of whom it must be independent;
- a *detemporalisation,* disengaging the operations from their actual time and duration: this process is fundamental to the passage from the world of actions to that of relations and operations.

Among the various types of pragmatic and conceptual proofs, we have singled out four main types which hold a privileged position in the cognitive development of proof: naive empiricism, the crucial experiment, the generic example and the thought experiment. Actually, the former two types do not establish the truth of an assertion; we talk of *proof* because they are recognised as such by their producers. As we show below, there is a fundamental divide between the first two sorts of proof and the latter two. Moreover, for the generic example and the thought experiment, it is no longer a matter of 'showing' the result is true because 'it works'; rather, it concerns establishing the necessary nature of its truth by giving reasons. It involves a radical shift in the pupils' reasoning underlying these proofs.

Moreover, we claim that these forms of proof form a hierarchy, one which is taken into account in the order of presentation below. Where a particular type of proof falls in this hierarchy depends on how much the demands of generality and the conceptualisation of knowledge are involved. Thus moving from the generic example to the thought experiment, for instance, requires moving from action to internalised action, as well as involving a decontextualisation, which is one sign of a decisive change in the construction of knowledge.

Naive empiricism

Naive empiricism consists of asserting the truth of a result after verifying several cases. This very rudimentary (and as we know, insufficient) means of proving is one of the first forms of the process of generalisation (Piaget, 1978). But arising from a collection of problems posed to fifteen year olds, Bell (1979) found that 25 per cent of them based their answers only on the verification of a few cases. We can therefore expect naive empiricism to constitute a form resistant to generalisation.

The crucial experiment

The expression 'crucial experiment', coined by Francis Bacon (*Novum Organum,* 1620), refers to an experiment whose outcome allows a choice to be made between two hypotheses, it having been designed so that the outcome should be clearly different according to whether one or other hypothesis is the case. (Whether this experiment allows the rejection of one hypothesis or not, it does not allow us to assert that the other is true.)

We use the same expression for a slightly different process, one of verifying a proposition on an instance which 'doesn't come for free', asserting that 'if it works here, it will always work'. Here is an example from Bell (1976, cp. 10, p. 12): 'Jayne shows a complicated polygon, she can definitely say that the statement is true.' This type of validation is distinguishable from naive empiricism in that the pupil poses explicitly the problem of generality and resolves it by staking all on the outcome of a particular case that she recognises to be not too special.

The generic example

The generic example involves making explicit the reasons for the truth of an assertion by means of operations or transformations on an object that is not there in its own right, but as a characteristic representative of its class. The account involves the characteristic properties and structures of a class, while doing so in terms of the names and illustration of one of its representatives. Below is an example taken from Bezout (*Notes on Arithmetic*, 1832, p. 23):

> The remainder on dividing a number by 2 × 2 or 5 × 5 is the same as the remainder on dividing the number formed by the rightmost two digits by 2 × 2 or 5 × 5 . . .
>
> To fix these ideas, consider the number 43728 and the divisor 5 × 5. The number 43728 is equal to 43700 + 28. However, 43700 is divisible by 5 × 5, because 43700 is the product of 437 and 100, and as 100 is 10 × 10, or 5 × 2 × 5 × 2, the factor 100 is divisible by 5 × 5. The remainder on dividing 43728 by 5 × 5 or 25 is therefore the same as that on dividing 28 by 25.

The thought experiment

The thought experiment invokes action by internalising it and detaching itself from a particular representation. It is still coloured by an anecdotal temporal development, but the operations and foundational relations of the proof are indicated in some other way than by the result of their use, something which is the case for the generic example. (For more on the thought experiment, see Lakatos, 1976.) Here, for example, is the proof that Cauchy gave for the intermediate value theorem in his *Cours d'Analyse* of 1821:

> It suffices to show that the curve with equation $y = f(x)$ will cross the line $y = b$ at least once in the interval which includes the ordinates which

correspond to the abscissae x_0 and X; however, it is clear that this will happen under the given hypotheses. Indeed, as the function $f(x)$ is continuous between $x = x_0$ and $x = X$, the curve with equation $y = f(x)$ and which passes firstly through the point with coordinates x_0, $f(x_0)$, and secondly through the point with coordinates X, $f(X)$, will be continuous between these two points; and as the constant ordinate b of the line whose equation is $y = b$ lies between the ordinates, $f(x_0)$ and $f(X)$, of the two points under consideration, the line necessarily passes between these two points, something it cannot do without meeting the above-mentioned curve in the interval.

An experimental study on types of proof

Presentation of the experimental setting

We chose for this study the problem of discovering and justifying a formula for the number of diagonals of any polygon. The 28 pupils aged thirteen and fourteen worked in pairs, though were only provided with one pen between two. The observer explained to them that

> you are to write a message which will be given to other pupils of your own age, which is to:
>
> > provide a means of calculating the number of diagonals of a polygon when you know the number of vertices it has.

(These last two lines were written on a sheet which was available to the pupils throughout the period of observation.)

The problem was given to the pupils without providing them with definitions of *polygon* and *diagonal*. This choice was made in order to allow the possibility of observing the (re-)construction of these concepts in the course of the solution, particularly with regard to refutations. In this way, we tried to place ourselves as close as possible to the focus of Lakatos' study (1976) which, along with the problem of proof, also examines that of the construction of mathematical knowledge.

The pupils were told that they had as much time as they wanted: *they* were to decide when they thought they had solved the problem. In fact, this activity formed the first part of the experiment. After a message had been offered by the pupils, the observer suggested difficulties that the recipients of the message could encounter in implementing their proposed method of calculation for certain polygons. In other words, in this second part, the observer offered counter-examples.

The experimental setting used thus consisted of two quite different parts, and the move from one to the other was achieved at the expense of breaking the 'experimental contract', that is to say involving the observer in a change of role from that of 'neutral observer' in order to offer counter-examples. For the majority of pupils, this breaking of the contract did not seem to have greatly affected their behaviour. It is true that the polygons the observer produced as counter-examples carried with them his authority, but this did not, for example, prevent pupils from rejecting these purported refutations.

Results of the problem solutions

The table below lists some of the wide range of solutions produced by the pupils during the first part of the experiment (about one hour). Eventually, more than half the pairs arrived at what we would call a correct solution. Only one pair, however, reached the classical formulation of the solution, $f_1(n) = n(n-3)/2$ in the first part of the experiment.

Pair	*First Part*
Christophe and Bertrand	$f_1(n) = n(n-3)/2$
Hamdi and Fabrice	n^2
Lionel and Laurent	n
Nadine and Elisabeth	$f(n+1) = f(n) + a(n+1)$ and $a(n+1) = a(n)+1$ where $a(n)$ is the number of diagonals which should have been added to pass from P_{n-1} to P_n.
Martine and Laura	$f_2(n) = (n-3)+(n-3)+(n-4)+(n-54)+...+2+1$
Olivier and Stéphane	$f_2(n)$
Georges and Olivier	$f_2(n)$
Pierre and Philippe	$n.s(n)$, where $s(n)$ is the number of diagonals at a vertex
Lydie and Marie	$n/2$
Naïma and Valerie	$n/2$
Antoine and Damien	$n/2$
Evelyne and Christine	$n/2$ or n
Blandine and Elisabeth	$n/2$ or $(n-1)/2$
Pierre and Mathieu	n

These results support the *a priori* analysis made of the procedures and conceptions that the pupils would bring into play. Even the solution $f(n) = 2n$, which does not appear in the table, occurred: it was strongly defended by Christophe against Bertrand. (See the Appendix to this article on pp. 231–5.) The potency of the square as a model for diagonals explains the dominance of the solutions of the form $f(n) = n/2$.

The types of proof observed

We are interested here in the stages of validation of those results which appear, in the eyes of the pupils at least, to be conjectures. In addition, we are only considering the first part of the observations, where the observer has not yet intervened in the solution of the problem.

Pragmatic proofs

(a) Naive empiricism

We include here those conjectures which were taken from looking at a few cases; the question of their validity did not explicitly come up. But, on the other hand, the pupils showed, in their words or deeds, their confidence in these assertions. Rather than a characteristic of the pupils themselves, naive empiricism appears to be a state in which they found themselves, and they stayed there for reasons to do with the situation or their relationship with the knowledge itself.

The fact that particular pairs did not get past this level of naive empiricism can be described in terms of an obstacle, one whose source is the social interaction. Wanting to be right despite a disagreeing partner can get in the way of getting involved in problems of justification. Thus Christophe supported the conjecture $f(n)=2n$ (verified only in the case of a seven-sided polygon) against Bertrand's, without showing either uncertainty or a desire to look for a justification. (See the Appendix for more details.) Lydie defended her assertion that $f(n)=n/2$ against Marie every step of the way, by means of *ad hoc* arguments in the face of refutations. In these two cases, the pupils took advantage of their partner's difficulties to promote their own solution; they were not really involved in a collective effort to solve the problem.

Social interaction can thus provide an obstacle when pupils with very different conceptions are brought together. This was true in the case of Pierre and Mathieu, whose conceptions of polygon and diagonal were essentially distinct. The complexity involved in unifying their points of view and the emotional intensity of the conflict formed an obstacle to their getting involved in the question of proof. These problems arise, like those from the choice between two solutions, but the conflict is such that it favours one reading of the situation in terms of a game in which there is not much to lose. (In all that follows, P_n refers to an n-sided polygon).

> After a very important discussion about what a diagonal actually is, and various proposals, the claim that $f(n)=n/2$ is arrived at from a consideration of P_4, P_6 and P_8: 'with a square, an eight-sided one and a six-sided one, so there you are, it must always be divided by two'. The counter-example P_5 which Pierre comes up with is dealt with by an *ad hoc* adjustment to the claim: 'even, you divide by two

. . . odd, you take one off it', which is confirmed by a laborious and contentious check on P_7. The *ad hoc* nature of this adjustment confirms the naive empiricism which guides the two pupils' activities.

In fact, for Pierre, it is now a question of a 'theory' which Mathieu can refute if he does not agree; a conjecture about which he declares that he 'do[es] not really think that is it, but you always have to try rather than stay in the same place'. However, the pupils fail to undertake any other validatory steps.

For the figures whose number of vertices is even you divide by 2 the number of diagonals with respect to the number of vertices. For those figures whose mimber of vertices is odd, you take away 2 from the number of diagonals with respect to the number of vertices.

Without refuting it, Mathieu denies the previous conjecture that: 'the rule has to apply to every case. From looking at P_5 and P_7, as represented below,

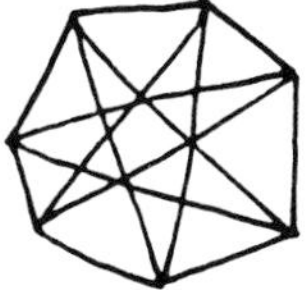
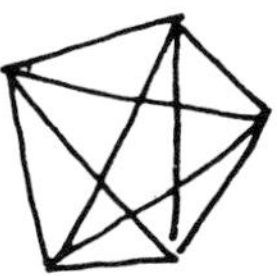

he produces the conjecture $f(n) = n$, expressed in the following way:

To find the number of diagonal, it must agree with the number of vertices.

Here too it is a naive conjecture: 'I think that it is rather . . . that there are as many diagonals as vertices'.

So now the two conjectures are concurrent, 'gotta choose one of them'. Pierre suggests a way out of the situation: 'We'll write down each of our theories and we'll try to rule out those that are wrong'. This proposal is not followed, but it shows that naive empiricism is not intrinsic to these two pupils.

Instead of getting into a discussion about proof, the pupils refer it to the observer. Pierre would really like to have the solution and as for

Mathieu: 'p'rhaps you think we've got it all wrong, or . . . or p'rhaps we've done it really well'.

Mathieu's fatalism and Pierre's impatience could comprise essential obstacles to their escaping from naive empiricism. To this can be added looking at the situation in terms of a riddle: 'it's a game . . . better to try', although one of little interest, of 'try anything you like'.

(b) The crucial experiment

The crucial experiment was observed as a means both of checking a result and as a weapon in discussions about validity between the two pupils from the same pair.

In every case, the crucial experiment was actually the checking of a proposition against a particular polygon with the deliberate intent of testing it. And thus, in the process, it involved the taking into account of generality. This goal is explicit in the work of Nadine and Elisabeth who, in this way, came up with a conjecture initially based on what could be called a primitive recursion.

From looking at P_4, P_5 and P_6 the pupils come up with the conjecture that $f(n+1) = f(n) + a(n+1)$ and $a(n+1) = a(n)+1$ where $f(4) = 2$ and $a(4) = 2$. Before checking it, they predict for P_7: 'you'd have to add five to it usually' and 'usually, with 7, you'd have 14 diagonals, if that ever worked'.

The experiment holds for P_7 convex, but before that it had failed for P_7 concave: 'if it's like in the figure, you've not got the same number of diagonals [. . .] it must be without angles'. Also, at least for Nadine, this proof by experiment on P_7 is insufficient: 'Normally, if you're completely right, . . . with 8 sides you'd find six more of them.' She relies on the crucial experiment to decide: 'try it with 15 and then if it works for that, well then that means that it works for the others'. In fact, this experiment is carried out on P_{10}, because P_{15} seems too complex from the outset: '. . . 10 sides you should find 35 diagonals'. The experiment they have in mind confirms this result.

(c) The generic example

In three cases generic examples were used to establish the truth of the proposition $f_2(n) = (n-3) + (n-3) + (n-4) +. . .+ 2 + 1$. But the proof thus obtained never carries the conviction of both pupils, even if an apparent collaboration has united them. It is, in fact, in each of these cases, a crucial experiment which overcomes the doubts of the sceptical partner. The difficulty of these proofs lies in the fact that the speakers need to be agreed on the generic character of the example used, and thus that they share the same conceptions of the objects in question: otherwise the explanation that is developed will appear to be crucially tied to a particular case. In this empirical context, having recourse to a crucial experiment appears to be legitimate as a tool in the debate about validity. Below we discuss the case of Georges and Olivier:

The construction of the sequence $(n-3)$, $(n-3)$, $(n-4)$, . . . , 2, 1 comes in response to 'a problem' raised by Georges while he is exploring the proposition that $f(n)=n.s(n)$ [where $s(n)$ is the number of diagonals at each vertex]: 'they [the diagonals] are doubling up'.

The question of a proof depends centrally on that of the first term of f_2. With the generic support of P_6, the pupils establish that this first term will be of the form $n-3$:

'The two segments which are next to the point you consider can't have diagonals, because they are like that. So, it's those on this side [. . .] if you take one, there are already two next to it ruled out.'

Once this is established, the construction sequence of f_2 is correct for P_6. Having announced the number of diagonals from each vertex, this consists of verifying it on a diagram step by step. However, this proof (based on a generic example) does not convince Olivier. He only believes the evidence of a crucial experiment with P_{14}.

Moreover, in the case of f_2, a discussion about reasons would be particularly difficult, as the difficulties in formulating messages attest. In effect, they involve expressing an iteration, and consequently a means of representation which is very intricate in natural language or requiring a high level of abstraction to be formulated in a more formal language (which would reduce the complexity to a linguistic one). This complexity can constitute an obstacle to the evolution of the kinds of proof used towards a more advanced level.

Conceptual proofs

(d) The thought experiment

Before including the proof style of a pair in this category, we require that the justification, which forms the basis of the validation of the proposition, should rest on an analysis of the properties of the objects in question. These properties are no longer evidenced on instances, but formulated in their generality. The action is internalised, invoked in the discourse which makes the proof explicit.

The thought experiment really appears as a means of underpinning the proposed propositions, in an effort to explain them. It does not involve particular situations. Decontextualisation, as can be seen with Olivier and Stéphane, is the central process of generalisation. The ideas involved are essentially based on perceptual experience and action. The reasons offered are bound up with actions, which are eventually internalised on the objects.

Expression of a thought experiment involves complex cognitive and linguistic constructions: at the linguistic level the difficulty is in expressing the operations on an abstract object (a class of objects). This ability must be operational to allow the construction of a proof. One elementary process of decontextualisation is erasing any traces of the particular in a formulation. But, as can be seen in the case of Olivier and Stéphane, such a process does not necessarily preserve relations.

The construction of a proof of the assertion below is the result of a long and deliberate search for reasons on $s(n) = n-3$.

In a polygon if you have x vertices the number of diagonals which go from one point will be x-3 because there is the point you are leaning from and the two points which join it to the polygon.

The first explanation rests on the generic example P_6: 'There are the two points where they are joined . . . that's already taken care of: there are three left, as it should be.' It is expressed in the following manner.

In a polygone if there are 6 points there will automatically be 3 diagonals for each point because in the boundary of the polygon there are two points which join it on: conclusion there are 3 which are diagonals.

But the expression of an explanation using an example is rejected as a proof 'there we've done an example . . . you mustn't use examples . . . it must be in general'.

Olivier proposes to introduce letters instead of numbers: 'you put *x* points';

In a polygone if there are x points there are automatically y diagonals for each point because in a boundary of the polygon there are two points which join it on: conclusion there are 3 which are the diagonals.

But replacing 6 by *x* and 3 by *y* fails to take into account the relation between the number of vertices and diagonals. The pupils then start looking in other directions. As Olivier suggests, 'there's not only one explanation'. The following attempt has the rhetorical style of geometry (see opposite). This explanation is, in fact, a formulation of a thought experiment.

Pupils must be able to express the properties of the objects concerned. The most common use ties the thought experiment to the generic example. It involves relying on individuals (particular cases), not as representatives of a class of objects, but as tools for linguistic expression: P_6 traced by Stéphane for his geometric proof is not a generic example of polygon. It means polygon.

(e) Calculation on statements

We return here to proofs which have nothing to do with experience. They are intellectual constructions based on more-or-less formalised,

If the points are
not aligned

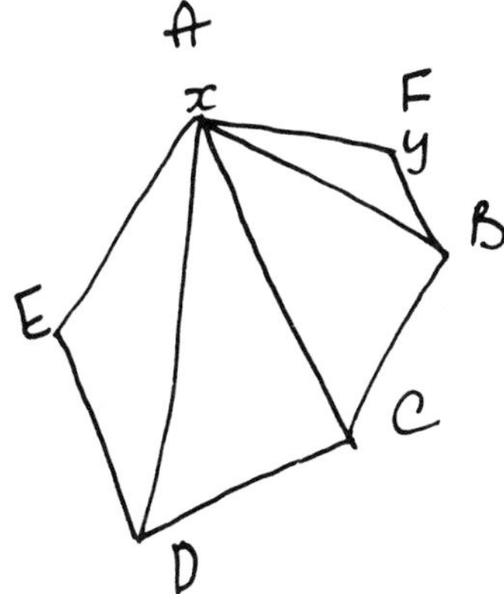

A which is adjacent to E and
F must have its diagonals
drawn to DCB which are the
points that are left.

more-or-less explicit theories of the ideas in question in the solution of the problem. These proofs appear as the result of an inferential calculation on statements. They rely on definitions or explicit characteristic properties.

We end by presenting below one of the two observed cases which reflect this type of proof, that of Antoine and Damien.

The claim asserted by the pupils is expressed in the following fashion:

To calculate the number of diagonals of a
polygon when you know the number of
vertices, you should divide the numbers
of vertices by two.

$$\frac{\text{vertices}}{2} = \text{no. of diagonals.}$$

It relies on definitions they adopted for polygon and diagonal: 'the diagonals all pass through the same centre' and 'the sides must be parallel two by two'. These fundamentals came about when the problem of the domain of validity of dividing *n* by 2 came up: 'and yeah, so, if it's not an even number, it doesn't work' (Antoine). 'It can't be an odd number since we've said that the sides must be parallel in pairs' (Damien).

Damien thinks that 'It must be possible to prove it [. . .] by saying that each side, as it shares a diagonal and that each side touches another . . . you can easily show it.'

However, having gained conviction, this proof is not made explicit.

Conclusions

We have shown that the analysis of characteristics of linguistic expression of proofs is insufficient to make clear their level. In particular, the thought experiment, because it takes place in the language of the everyday using a primitive form of 'proper names' (for example, the name of a particular polygon), can seem to bear the hallmarks of a lower level of proof: generic example. In the end, it is knowledge about the *process* of production of the proof that allows a decision to be made about its effective validity and its level.

The hypothesis we had made about a hierarchy among the types of proofs has also been supported. But an analysis of the observed processes of validation allows us to go further and assert the existence of a break between naive empiricism and the crucial experiment on the one hand, and the generic example and the thought experiment on the other. This divide can be characterised as one of passing from a truth asserted on the basis of a statement of fact to one of an assertion based on reasons. It is a question of an actual change in the way of thinking about the problem, that is to say in the way of actually conceiving of and formulating the problem of the validity of an assertion. The source of this change can reside in a desire to get rid of an uncertainty, but a frequent obstacle in its effective realisation comes from the nature of the pupils' conceptions of the mathematical ideas at stake, or even the linguistic means that they are able to construct or deploy.

We also recognise a connection between naive empiricism and the crucial experiment, when the latter is used at the end of a proof. Passage from the first to the second type of proof corresponds to taking into account the need to assure the generality of the supported conjecture. However, these two types hark back to the same empirical rationality (that is, one drawn from experience), according to which the accumulation of facts produces conviction in an assertion (Fischbein, 1982, p.17). But although naive empiricism disappears once conceptual proofs are brought into play, the crucial experiment can continue as an ultimate test to guarantee conviction, most noticeably when the assertion has been founded on a generic example. We find here an example of an operational cohabitation between empirical pragmatism and logical rationalism which Fischbein (op. cit.) suggests and which he considers as involving two types of rationality of practical validity differing in the degree to which empirical pragmatism retains its usefulness in everyday practice outside of mathematics. Thus, the crucial experiment means something different in social interaction, where it becomes a means of resolving completely a conflict over the validity of an assertion, or over the choice between two conjectures. We no longer consider it as a means of proof, except when it constitutes the refutation of an assertion. On the other hand, it brings a certain support to one of the two offered solutions, while not validating it entirely; its essential function is therefore to afford a defence against opposition.

Another connection is that between the generic example and the thought experiment. Passing from the former type of proof to the latter relies on a linguistic construction which involves a recognition and differentiation between the objects and relations involved in the solution of the problem; in other words a cognitive construction. A generic example constitutes a transitional stage in moving from pragmatic to conceptual proofs, in that it always requires a negotiation of the generic character of the example employed. This fragility encourages an evolution towards the thought experiment, which detaches itself from the particular.

Finally, we have made reference in our observations to proof, but it is only intended in principle to evoke the need to produce a 'mathematical' proof. The attempts of certain pupils to establish a proof by mathematical means runs up against the difficulty of providing them with a justification in the specific setting of the problem to be solved. The practice of proof requires reasoning and a specific state of knowledge at one and the same time. In addition, it involves a commitment to a problem-solving approach which is no longer one of effectiveness (a practical requirement) but one of rigour (a theoretical requirement).

References and further reading

Balacheff, N. (1987) 'Processus de preuve et situations de validation', *Educational Studies in Mathematics,* **18**(2), pp. 147–76.

Balacheff, N. (in press) 'Treatment of refutations: aspects of the complexity of a constructive approach to mathematics learning', in E. von Glasersfeld (ed.) *Constructivism in Mathematics Education.* Dordrecht: Reidel.

Bell, A.W. (1976) *The Learning of General Mathematical Strategies*, PhD, University of Nottingham.

Bell, A.W. (1979) 'The Learning of Process Aspects of Mathematics', *Educational Studies in Mathematics,* **10**(3), pp. 361–87.

Fischbein, E. (1982) 'Intuition and Proof', *For the Learning of Mathematics,* **3**(2), pp. 9–18.

Lakatos, I. (1976) *Proofs and Refutations.* Cambridge: Cambridge University Press.

Piaget, J. (1978) 'Recherches sur la généralisation', in *Etudes d'Epistemologie Cognitive*, vol. XXXVI. Paris: Presse Universitaire de France.

Sémadéni, (1984) 'Action Proofs in Primary Mathematics Teaching and in Teacher Training', *For the Learning of Mathematics,* **4**(1), pp. 32–4.

Vergnaud, G. (1981) 'Quelques orientations théoriques et méthodologiques des recherches françaises en didactique des mathématiques', *Actes du Vième Colloque de PME*, vol. 2, pp. 7–17, Edition IMAG, Grenoble.

Nicolas Balacheff is Maître de Conférence at the University of Grenoble, Grenoble, France.

Appendix to Chapter 24

You Can't do that!

Edited by Nicolas Balacheff

Cartoons by d'Eric Coulomb

The original dialogue is by Chris (on the left) and Bert (on the right)

Bert and Chris go back to the 7 - sided polygon
If you have a number and divide it by 2, you get 14.
Wait. there are 7 ....
Wait , let's start again. There are 7 corners by ...take away 3 to find..
So you know...you get double.
· No..no..look, 4.. 7 times 4, 28 ..divided by 2..that's 14.
That's what I said...it's 7 and 7, isn't it?
Not at all, look ...each diagonal appears twice and dividing by 2 will give each diagonal once.
That's a complicated trick. Some people won't get it.
Anyway you haven't provoved it. You're not allowed to say what you said.
Wait! Let me say something..You multiply the number of corners by 2, so if you've got 7 corners, that's 14, so you know for certain that there are 14 diagonals.
But how do you know, you haven't proved it..
People aren't stupid they count the number of corners.
But they don't want to draw it. They want to calculate it!
So what have we done? Didn't we draw something?
Yeah but they...but they don't want to draw... they want a rule, that's what they want!
Ok tell me your trick. I don't get it ... you get each diagonal once.
This trick looks fishy to me.
OK... if you've got 8 - 3, that makes 5. It'll be 5 for each corner, so ... that's 5 times 8. That's 40, divided by 2, that's 20.
That'll be 20. Wait. Let's see if it really is.
'Cos 8 and 8 isn't 20 .. but it works with 7.
Yeah but .. maybe it's you .. maybe it's luck that we started with 7 and it worked ... 7 and 7 ... 14, so ...
So that's not it. It isn't the right way.
Oh! You are stupid!

Come on take a polygon with 7 sides...uhh...each corner has got two neighbours .. and it's got....5 diagonals.
Hey..wait. Let's see. make one here...make one..
Yes you do...to calculate it.
No. You don't need to draw it
Bert draws all the diagonals from one vertex of the polygon that Chris has just drawn.
Only 4 diagonals! No...no...We forgot itself! 7 - 2 + itself. You can't draw a diagonal to itself!
So that's it..yeah!
Oh..no..no..do...you have to do the same for each corner
OK..wait..wait. We'd better check out what you said..yeah..'cos
Yeah..wait.. I'll explain.
Yeah...let's multiply what we got by the number of points, that will be the same thing as starting from each corner. That's it...yeah.
Given the number of corners in a polygon, starting from each point, the number of corners - (its 2 neighbours plus itself). Multiply what you get by the number of corners.
So for 7 you get...you get 4...4 times 7! 'Cos there are 7 corners.
Yeah..so we're going to count them.
Uhhhh!
No! It isn't right. It was OK before.....but....since there are some that....some like AF and FA....Noooooo!
....Yeah...got it...... think I've got it...ummm....take away the number of corners from what you get...'cos...
'cos the diagonal AF is...it's the diagonal FA...BF....no it doesn't work....uhhh.

Chris counts again the diagonals of a seven-sided polygon
14!
So that's 7 and 7 ...14!
That'll do it...that's the number of sides of the polygon...double...go on..do it with 8 sides..you'll see.
Yeah, sure ..that'll be 16.
But we can't say that.. we haven't proved it we can't be sure it's right.
What...prove it all over again.
How do you know it's double.
Inside the brackets...if this thing has 7 corners..there's no need to prove it. See you don't need to ..you put..look.
Why double?...how's that?...you don't know what you're talking about.
Yeah I do know...that's it...that's what we're not allowed to put.
I know...I think I've got it. I think I've got it. Wait...give me the pen ....multiply...multiply by each corner to get ...wait .. you have to multiply what's here by the number of corners.
Oh so you're saying some could get counted 3 times.
But ...but ... there are the diagonals that get ... that would be counted twice ... and ... No! Every diagonal gets counted twice.
That's right!
No .. no not at all ...not at all.. AF has only been counted twice ... when you draw all the diagonals through A and all the diagonals through F .. and through B, it's all the same thing ..
OK, so it's twice then .. count them twice .. so that's it.
It's like dividing by 2.
Knowing the number of corners in a polygon, from each corner there will be, the number of corners - (it's neighbour + itself). We have to multiply what we found by the number of corners (there are the same number of diagonals for each corner). BUT each diagonal has been counted twice. The number of diagonals must be divided by 2 to get each diagonal only once.

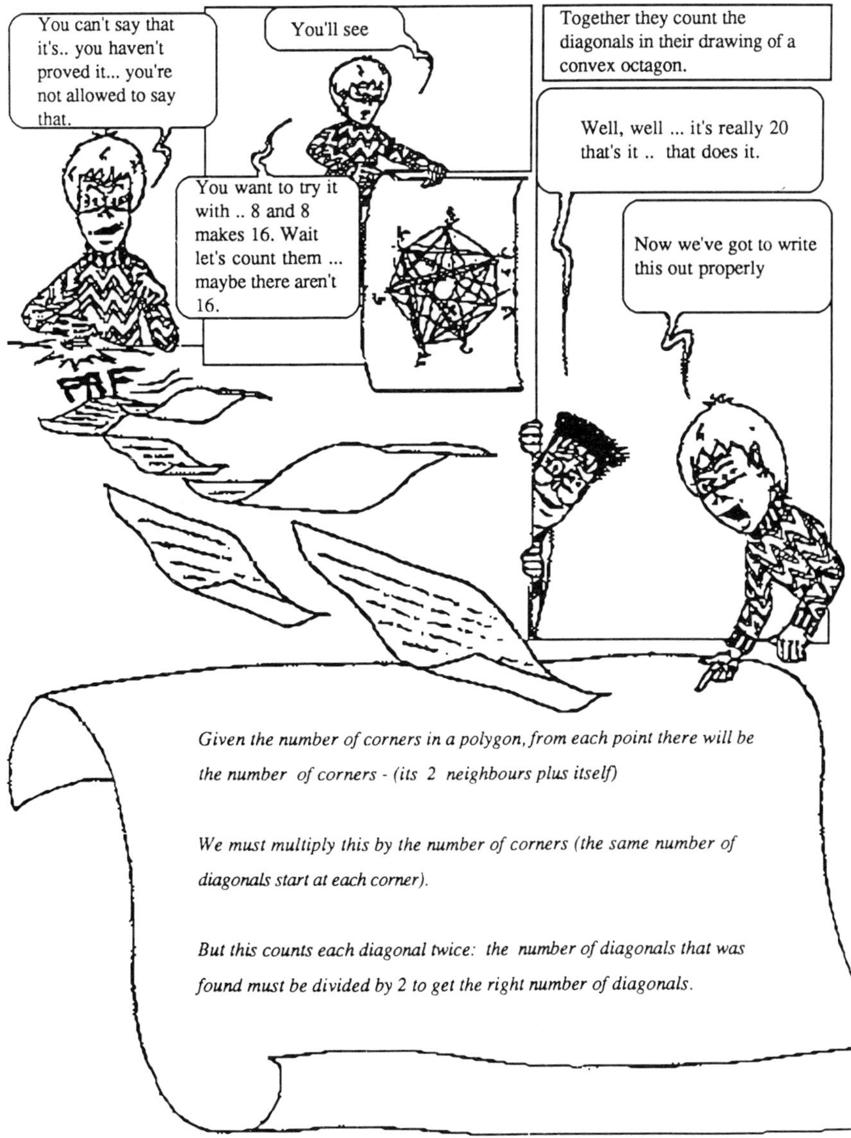

(A number of people worked on translating this cartoon: see the Acknowledgments p. ix for details.)

SECTION IV

Mathematical Education Issues

Introduction

There is no clear divide between mathematical and mathematical education issues, as many of these articles bear witness. For instance, games are often seen as an enjoyable way of practising and consolidating mathematical skills and concepts. Janet Ainley examines the widespread use of games in the teaching of mathematics and offers a rationale for their justification in terms of what mathematics is, exploring the potential of games as contexts for using mathematical thinking processes and for meaningful problem solving. With a move away from a purely content description of mathematics, other ways need to be developed for talking about what it means to do mathematics. Eric Love's piece provides a thorough analysis of the variety of ways which have been produced for describing mathematical activity, and hence its evaluation.

There has been considerable recent discussion about the roles and dissemination of the burgeoning research work in mathematics education. In particular, a number of groups are working at the notion of 'teacher *as* researcher'. 'Should teachers be interested in research in mathematical education?' is the challenging question posed by Rosalinde Scott-Hodgetts, which she explores by means of examples of research, together with an analysis of a few of the intents of the research enterprise and the sometimes conflicting perceptions and values of researchers and teachers.

Tom Cooney's article provides an example of recent research about teachers and the various ways in which they make classroom decisions. It emphasises the importance of an overt awareness of decision making in contributing to successful teaching. One example of how an apparently abstract theory can unify and illuminate a number of apparently disparate issues is provided by Barbara Jaworski's article on constructivism. In it, she examines some current concerns about the mathematics classroom and suggests that a constructivist philosophy can provide insight into their common causes.

John Mason chooses the recently re-emerging topic of mathematical imagery and describes how it can be drawn on and worked on (by means of specific exercises) in mathematics classes to aid mathematical understanding. The final two pieces, by David Wheeler and Dick Tahta, inform each other (and us!) about certain aspects of the conduct of and justification for 'investigations'. Each is written by a sometime editor of *Mathematics Teaching*, house journal of the Association of Teachers of Mathematics, which is widely regarded as having been extremely influential in the promulgation of pupils' own investigative mathematical activity in Great Britain. Both take a sharp look at the question of the justification for such activity, and Dick Tahta in particular argues keenly for such activities to be closely linked to classical mathematical content. His article provides an appropriate concluding piece in that it shows how inextricably linked are questions about mathematics, its teaching and its learning.

25

Playing games and real mathematics

Janet Ainley

Playing games in mathematics classrooms was considered sufficiently important for *Mathematics in School* to have devoted an entire issue to games (Volume 15, No. 1, January 1986). Most articles are concerned with describing particular games, and pupils' reactions to them; indeed most literature on games seems to be of this kind. However, a few authors do attempt to discuss the rationale for including games in the mathematics curriculum. As so little has been written in this area, it seems sensible to focus initially on the lead article in this collection, which attempts to provide such a justification.

In 'Games. A rationale for their use in the teaching of mathematics in school', Paul Ernest (1986) reviews some research into the use of games, and uses the results to construct an argument for the effectiveness of games as a vehicle for teaching mathematics. Ernest claims that 'games teach mathematics effectively' in four ways; by providing reinforcement and practice skills, by providing motivation, by helping the acquisition and development of concepts, and by developing problem-solving strategies. The first two of these seem unequivocal: games can provide motivation for many children. Within a game, routine calculations are often repeated many times, and great facility with numbers can be acquired in this way, as most darts players demonstrate.

The second two claims seem less well-founded. Ernest supports them by referring to research involving particular games which were designed to force awareness of specific concepts or the use of certain strategies. Many games which have an ostensible mathematical content do not contain either of these features, and so it would be misleading to make these claims for *all* mathematical games. Ernest ends with the following claim:

> The evidence reviewed . . . suggests that games are an effective way of teaching mathematics, both in terms of attaining mathematical objectives and in terms of motivating students to learn.
>
> The evidence strongly suggests that if games are to contribute to the effective teaching of mathematics they must be fully incorporated into the mathematics curriculum. During the teaching of a specific topic, or directed at a particular objective, games should be
>
> 1 selected on the basis of the desired objectives
> 2 incorporated into the teaching programme.

As well as questioning the notion that games can *teach* mathematics, I should like in this article to suggest that Ernest's claims for the value

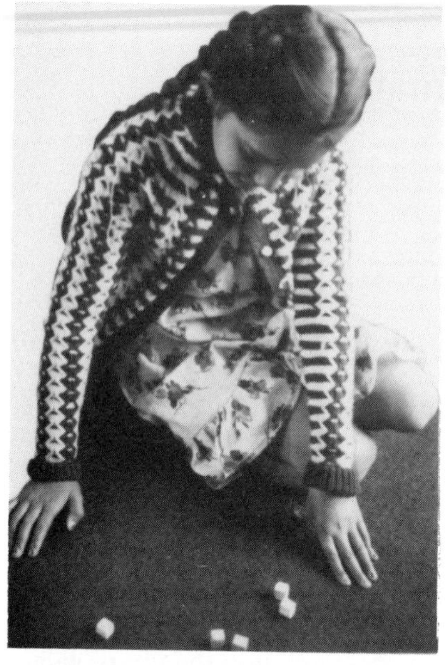

of games overlook some of the most important aspects of mathematical games, ones which not only enable children to *learn* mathematics, but also provide rare opportunities for children to *do* real mathematics in the classroom.

What are mathematical games?

Many games found in classrooms, and outside them, may appear to have mathematical content. Indeed, almost all organised games contain some element of scoring, which involves at least some counting. Games such as Monopoly and Scrabble involve making decisions about how to maximise scores, and this in turn requires calculation, but these are not essentially mathematical games. Their design is not based on a mathematical structure, and the calculation of scores is not the most important aspect.

Enthusiasts often claim that games of strategy such as chess, bridge and backgammon encourage mathematical thinking, despite their lack of obvious mathematical content. Playing such games may indeed involve the use of mathematical processes, particularly when they are played at a high level, but these games too are designed on essentially arbitrary rules rather than on a mathematical structure.

Another category of apparently mathematical games are those in which a winning move depends on getting a piece of mathematics 'right', but in which the rewards are unconnected with the mathematics. Perhaps the most obvious examples of these are computer games in which answering the 'sum' correctly allows the player to drop a bomb or fire a missile. Many non-computer games designed for practising basic computational skills also involve arbitrary, though perhaps more socially acceptable rewards. Some examples of this type of game can be found in *40 Maths Games to Make and Play* (Williams and Somerwill, 1982). 'Save the Wildlife' is typical of these; players throw two dice, and multiply the resulting numbers to decide which of the wild animals illustrated (and numbered) on a map of the world they are able to 'save'. Although mathematics is a central feature of games like this one, some external arbiter (human or electronic) is needed to judge whether the response is 'right or wrong'; there is nothing in the structure of the game to enable the player to decide if she is right, or to help her correct a mistake.

The most effective mathematical games are those in which the structure and rules of the game are based on mathematical ideas, and where winning the game is directly related to understanding this mathematics. These games, in contrast to many of the games already mentioned, are often very simple. The equipment needed to play them is minimal, as are the rules which must be learned, and yet these games are very engaging and satisfying to play. Two widely-known examples of such games are Fizz-Buzz, a verbal game based on counting and multiplication tables, and Nim, which has many versions, all of which depend on taking counters away from a given starting number of, or arrangement of counters, and forcing your opponent to remove the last counter. Both these games illustrate two important features of true mathematical games: there is a structure within the game which makes checking and correcting easy (the use of counters in Nim and the order of the players themselves in Fizz-Buzz), and the games are adaptable. Both games provide a basic structure within which details, such as the numbers used, can be changed to make the game simpler or more challenging.

A large number of games designed to contain all these features of true mathematical games are included in the materials produced by the Primary Mathematics Project (Skemp, 1988). These games are integrated into a mathematics programme for primary schools which is based entirely on practical activities, and each focuses on a particular mathematical idea. Many of the games use existing game structures, adapted to embody these ideas. Below are just two examples: the first game is based on number bonds to ten, and the second on multiples.

Crossing

This game is for 2 or 3 players. It uses the board illustrated overleaf. Each player has 3 counters, and chooses three 'lanes' on the board in which they are to move. A 1–6 die is used.

F I N I S H								
10	10	10	10	10	10	10	10	10
9	9	9	9	9	9	9	9	9
8	8	8	8	8	8	8	8	8
7	7	7	7	7	7	7	7	7
6	6	6	6	6	6	6	6	6
5	5	5	5	5	5	5	5	5
4	4	4	4	4	4	4	4	4
3	3	3	3	3	3	3	3	3
2	2	2	2	2	2	2	2	2
1	1	1	1	1	1	1	1	1
S T A R T								

The object of the game is to move all 3 of your counters to the finish. When a player throws the die, she may move any of her counters forward by that number of squares. The shaded squares are 'no parking' zones; if a counter lands on one of these at the end of a move, the counter must be returned to the start. The exact number must be thrown for each counter to land on finish.

Multiples Rummy
This is a card game for 3, 4 or 5 players. They play with a double pack of number cards 2–30. Each player is dealt 5 cards, and the remaining pack is placed face down, with the top card turned up.

Players may put down any three cards which are all multiples of the same number. Play proceeds as in rummy; each player in turn may pick up either the face-up card, or the top card face down, puts down any trios they can make, and discards one card onto the face-up pile. The first player to get rid of all her cards wins that round, and scores 0. Other players score the total of the cards left in their hands. The one with the lowest score after several rounds wins.

What games can and cannot offer

Whatever the nature of the games, Ernest's phrase 'games *teach* mathematics' seems to be misleading; at most, games can help children to learn mathematics. This is not simply a linguistic quibble. If teachers use games in the hope that *the games* will teach their pupils particular pieces of mathematics, they will be sadly disappointed. Children will certainly learn from playing games, but *what* they learn will vary enormously, just as what children learn when working from a textbook varies. A well-designed game may create a good environment for learning some mathematics, but it will not ensure that the children learn the mathematics, and more importantly it will not replace the teacher. The teacher's role in stimulating mathematical learning during the playing of a game, and monitoring the learning which is going on, is vital.

In describing some studies of the effects of including games in the mathematics curriculum, Ernest claims:

> It is quite likely that this success is related to the positive effect of games on motivation and attitude reported in some of the studies.

Although it is undeniable that games can provide motivation, focusing heavily on this feature may in the long term have detrimental effects on children's attitudes to mathematics. Games are often offered as a reward for those who have finished their 'work'; the hidden messages are clearly that real mathematics cannot be fun, and that games are not difficult 'work'. Incidentally, this also results in those pupils who least need extra motivation getting most of it, and vice versa.

Games may also be seen as sugaring the bitter pill of learning, by creating situations in which children repeatedly practise skills which would seem tedious if presented as paper-and-pencil exercises. It is true that many children will gain increased fluency with number in this way. When children play such games their response is often comments like, 'That was great! We didn't do any maths, we just played games'. In the short term, this may be rewarding for the teacher, who knows that they *were*, in fact, doing some mathematics. In the long term, however, we seem to be tricking pupils into doing mathematics despite themselves, and if we never make it explicit that playing the games *is* doing mathematics (or at least as much 'doing mathematics' as much of what goes on in classrooms), we may be denying them the opportunity to see that real mathematics can also be fun. Perhaps more importantly, we may be denying pupils the opportunity to realise that *they* are capable of doing real mathematics.

Real mathematics

Real mathematics here means mathematics which is important and meaningful to children, *and* doing what real mathematicians do, using mathematical processes and thinking in a mathematical way. These two meanings are related since if children are thinking mathematically then the mathematics that they tackle is more likely to become important to them personally. Equally, if children engage in problems and activities which are important for them, they are more likely to see the value of mathematical processes. In the rest of this article, I aim to show how mathematical games can enrich the curriculum by providing children with opportunities to experience mathematics which is real in both these senses.

Reading, writing and mathematics form a large part of the curriculum for children in the early years of schooling. When children learn to read, they can straight away begin to use reading in the same way, and for the same purposes, that adults do; they can read for pleasure, to get information, etc., and there is a wide range of children's books and comics designed for them to do just that. The same is true to some extent of writing; children can write for their own pleasure, to communicate with others, to label their possessions, etc. Reading and writing are important and useful for children independently of their school work.

When children learn mathematics, however, there is very little that they can do with it, except to complete exercises set by someone else. Certainly most children will have a few everyday contexts in which they may use some mathematics – spending pocket money, following a knitting pattern, compiling football league tables – but these are fairly few, and in general the mathematical content is at a low level. Some children will investigate bits of mathematics simply for the pleasure of doing it, but there is very little that compares with comics. Many commercial mathematics schemes attempt to bring some 'realism' into the curriculum by including everyday problems which mathematics can help to solve, such as carpeting a room or paving the area around a swimming pool, but in general these are everyday problems for adults, and not for children.

Mathematical games are one way of providing the equivalent of children's books and comics; within a game there is a context for using some mathematics that you have learned, and that context is real for children because they can engage with it and the outcome matters to them. This has very little to do with the reality of everyday life. Some games may model everyday situations, but the appeal of adventure games such as Dungeons and Dragons, and its computer counterparts like *L* indicates that fantasy games can be equally engaging.

Prediction

In adult life perhaps the most common use of mathematics is for making predictions. The predictions may range from the apparently trivial ('If I buy those new shoes, I won't have enough left for the phone bill'; 'If I leave at 2.15, I'll have enough time to go to the bank before I catch the train') to very detailed technical calculations used by engineers and scientists. What they have in common is that people are using some mathematical knowledge to help them predict the outcome of events. Getting the prediction wrong may have more or less serious consequences, depending on the context, but that is exactly what makes getting such predictions right satisfying. It gives you control over your environment. However, since wrong predictions about things that matter will inevitably have some unwelcome consequences, children are rarely given genuine opportunities to use their mathematics in this way.

Within a mathematical game, many situations will occur where making predictions (based on mathematical knowledge) is clearly a valuable strategy. Getting the prediction right gives the same feeling of satisfaction and control, but making a wrong prediction may mean that you lose the game. What hangs on the accuracy of your prediction is important, but not dangerous.

In some games you may make a prediction about the consequences of a particular move simply in order to decide whether to go or not; it may be better to miss a turn than to make a move which will ultimately make your position worse. Such a position could easily arise in Crossing. Adding the simple rule that once a counter is touched it must be moved transforms even simple board games into games of prediction. Equivalent rules may be devised to have the same effect on card games, and in verbal games a player may be committed to standing by the first thing she says. In Crossing and in Multiples Rummy there may be several possible moves open, and several predictions may be necessary to decide which is 'the best'.

Conjecturing

Games like these stimulate conjecturing, that is, trying out an idea and seeing the consequences in a situation where it is easy to change to a different strategy if the first is unproductive. In most games, it is only ever possible to make partial conjectures about the effects of any one move, since the situation for your next move is unknown. Your opponent's move may have an effect on your position, or there may be a random element, such as the throw of a die or the turn of a card. In other situations, children are often unwilling to try out ideas unless they are sure that they are correct, and so do not naturally make conjectures. They may associate *modifying* a conjecture with admitting to having made a mistake. Within a game, conjecturing is both natural and safe; games can provide opportunities to talk explicitly about the process of conjecturing.

The ever-changing situations, which are what make games interesting, also have a potentially powerful effect on children's learning. Skemp (1979) uses the term 'intelligent learning', as opposed to 'rote' or 'memory learning', to distinguish learning which is based on relational understanding. Because rote learning may initially produce the best results (i.e. red ticks and adult approval) for the minimum effort, many children rely on trying to learn mathematics 'off by heart'. Playing mathematical games discourages rote learning, since you never know in advance what the situation will be when you take your turn. Even if there is no random element in the game, the moves made by other players create a wide variety of situations, and it would be impossible to learn by rote the best move for each situation which may occur. Children who learn some of their mathematics by playing games will soon experience the benefits of intelligent learning and relational understanding.

Generalising

Since it is not feasible to memorise the best moves for all possible situations in a game, it is a natural strategy to begin to devise *generalised* strategies for playing a particular game. If the game has rules which reflect a mathematical structure, these strategies may be in the form of mathematical generalisations. In Crossing, there is no obvious strategy which is likely to improve your chances of winning, but some children try out different possibilities. One group of six year olds decided that a good strategy might be to try to get one counter to the finish before moving any of the others. This led one of them to make another kind of generalisation. Two of the children threw 4 on their first turn, and the third, Claire, threw 3. When one of the others threw 6 on the next turn, and got one counter home, Claire turned to the teacher and asked 'Is there a seven on that dice?' Claire seemed to have moved away from focusing on the numbers which were actually thrown, to looking for number bonds to ten to get home in two moves.

In other games which have rules that reflect a mathematical structure, these strategies may be in the form of mathematical generalisations. For example, in Multiples Rummy players often develop general strategies about cards which are good to keep, and those which you should always discard. Obviously, it is a good strategy to get rid of high numbers, because of the scoring, but some high numbers are also multiples of several different numbers, and so are useful in making up trios. One group of top juniors used the term 'nasty numbers' for the large primes which always end up on the discard pile.

Generalising is an important process in real mathematics, and it is one which often seems to occur spontaneously when children are playing games, even in games which have little or no mathematical content. This may provide a context in which the process of generalising could be discussed explicitly.

Checking and justifying

Another important aspect of what real mathematicians do is checking their own conjectures, and justifying them to colleagues. Within the normal classroom situation, there are few opportunities and little incentive for children to do this, if they know that ultimately their work will be assessed by their teacher. Typically, teachers encourage children to check their own results, but young children find this difficult to do, and can often see little point in doing it. In the context of a game, there is a clear purpose for checking your own conjectures; once a move has been made, it cannot be undone and may have unwelcome consequences. This is another situation in which a teacher may want to intervene explicitly to talk about the value of a mathematical process.

Since cheating is something that most children are very conscious of, there is also a strong incentive for players to check each other's mathematics, challenging moves which they think are unjustified. If this aspect of playing games is encouraged, games can provide a meaningful context for discussion about mathematics, where clear communication has a real pay-off. Many games can be played at varying levels of sophistication, according to the expertise of the players, even without making changes in the rules. The random element in dice and card games also works as an equalising factor, and these two features mean that it is often possible for children of differing ages and abilities to play against each other. This is clearly demonstrated in games such as Monopoly and Scrabble, which all members of a family might play together. In the classroom, encouraging mixed-ability groups to play games together can have organisational and social advantages as well as educational ones.

Games and competition

An understandable worry about including games in mathematics, or in any other subject, is that this may introduce an added element of competition into the classroom. The extent to which school is seen as a competitive environment varies enormously both among schools and among individual children, though sadly the current political climate seems likely to favour competition rather than co-operation in the future. Teachers who work hard to achieve a co-operative atmosphere in their classrooms may feel that the introduction of games would be counter-productive.

There is a distinction, which is perhaps important here, between games in which you win simply by your own skill and luck, and those in which you can also increase your chances of winning by making moves which hinder your opponent. This is nicely illustrated in some of the most popular televised sports. Golf and darts both rely entirely on the individual skills of players. A player cannot have any effect, except a psychological one, on her opponent's performance. In contrast, a snooker player wins by a combination of skill at potting balls and skill at creating difficult situations for her opponent. Tennis and football rely entirely on the interaction of the players. Of the mathematical games already discussed, Crossing is like golf, Multiples Rummy is more like snooker, though novices may play *without* blocking tactics, and Nim is more like tennis. Using only games which do not involve interaction between players may avoid some of the less desirable aspects of competition, though these games often lack the opportunities for developing generalised strategies.

There are also games which can be played co-operatively; Fizz-Buzz is an obvious example. However, my own experience when working with the Primary Mathematics Project was that the majority of *children* are happy to play co-operatively, regardless of the game they are playing. In the true Olympic tradition, winning seemed less important to them than taking part, and very little encouragement from the teacher was needed for them to help players who were struggling. This co-operative atmosphere within games can also be encouraged by changing them into games for teams rather than individuals. Sharing ideas with colleagues is an important part of doing real mathematics.

What games can offer teachers

Most of this article has been about what mathematical games have to offer children, and little reference has been made to teachers. Groups of children playing games in mathematical lessons have one obvious practical advantage for their teacher: those groups will need only a small amount of her attention, and so there is more time to spend with the rest of the class. However valuable this is, it would be a pity if the teacher *never* spent time joining in with games, or even just watching what is going on, since she would then miss a rare opportunity to observe her pupils doing real mathematics. The difficulty of making judgements about children's understanding from the results of written (and even oral) tests is well researched. In contrast to this, when children are playing games their thinking is much more transparent. Their actions reveal much about their thinking strategies. For example, when watching a group playing Crossing it becomes clear which children are using counting on, and which are using known number facts, to predict the effect of a particular move. Even if the rules prohibit moving the counter, fingers and eyes move.

Opportunities for careful observation do not only occur in games which involve moving counters: in the context of playing any mathematical game, it is easy and natural for a teacher to question children about their thinking ('Why did you choose that move?', 'Could you have played a different card?', 'Do you agree that the move is allowed?'), without all the problems of a more obvious assessment. If we really want to know about chiidren's attainment in mathematics, we need to watch them doing some real mathematics: we may be surprised at what we see.

References

Ernest, P. (1986) 'Games. A Rationale for their Use in the Teaching of Mathematics in School', *Mathematics in School*, **15**(1), pp. 2–5.

Skemp, R. R. (1979) *Intelligence, Learning, and Action*. Chichester: Wiley.

Skemp, R. R. (1988) *Structured Activities for Primary Mathematics*. London: Routledge.

Williams, M. and Somerwill, H. (1982) *40 Maths Games to Make and Play*. London: Macmillan.

Janet Ainley is Lecturer in Mathematics Education at the University of Warwick.

26

Evaluating mathematical activity

Eric Love

Mathematical activity

In the beginning it was easy. There were interesting, loosely defined problems: the children worked at them and did mathematics – or, as was said, engaged in mathematical activity. At that time it was a revelation to many teachers that they could get pupils to explore their own mathematics. Knowledge of teaching in this way became more widespread mainly through college teacher training and PGCE courses, and, for practising teachers, mostly by personal contacts from meetings, or working groups within ATM.

In contrast to the tasks set by the teacher – doing exercises, learning definitions, following worked examples – in mathematical activity the thinking, decisions, projects undertaken were under the control of the learner. It was the learner's activity.

As well as having pupils working at their own mathematics, the teachers were also reacting against the notion that problems must be well-defined in a narrow sense: whether the 'word problems' of junior and lower secondary texts, or the scholarship problems for potential Oxbridge candidates. Children were given 'starting points', or worked at 'problem-situations', or 'investigated such-and-such'. Here, defining the problem that they were to work on was seen as essential if they were to make the problem their own. The teachers viewed mathematics as a field for enquiry, rather than a pre-existing subject to be learned.

The work of children was seen as paralleling that of professional mathematicians. Those creators were attempting to solve problems, and they needed not merely a grasp of previously ready-made results and ideas, but also the ability to create classifications and relationships, and to test and criticise these both internally and against other social constructions. There was a recognition that mathematical problem solving and thinking required similar abilities to those needed for creating mathematics.

The teacher's job was now that of providing children with situations – starting points – intended to initiate constructive activity. When they were engaged upon such activity – which would involve them in setting their own goals, making decisions about the course of the work, and carrying out the work – the teacher would, in the words of Madeleine Goutard, 'help the pupils follow their own intentions through, strengthen their own intuitions and carry their own creations to a higher level' (Goutard, 1968).

This Edenic vision could not last long before a host of questions concerning the relationship between such activity and more conventional mathematics teaching and learning arose.

- Why did we want children to undertake it: was it to foster the development of different kinds of mathematical thinking from those conventionally taught?
- In these mathematical activities, how could we describe the mathematics involved?
- If these activities involved important aspects of mathematics, could the activity itself be used as a means of assessing the children's grasp of this mathematics?
- What kinds of 'problem-situations' helped to promote mathematical activity? Did it matter what problem the activity started from?
- Could mathematical activity be taught? What would the teacher have to do?
- Was it possible for activity of this kind to give rise to 'ready-made' results and insights; could it be used to help children learn pre-existing results?
- How important was the mathematical content of the activities; were polyominoes as good as Pythagoras for this purpose?
- How could we decide on the value of the activity? Was this piece of work 'better' than that or, if that soon became a non-question, in what ways did these pieces differ? Are these two more alike than those?

The thinking about these questions – and the partial answers provided – then started to interact with the activities themselves. From some starting point the children would 'almost certainly' encounter particular ideas or results while investigating; from some other they would gain experience in classifying, or in systematically considering all cases. In a desire to include this valuable activity in the examination-dominated system, assessment schemes for children's activity were produced; some thought there were investigating skills that might be taught. Since such activity took time, the idea of an extended piece of mathematical work – an investigation – was born.

In the early writings on mathematical activity, there is no mention of 'investigation' in the sense of 'doing an investigation'. It is interesting to see this construction develop from descriptions of pupils as 'investigating such-and-such', or 'carrying out an investigation into such-and-such', no doubt originally as a shorthand, but soon taking on a life of its own. The path to formalisation had begun.

In the last decade 'investigations' have become institutionalised – as part of formal requirements for assessment of courses, for example, in the Mathematical Association Diploma, the Open University Mathematics Foundation Course, and in GCSE. They also appear in the official recommendations of Cockcroft and HMI.

Such a development is a typical one in education – the often commented upon way in which originally liberating ways of working become formalised and codified, losing their purpose as they become adapted for different ends or by those who have no personal commitment to the underlying intentions.

Describing mathematical activity

Once we start to think about the place of mathematical activity in the mathematics curriculum, it becomes necessary to distinguish it from other mathematical work and to say what is of value in it. The problem of evaluating mathematical investigations by children is the problem of finding ways of describing what they have done. The difficulty of this is indicated by some observations.

(a) Starting points are so diverse that investigations arising from different ones – which may involve, for example, generalising number patterns; spatial organisation; analysis of games of strategy – seem to have little in common. Even in problems that appear to be comparable – say, different ones involving generalising number patterns from geometrical configurations – the contexts are likely to give rise to different activity.
(b) We cannot describe the activity solely by giving the starting point. Even from the same point, different children, or the same child at different ages, or with different teachers, may do very different things. Thus they may turn what seemed to be a fairly well-defined numerical investigation into one involving geometrical shapes.
(c) It is not adequate – or perhaps even possible – to list what the children have done in their investigation ('She found the number chains 1–18'). These descriptions will be too particular to define the activity. From the same starting point, different problems will be created and other paths might have been chosen. It is the essence of mathematical activity that learners will have control and so take different directions.
(d) It is inappropriate to describe activity in terms of how far the children utilise 'ready-made' mathematics – mathematics that they have worked at previously. Usually the mathematics in such activity is at a much lower level than that which they are able to work at directly in other lessons. Thus sixteen year olds hardly ever use algebraic manipulation, nor do degree students use differential equations. The mathematical aspects of the activity are not captured in this way.
(e) We cannot describe the activity by the quality of the results produced: even with research mathematicians what seem plausible lines of attack, pursued effectively, may still not produce anything worthwhile. It is not reasonable to expect our pupils to be innovative mathematicians.

These observations are warnings about the traps of producing descriptions that are either too general or too specialised. Some writers have, however, attempted to describe mathematical activity in a general way that is also sufficiently detailed to distinguish different aspects of activity. The most important such classifications are in terms of:

- content/process (Bell)
- strategies (Polya, Schoenfeld)
- mathematisation (Wheeler)
- phases of investigation (Polya, Mason)

I shall give a brief summary of these before outlining some of the problems in seeing them as descriptions of mathematical activity.

Content and process

Here mathematics is seen as having two aspects to it: 'content' (the pre-existing conceptual structures), and 'process' (the activity of making mathematics). Alan Bell has made the following distinction:

> Content represents particular ideas and skills like rectangles, highest common factor, solution of equations. On the other side there is the mathematical process, or mathematical activity, that deserves its own syllabus to go alongside a syllabus of mathematical ideas; I would express it as consisting of abstraction, representation, generalisation and proof. (Bell, 1982)

Bell amplifies these categories, including more detail, and a course for lower secondary pupils based upon these ideas, *Journey into Maths* (Bell *et al.*, 1978–9), gives lists of both content and process objectives for each topic. Many of the process objectives are similar to the Polya strategies (see below).

Strategies

George Polya (1945), and others acting on his inspiration, have identified strategies – Polya calls them *heuristics* – that are used by mathematical problem solvers. The strategies may have very different levels of generality, ranging from:

> Draw a diagram.
> Examine special cases.
> Introduce notation.

to the more specific:

> Noticing quantities that increase or decrease together.
> Listing all possible cases.

The idea of 'strategies' bears an uneasy relationship to that of 'skills'. The Cockcroft Report (DES, 1982, p. 71) describes 'general strategies' as 'procedures which guide the choice of which skills to use or what knowledge to draw upon'. The word 'skill' itself is used in a much more restricted sense than strategy:

> Skills include not only the use of the number facts and the standard computational procedures of arithmetic and algebra, but also, any well-established procedures which it is possible to carry out by the use of a routine. They need not only to be understood and embedded in the conceptual structure but also

to be brought up to the level of immediate recall or fluency of performance by regular practise.

This intended distinction creates its own problems, as we shall see.

Mathematisation

David Wheeler suggests that mathematical activity – which he sees as the essence of mathematics – should be understood 'not by its theorems, models or algorithms, but by its way of thinking, a mode of mental activity that has yielded a variety of objectifications that we call mathematics' (Wheeler, 1982). Thinking in this way – mathematising – is engaging in 'the process by which mathematics is brought into being'. Wheeler writes of it:

> Although mathematization must be presumed present in all cases of 'doing' mathematics or 'thinking' mathematically, it can be detected most easily in situations where something not obviously mathematical is being converted into something that most obviously is. We may think of a young child playing with blocks, and using them to express awareness of symmetry, of an older child experimenting with a geoboard and becoming interested in the relationship between the areas of the triangles he can make, an adult noticing a building under construction and asking himself questions about the design, etc.
>
> [Here] we notice that mathematization has taken place by the signs of organisation, of form, of additional structure, given to a situation.

Because of the difficulty in pinning down mathematisation, Wheeler feels he can only offer 'clues as to its presence', and gives some of these as 'structuration', 'dependence', 'generating equivalence through transformations'. The full list is given in Appendix A. Other authors (for example, Mason *et al.*, 1984) would include specialising, generalising, conjecturing, convincing, as mathematical activities under the general heading of mathematisation.

Phases of investigation

Mathematical activity has also been characterised in terms of the stages of solving mathematical problems, and the mental states associated with these. Again, Polya (1945) was one of the earliest to try delineating these stages. He describes them:

> understanding the problem
> devising a plan
> carrying out a plan
> looking back

Others use different words ('Entry, Attack, Review' or 'Problem Formulation, Implementation, Evaluation, Conclusion'), but the idea is the same. This process is often described as being cyclic. Diagrams illustrating this frequently show a loop indicating an iterative procedure. The one overleaf is from Davis and Hersh (1981):

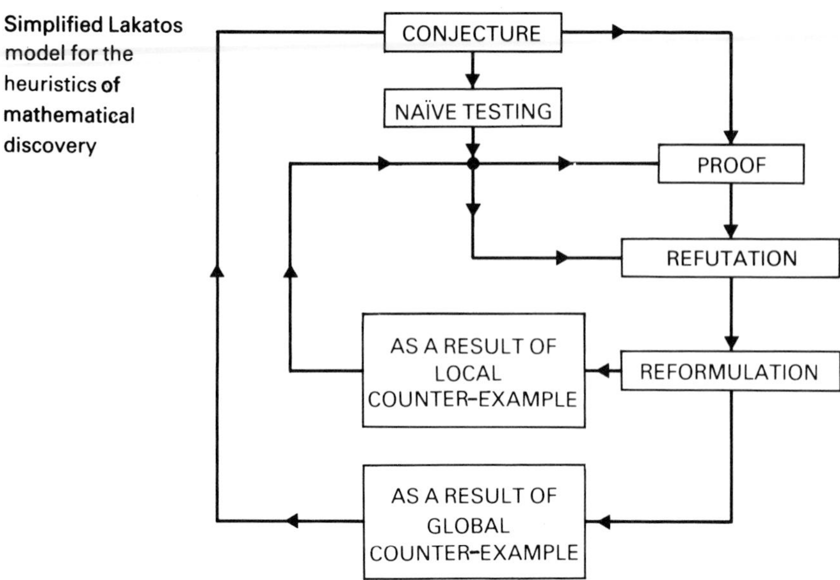

A list of 4 or 5 stages does not provide much of a basis for describing activity: such lists are often amplified by combining them with a list of strategies that can be found in the different stages. For example, the stage of problem formulation could be associated with these strategies:

identifying factors
generating variables
selecting variables
formulating sub-problems
representing through diagrams.

The trouble with such lists is their detail. They help in identifying aspects, but their particularity fails to help us to decide whether some aspect that is not included in the list is mathematising or not.

In another interesting attempt to broaden the idea of phases, John Mason and others have attempted to associate emotional states with these phases:

> getting started, getting involved, mulling, keeping going, insight, being sceptical. (Mason *et al.*, 1984)

While this does suggest that there are wider things at stake, it is still very closely tied to the phases, and subject to the determinism those categories seem to instigate. What happens is that the aspects start out as being descriptions, but become prescriptive – they are things that *must* happen in each activity.

Development of the descriptions

While the previous descriptions have arisen from educators thinking about mathematical activity, there has been a more practical development.

Groups of teachers faced with the problem of assessing the reports written by pupils after carrying out an investigation have needed to characterise them. Their descriptions typically include an amalgam of several of the aspects outlined above, organised into a few broad categories, each with more detail within:

> problem formulating, strategies used, mathematical argument, evaluation, communication.

These are in part phases, and in part kinds of mathematical thinking.

Historically, the first classification of this kind was produced by the ATM N and F study (ATM, *Mathematics for Sixth Formers,* 1977), and subsequently adapted by Wyndham School, Cumbria, for an O level which included investigative work. More recently, other versions have been widely disseminated and adopted (for example, the TEAM materials, 1985, and the Draft Grade Related Criteria for Mathematics, SEC, 1985 an extract from which is shown below).

The pupil at grade F will be able to	**The pupil at grade C will, in addition, be able to**
decide the relationship to be established or the features to be investigated;	
use drawings and sketches to clarify a situation;	
decide on the steps to be carried out and the order in which to carry them out;	adopt a systematic approach, for example by ordering and categorising information, deciding what has to be measured, selecting appropriate variables;
decide the information to be obtained and use data from available sources, collecting it or generating it as appropriate;	
	identify important variables or features which can be ignored;
explore a situation by experiment, trial and error or testing of a special case;	carry out trial and error methods in a systematic way or enumerate all possible cases;
recognise, continue and extend patterns.	make a conjecture about a pattern or relationship or postulate a general rule and attempt to verify;
	attempt to generalise from experience of two or three examples or special cases.

Each of the sections of these contains a rather diverse set of criteria, often grouped together for no apparent reason.

The reason is, in fact, an empirical one: these were felt by the teachers to be the sorts of things a pupil – or two pupils of similar attainment – would do on different occasions.

The main problem here is that the categories lack any sense of development. Thus, 'make[s] a conjecture about a pattern' does not distinguish between trivial and deep instances: it is not concerned with the quality of the thinking. In practice, this issue is side-stepped by tacit agreements about the meaning of the phrases and about quality amongst the teachers concerned. It still leaves untouched the problem of the wider dissemination of the assessment criteria, and also of how to describe the development of the pupil's mathematical activity.

Problems with the descriptions

All of these descriptions have drawbacks which have acted against their widespread adoption. This section looks at some of the problems associated with them.

Mathematical processes rather than general thinking processes

The justifications of mathematical activity in terms of processes have parallels in many curriculum areas. Teachers of science, design, and technology would all say that they wish to get pupils to generalise, to explore systematically, to classify, and so on. Mathematicians seem to be engaging in a form of cultural imperialism here: the strategies mentioned are more plausibly described as general thinking processes, rather than specifically mathematical ones. A recent instance is the justification for including Logo in the mathematics curriculum (not now, typically, in terms of its turtle geometry, but because of the kinds of thinking it promotes and the ways it encourages children to devise and commit themselves to their own problems). The children might just as readily be said to be doing computer science as doing mathematics.

It may seem that this distinction does not matter and that mathematical thinking occurs when these general processes are applied to mathematical objects. However, this merely shifts the issue: how do we recognise a 'mathematical object' – if, indeed, such a thing exists? Although pupils themselves are unlikely to distinguish between mathematical and non-mathematical thinking of this kind, the teacher or, more generally, the mathematical educator needs to know what it is he is trying to do. The notion of mathematising is an attempt to be specifically mathematical – although there again some of the words used seem of wider applicability.

Dichotomising

The content/process distinction suggests that problem solving, and investigatory work in the classroom, are complementary to other aspects of school mathematics:

> Research shows that these three elements – facts and skills, conceptual structures, general strategies and appreciation – involve distinct aspects of

> teaching and require separate attention. It follows that effective mathematics teaching must pay attention to all three. (DES, 1982)

The learner, in order to come to understand mathematics, must engage with and develop all of these aspects. At its best the dualist content/process view can act as a kind of yin and yang, a dialectic where the process is used to develop content which in turn gives rise to problems that are resolved by using mathematical thinking. However, the relationship is more problematic than this view of complementary aspects suggests. The dualism creates a special problem: turning process into content.

'Content', an essentially static notion (as the metaphor indicates), contrasts with 'process' which is intended in a dynamic sense. It might seem that 'process' is simply another word for mathematising, but the change from verb to noun has, as usual, some significance. This static/dynamic distinction does disservice to the complexity. It is difficult to think of 'content' as other than something external and fixed. However, any proper description needs to take account of the dynamic of learning new mathematical ideas. Learners personally construct their own content, they understand and incorporate new ideas in their own way, with their own networks of associations, beliefs and valuations.

However, even more importantly, process – and especially processes – can become reified into a static content with various aspects being treated as identifiable things that can be acquired by a learner (for example, particular strategies). In the quotation above, this shift can already be seen happening with Bell's assertion that 'it deserves its own syllabus to go alongside a syllabus of mathematical ideas'. One result of specifying 'process' aspects in the GCSE National Criteria has been that Examining Groups and schools have started to formalise these, i.e. the 'processes' are becoming additional 'content' to be learned and tested.

A similar effect can be seen happening with the famous Cockcroft paragraph 243 recommendations, where the response of some teachers has been to create lessons specifically devoted to discussion or practical work, rather than to treat these as means of doing mathematics.

Strategies and skills

The strategies described above are plausible and have been identified in many instances of actual problem solving. However, by a twist that seems characteristic of this area, as soon as we pin them down, we run into trouble. When we observe skilled problem solvers in action and see what they do in terms of 'strategies', it does not follow that such strategies exist as things in themselves.

There are two problems. One is the difficulty in identifying the existence of a general strategy. The strategies have different degrees of generality, and the more general the strategy, the more difficult it is to know what would count as evidence of showing a grasp of it; or whether children are exhibiting control of these strategies. It seems straightforward to see whether children can 'recognise and extend a pattern'. But it becomes more difficult to tell whether children can 'develop systematic methods to obtain all possibilities', and not just repeat a learned method in one instance. And it is altogether more uncertain whether children are showing that they 'know how to seek reasons'.

The other response to this is to see the simpler strategies as being skills and the more complex ones as being composed of sub-skills. As soon as we do this, however, the skills/strategies have become content again. When this happens, less tangible features of mathematical activity, such as whether children are developing their mathematical judgement, are inevitably lost.

Identifying phases

While it seems plausible that mathematical activity will fall into phases – for it will have a beginning, a middle, and an end – it is difficult in practice to distinguish the phases described above. For example, although there will be some initial problem worked at, it is likely to be loosely formulated at that stage, and as the initial problems are worked upon they are refined or changed into new ones. There is not even a cyclic process taking place here, but rather attention is being given to different aspects in a continual to-ing and fro-ing.

As with the other descriptions, seeing activity in terms of phases can lead to either the teacher or the learner being seduced into schematic behaviour. In this case, learners or teachers adopt the reified structure and carry out the phases in a particular order, without regard for the particularities of the problem they are working on.

Beliefs about mathematics

When we attempt to isolate the knowledge that the learners have by describing them as 'strategies', something important is lost. The strategies are not things in themselves, but a surface manifestation of underlying values and attitudes. These, usually implicit, beliefs children have are, of course, in large part acquired from their teachers and thus are bound up with the way their teachers see mathematics – with *their* implicit beliefs about the nature of mathematics.

Tom Brissenden polarises beliefs about mathematics between seeing 'mathematics as a body of knowledge' and seeing 'mathematics as a way of knowing'. The characteristic effects of these beliefs are very different:

> The body of knowledge outlook leads the learner to believe that mathematics, by its nature, has to be learnt in an uncritical way. . . To view mathematics as a way of knowing implies that the learner has an active role, has to instigate rather than merely respond or listen, and in particular, has to develop critical powers. (Brissenden, 1980, p. 72)

The force of this is echoed by the philosopher Gilbert Ryle's (1951) distinction between *knowing-how* and *knowing-that*. Ryle contrasts factual knowledge (knowing-that) with knowledge of how to carry out actions and procedures. In the latter case we can ask whether someone knows *how* to carry out their actions wisely, carefully, with insight, rather than clumsily or superficially. This implies that there are 'values' or 'attitudes' embedded in knowing-how – and that these can only be acquired by learners through learning in certain particular ways. Although this distinction appears similar to the content/process dichotomy, we are not now dealing with two complementary ways of learning mathematics. The assertion is that some ways of attempting to teach mathematical activity will act against it happening.

The point here is that it is misleading to adopt a simple view of the relationship between the acquisition of strategies and being able to act mathematically. If pupils are to be able to use mathematics as a way of coming to understand and gain insight into their world, it will not be enough that they can demonstrate mathematical strategies. If they are to mathematise, to take part in 'knowledge getting', more is needed. The values are all pervasive – they will be embedded in the ways in which the teacher devises for children to meet strategies and skills; and in how children are allowed and encouraged to operate in devising their own problems. Acquiring the general strategies is not in itself equivalent to engaging in the process of knowledge getting.

How can we know the dancer from the dance?

There is a (possibly fatal) flaw shared by all of the above descriptions. In attempting to define the process we are always looking at products. Such products may be written, spoken, enacted: but they are always *after* the event. It is inevitable, therefore, that the categories we create to describe the process are static impositions – products – on the process. This can be seen in the reification of strategies, where such strategies appear to exist as things, although they do not necessarily exist at the level of consciousness of the individual problem solver.

There are twin dangers: first, that the descriptions arising from the products appear to imply that particular processes must, or should have happened. These assumed processes then are used as a means to describe the activity. Mathematical activity then becomes so identified with the processes, that children will be seen as engaging in it only in so far as they seem to exhibit aspects of the descriptions. Secondly, and even more disastrously, teachers' actions are affected – so that they teach processes or strategies directly in the belief that they are then getting their pupils to act mathematically.

Mathematical activity without descriptions

The descriptions might seem to be thoroughly discredited by the comments of the last section. If this were the case, it would be legitimate to ask what descriptions can we put in their place? Each of the descriptions is in some way an attempt to avoid the deficiencies of the others, and yet fails in similar ways. This happens not because the descriptions are inadequate, but because we have an unavoidable problem. We cannot avoid making reifications of processes; creating concepts in order to describe activity, i.e. to give meaning to it, is deeply ingrained in our ways of thinking. But equally, the activity will never be subsumed under such concepts – something vital will always be lost. The best we can do is to be aware that we are creating such concepts rather than uncovering existing ones, so that we are not misled into thinking that we have found the 'truth'. All we ever have is some temporary resting place, strong enough to bear our weight for the time being, but liable to collapse under us if we try to build on it.

In other curriculum areas where the same issues occur, educators have shifted the problem away from pupil products by focusing on the ways in which the pupils will learn, i.e. the kinds of process they will go through.

Thus a middle school social studies course (Man: A Course of Study) which the psychologist Jerome Bruner helped devise, has a conception of engaging pupils in the knowledge-getting process. The aims of the course are:

1 To initiate and develop in youngsters a process of question-posing (the inquiry method);
2 To teach a research methodology where children can look for information to answer questions they have raised and use the framework developed in the course (e.g. the concept of the life cycle) and apply it to new areas;
3 To help youngsters develop the ability to use a variety of first-hand sources as evidence from which to develop hypotheses and draw conclusions;
4 To conduct classroom discussions in which youngsters learn to listen to others as well as to express their own views;
5 To legitimize the search; that is, to give sanction and support to open-ended discussions where definitive answers to many questions are not found;
6 To encourage children to reflect on their own experiences;
7 To create a new role for the teacher, in which he becomes a resource rather than an authority. (Man: A Course of Study, 1970, p.7)

What is most striking about this list is that it does not delineate the outcomes the pupils will have, what strategies they will acquire, but rather it focuses on the ways in which they will learn. The guidance in these aims attempts to influence the ways in which the teachers will act.

For mathematics, teaching can act to sustain a belief in mathematics either as a body of knowledge or as a way of knowing, and the conditions and atmosphere that a teacher creates will strongly influence how and what the children learn. In attempting to foster mathematics as a way of knowing, a key feature is the adoption by children of a critical attitude towards their own learning, the ability to 'think for themselves in mathematics'. To do this children need to be allowed to engage in such activities as:

- Identifying and initiating their own problems for investigation.
- Expressing their own ideas and developing them in solving problems.
- Testing their ideas and hypotheses against relevant experience.
- Rationally defending their own ideas and conclusions and submitting the ideas of others to a reasoned criticism.

The traps of describing mathematical activity are not, however, avoidable by knowing about them. The movements towards formalisation are part of the tension between change and stability that is always with us. It is heady, living dangerously, having your pupils explore unknown territory; but such excitement will almost inevitably become subdued by putting up direction posts to particularly interesting areas. This is something an individual teacher can be alert to (even if it is difficult to avert). Helping other teachers gain entry into working with their pupils in these ways is more problematic. Here the traps of formalisation are much harder to avoid, particularly in writing. The effects of the demands for investigative work in GCSE and elsewhere will mean that the form will increasingly be taken for the substance, and the process of renewal will need to start all over again.

Appendix A

Clues to the presence of mathematisation (from Wheeler, 1982):

> *(a) Structuration*: 'Searching for pattern' and 'modelling a situation' are phrases which grope towards this aspect. But our perceptions and thoughts are already structured; reality never comes to us 'raw'. So mathematization is better seen as 'putting structure onto a structure'. Existentially, it seems more like discovering or restructuration since what we have brought into being seems new to us. The 'eureka' feeling is an extreme case, marking the release of energy brought about by a new structuration.
> *(b) Dependence:* Mathematization puts ideas into relation and coordinates them; in particular it seeks to establish the dependence of ideas on each other.
> *(c) Infinity:* Poincaré points out that all mathematical notions are implicitly or explicitly concerned with infinity. The search for generalizability, for universality, for what is true 'in all cases', is part of this thrust.
> *(d) Making distinctions:* This seems to be the fundamental mental action underlying the construction of mathematical sets and mathematical relations.
> *(e) Extrapolating and iterating:* These are the main mental actions for producing new things out of old ones.
> *(f) Generating equivalence through transformation:* This is the most powerful of all since it generates stability (equivalence) out of flux (transformation).

References

Ahmed, A. G. and Bufton, N. (1985) *Teachers Evaluating and Assessing Mathematics (TEAM)*. Southern Region Examination Board and West Sussex Institute of Higher Education.

Bell, A. W. (1982) 'Teaching for Combined Process and Content Objectives', *Proceedings of the Fourth International Congress on Mathematical Education*. Boston: Birkhäuser p. 587–90.

Bell, A.W., Rooke, D. and Wigley, A. (1978–9) *Journey into Maths*. Glasgow: Blackie.

Brissenden, T. H. F. (1980) *Mathematics Teaching: Theory in Practice*. London: Harper & Row.

Davis, P. J. and Hersh, R. (1981) *The Mathematical Experience*. Brighton: Harvester Press.

DES (1982) *Mathematics Counts* (The Cockcroft Report). London: HMSO.

Goutard, M. (1968) 'An Aspect of the Teacher's Role', *Mathematics Teaching*, **44**, pp. 16–19.

Man: A Course of Study (1970) *Evaluation Strategies.* Washington D.C.: Curriculum Development Associates.

Mason, J. H. *et al.* (1984) *Thinking Mathematically*. London: Addison-Wesley.

Polya, G. (1945) *How to Solve It.* New Jersey: Princeton University Press.

Ryle, G. (1951) *The Concept of Mind.* Harmondsworth: Penguin.

Schoenfeld, A. H. (1985) *Mathematical Problem Solving.* New York: Academic Press.

Secondary Examination Council (1985) *Draft Grade Related Criteria for Mathematics.* London: SEC.

Wheeler, D. (1982) 'Mathematization Matters', *For the Learning of Mathematics*, vol. 3, no. 1, pp. 45–47.

Eric Love is a mathematics advisory teacher with Cumbria Local Education Authority.

27

Why should teachers be interested in research in mathematics education?

Rosalinde Scott-Hodgetts

Teachers and researchers – us and them?

For many teachers, the word 'research' has decidedly negative connotations: research, they believe, is the concern of ivory-tower academics who are far removed from the reality of the classroom and unaware of the needs of either pupils or teachers. I would like to suggest that this attitude is in some ways similar to those which lead to assertions that 'those who can't, teach' or that 'teachers have an easy life – short hours, long holidays'. The common factor is the grain of truth which lies behind these beliefs: it cannot be denied that there are members of the teaching profession who do the minimum work necessary to ensure survival; it is equally true that there are educational researchers who have lost touch with the classroom. On the other hand, just as there are caring, committed and brilliant teachers in schools, there also exist researchers whose primary motivation is the possibility of contributing to the emergence of more constructive learning/teaching environments.

For them, it is clear that they must continually update and extend their classroom experience, not only through their involvement in classroom situations in the role of researcher, but also to improve their own teaching skills and strategies. Only in this way can they remember and understand the pressure of classroom life.

Finally, it should not be forgotten that many researchers are themselves practising teachers, in schools as well as in colleges. More and more teachers are involving themselves in projects where they use existing research findings as a starting point for their own classroom studies – perhaps the most powerful way in which research can be put to use.

I haven't got time!

The ever-increasing expectations made of teachers are almost incredible; it is not surprising, therefore, that many feel that they have difficulty simply 'keeping their heads above water'. The lack of time and support for teachers wishing to pursue research-based activities is depressing, and is largely outside the control of the individual teacher. The most enthusiastic teachers find that there is little alternative, in the short term, to donating more of their precious, shrinking leisure time if they are determined to carry out their own research, or just to find out more about the work of others. It is, perhaps, surprising that many do make the choice, and feel that it has been worthwhile (Lolley *et al.*, 1987). To understand why this is so, it is necessary to look at the long-term implications of 'research awareness'.

I said earlier that a driving force for many researchers (practising teachers and others) was the idea that they could have a positive influence on what happens in their own classroom, and perhaps in classrooms generally. If they work effectively to produce results of direct relevance to teachers and learners, then clearly the potential is there for teachers to gain insights which lead to constructive changes in, for example, curriculum development or classroom interactions. This is particularly true if teachers are able to replicate the researcher's study within their own school context, in order to see how their own situation compares and contrasts with that reported. Consideration of the similarities and the differences which arise can prove most enlightening, and in the long-term could actually inform decisions aimed at lightening the teacher's load, by making the learning/teaching process more efficient.

In fact, many teachers see research as an integral part of their role, and a great many engage in classroom research, although they might not label their activities in that way.

Things to think about

Where researchers working in higher education are at an advantage is that research is an *expected* part of their job, and they are allowed time and resources to support their studies. Because of this, they are often able to engage in in-depth and/or large-scale projects, and are sometimes able to draw conclusions which are likely to be of relevance to a very large number of pupils and teachers, rather than be specific to a particular school context.

One problem is that researchers are often not equipped – either in terms of experience or facilities – to disseminate their results widely. A lot of existing research is effectively inaccessible to the majority of teachers, partly because it is disseminated in specialist journals, and in some cases because of the style in which it is reported. Ideally, I believe, reports of research studies should be compiled to form concise, comprehensive anthologies, widely available to teachers. These might come to be considered as a time-saving resource; they could be used in similar ways to good textbooks or schemes, where the teacher selects 'items' which can be useful in developing an appropriate teaching/learning scheme. In the case of the textbook/scheme an example might be selected as a starting point for a range of mathematical investigations; in the case of the research anthology, an example of a researcher's work might be used as starting point for a range of classroom investigations by the teacher; alternatively, a particular research finding might be used to inform the choice of textbook/scheme examples!

Some progress has been made towards the goal of making research findings readily available in the form suggested (Bell *et al.*, 1983; Dickson *et al.*, 1984; Hart, 1981), and although greater efforts must be made in this area, there is undoubtedly enough material already available to provide a variety of starting points for interested teachers. Within mathematics education alone, reported research covers a vast range of themes and issues, from consideration of children's understanding of specific mathematical topics to social issues like gender and race, and affective factors like maths anxiety and pupils' expectations of teachers.

To give a 'feel' for the possibilities, I think it might be useful to provide examples of findings which made *me* think about, and modify, my own teaching strategies when I first read them. You may feel that the results which I have selected as illustrations are 'obvious'; my own experience in this respect is varied – sometimes I am genuinely surprised by things I read; more often I find evidence which supports beliefs I already had, but which is helpful both in validating my instinctive feelings and suggesting novel (for me) ways of addressing identified problems. I have restricted my selection to research summarised in the three books already referenced, but give references to the original work below, for those readers who have access to good library facilities.

Language and symbolisation

A vast amount of research has been conducted in this area, and all I intend to do is to provide some 'snapshots' which motivated reflection on my part.

In one study, three hundred secondary pupils on CSE courses were tested to probe their understanding of words which are used in mathematics, including mathematics examination papers (Otterburn and Nicholson, 1976). The instructions they were given were as follows:

> On the left of the page is a list of words used in mathematics. In column (1) put *Yes* if you understand what the word means, *No* if not. In column (2) put the *Symbol* for the word if it has one (not all words have them). In column (3) *Draw a Diagram* or use *Numbers* or *Symbols* to show what the word means. In column (4) *Describe in Words* what the word means, use an example if you like.

An example was provided:

	(1)	(2)	(3)	(4)
Word	Yes/No	Symbol	Draw a diagram	Describe in words
Plus	Yes	+	OO + OO = OOO OO O OOO OO OOO 4+5 = 9	Add, e.g. four plus five are nine

Responses under the last three columns only were regarded as significant – rather than a 'yes' in column one.

Some examples of the results are given below:

Word	**Correct***	**Percentage Blank**	**Confused**
Minus	99.7	0.3	0
Fraction	91	8	1
Prime Number	52	34	13
Square Root	40	44	16
Rotation	37	60	3
Factor	32	62	6
Ratio	25	71	4
Multiple	20	45	34
Similar	19	67	15
Mapping	16	81	3
Integer	15	76	9

*Correct: if any reply in the last three columns indicated a correct interpretation of the word.

Another researcher went on to investigate the extent to which pupils were held back by lack of mathematical vocabulary (Nicholson, 1977), and found that roughly speaking the middle 50% of the whole 'ability' range are significantly disadvantaged by this factor.

Do you know what specialist terms occur in mathematical problems, and their relative frequency of occurrence?

Are you surprised by any of the results above? Do you think you would find a similar pattern if you gave short diagnostic tests to your pupils? Why not try it and see?

Since I have been aware of the results of this and other related research I have noticed two changes in my own teaching. The first is an increased ability to recognise mathematical errors resulting from an incorrect or partial understanding of particular words within the mathematical context. The second is that I realise how 'sloppily' I use words in the mathematics classroom – thus causing some of the problems. Improvement is a gradual process!

Even at the primary level there is a mis-match between 'good practice' in language teaching and the way in which terms are introduced within mathematics. For example, analysis of primary texts and workcards – eight schemes in all – revealed 18 different words, phrases and symbols used to denote addition (Preston, 1978). One particular text, supposedly designed for children of average and below average 'ability' uses 14 of the 18 alternatives in two pages!

The way in which terms are introduced within a particular context adds to the confusion.

An interesting example is given by Ginsburg (1982). Patty, aged 8, associated the word 'plus' only with a written algorithm for addition. This was particularly interesting because she was using an 'incorrect' algorithm.

For example, for '10 plus 1' she wrote:

$$\begin{array}{r} 10 \\ +\ 1 \\ \hline 20 \\ \hline \end{array}$$

When asked to draw marks on her paper to find out what 10 and 1 made, the conversation ran thus.

Patty: 'Altogether it would be 11.'
Interviewer: 'OK, what about 10 plus 1, not altogether, but plus?'
Patty: 'Then you'd have to put 20.'
Interviewer: 'What if we write down on paper, here's 20, now I write down another 1, and you want to find out how much the 20 and 1 are altogether.'
Patty: 'It's 21.'
Interviewer: 'OK, now what would 20 plus 1 be?'
Patty: '20 plus 1?'
She wrote:

$$\begin{array}{r} 20 \\ +1 \\ \hline 30 \\ \hline \end{array}$$

It has also been proposed that words in mathematics fall into various categories (Shuard and Rothery, 1984):

1 Those which are found almost exclusively within the context of the mathematics classroom, e.g. trapezium, square root, hypotenuse. The potential problem with these words stems from our tendency only to define them once, and then assume that if they have apparently been understood there is no need to negotiate meaning later, or to give reinforcement.

2 Those which are found in 'everyday' English and in mathematics, but have radically different meanings depending on context, e.g. difference, prime, similar, index. Here the problem is to differentiate between the conflicting meanings.

3 Those which are used in both contexts with more or less the same meaning, e.g. square, diagonal. You sometimes cannot win either way: in these cases it might prove difficult to convince children who have realised that mathematics is full of jargon that the meaning in mathematics really *is* the same!

Again, it is useful to reflect upon the likelihood of your pupils finding themselves in difficulties, and to plan to pre-empt such problems in future by, for example, ensuring that you regularly negotiate the meaning of words, and symbols, within the mathematics classroom.

Interpretation of graphs

Distance–time graphs are often used as examples where pupils are asked to pick out different rates of travel, arrival times, etc. Such an example was given to large numbers of 13, 14 and 15 year olds (Kerslake, 1981), and the majority of the sample answered the questions quite well. When interviewed later, however, it became clear that many pupils had incorrect perceptual interpretations of the graph. They were subsequently given examples of graphs some of which could *not* represent journeys, and were asked to describe what they thought they showed.

> Which of the graphs below represent journeys? Describe what happens in each case.

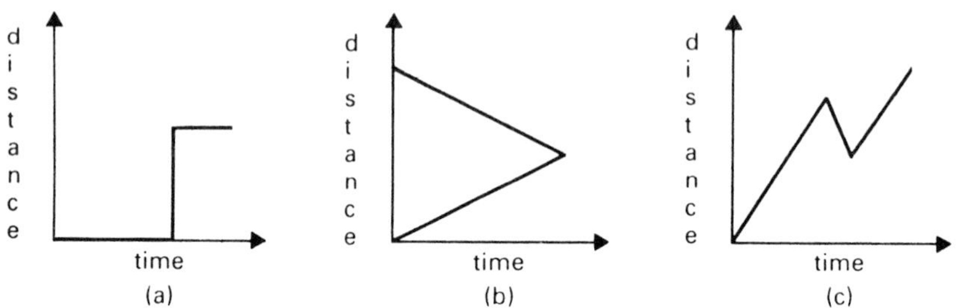

Answers demonstrating understanding (as percentages):

	13 years	14 years	15 years
(a)	9.5	8.4	15.0
(b)	11.1	9.3	15.7
(c)	14.7	17.2	25.2

In the case of graph (a) a few pupils did recognise that the graph could not represent a journey, some pointing out that according to the graph a certain distance had been travelled in zero time. Other responses, however, showed basic lack of understanding, or a pictorial frame of reference – 'a graph is a picture'.

For (a) descriptions included:

> 'went along a corridor, then up a lift, then along another corridor'
> 'going east, then due north, then east'
> 'went along, then turned left, then turned right.'

For (b):

> 'going along, then turning left'
> 'going North-East, then North-West'
> 'going back the way he came.'

For (c):

> 'climbing a mountain'
> 'going up, going down then up again.'

This particular example interested me because whilst I had met similar problems with pupils, I had not really given my attention to preventing the problems rather than taking remedial action. A more comprehensive response was made by a student on a Master's course at my current institution, South Bank Polytechnic. The student concerned, Saw Hoon Teah, is a mathematics teacher in an inner London school. Like me, she was intrigued by the above research results; we had also noticed that one of the questions from the Joint Matriculation Board/Shell Centre for Mathematical Education (1985) was of similar type, requiring a commentary on a hurdles race involving three people.

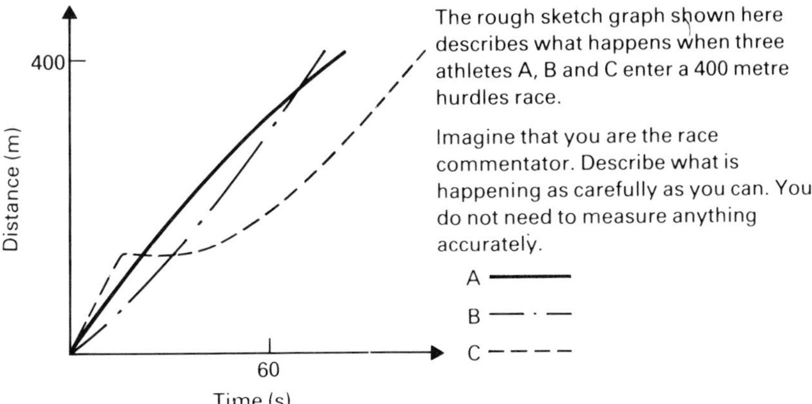

400
Distance (m)
60
Time (s)
The rough sketch graph shown here describes what happens when three athletes A, B and C enter a 400 metre hurdles race.
Imagine that you are the race commentator. Describe what is happening as carefully as you can. You do not need to measure anything accurately.
A
B
C

Saw Hoon decided that she would first test to see if her pupils were holding misconceptions similar to those described above, and having determined that they were, she designed and implemented a teaching/learning module to remediate the situation, and to use as an introduction to graphs for future pupils.

The problems which Saw Hoon's pupils were having reflected those reported in the research.

For example, consider the responses of one pupil to the following problem:

Hoisting the Flag

Every morning, on the summer camp, the youngest boy scout has to hoist a flag to the top of the flagpole.

(i) Explain in words what each graph below means.

(ii) Which graph is the most realistic?

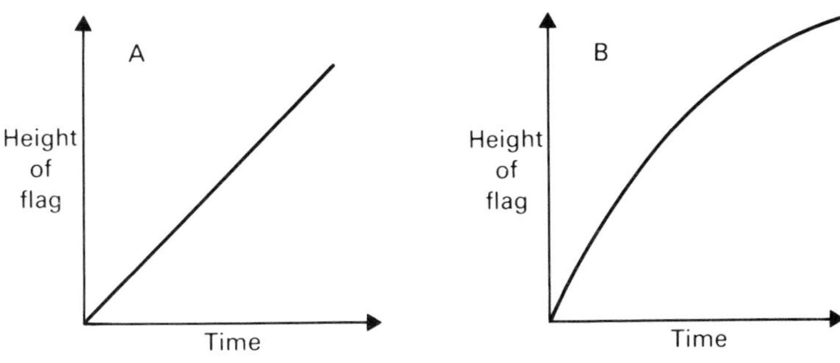

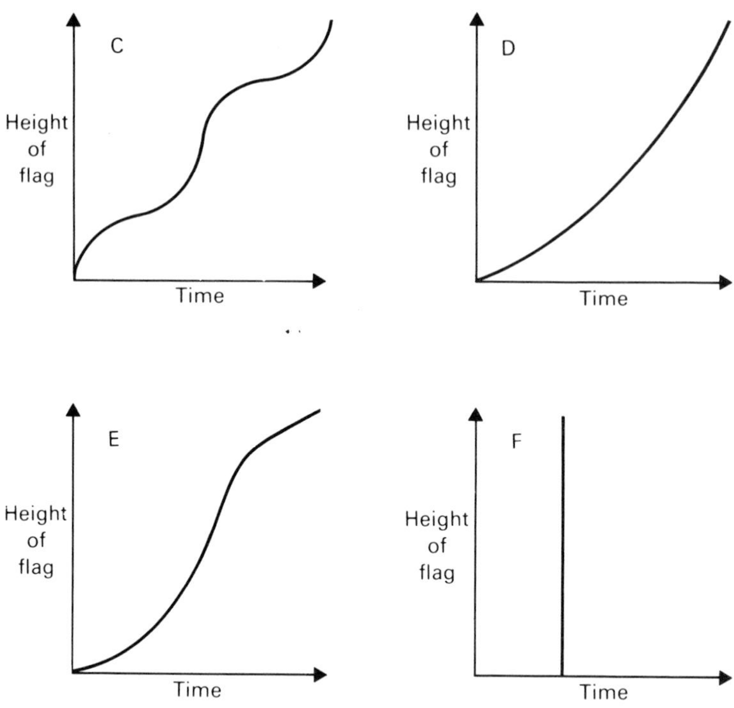

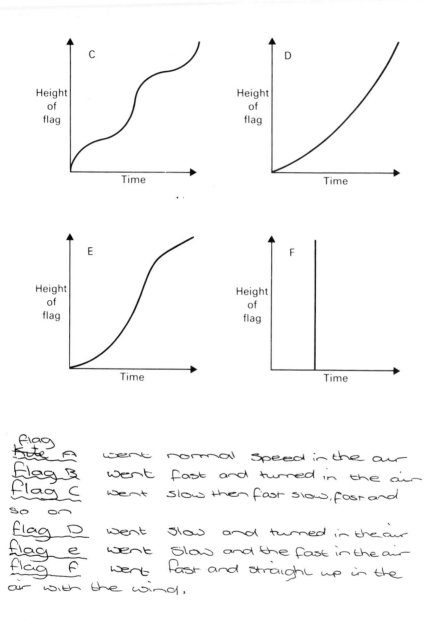

~~Kite~~ flag A went normal speed in the air
flag B went fast and turned in the air
flag C went slow then fast slow, fast and so on
flag D went slow and turned in the air
flag e went slow and the fast in the air
flag F went fast and straight up in the air with the wind.

The programme of work devised to overcome these misinterpretations was varied, including use of computer software and laboratory experiments, as well as written tasks. Contexts used included traffic, filling bottles, athletics, sizes of buildings and towns, levels of happiness and exhaustion over time and feeling hungry! One example which demands a high level of understanding for success is shown below.

Bottles

Here are 6 bottles and 9 graphs.

Choose the correct bottle for each graph. Explain your reasoning carefully.

For the remaining 3 graphs, sketch what the bottles should look like.

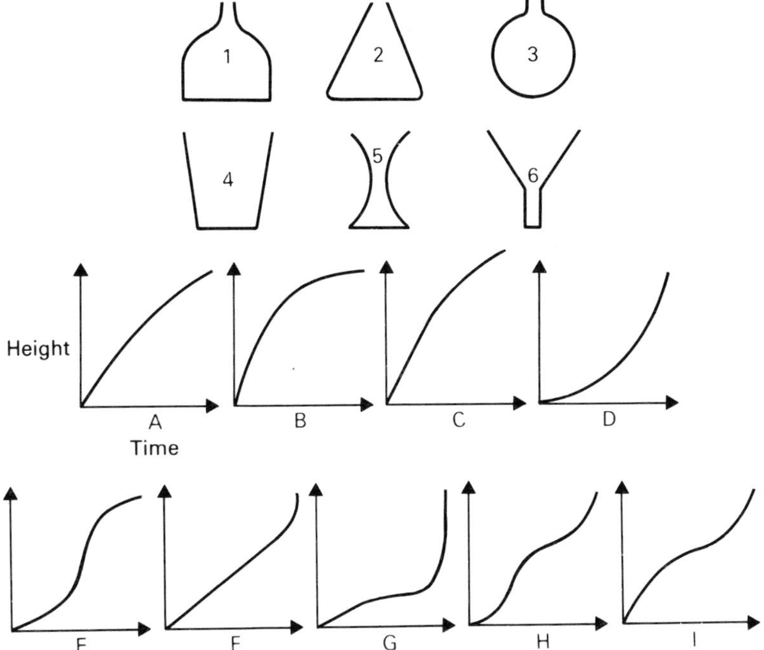

At the end of the module Saw Hoon felt that her pupils had gained a far deeper understanding of the topic, and, perhaps as importantly, had been well motivated throughout the implementation of the scheme. This was not the first 'mini-research' project for Saw Hoon – her first such venture involved the design and evaluation of materials related to children's understanding of decimals, which included her pupils in the invention of some very innovative games. She is now determined to continue with similar schemes in future – mainly because she is excited by the way in which her pupils have responded, in terms of performance and improved levels of interest and independence.

How to get started

The examples I have given are fairly arbitrary. If you do decide that you would like to see what research has to offer you as a mathematics teacher, I hope you will find the time to look at some of the books for which references are given at the end of this article. To do so will give you a more balanced picture of the range of available research in the field of mathematics education.

It may be that you have already got a good idea of the area in which you would like to undertake some research, and want to find out what has already been done in that particular area; if so you will need to find out about the wide variety of journals which carry articles on mathematical education. Ways of accessing this detailed information are outlined in the final chapter of one of the books listed (Bell *et al.*, 1983).

Sharing

Finally, if you *are* able to complete some research alongside all your other tasks, and want to share your thoughts and findings with others, there are various journals which might be willing to publish your work. Once you have decided exactly what it is you want to say, and how you want to say it, look at the different publications and see which best suits your preferred style. By making your results available you may save a fellow teacher some time, or give them an inspiring starting point for their own research activities.

References

Bell, A., Costello, J. and Küchemann, D. (1983) *A Review of Research in Mathematical Education: Part A*. Windsor: NFER/Nelson.

Dickson, L., Brown, M. and Gibson, O. (1984) *Children Learning Mathematics*. London: Holt, Rinehart and Winston.

Ginsburg, H. (1982) *Children's Arithmetic: How They Learn It and How You Teach It.* Austin, Texas: PRO-ED.

Hart, K. (ed.) (1981) *Children's Understanding of Mathematics: 11–16.* London: John Murray.

Kerslake, D. (1981) 'Graphs', in Hart, K. (ed.) (1981) op. cit.

Lolley, M., Davies, S. and Scott-Hodgetts, R. (1987) 'Teachers as Researchers', *Mathematics Teaching*, **118**, pp. 46–7.

Nicholson, A. (1977) 'Mathematics and Language', *Mathematics in School*, **6** (5), pp. 32–4.

Otterburn, M. and Nicholson, A. (1976) 'The Language of (CSE) Mathematics', *Mathematics in School,* **5** (5), pp. 18–20.

Preston, M. (1978) 'The Language of Early Mathematical Experience', *Mathematics in School*, 7 (4), pp. 31–2.

Shuard, H. and Rothery, A. (eds) (1984) *Children Reading Maths.* London: John Murray.

Rosalinde Scott-Hodgetts is Principal Lecturer in Mathematics Education at the Polytechnic of the South Bank, London.

28

Teachers' decision making[1]

Tom J. Cooney

(*Editor's note*: This article refers to classes in the USA. Pupils of whatever age are referred to as 'students' and a rough guide to the age of the pupils can be gained by adding 5 to the grade number. Thus fifth grade is 10–11 year olds, first grade is 5–6 year olds, ninth grade is 13–14 year olds. Elementary school is primary school.)

Teachers are sometimes likened to actors on stage; they emote and enthuse in order to capture the imagination of the audience. While teachers may need to be good actors, the process of teaching also includes *re*acting. Teaching is an interactive process, one in which the teacher plays off the students and the students play off the teacher. It is a process of gathering information, making a diagnosis, and constructing a response based on that diagnosis. While much of this process may be quite automatic, some situations require conscious decision making. The act of generating and considering alternatives in constructing a response – that is, making an instructional decision – is of paramount importance in teaching.

Shroyer (1978) used the term 'critical moments' to denote those moments of classroom teaching when there is an occlusion in the instructional flow. Perhaps a student demonstrates an unanticipated learning problem or gives a particularly insightful response. Such unexpected events cause the teacher to reflect on the interaction and to process certain information in order to construct a reaction. Episodes that depict critical moments are presented later in this article to provide a context for considering teaching as a process of decision making.

The decision-making process

Various researchers have studied teachers' decision-making processes (Shavelson, 1976; Peterson and Clark, 1978). Regardless of the theoretical prism through which the processes are viewed and studied, several aspects remain constant: teachers gather and encode information, generate alternatives, and select a course of action.

In Peterson and Clark's study (1978), a scheme consisting of four paths was developed for describing teachers' decision-making processes. The investigators found that Path 1 was most frequently traversed; Path 2 was the second most traversed; student achievement was negatively correlated with Path 3; and Path 4 was positively related to higher learning outcomes. Peterson and Clark's study emphasizes two aspects of teaching central to

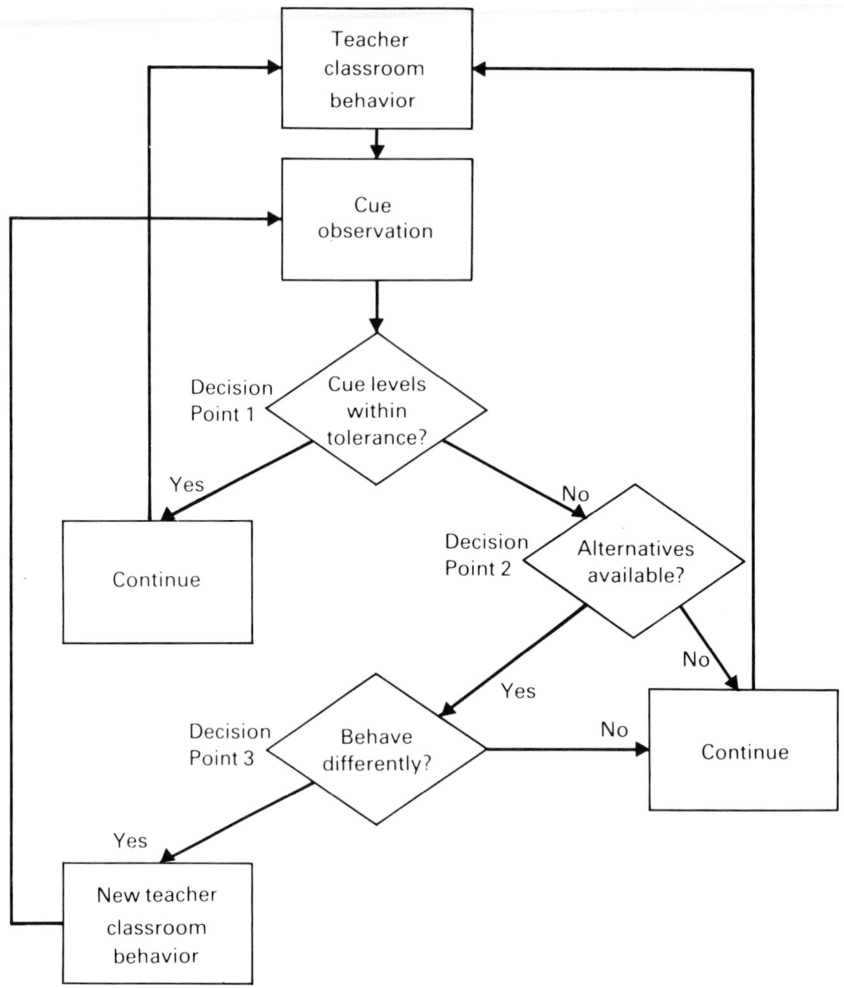

Paths Identified from the Scheme

Decision Points	Path 1	Path 2	Path 3	Path 4
Student Behavior Within				
Tolerance?	Yes	No	No	No
Alternatives Available?	—	No	Yes	Yes
Behave Differently?	—	—	No	Yes

Scheme for analyzing decision making by teachers

decision making: (1) the decision-making process is related to educational outcomes, and (2) a critical part of the decision-making process is the generation of alternatives. The generation of alternatives is considered central to viewing the teacher as a decision maker and is deemed essential for a flexible and creative teacher. Peterson and Clark's analysis helps provide a means by which we can consider the role alternatives play in the decision-making process.

Types of decisions

Teachers make different types of decisions. Some are related to the content, including its selection, and the selection of teaching methods. Other decisions relate to the more interpersonal aspects of teaching, that is, affective concerns. Still other decisions involve management considerations, including the allocation of time. I will use this triadic scheme of classifying decisions as cognitive, affective, or managerial to focus on the various types of decisions that teachers make. I must emphasize, however, that these three categories are not in any way mutually exclusive. Teaching is too complex to permit such a simplistic view. In the real world of the classroom, classification schemes are seldom clearly exhibited. Nevertheless, the classification seems appropriate at least for the purpose of examining factors that influence decisions.

Cognitive decisions

There are two phases of teaching. The *preactive phase* is what transpires before the teacher begins interacting with students. It typically involves lesson planning. The *interactive phase* involves the classroom interaction between students and the teacher. Content related decisions, as well as other types of decisions, are made in both the preactive and interactive phases.

A content decision that occurs in the preactive phase is deciding which content to present and which to exclude from the instructional program. Cooney, Davis and Henderson (1975) identified the following factors that affect teachers' decisions in selecting content: (a) requirements or regulations from governing bodies, such as state departments of education, (b) objectives developed by a teacher, department, or a more inclusive group, (c) the expected use of the content to be taught, (d) the student's interest in the content as well as the teacher's interest in teaching it, (e) the predicted difficulty of the content, and (f) authoritative judgments expressed by professional groups or prestigious individuals within the field. In many cases decisions related to topic selection are passive and based primarily on what appears in textbooks. Nevertheless, a decision is made.

Another type of content decision concerns how the content within a topic will be interpreted or presented. Consider the concept of fraction. One can conceive of a least ten different interpretations of fraction: parts of a region, parts of a collection, points on the number line, fractions as quotients, fractions as decimals, repeated addition of a unit fraction, ratios, measurement, operators, and segments. Decisions must be made on which one or which combination of interpretations to use in teaching fractions. Similarly, there are various means of interpreting other mathematical topics. Such interpretations provide a variety of alternatives to consider when presenting content.

Decisions are also made with respect to strategies of presentation. A variety of materials, such as rods or paper folding, can be used to present different interpretations of the content. Another strategy decision has to do with the use of examples and nonexamples. Suppose the teacher wants to develop the concept of line symmetry for the class. A matrix similar to the one below could be constructed with students providing the samples.

	Mathematics	Real World Applications
Example	rectangle	a human face
Nonexample	parallelogram	a human hand

Such an activity can provide a mixture of examples and nonexamples and relate the concept to life-like situations. Other cognitive decisions include deciding how to justify theorems, what prerequisite knowledge should be reviewed, or whether to use an expository or a discovery approach.

Cognitive decisions are also made in the interactive phase of teaching. Several classroom episodes are posed below to highlight the nature of these types of decisions.

Episode 1

Mr Smith's class is learning the Pythagorean Theorem. Students had used unit squares to construct larger squares on the legs of right triangles ABC and DEF.

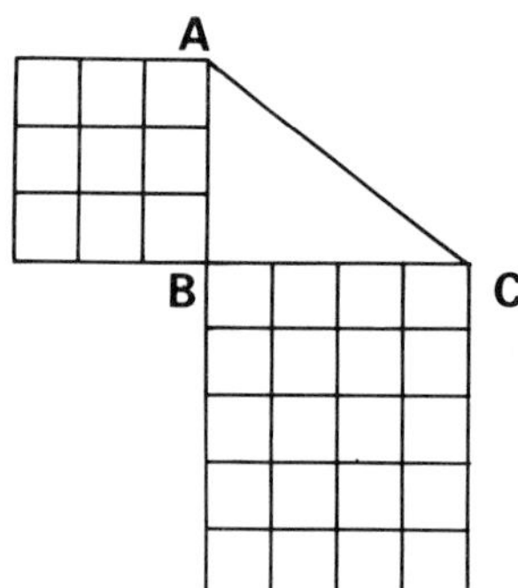

These unit squares were then rearranged to form a larger square of unit squares on the hypotenuse. The following dialogue between the teacher and two students, Billy and Chuck, then transpired.

Teacher: Now consider the right triangle with legs of length a and b and hypotenuse c. (*He draws triangle ABC on the board.*) What does the theorem say about this triangle?

Billy: $a^2 + b^2 = c^2$.

Teacher: Okay. Very good. Now suppose we have a different right

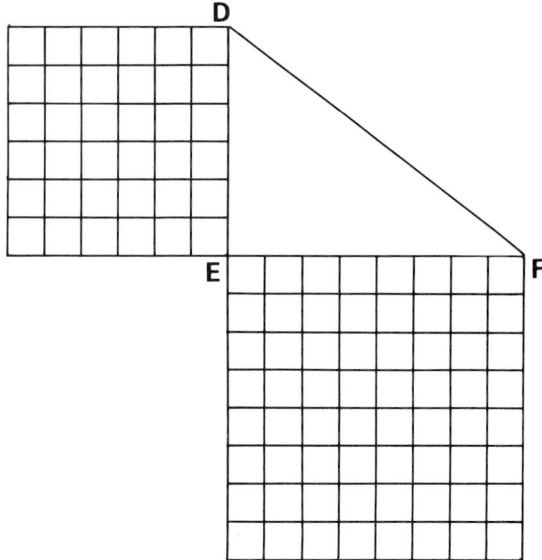

triangle with legs of length *a* and *c* and hypotenuse *b*. (*He draws this triangle on the board.*) Now what does the theorem say?

Chuck: The theorem won't work for that triangle. It doesn't apply.

Apparently, Chuck had not grasped the meaning of the theorem. Perhaps he thought of mathematics only in terms of symbols and not in terms of meanings behind the symbols. What alternative actions exist? Possibilities include the following.

(a) Call on another student to state a relationship.
(b) Tell Chuck the theorem does apply and state the correct response.
(c) Ask Chuck to clarify what 'doesn't apply' means.
(d) Ask him to state the conditions under which the theorem does or does not apply.
(e) Ask another student if he or she agrees.

The issue is not which alternative is necessarily better for all situations. Rather, the focus should be on the identification of possible alternatives and the decision as to which one seems best suited in a particular context. The making of a wise decision requires the consideration of various alternatives in light of what is known about a particular student in specific situations.

Episode 2

Ms Jones was reviewing linear functions when the following dialogue occurred.

Teacher: What do we mean, class, by linear function? How would we define it, Mary?

Mary: I don't know. I forgot.

Teacher: Carla?

Carla: Well, it has something to do with a straight line.

Teacher: That's true, but we need more.

Evidently Ms Jones perceived that students were struggling with the apparent goal of stating a definition. At this point, several alternatives could be considered, including the following.

(a) Call on another student and press for a correct definition.
(b) Provide some sort of hint on how to 'start' the definition and give Carla or another student a chance to state the definition.
(c) Abandon the instructional goal and identify a new goal.

The dialogue continued.

Teacher: Jan?

Jan: Things like $f(x) = 2x + 3$ and $f(x) = 4x - 10$. These are linear functions aren't they?

Teacher: Yes. That's good. Okay, now let's see how we can graph some linear functions.

The teacher seemed satisfied with the two examples. Was she unclear about the content being taught or at least unclear over the distinction between definitions and examples? Did the teacher make a conscious decision to accept examples rather than a definition? If so, what factors influenced her decision? What was the likely impact of the discussion on the students? Were they confused about what constitutes definition?

We cannot be sure what cues Ms Jones attended to when she made her decision to accept the answer, or if she considered any other alternatives. In short, we do not know what information this teacher processed in making the decision. But we do know that for whatever reason a response which was not an answer to the teacher's question was finally accepted. The response may have been accepted as a compromise if Ms Jones perceived that the task was harder than anticipated (and thus the goal was changed). Or it may have been accepted without Ms Jones reflecting on the nature of the instructional request.

Consider another situation observed in an elementary school classroom.

Episode 3

Mr Costa's class was discussing the addition of whole numbers. At one point the discussion focused on a word problem that entailed finding the sum of 1970, 330, and 31. The following dialogue occurred.

Teacher: So what numbers do we need to add?

Sonya: 1970, 330, and 31.

Teacher: Okay. Albert, why don't you show us on the board how to add those numbers? (*Albert goes to the board and writes the following.*)

$$\begin{array}{l} 1\,9\,7\,0 \\ 3\,3\,0 \\ \underline{3\,1} \\ 8\,3\,7\,0 \end{array}$$

Albert: The answer is 8370.

Albert's difficulty and misconception are clearly evident. What alternatives exist for the teacher?

(a) Ask another student to come to the board and find the sum.

(b) Show Albert and the class how the numerals should be arranged.
(c) Use the idea of place value to explain briefly how the numbers should be added.
(d) Stop the lesson to review in some detail the process of adding whole numbers.

In this particular case, the teacher decided on option (b). The effect seemed to be a continuation of the class discussion in a fairly uninterrupted manner, although an observer might wonder if Albert's confusion had really been resolved.

The following episode highlights the importance of generating alternatives when a lesson goes poorly, and the importance of generating alternative strategies when planning a lesson.

Episode 4

Mrs Lincoln, a seventh-grade mathematics teacher, was teaching her class how to factor whole numbers into their prime factors. She began by quickly stating the definition of *prime number* and giving two examples of prime numbers. No nonexamples were given. She then presented two demonstrations of how to obtain the prime factorization of a whole number. Students had obvious difficulties, including the mistakes below, as alleged by prime factorizations of the numbers of the left.

$$\begin{aligned} 12 &= 4 \times 3 \\ 8 &= 5 + 3 \\ 40 &= 4 \times 10 \\ 24 &= 16 + 8 \end{aligned}$$

Mrs Lincoln recognized there was a problem; she repeated the definition, and gave one more demonstration. Students returned to their worksheets, but few corrections were made as they were still quite confused.

Several comments are relevant. First, the students lacked basic prerequisite knowledge with respect to the concepts of prime number and factor. Had the teacher placed greater emphasis on teaching these concepts, particularly through the use of examples and nonexamples of prime numbers and by comparing factors with addends, students would likely have done better.

Second, it seems clear that Mrs Lincoln had few instructional alternatives to draw on. The role examples and nonexamples can play in designing instructional strategies was mentioned earlier. Kolb (1977) developed a model for predicting the effect of various strategies, including the use of examples and nonexamples for teaching mathematical concepts.

Basically, Kolb's model suggests that examples and nonexamples of concepts produce more learning than presenting characteristics of concepts when students have little prerequisite knowledge. For students with a higher degree of prerequisite knowledge, discussions that focus more on the attributes of a concept, for example, necessary and/or sufficient conditions for concepts, are more effective than focusing on specific examples and nonexamples. The model is complex and involves considerable detail. However, it does highlight the importance of using examples and nonexamples particularly for students with poor conceptual backgrounds.

In Episode 4, it was clear that many students did not understand the concept of prime number nor of factor. For them an instructional alternative should have been generated which entailed extensive use of examples and nonexamples. Iteration of the strategy 'define and give one or two examples' was not productive.

Affective decisions

Teachers need to be sensitive to students and provide ample affective support for them. Instructional decisions involving affective considerations are sometimes based on the teacher's perception of how students are interacting with the content. Comments like 'Why do I have to learn this?' are not atypical in mathematics classrooms. The way in which such questions are handled depends on what the teacher perceives to be the reason for such a comment. If the student is asking 'How does this content fit with other topics that we have studied or will study?' or 'How can the content be applied to help me solve problems in the real world?' then a response dealing with the substance of the discipline is appropriate and, hence, is primarily cognitive in nature. But if the student is really asking 'Why am I not doing better in learning this?' then a response oriented toward building the student's confidence appears more appropriate. Thus a teacher is faced with an instructional decision. Within the affective domain in particular, hidden meanings must be attended to as well as the overt context of the remark, in order to generate viable alternatives.

Bishop and Whitfield (1972, p. 35) offered the following situation, which suggests the need for an 'affective' response:

> If a man can run a mile in four minutes, how far can he run in an hour? A 12-year-old pupil answers: 'Fifteen miles.' On being questioned about the reasonableness of the answer, he replies: 'Well, math is nothing to do with real life, is it?'

Should one expect that a substantive discussion on the relationship or applicability of mathematics to the 'real world' would resolve the problem? Perhaps, but it is also conceivable that the student's response has less to do with mathematics *per se* than it does with an affective problem associated with learning mathematics.

Consider the following two episodes.

Episode 5

Donald has considerable trouble learning mathematics. The current lesson is on solving linear equations of the form $ax + b = c$. Donald is doing rather poorly. The teacher has emphasized that it is important in solving equations to have only one equals sign (=) per line. Donald, along with other students, is sent to the chalkboard to practice solving equations. Donald typically does not do well when performing at the board. The equation to be solved is $2x + 4 = 7$. Donald's solution is:

$2x + 4 = 7 = 2x + 4 - 4 = 7 - 4 = 2x = 3 = x = 1\frac{1}{2}$

Episode 6

Pat is a C student in geometry. The class has been studying constructions using a compass and a straightedge. Most students are quite proficient in bisecting a line segment as shown on the left. However, Pat persists in bisecting a segment in the manner indicated on the right.

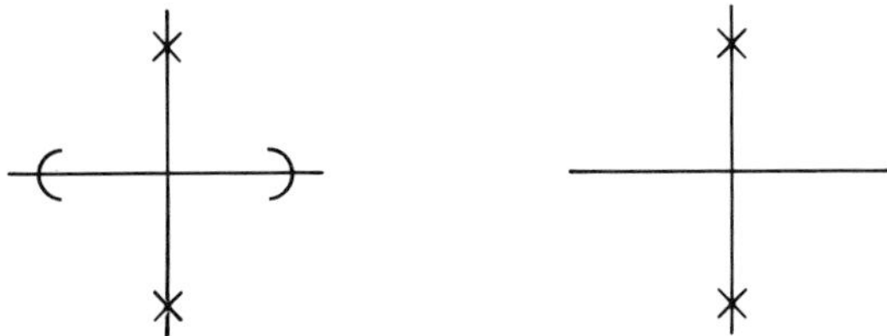

The teacher has continually emphasized to Pat that while her procedure is mathematically correct, it is not the most efficient way and not the method to be used in class. Nevertheless, when asked to find the midpoints of the sides of a triangle, Pat resorts to the second method.

If one were to consider only affective concerns to the exclusion of cognitive ones, then decisions would be easier. But often affective decisions must be tempered with cognitive concerns, as evidenced in Episodes 5 and 6.

In Episode 5, the teacher reinforced Donald with considerable praise for obtaining the correct answer. As a result, Donald felt proud but other students asked if they could solve equations using only 'one' line. The teacher seemed intent on emphasizing affective outcomes; desirable affective outcomes were paramount to the teacher. In Pat's case, the teacher was very sharp and critical. Pat probably wouldn't make the same 'mistake' again, but at the expense of a loss of enthusiasm for the subject. For this teacher and this situation, cognitive outcomes were evidently of higher priority than affective outcomes.

Many decisions involve striking a balance between cognitive and affective outcomes. Recall Chuck's response concerning the Pythagorean theorem. Chuck had a misconception regarding the theorem. But the teacher might select an alternative action having considerable affective overtones. That is, an alternative might be selected which best ensures Chuck's feelings would not be hurt or best ensures Chuck's continued participation in class discussions. This situation highlights the necessity of considering a number of factors, both cognitive and affective in nature, when making instructional decisions. Artistic teachers are often able to promote both desirable cognitive and affective outcomes. One type of outcome need not be sacrificed for another. But the task of striking a balance is not always easy; it requires careful consideration of several alternatives of action.

Research generally indicates that the warm, supportive teacher is more effective than the critical teacher. Tikunoff and others (1975) conducted an ethnographic study of second and fifth grade teachers teaching reading and mathematics in which many teaching variables, affective in nature, were found to be related to achievement. The investigators characterized the significant variables as being related to 'those familial interactions in the home which have been attributed traditionally to the successful rearing of children' (p. 22).

Rosenshine and Furst (1971) also suggest that the warm, supportive teacher is more effective than the critical teacher. However, Brophy and Evertson (1976) found that in high socioeconomic status (SES) classrooms praise was negatively related to student learning gains, whereas students in low SES classrooms prospered in warm, supportive classroom atmospheres. This suggests that affective variables may be contextual in nature in terms of how they relate to achievement.

Teachers make continual assessments of students' affective status in the classroom. Although universal quantification is difficult to justify, generally the 'familial' variables identified by Tikunoff and others (1975) seem to characterize the effective teacher. But individual instructional decisions may not be unidimensional in value. That is, one may have to strike a balance between cognitive concerns and affective ones when assessing expected payoffs of various teaching behaviors.

Managerial decisions

Managerial decisions relate to time allocation, organization of classroom activities, and control of disruptive behavior. Some of these decisions can be made in the preactive phase of teaching while others, especially those related to 'control' problems, are more specific to the interactive phase of teaching.

Consider Episodes 7 and 8, which involve decisions related to how time is allocated.

Episode 7

A student is subtracting fractions and keeps making mistakes similar to the one below.

$$\begin{array}{rcl} 4\ 1/8 & = & 3\ 11/8 \\ \underline{-1\ 7/8} & = & \underline{1\ \ 7/8} \\ & & 2\ \ 4/8 = 2\tfrac{1}{2} \end{array}$$

After the teacher poses several questions, it is clear the student is quite confused.

Episode 8

A geometry teacher is discussing the importance of the parallel postulate in Euclidean geometry. The teacher has emphasized that many theorems in their geometry books are based on the parallel postulate. As an illustration, the teacher argues that the theorem, 'The sum of the measures of the angles of a triangle is 180 degrees,' follows from the parallel postulate. A bright student asks, 'If we didn't have the parallel postulate, does that mean the measures of the angles of a triangle would be different than 180 degrees?'

In Episode 7, should content be reviewed for a single student or for a few students at the risk of 'wasting' the time of other students? In Episode 8, should class time be taken to pursue the thought initiated by the bright student? Or should the student be informed that the question was a good one and it would be followed up sometime *after* class? What are the expected results of the two alternatives? The decisions will clearly affect how time is allocated. What is not so clear and is quite value laden is deciding how to strike a balance between discussions of a tangential point for a few students compared with discussions that benefit the remaining students. Given that instructional time is a scarce commodity, allocation of that commodity is critical to determining what is learned.

Some decisions on time allocation occur in the preactive phase of teaching. Ebmeier and Good (1979) found that fourth-grade mathematics teachers could improve achievement by emphasizing six aspects of instruction with tentative time allocations: development (about 20 minutes), homework, emphasis on product questions, seatwork (10 to 15 minutes per day for practice), review/maintenance, and pace (consider the rate of instruction and increase if possible).

Berliner (1978) reported a great deal of variance among teachers in how they allocate time for mathematics instruction, particularly for specific topics, such as fractions, measurements, decimals, or geometry. At the elementary level, the time allocated for mathematics instruction varies considerably from one day to the next because of contextual situations, for instance, if students come back late from a music class or a social studies project takes longer than expected. At the secondary level, the allocated time is more constant, but even within that allocation, a teacher may decide to take care of administrative tasks or attend to other non-mathematical activities. Thus, a decision of one sort or another may significantly affect the amount of time devoted to the study of mathematics.

Another type of decision, which occurs in the interactive phase of teaching, is the decision on how long to wait for students to respond to a question. Rowe (1978) defined two kinds of wait time: (1) the pause following a question by the teacher and (2) the pause following a student's response (usually measured in terms of seconds).

Rowe (1978) found that elementary science teachers typically wait less than one second before commenting on an answer or before asking an additional question. When the two types of wait time were increased, Rowe reported that the length of student responses increased, failures to respond decreased, students' confidence increased, disciplinary problems decreased, slower students participated more and, in general, students were more reflective in their responses.

Consider the likely payoff if wait time of less than one second predominates. Can problem-solving abilities be nurtured and promoted when wait time is consistently less than one second? Not likely. It seems highly desirable for teachers to be explicitly aware of concepts such as 'wait time' in order that alternatives can be generated which are consistent with their instructional goals. This is not to claim that awareness of such concepts will yield completely 'rational' decisions in the sense that an explicit and highly recognizable decision-making strategy can be readily identified. But it is the belief here that whatever commonsensical decisions are made in the classroom, they can be enhanced by an explicit awareness of alternatives and by having a variety of pedagogical concepts, of which wait time is one, on tap.

Another aspect of managerial decisions involves the very-present problem of discipline. To deny that teachers are concerned and conscious of potential and actual classroom disruptions is to be oblivious to the realities of classroom teaching. Consider the following episode.

Episode 9

A first-year geometry teacher was discussing the proof of a theorem with the class. In the back of the room a student who was the band's drum major was twirling her baton. After a minute or so, the young teacher noticed her behavior. The teacher's confusion about alternatives was mirrored on his face. Apparently, alternatives did not exist since the teacher avoided the situation. But the impact on the class of the indecisiveness could not be discounted.

Perhaps the response of 'do nothing' was the best alternative. But consider the alternative prior to the specific incident. Could the teacher have moved about the room (as was not the actual case) and, as a result, increased his awareness of any potential problems? Did not the decision, determined consciously or unconsciously, to stay in front of the class in a small area inhibit his ability to monitor the student's behavior in the back of the class? Had he decided to move around the room and consciously monitor student behavior, could the embarrassing incident have been avoided? Probably so.

The ability of a teacher to monitor classroom events has been the focus of various investigations. For example, Kounin (1970) studied a number of variables with respect to classroom management and their relationship to achievement. One of the variables identified was called 'withitness'. This variable dealt with teachers communicating that they know what is going on regarding children's behavior and with their ability to attend to two issues simultaneously. Kounin found withitness to be a strong correlate of achievement. Brophy and Evertson (1976) also found that more successful teachers were more 'withit' than less effective teachers. Thus it appears that a teacher's ability to monitor simultaneous classroom events is an important factor in maintaining control and in positively affecting achievement.

There are no explicit directions for solving management problems. But alternatives can be identified for preventing and coping with situations. Perhaps an explicit awareness of possible alternatives can assist teachers in making those difficult decisions and provide greater confidence in themselves for believing they can control classroom events.

Conclusion

Teachers have an immense amount of common sense and good judgement. Many creative teachers have a wealth of alternative methods for dealing with a wide variety of classroom situations. But common sense can be enhanced by an explicit awareness of the importance of generating alternatives and by an explicit knowledge of various pedagogical concepts and principles. Practitioners' maxims and research in concert can play an important role in the generation of alternatives. The art of teaching can be improved by consciously considering alternatives and by expanding the knowledge base for generating alternatives.

Another aspect of improvement can arise from reflecting on why certain alternatives are selected. Value judgements, perceptions about what constitutes the teacher's role, and what constitutes mathematics, all provide a sort of filter through which some alternatives pass and others do not. Perhaps a realization of what factors contribute to the selection of alternatives as well as an awareness of the decision-making process itself can provide a basis for several outcomes; additional insights into the teaching process, a richer use of the teacher's knowledge base, and an avenue for teachers' further professional development.

Note

1 The author would like to express his appreciation to Dr Stephen I. Brown of the University of Buffalo for his helpful comments in writing this article.

References

Berliner, D. C. 'Allocated Time, Engaged Time, and Academic Learning Time in Elementary School Mathematics Instruction.' Paper presented at the 56th Annual Meeting of the National Council of Teachers of Mathematics, San Diego, April 1978.

Bishop, A. J. and Whitfield, R. C. *Situations in Teaching*. London: McGraw-Hill Book Company (UK) Limited, 1972.

Brophy, J. E. and Evertson, C. M. *Learning from Teaching: A Developmental Perspective*. Boston: Allyn and Bacon, 1976.

Cooney, T. J., Davis, E. J. and Henderson, K. B. *Dynamics of Teaching Secondary School Mathematics*. Boston: Houghton-Mifflin, 1975.

Ebmeier, H. and Good, T. L. 'The Effects of Instructing Teachers About Good Teaching on the Mathematics Achievement of Fourth Grade Students.' *American Educational Research Journal*, **16** (Winter 1979): 1–16.

Kolb, J. R. *A Predictive Model for Teaching Strategies Research, Part I: Derivation of the Model*. Athens, Ga.: The Georgia Center for the Study of Learning and Teaching Mathematics, 1977.

Kounin, J. S. *Discipline and Group Management in Classrooms*. New York: Holt, Rinehart and Winston, 1970.

Peterson, P. L. and Clark, C. M. 'Teachers' Reports of Their Cognitive Processes During Teaching.' *American Educational Research Journal*, **15** (Fall 1978): 555–565.

Rosenshine, B. and Furst, N. 'Research in Teacher Performance Criteria.' In *Symposium on Research in Teacher Education.* Edited by B. O. Smith. Englewood Cliffs, N.J.: Prentice-Hall, 1971.

Rowe, M. B. 'Wait, Wait, Wait, –.' *School Science and Mathematics,* **78** (March 1978): 207–216.

Shavelson, R. J. 'Teachers' Decision Making.' In *The Psychology of Teaching Methods (Yearbook of the National Society for the Study of Education).* Chicago: University of Chicago Press, 1976.

Shroyer, J. C. 'Critical Moments in the Teaching of Mathematics.' Paper presented at the annual meeting of the American Educational Research Association, Toronto, March 1978.

Tikunoff, W. J., Berliner, D. C. and Rist, R. C. *An Ethnographic Study of the Forty Classrooms of the Beginning Teacher Evaluation Study Known Sample* (Tech. Rep. 75-10-5). San Francisco: Far West Laboratory, 1975.

Tom Cooney is Professor of Mathematics Education at the University of Georgia, Georgia, USA.

29

'Is' versus 'seeing as': constructivism and the mathematics classroom

Barbara Jaworski

Introduction

Constructivism[1] is a philosophical stance through which it is possible to view many of the important issues in education. In particular, there are issues, current in mathematics classrooms, which may be viewed through a constructivist perspective. The purpose of this article is to suggest how constructivism can offer a way of perceiving mathematics teaching and learning which has the effect of unifying the underlying concerns in some issues.

Look at the figure below.

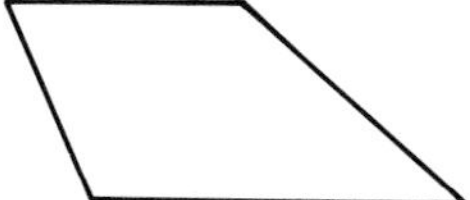

What is it?
What *shape* is it?
What would be your reaction to someone who said it was a square?

A class of 12 year olds had been asked by their teacher to name the above shape, which he had drawn on the board. Someone said that it was a *trapezium*. Some pupils agreed with this, others disagreed.

The teacher said. 'If you think it's not a trapezium then what *is* it?' One boy said, tentatively, 'It's a square . . .'

There were murmurings, giggles, 'a square?!'. But the boy went on '. . . sort of flat.'

The teacher looked puzzled, as if he could not see a square either. He invited the boy to come out to the board to explain his square. The boy did. He indicated that you had to be looking down on the square – as if it were on your book, only tilted. He moved his hands to illustrate.

'Oh,' said the teacher. 'Oh, I think I see what you mean . . . does anyone else see what he means?' There were more murmurings, puzzled looks, tentative nods.

The teacher then drew onto the shape, modifying it to produce the figure overleaf.

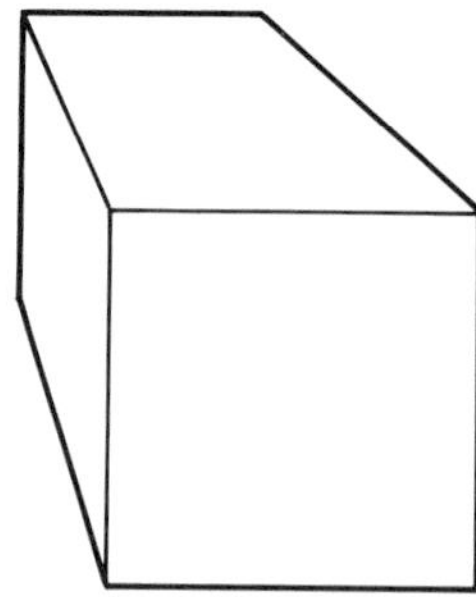

There were Ohs! around the class.

Some issues of current concern in mathematics education

If you were asked to name some of the important issues current in mathematics education, what would you offer?

I have chosen to consider five questions which have had currency with mathematics teachers with whom I have worked recently, and which lead to issues concerning the teaching and learning of mathematics.

1 *What* is *mathematics?*

At first sight this might seem a strange question for mathematics teachers, but many of us have been asked by a parent or pupil to justify what is mathematical about a particular problem or activity.

The question can underlie much of what takes place in mathematics classrooms. The beliefs of teachers and pupils about what mathematics *is* frequently influence what mathematics is done. If children believe that mathematics is a collection of rules, for example, then their learning might be influenced by their search for rules to memorise and attempt to apply. If teachers think of mathematics as a rigid formal system they might remain unaware of alternative concepts or ways of perceiving mathematical ideas.

My own school experience left me with a very formal view of mathematics in which I believed in the absoluteness of important results with which I had been presented. I should have been very unwilling to accept the figure on p. 287 as a square. It would not have fitted the definition which I had been given. The teacher in the anecdote also found it hard to see a square but he was prepared to let the boy explain, and from the boy's stumbling explanation the teacher and the class came to see the figure *as if* it were a square. This in no way alters the formal definition of a square. Indeed, there are times when it would be inappropriate to see this figure as a square. However, the *seeing as* opens up a wider area of perception. It allows new perspectives (the pun is intended!) on what is mathematically admissible as a square, given appropriate circumstances, and this might lead into areas of mathematics such as projective geometry or topology which had not previously been considered.

2 *How should a teacher try to communicate mathematics to her pupils? When is it appropriate just to tell them a result?*

The teacher in the anecdote did not give the boy a formal definition of a square. Maybe he judged that this would be inappropriate in the circumstances, although there might be other occasions when he *would* provide a definition, where perhaps he considered it important to the thinking of the pupils. Judgement of when it is appropriate to tell pupils a result requires considerable experience, sensitivity and knowledge of the pupils concerned. Also, implicit in *telling* is the notion that there exists truth or knowledge to be told and questions arise about the nature of this knowledge and whose knowledge it is. Even the most uncontroversial definitions have resulted from agreement in negotiation between mathematicians, and it is dangerous to view them as being absolute or God-given.

For example, when pupils work on mathematics using the computer language LOGO, there are often problems for them in knowing when a difficulty stems from the syntax of the language or from their mathematical inexpertise. A teacher trying to be helpful may judge that telling about syntax was a necessity while telling about mathematics may unduly constrain the pupils' thinking. Such judgement implies that the nature or quality of syntactic knowledge is somehow different from that of mathematical knowledge.

As another example, the question of whether 1 is or is not a prime number has long perplexed mathematical thinking. Clearly there are times when it is important to decide one way or the other, and pupils might expect the teacher to tell them which is the case. However, it could be more important for pupils to perceive that such dilemmas are possible and within their power to resolve and decide than just to receive an anodyne definition from the teacher. Pupils' perceptions of the origins of definitions will not develop if they are never themselves challenged with the need to define. The result – 1 is *not* a prime number – needs to be seen by pupils as being a decision by mathematicians, rather than as being a property of the number 1. The concept of definitions which are a result of convention rather than being in any sense intrinsic in the mathematics is a difficult one which pupils will only appreciate through experience.

3 *What constitutes a* productive *mathematical task for pupils in the classroom?*

As mathematics is not to be found just lying around to be picked up, a teacher has to find ways of making mathematical concepts available to pupils. Activities are developed to bring pupils up against particular concepts and might be expected to be measured against their success in this. What about the teacher in the anecdote – was he happy with the outcome of the pupils' responses to his drawing of the figure and his question about it?

The *productivity* of an activity must be measured both against the aims under which it was invented and against the outcome when it takes place. Too strict an adherence to the aims might restrict the outcome, but a more open-ended approach in practice may prevent the aims ever being achieved. If, in the anecdote, it had been the teacher's aim to test pupils' understanding of certain definitions of particular shapes, he might not have been too happy to accept that the figure drawn was a square. Compared against the usual definition of a square, it might have left some pupils very confused. Yet to *insist* on the usual definition could have implied that the boy was wrong, with the possibility of many unfortunate consequences as far as the boy was concerned and a loss of opportunity to broaden the mathematical experience of the other pupils.

4 *How do a teacher's questions influence the thinking of her pupils?*

It may be believed that a teacher can encourage pupils to be thinking and reflective mathematicians by asking the sort of questions which genuinely stimulate mathematical thought. Jim Smith (1986) suggests that such a questioning approach might constitute 'teaching-without-telling', that the right questions could enable pupils to produce the mathematics for themselves.

In her response to Jim Smith, Janet Ainley (1987) emphasises the *purpose* behind teachers' questions. She analyses some of the different types of questions which are asked in mathematics classrooms and maintains that, even with more 'open' questions, there is still an element of emphasis which the teacher's question conveys. Teachers do not ask questions at random or without purpose, or at least this is what pupils perceive. For example a question of the type 'How many xs can you find?' might suggest that, whether there are any xs to be found or not, x is something which it is important to look for – otherwise why would the teacher ask?

However, the teacher's purpose may not have been to put emphasis on the x so much as on the 'how many?'. The answer to 'how many?' might be 2 or 5000, or none or an infinite number, and the teacher may have wanted pupils to perceive these possibilities, simply using x as a device. Thus teacher and pupils get at cross purposes in the focus of their attention and possibly in their interpretations of what mathematics emerges.

Questions in the classroom can convey very complex messages which to a great extent depend on the conventions and expectations prevailing, and the teacher needs to aim not only for her own intended emphasis to be clear, but to circumvent other interpretations which might be made. This is a tall order.

5 *How can a teacher assess pupils' mathematical progress? How is it possible to standardise the teaching of mathematics – either in terms of syllabus or in terms of grading?*

When mathematics is presented formally with strict procedures, rules, theorems and results, it is possible to test pupils' ability to reproduce it. Pupils can be seen to quote theorems, apply rules and follow procedures. However, such testing probably says little about the pupils' overall mathematical understanding. Some form of diagnostic testing is necessary to find out what mathematical meanings pupils have made and what construction they have put on the various rules and procedures in trying to reach some overall coherence. Devising appropriate activities for any pupil depends on having some notions of the pupil's current images of the area of mathematics in question, to avoid creating bewilderment and confusion. If mathematics teaching is seen in terms of creating opportunities for pupils to encounter mathematical ideas and concepts and to develop their own powers of asking and answering mathematical questions, then assessment needs to be designed to provide feedback to the teacher for the creation of appropriate activities or tasks.

Assessment is also seen as having to provide information about pupils which will allow their performance to be measured relative to each other. There are many pressures from industry, from parents, from government, from higher education and so on for standardisation which will allow categorisation of pupils' achievement. In order for this to be possible, the curriculum has to be finely specified and syllabuses and ways of working prescribed. This can militate against the provision of opportunity to challenge pupils according to their experience and needs. Testing for standardisation can lead to teaching for the tests, so that pupils can be seen to be successful. Alan Schoenfeld (1982) puts it succinctly:

> All too often we focus on a narrow collection of well-defined tasks and train students to execute these tasks in a routine, if not algorithmic fashion. Then we test students on tasks that are very close to the ones they have been taught. If they succeed on those problems, we and they congratulate each other. . .
>
> To allow them and ourselves to believe that they 'understand' mathematics is deceptive and fraudulent. (p.29)

These five issues may be seen to have an underlying theme which has to do with the nature of mathematical knowledge, the methods available to the teacher for communicating mathematically with the pupils and the constructions which pupils put on the mathematics which they encounter in the classroom. A teacher may have a clear, coherent mathematical story which she wishes to convey to her pupils, and she may provide them with a good explanation as she sees it. However, it is only good for pupils if it fits their experience and needs. In the words of John Mason (1987), 'experience is fragmentary' – pupils come to the mathematics classroom with a diversity of experiences to which they attempt to relate what they do and hear, constructing stories which form the basis of their understanding. Their mathematical stories may be very different from the teacher's, depending on what they stress and ignore. Whether pupils have a coherent story in either the teacher's terms or their own will depend on the sense which they make. Mathematical meaning varies from one individual to another and communication depends upon the ability to share each other's meanings. As Alan Bishop (1984) writes:

> Given that each individual constructs his own mathematical meaning how can we share each other's meanings? It is a problem for children working in groups, and for teachers trying to share their meanings with the children individually . . .
>
> If meanings are to be shared and negotiated then all parties must communicate . . .
>
> Also communication is more than just talking! It is also about relationship.

A distinction between simply 'saying things' to someone and communicating with them was made quite strongly by Ernst von Glasersfeld (1983) who urged that we should explore the nature of communication:

> As teachers we are intent on generating knowledge in students. That after all is what we are being paid for, and since the guided acquisition of knowledge, no

> matter how we look at it, seems predicated on a process of communication we should take some interest in how that process might work . . .
>
> Although it does not take a good teacher long to discover that saying things is not enough to 'get them across', there is little if any theoretical insight into why linguistic communication does not do all that it is supposed to do.

Discussion and negotiation in the classroom are vital, not only in terms of the mathematics which is superficially being considered, but in terms of the deep-rooted expectations and conventions which influence the mathematical stories which are being constructed. Imre Lakatos (1976) presents a classroom dialogue in which teacher and students examine a geometrical problem and discuss their perceptions of it. As the discussion proceeds definitions are questioned and nothing seems sacred in an attempt for each student to get to the roots of the mathematical proof involved. Is this achievable in practice?

What constructivism is

Constructivism is an abstract philosophical stance about knowledge and its relation to the world and to people's attempts, through their experiences, to try to rationalise the world. Its span is much broader than education. However, there are very powerful practical implications for mathematics education from a constructivist way of thinking which relate directly to the issues discussed above.

Ernst von Glasersfeld, who was quoted above, is one of the world's leading proponents of constructivism as a philosophy which has important consequences for education and in particular for mathematics education. He was challenged at a conference on the Psychology of Mathematics Education in 1987 by a mathematics educator, Jeremy Kilpatrick, to re-examine some of his claims about the consequences which he suggests. The debate which this encouraged seemed to get at the very roots of what constructivism has to offer to education.

Kilpatrick (1987) quoted two principles which according to von Glasersfeld define a constructivist view of knowledge and learning.

1 Knowledge is actively constructed by the cognising subject, not passively received from the environment.
2 *Coming to know* [my italics] is an adaptive process that organises one's experiential world; it does not discover an independent, pre-existing world outside the mind of the knower.

These may be simply paraphrased to say that the learner is not *given* knowledge, but actively constructs it herself, and that learning, or coming to know, is a process of adapting one's view of the world as a result of this construction.

The anecdote at the beginning of the article offers a simple example of the second principle. You might believe that a square is a well-defined mathematical object with an independent existence that defies interpretation, i.e. that things either are or are not squares. This is the Platonic view. To know a square is to compare it with its heavenly prototype and find sufficient agreement between the pragmatic earthly object and its perfect counterpart. Such comparison with the object in the first figure would be unlikely to allow the object to be named a square. Yet the boy's perception seems stunning when insight gives us a glimpse of his thinking. Are we ready to adapt our rigid image of a square to include this new perspective? It is no longer so much a question of what is or is not, but rather of what we perceive and how useful it is.

As human beings struggle to understand the world around them, the best they can do is to conjecture hypotheses to explain what they observe and test these against further experience and observation. They may struggle to search for objective truths about existence, but yet have no means of verifying if truth has been found as this would require comparisons which are beyond human scope. The constructivist's position is that we can never *know* objective truth, even if it exists – all we can do is struggle to explain what we observe, to identify theories which *fit* our observations.

Von Glasersfeld (1983) suggested that there are two metaphors for explaining the world around us, encapsulated in the words 'match' and 'fit'. In order to open a door a key has to *fit* the lock. Many keys will do this, and it makes no difference which of these we use. We do not have to find one key which *matches* the lock exactly.

In explaining the world around us or the world of mathematics it is necessary, and indeed possible, only to find theories which *fit* what we observe or perceive. Such a theory is *viable*. Biology offers examples of this. Survival of an organism occurs when the organism finds a *viable* means of existence. It does not have to be the *only* means of existence, or even the best. What is overwhelmingly powerful is the constraint against which viability fails. The organism dies.

After a number of activities designed to help pupils appreciate Pythagoras' theorem for right-angled triangles, one pupil, Paul, believed that the 'sum of squares' method would give him the *area* of the triangle (rather than the hypotenuse). In a subsequent exercise in which he was required to find areas of triangles, he performed the Pythagorean algorithm correctly but, in comparing his result with the area obtained by another method, discovered inconsistency. It was only after being puzzled by this inconsistency and having a lengthy discussion with his teacher that Paul abandoned the algorithm as a viable means of finding area.

Von Glasersfeld (1982) claims that Piaget's thinking was primarily constructivist. In discussing Piaget's 'action schemes' he writes:

> The relation of 'knowledge' and the 'real world', thus, is reciprocal because any cognitive structure is likely to be modified when it clashes with a constraint. To the organism, the environment manifests itself *only* through such clashes, and the organism can therefore conclude no more than that those structures and schemes which have *not* clashed with the constraints of the world constitute a viable way of managing. This is analogous to saying that the biological organisms that are alive at a given moment, are *viable* because they have so far managed to survive.

In the example, Paul had to abandon the Pythagorean result in his struggle for understanding area. The difference of the results was the constraint that made their co-existence unviable and the teacher helped Paul to judge which of them was incorrect. Thus Paul modified his beliefs about area by rejecting a theory which was contradicted by a constraint.

Von Glasersfeld points out that the cognitive organism (Paul in this case) has more opportunity to achieve viability than does the biological organism as cognition builds on modification. Biology, however, is unremitting – the species as a whole adapts because individuals are not all the same and those which are not viable are eliminated and do not reproduce!

In considering the connections between constructivism and the teaching and learning of mathematics, the pragmatism forced by a classroom environment might be seen as throwing up constraints which have to be overcome before learning may be achieved. Thus there are both mathematical constraints and social constraints challenging viability in learning mathematics.

Constructivist implications for mathematics teaching

Kilpatrick (1987) paraphrases von Glasersfeld (in press) as having identified five consequences for educational practice that follow from a radical constructivist position.

(a) Teaching (using procedures that aim at generating understanding) becomes sharply distinguished from training (using procedures that aim at repetitive behaviour).
(b) Processes inferred as inside the student's head become more interesting than overt behaviour.
(c) Linguistic communication becomes a process for guiding a student's learning, not a process for transferring knowledge.
(d) Students' deviations from the teacher's expectations become means for understanding their efforts to understand.
(e) Teaching interviews become attempts not only to infer cognitive structures but also to modify them.

It is Kilpatrick's thesis that although these five consequences fit the constructivist stance, they appear to fit other philosophical positions as well, and by inference, that belief in them does not imply espousal of constructivism. It is a nice point that constructivism *fits* these particular beliefs rather than matches them. However, whether these beliefs are a consequence of constructivist thought, or whether they are principles which constructivism supports, is less important than how constructivism can influence thought about teaching and learning mathematics.

The first of von Glasersfeld's two principles suggests that knowledge is actively constructed by the pupil, not passively received from the environment or the teacher. Here the mathematics classroom is the environment, and pupils are the cognising subjects. Although it might be seen as the pupils' responsibility actively to construct mathematics for themselves, it is unreasonable to expect that they will do it solely of their own accord. This is particularly true in the case of mathematics which, unlike physics or geography, is not an observable part of the environment, but exists within people's minds. The teacher is the mediator between pupils and mathematics. The issues discussed earlier highlighted the difficulties which teachers face in this role. The 'consequences' above suggest ways in which the role might be interpreted to help pupils with their mathematical construction, for example, as in (a) above, using procedures which aim at generating understanding rather than inducing repetitive behaviour. The Cockcroft Report (DES, 1982) in paragraph 243 suggested certain elements of classroom practice which would contribute to pupils' understanding, and some examples of these elements in practice may be found in Jaworski (this volume).

Construal of the social nature of the classroom environment takes place along with construal of mathematics. Pupils have developing expectations of what it means to learn mathematics in school. Teachers need to ensure that this is positive in terms of pupils actively working on mathematical ideas rather than merely expecting that the mathematics will happen to them.

In order to help pupils make sense of mathematics, the teacher needs to gain insight into their thinking. In pragmatic terms, the teacher has responsibilities for interpreting the curriculum, for delivering the syllabus and for ensuring that pupils achieve their best in terms of examination results on which their futures may depend. This implies that there must be communication between teacher and pupils so that the teacher may know what construal is taking place.

The second of von Glasersfeld's principles states that *coming to know* is an adaptive process that organises one's experiential world; one does not discover an independent, pre-existing world outside the mind of the knower. Traditional testing has often presumed such a pre-existing mathematical world, but if testing is truly to reflect the meanings which a pupil constructs, stereotyped tests will not do. The teacher has to somehow get inside the minds of her pupils. Consequences (b)–(e) above are related to this. Linguistic communication becomes supremely important – teachers encouraging pupils to talk, and listening to them; providing opportunity for pupils to talk and listen to each other; encouraging open negotiation of meanings without fear of being thought foolish or wrong. Teachers need to use pupils' apparent misconceptions in order to gain insight into their images and constructions. In the case of Paul above, for example, the teacher was very surprised to learn what use Paul was making of the Pythagorean result, but it gave him insight into Paul's thinking so that he was better able to be of help in suggesting ways to proceed.

Paul was challenged to reconsider his mathematical construction when a constraint arose in the form of an inconsistency in his results. Unfortunately, pupils are not always aware of inconsistencies and might not always examine their beliefs in a way which reveals inconsistency. Teaching interviews were designed as a research tool to learn about children's thinking and the constructions they made. They are not easy to adopt in a classroom environment where the teacher finds it difficult to talk at length to individual pupils. However, a modified form of the teaching interview occurs whenever a teacher talks with and listens to one or more pupils in the classroom. The teacher needs to be on the lookout for inconsistencies in pupils' thinking so that she can ask questions or design activities that will introduce the constraints which challenge misunderstanding.

Constructivism offers no panacea to teachers in coping with the issues of teaching and learning, but it may provide insight into the reasons why making mathematical sense is no easy task. If learning is seen as the continuous act of making sense and fitting into experience, rather than the absorption of preordained mathematical knowledge, and if teaching is seen as the provision of *opportunity* to make sense and encounter constraints rather than to convey knowledge, then relationships in the mathematics classroom may take on a different form and the environment become more oriented towards a coherent building of mathematical concepts.

Notes

1 Constructivism in this article should be interpreted as Radical Constructivism. This is distinguished from *simple* (or *trivial*) Constructivism which might be said to embrace the first of von Glasersfeld's principles but not the second.

References

Ainley, Janet (1987) 'Telling Questions', *Mathematics Teaching*, **118**, pp. 24–26.

Bishop, Alan (1984) 'Research Problems in Mathematics Education II' *for the learning of mathematics,* vol, 4, no. 2, pp. 40–41.

DES (1982) *Mathematics Counts* (The Cockcroft Report). London: HMSO.

Kilpatrick, Jeremy (1987) 'What Constructivism might be in Mathematics Education', in PME-XI proceedings, Montreal.

Lakatos, Imre (1976) *Proofs and Refutations.* Cambridge: Cambridge University Press.

Mason, John (1987) 'Teaching (pupils to make sense) and Assessing (the sense they make)', *Perspectives* 34, University of Exeter.

Schoenfeld, Alan. (1982) 'Some Thoughts on Problem-solving Research and Mathematics Eduction', in F. K. Lester and J. Garofalo (eds) *Mathematical Problem Solving: Issues in Research.* Philaelphia: Franklin Institute Press.

Smith, Jim (1986) 'Questioning Questioning', *Mathematics Teaching*, **115**, p. 47.

von Glaserfeld, Ernst (1982) 'An Interpretation of Piaget's Constructivism', *Revue Internationale de Philosophie*, pp. 142–43.

von Glaserfeld, Ernst (1983) 'Learning as a Constructive Activity', in PME-NA proceedings, Montreal, September-October 1983.

von Glaserfeld, Ernst (in press, 1988) 'Constructivism', in T. Husen and N. Postlethwaite (eds) *International Encyclopaedia of Education: Supplement Vol. 1.* Oxford: Pergamon.

Barbara Jaworski is Lecturer in Mathematics Education at the Open University.

30

Imagery, imagination and mathematics classrooms

John Mason

If artists are people who best express themselves by manipulating physical objects and by leaving some sort of trace (picture, pot, sculpture, music, magnetic-tape . . .), and poets are people who best express themselves by manipulating words, then mathematicians are people who express themselves by manipulating succinct symbols. But the symbols, like the pictures and the poems, are only the end product. What do the symbols stand for?

I consider mathematics to be an action which takes place mostly inside people, and that what is written down is an artefact, a mere vestige of the real action. Put another way, I consider mathematics to be concerned with *seeing, expressing* and *manipulating* generalities, mostly in the domains of number, space and relationship. The seeing takes place internally, in the imagination; hence the title of this article.

> **Exercise 1**
> Imagine a cube. Balance it on one face. The vertices lie on two layers, four vertices in each layer.
> Balance it on one vertex. How many layers are there now? How many vertices are in each layer?
> Balance it on one edge. How many layers are there now? How many vertices in each layer?

Not everyone finds such an exercise straightforward the first time they try it, but with a little practice everyone can find *something* to do which enables them to answer the questions. Some people report that they actually 'see' a cube, while others deny pictures, but have a sense of, or awareness of a cube. Some people experience a sort of 'radar screen', with a frequent need to refresh the bits of their image that they are not attending to. They also find it helpful to repeat the instructions to themselves, subvocally, to help strengthen and sharpen their image.

It is easier to imagine a cube if you have a cube-like object or a diagram of a cube in front of you. But even with a diagram, it is necessary to look 'through' it, rather than at it, making use of the powers of the imagination. The diagram can act as scaffolding or support for the mental screen, stabilising the image, but if the diagram becomes the sole object of attention then it can hinder rather than help thinking. The cube exercise demonstrates the power of a diagram to extend the mental screen, and to release the powers of imagery to work on the question at hand.

I take 'imagination' to mean the inner experiences of pictures-in-the-head, sounds-in-the-head, internal-muscular-response and fuzzy-senses-of; in short, all inner modes of experiencing, including inner analogues of outer senses such as seeing, hearing, feeling and perhaps even tasting and smelling. These may be stimulated by immediate sense, by recall of past experience, or freshly constructed. (To see that fresh construction is possible, imagine Lake Windermere drained of all water, filled with whipped cream, with a huge cherry on top, and surrounded by fan wafers that tinkle in the wind like wind chimes.) Later, it may become useful to make distinctions, and to restrict the meaning of the word 'imagination', but as when young children learn a new word by first expanding its meaning then later contracting it, so it may prove useful to remain for the present in our expansion phase.

Intentionally invoking the various powers of imagination produces *imagery*. The cliché 'I see what you're saying' suggests that it helps our listeners if we are good at 'saying what we are seeing'. Learning to speak directly from imagery, to describe so vividly that imagery is evoked in others, is part of the art of teaching. Helping pupils to give vivid descriptions is part of 'working on imagery', and can take place in any lesson.

Although the words 'imagery' and 'seeing' are based on pictures, I find it useful to encompass a wide variety of inner experiences by the word 'imagery'. In each of the following examples, try to pay attention to 'how you do it', as much as to the doing itself.

Exercise 2a
What letter comes seven before p? How did you find out?

Many people report only *hearing* the letters, marking some by extra emphasis. Others *see* or *sense* certain letters in order to enable them to count backwards. The difficulty of imagery lies not in the doing, but in the negotiating of a language to speak sensibly about what happens in our heads. Since this is where mathematics really happens, it seems a worthwhile endeavour.

Exercise 2b
Repeat the seven-times table. Where do the answers come from?

Try to catch yourself getting the answers. Extend the table beyond 12 if necessary! For most of us, the tables are a completely automatic response, yet even so we have to keep track of where we are in the table, and, if we reach into products not previously memorised, we have to find some way to store numbers and do calculations. It can be done, with only a little practice.

Exercise 2c
What are the roots of the following quadratic equation in a?
$xa^2 + ca + b = 0$.

Some people find that the memorised formula gets in the way, others report that the formula really consists of slots, so they can put the appropriate letters in the slots. The point of Exercises 2a-c is that no matter how you think you did them, that is part of what I mean by the powers of imagination producing imagery.

To see that there are several kinds of imagery which can be evoked and which, with practice, can even function independently, recall that when walking down the street, washing dishes, driving a car, etc., most people have an active inner life of imaginary conversations, pictures of other places and so on.

Exercise 3
Start counting silently to yourself 1, 2, . . .
You can count silently and be centred in your language, and you can establish a count that just happens inside you without employing all your attention. Now keep the count going, silently, and at the same time imagine a square – it might even change size, and rotate.
Keep the count going, and the square rotating, and silently recite a formula such as the quadratic formula or area of a trapezoid, the sum of arithmetic and geometric progressions, etc.
Imagine yourself getting into your bed at home.
Look out of a window near you.
Listen to the sounds around you.

You can be 'aware of' a square, have a 'sense of' a square without being able to see it firmly and completely. The same is true of your bed. You can also use a form of peripheral vision to see out the window without really being present in the seeing, and as soon as your attention is attracted by some movement, the count, or the square, disappears. Imagine the power that could be brought to bear if all of these were employed towards a common aim.

The following examples can be and have been used with pupils of various ages from 5 to 95. Their mathematical content is the least important aspect here, because our concern is with imagery. Once you are familiar with evoking imagery, you can focus on the mathematics. More important are the directness of the language used to try to evoke imagery, and the conjecturing atmosphere in which participants are invited to sharpen their images, to describe them vividly to others, to listen attentively and to respond to others' descriptions, to make conjectures and modify them, to try to convince others. It sometimes helps to hear rather than read the instructions, and then to repeat them silently until an image is established.

Exercise 4
Imagine a circle (not a disc!); let it move around in 'the' plane, changing size and position. Get a sense of all its possible movements and positions.
Now fix a point on the circle, and let the circle move around as before, but always passing through (coincident with) the point. Get a sense of the restrictions to movement.
Now fix a second point. Get a sense of the restrictions to movement.
Now fix a third point.

Repeat for a square.

To utter what you experience is to announce a theorem; to describe vividly what you experience is to offer a form of proof. Whereas the cube example was reasonably static, this exercise demonstrates the power of movement. Computer animations can display such dynamics beautifully, but they yield a different experience from doing it for yourself in your head. When the image is more or less under your control you own it, rather than trying to work out what 'the program' is doing and why. Animations are an excellent way to support dynamic imagery by providing experience to refer back to.

Exercise 5
Imagine a situation in which the calculation 43 subtract 27 is needed.
Imagine yourself mowing a lawn each week. If the grass grows faster, and/or the lawn gets smaller, and/or the mower is replaced by a larger one, in each case, will it take longer or shorter to mow?

Some pupils try to treat mathematics at arm's length, expecting perhaps that it is all just supposed to happen. Exercises like these can help pupils literally to enter a situation and make it their own.

Exercise 6
Imagine a bag of marbles. Five more are put in, then three removed.
How have the contents of the bag changed? Now imagine six more are removed. How have the contents changed?

This exercise illustrates the observation that practical materials (actual bags and marbles) can sometimes get in the way. By having actual bags with marbles present, it is likely that pupils will be fixated by the particular number of marbles in the bag. There is a significant difference between imagining a bag, and actually *seeing* a bag in front of you. Manipulation of physical objects can support imagery, but it can also distract from seeing 'through' the particular to the general.

Six year olds are perfectly capable of this sort of mental exercise, which can support both the idea of negative numbers, and numbers as operators. Pupils can develop and negotiate a language for talking about these sorts of situations which does not involve the number of marbles in the bag at the start – a relative rather than an absolute language.

Physical objects (and computer screens) have a particularising quality whereas corresponding mental images are much more general. It may help to stabilise your mental screen to have an appropriate object to look at, but over-dependence on particular objects, and on actually doing the actions physically, may not by itself evoke sufficiently powerful and general imagery. The whole point of Exercise 6 is that the number of marbles to start with is both unknown and irrelevant.

Exercise 7
'Here are some words we have been using in class recently: *divided by, shared by, divided into, equal parts, distributed into, . . .*
Imagine some situations to which they apply. Construct a sentence or two which describe your imagined situation, and which use these words. Now use the words to describe the sorts of questions we have been working on this week.'

This exercise is presented as a quotation to illustrate a technique for helping pupils to realise that they can and should try to formulate their own story about what happens in the classroom. The moment pupils leave a classroom, their attention is usually on what comes next. By spending time in a lesson linking ideas and terms with images, literally *reconstructing* their own account of a topic, there is more chance that they will be able to recall the ideas later in a usable form.

Exercise 8

Imagine a vertical number line. Stand on it somewhere. Go up three places. Go down five places. Double your distance from zero. Go up four places. Go half-way towards zero. You should be back where you started. How could I know this without knowing where you started?

As presented, these exercises are simply ink on paper, mere vestiges of stimulating events. They are not of themselves useful or engaging. They need to be lifted off the paper, and the only way I know to do this is to invoke imagery, to employ the many powers of imagination, which themselves depend on an appropriate mathematical atmosphere in the classroom, and on a supportive, interested and engaged attitude being manifested by the teacher.

After inviting people to imagine something, I usually spend considerable time getting individuals to tell each other, and then the group as a whole, what they are seeing. I work on helping them reach a succinct but vivid style of direct description (using imperative forms like 'imagine . . .' can be very effective) rather than talking vaguely 'about' what they are seeing, in abstract and general terms.

From these descriptions several points usually emerge. The first is that there are widely differing descriptions of the mental screen, with different people attending to quite different aspects. Usually some mathematical question emerges, if I have not posed one, and so there is plenty to investigate. Although I usually ask people to work solely in their heads, there is a lot to be learned about the nature of images and the role of diagrams by permitting pictures/diagrams, etc. on paper. Many teachers report that pupils are reluctant to draw diagrams for themselves. By experiencing the power of extending the mental screen, using part of your own image, pupils may begin to want to draw diagrams for themselves.

It may be that one or two of the exercises provoked an image of yourself in your own classroom, 'trying' the exercise with your pupils. Few activities can be 'taken' into the classroom as they are. Rather, they need subtle modification to make them appropriate to the particular circumstances of pupils, teacher and context. Preparing for a lesson calls upon the very same powers of imagery that we use in mathematics. One final example:

Exercise 9

Imagine yourself in front of a class about to introduce a task or activity. You have an image of pupils working away at your task. How do you describe the task so that a similar picture is evoked in them?

Posing a question to others, or initiating activity, is always problematic. Very often the imagery is so vivid, the task so clear to the teacher, that the description is incomplete and open to a variety of interpretations.

For example, a teacher had given each pupil in a class of 7–8 year olds a sheet of paper containing squares divided into quarters. The teacher posed the question 'How many different ways can such a square be coloured with two colours?' and imagined the pupils colouring in each quarter in a single colour, and confronting the question of what 'different' means. Some pupils surprised him by colouring parts of the quarter squares in different colours and making little sense of his question.

This last example suggests that our expectations are often in the form of images, and that we often expect other people to share those images, even when we speak in general terms *about* them rather than vividly *from* them. Young children show this very clearly, for when asked to talk about some event, their choice of words suggests that they believe everyone shares their inner world. I suggest that we are all like that to some extent!

Imagery can be effectively employed to prepare for a lesson, by imagining typical or potential moments in the lesson. By rehearsing both words (subvocally) and images (mentally), potential difficulties and awkwardnesses can be foreseen. By visualising several different ways of dealing with potential situations – the end of the lesson, responding to typical pupil questions or responses – you can free yourself from the tyranny of your automatic reactions. Suddenly, in the moment, you may find one or more of your alternative responses coming up inside you, and acted upon, almost before you are aware of it.

If the perspective of mathematics presented at the beginning has any substance, then one central task of a mathematics teacher is to help pupils to discover and develop their inherent imaginative powers:

- by establishing a conducive atmosphere (which in mathematics means a conjecturing atmosphere) where everything said can be taken as a conjecture intended to be modified, altered or abandoned;
- by providing important foci on which to exercise those powers, and not just a smorgasbord of activities to keep pupils engaged for whole lessons;
- by assisting pupils to reflect or otherwise become aware of their powers.

The best way for anyone to help others in this area is to work on themselves: to work at evoking imagery vividly; to work at becoming aware of their own images; to work at helping pupils describe what *they* are seeing; to act as a role model of an inquisitive mathematician who has, not answers, but mathematical processes for reaching conjectures and for convincing themselves and others.

Further reading

If you are interested in pursuing some of the ideas mentioned in this article, then *Geometric Images* by R. Beeney *et al.*, 1982 (published by the Association of Teachers of Mathematics) is an excellent source.

John Mason is Director of the Centre for Mathematics Education at the Open University.

31

Investigating investigations

David Wheeler

On the face of it, a lot of reported investigations of mathematical situations show us children trying to reach knowledge about things hardly worth knowing. I'm not terribly moved to know the sum of the dots on the visible faces of a die in all possible positions, or to master a rule-modification in the game of Frogs, or to establish the impossibility of drawing 5 lines so that they yield 3 crossovers. I feel it would be no particular loss to me if I didn't know any of these things. On the other hand, I do see that it would be, if not a loss, at least a serious inconvenience, if I didn't know how to find an integer equivalent to 4^3 (and have lots of other associations with this symbol).[1]

Maybe I would have more interest in the dot sums, frog moves, line crossovers, etc., if I were somehow involved in the investigations myself. Indeed, I can put it more positively than that and say that I have on occasion (though not frequently) found myself working at these and similar questions as if they mattered. At those moments the puritan in me slept and the activity seemed to justify itself: 'I'm enjoying myself, aren't I?'

One could say, as perhaps some of you are saying, that the mathematical end-points of classroom investigations do not have to be particularly significant, that it is more the experience of the processes involved that matters: the journey not the destination. I see there may be some force in that, but I then think, say, about solving crossword puzzles, an activity I engaged in quite avidly at one time but repeat only occasionally now. It is, no doubt, the processes involved in doing them, the struggle with the requirements of the tasks, that generate the fascination and the satisfaction. The final diagrams are of no consequence except to mark completion and release of energy. One finds that one must learn how to solve crossword puzzles, so there is some residue from the solving activity that gets applied to future examples, some learning of common processes and principles. But I stopped giving time to this when I found that solving puzzles only led to solving more puzzles, and that I had no wish to become a master solver. Now I take an occasional dip for the fun of it. If I have got anything more generally applicable out of the activity, I am not aware of it.

I kick off in this way because the ATM, through the journal *Mathematics Teaching* in particular, has made great efforts for some years to validate mathematical investigations as a classroom activity. Now these efforts have received the accolade of a Cockcroft award. Rather like a Labour Party supporter, only happy in opposition, I want to make sure that we continue (or resume) asking what mathematical investigations are all about. The debasement of meaning that has quickly followed the official endorsement of 'mathematical problem solving' in North America and elsewhere shows what could happen to the conception of mathematical investigations. A safeguard is 'to think in a complex way about complex questions', to acknowledge that when it comes to questions of worth, of 'what matters', the validity of one's answers may be both local and global, or maybe not; both individual and collective, or maybe not; immediate and long-lasting, or maybe not; personal and professional, or not. And so on.

A lesson that investigations teach us is that experiment plays an important part in mathematical thinking. In some situations we perform experiments to collect some 'data', for instance by drawing lines and counting the crossovers. In others we perform the experiment of matching some phenomenon to other things we know until we find a fit, for example by projecting the values of $x^2 + 3y^2$ onto a modulo 7 coordinate grid to give a repeating pattern. We may perform the experiment of altering some variable in a situation to see if an interesting new problem emerges, changing the jump rule in Frogs for example, [. . .].

The word 'experiment' may seem a little reckless (and haven't we all read somewhere that mathematics is not an experimental science?). I'll stick with it, though, for a couple of reasons. The first is that it carries the useful message that one can quite often take certain actions in mathematical situations to establish what is the case: 'I don't know for sure, but I will find out.' The second is that even in the 'experimental sciences' the experiments are not only about the behaviour of liquids in test-tubes, say, but about the confirming and denying of hypotheses, which are relations between ideas. If experiments are essentially tests of the connections between ideas, the application to mathematical situations is uncontroversial. Indeed, one might even allow that a proof is the end-result of an experimental process since each link has to be mentally tested for the security of its connection to the assumptions and hypotheses that precede it. This emphasis is faithful to the effort and inventiveness that we find we have to put into the construction of a sound proof. [. . .]

Experiments are not to be confused with thoughtless trials. Researchers always talk about 'designing experiments', which indicates that there must be some element of planning and managing to an experiment. I'll choose to put the stress here on 'managing' since 'planning' may imply knowing in advance exactly what to do with the result of an experiment, whatever that result is. This is not usually the case with the experiments undertaken in an investigation, especially in the early stages.

However, an experiment must be intended – that is, it must be meant to do something – and it must be monitored to make sure it doesn't go wrong and, at the end, interpreted. All this implies that it takes place in a controlled context.

Investigations have to be 'managed' sometimes, as in 'I managed to solve the problem'. The idiom is helpful, I think, just because it doesn't have to meet very stringent conditions. 'I managed to' tells us just enough; I might have tackled whatever I was doing clumsily, inefficiently, long-windedly, unimaginatively, etc., but at least I 'managed to' so I must have 'managed it'. It is also worth asking about students who have *not* managed their anxiety. Managing an investigation certainly involves not only managing the technical and mathematical tools, but the affective components too. Solving problems and investigating situations (and even mastering conventional mathematics) are risk-taking activities and require courage as well as skill. It would be good if some writers (without being sentimental about it) would give some attention to these often unspoken aspects.

A problem for the teacher may be to decide when and how to intervene in the matter of managing investigations. Would it help the pupils to be given some tips in advance about systematic thinking, say? Probably not. Piagetians would no doubt say that systematic 'hypothetico-deductive' thinking must wait on the development of the 'formal operations' stage in each person and that many secondary school pupils haven't reached it. De Bono has written a shelf full of books showing that rule-bound (systematic?) thinking is an obstacle to solving problems. The only virtue of systematic thinking is its economy in the use of time and energy, and since economy is an attractive quality to most people, one might take the opportunity to demonstrate economy by comparing different ways of doing things and hope that the inference is made. To try to *teach* systematic thinking is probably a mistake, even if we knew how. Our human tendency to form habits and the algorithmic leanings of mathematics should perhaps be balanced, not reinforced.

Finally, I offer a thought for consideration: one way to avoid being wedded to error is to make lots of them.

Note

1 The specific examples mentioned here and elsewhere in this section are not important for the general argument. They are references to investigations reported in the issue of *Mathematics Teaching* in which this chapter first appeared.

David Wheeler is Professor of Mathematics at Concordia University, Montreal, Canada.

32

Lucas turns in his grave

Dick Tahta

'Mathematics for all' became a powerful post-War slogan as an overtly elitist system of secondary education began to change. But the conviction that young people should not be denied mathematical experience can easily develop into an assumption that they *must* have this experience – whether they like it or not. And the evidence is that an enormous number continue not to like it.

There are various ways of fudging round this fact. 'If only the subject could be taught better,' say the advisers, and the inspectors and the teacher trainers, understandably forgetting that the situation was no better when they were in the classroom. 'If only the subject could be organised better', say the curriculum developers, the project directors and the textbook writers, possibly also forgetting that such reformulation has always been part of the mathematical enterprise, and that it has not always made things clearer or easier for *learners*.

Over the last few decades, the state of mathematical teaching has certainly seemed to some people to be sufficiently calamitous to justify new descriptions of the subject itself. Such proposals are often taken up with enthusiasm by a relatively small number of teachers, but usually fail to command any permanent universal assent. 'Let us not deny young people access to some twentieth-century mathematics,' said some enthusiasts in the 1960s. 'Mathematics is about relations,' they said, and tried to find ways of offering these to pupils. But the structuralist view of mathematics does not seem to have resolved classroom problems any better than, for example, an earlier commerce-based approach, one to which we now seem to be returning.

Other descriptions of mathematics were also developed; for instance, the notion that we are all mathematicians without always knowing that we are. A persuasive example comes from the physicist Richard Feynman, reporting a conversation overheard in the cafeteria when he was a student. One girl was explaining to another that if you wanted to make a straight line you go over a certain number to the right for each row that you go up. She went on to say: 'Suppose you have another line coming in from the other side, and you want to figure out where they are going to intersect; suppose on one line you go over two to the right, for every one you go up, and the other line goes over three to the right for every one it goes up, and they start twenty steps apart. . .' She then worked out where the intersection was. It turned out she was explaining how to knit Argyle socks!

In the same spirit, it has recently seemed attractive to emphasise that mathematics is a process, a human activity involving conjecture and refutation, classification and construction, problem solving and investigation, and so on. Such emphasis can soon lead to the making of trivial distinctions and pedantic reservations. But it does seem that the development of mathematics has always been accompanied by a lively self-awareness of the activity itself, and that currently there is a certain concentration on the exploratory and empirical aspects of mathematical investigation.

That there is indeed an *inductive* element in the mathematical process is not so easily dismissed nowadays as it was when, for example, the seventeenth-century French mathematician, Pierre Fermat, attacked the ideas of his English contemporary, John Wallis. Wallis seems to have been one of the first to describe explicitly his own method of arriving at general results by induction from particular cases – an activity which is often invoked in many of the 'investigations' which are currently being proposed for pupils. He countered Fermat's very strong criticism by claiming that he was trying to get beyond the particular problems and solutions current in his time, that he was searching for general methods of investigation rather than the discovery of new truths. 'But that which I aim at, in discovering these Methods, is not so much for this one Question (which perhaps may not deserve it) as to give a Pattern how other Numerical Questions of like nature (or even more perplexed than this) may in like manner be solved. . .'

Inevitably, new methods prove their worth by being successfully used to solve old problems. Wallis applied his new techniques to some classical quadrature problems. His generalising approach led him and his successors, notably Isaac Newton, to consider an extension of the index notation to include a fractional, negative and ultimately any real number, power. It is this long, hard struggle to extend meaning that lies behind the simple phrases – 'powers of x' or 'the exponential function' – of a traditional mathematics syllabus. And most elementary classroom approaches to these topics have tended to invoke, albeit unconsciously, Wallis' inductive approach. The development of 'mathematics for all' has meant, to some extent, that the more rigorous demands of a syllabus designed primarily for a small, selected minority of pupils have had to be modified considerably. Thus a very detailed analysis of the exponential function tends to be replaced by a trust in the symbolism, a traditional appeal to a sense of 'continuity'. So much so, that, for example, it might now appear very strange to many to consider precisely why it is the case that $\sqrt{2} \times \sqrt{3} = \sqrt{6}$. (In fact, this would have been a strange request for many mathematicians in the past; it was not considered to need proof until the nineteenth century.) Moreover, the development of 'algabraic' calculators will encourage the current trend away from the traditional demand that students have a very highly practised facility with algebraic manipulation. 'Powers of x' is losing its force as an item on the syllabus.

In this context, it is not surprising that there is currently a lot of interest in a process curriculum. If we are not completely clear *what* mathematics could and should be taught to all pupils, we can at least try to give them the experience of 'mathematising', by offering them accessible situations which they might approach more or less in the way that professional mathematicians would do. And various recent publications suggest that there is no shortage of such situations, whether these are classically inherited problems – from mainstream mathematics, but also very often from the recreational literature – or cunningly-contrived modern versions.

Various issues arise when the classical inheritance is raided in this way. First, there is the problem of classification, of distinguishing between triviality and importance. Thus in the well-known and influential ATM publication, *Points of Departure*, the first collection of 75 miscellaneous situations is categorised as follows: patterns in number; spatial; symbolisation; games and puzzles; structure; suitable for younger children; mainly for 14+ or sixth form. This somewhat *ad hoc* and heterogeneous scheme is not maintained in the second collection, whose eclectic range may be indicated by the last few entries; bell-ringing, elephant walk, frogs, folding stamps, enclosures, dotty variations, transforming triangles.

There are also such questions as the following. How can one decide when and why any particular item is to be used? How far is it to be taken? How far is it sensible or worthwhile to depart from the main focus of traditional mathematical interest? For example, the first item in the ATM collection, called *Routes*, presents a square grid which is to be traversed in as many different ways as possible, starting from the bottom left and moving either upwards or to the right. *Try other points. Can you spot more patterns? Can you generalise them? Can you explain or prove them?* It is not clear from the context whether the main emphasis is supposed to be on the inductive process, on conjecture and proof, or on the classical content – Pascal's triangle, binomial theorem, and so on. Perhaps these are and should be equally important. But it is significant that this item is not listed under the 'combinatorial' sub-category and that the set questions move on, first to an extension of the theme on an isometric grid, and then to the now almost universal 'creative' invitation: *Invent your own grid and rules for moves.*

There are some teasing inconsistencies in all this. Is the sub-text here saying that 'anything goes', that exploring the implications of your rules is just as valid as exploring those enshrined by tradition? Does it matter how far the development of the problem of routes on a square grid goes? Is the work intended for any particular age-group? (The item does not get classified into either of the age-groups – younger children, 14+ or sixth form – of the categories provided in the first pamphlet.) If the thrust of the investigation is towards the creative development of other rules, then it is surprising that the initial situation is presented in such a very constrained way. Why should moves be restricted to the upwards and right direction only? Why, for that matter, should they be restricted to lines of the grid? Why should anyone get involved with this problem in the first place?

There are perfectly reasonable pedagogical answers to these questions. But it is worth emphasising here that the background knowledge about the original context of the situation has been kept very firmly suppressed: 'the ladder has been raised'. With hindsight, we can now trace a development in which a way of teaching the binomial theorem to sixth formers becomes a way of making some combinatorics accessible to first formers, and then becomes an optional item out of many others that could exemplify some aspect of a process-centred curriculum. However natural and well-intentioned it might be, this transition can result in a profound mystification for the pupil about what it is that is being studied. Indeed, it might be just as mystifying to some teachers. Why should it not be made explicit that the first few items in the ATM collection, for example, are concerned with binomial coefficents, Chinese remainders, multiples, sums of squares, slopes of lines, equivalence classes, and so on?

Is it merely an accident that some situations that are currently used as 'starting points' have some historical antecedents, some connection with classical mathematics? In due course, inventive teachers and their equally inventive pupils would be able to generate completely original situations to work on. But this would be to deny the current evidence that the most successful situations for investigation are almost invariably based on some classical content. This is not because such content is inviolate and unchanging; rather, it is that process and product are in fact indivisible aspects of a discipline, and that content is equivalent to form, in the sense that each determines the other.

To recapture this essential indissolubility of matter and method requires a considerable effort of reinterpretation and reconstruction. Much of the mathematics that is enshrined, either in the traditional texts or in recent innovatory suggestions, tends to be offered out of context, often without any accompanying explanation of what the problems actually were that the particular piece of mathematics is elucidating. On the one hand, syllabus items such as 'powers of x' tend to obscure the underlying inductive extension of index notation, and, on the other hand, arbitrarily presented situations for investigation, like routes on a square grid, can ignore the mathematical purposes for which they were originally designed.

Consider, as a further exemplifying case study, the problem widely known as *The Tower of Hanoi*, which is also given in the ATM collection. This affords a startling example of the ability of mathematicians to ignore certain aspects of a situation when it suits their purpose to stress other aspects. The combinatorial puzzle about shifting piles became popular among teachers during the very years in which Hanoi was involved in one of the grimmest human conflicts of recent years. It seems strange, if not distasteful, that the name should be invoked in classrooms, without any further reference to its other significance. It seems strange, if not culturally insensitive, that it should often have been introduced with a rigmarole about priests moving heavy discs until the world ends.

Where and when and why did this puzzle originate? It was certainly around in the books of mathematical recreations before it was brought into classrooms. It was, in fact, invented by Edouard Lucas and described in his *Récréations Mathématiques*, published in 1883. The story about the toiling priests was a fanciful invention of his to suit the conventions with which mathematical puzzles were offered to a lay public. The reference to Hanoi reminds us that Indo-China was once a French sphere of influence. We may safely suppose that this nineteenth-century pleasantry would not amuse the present-day Vietnamese, of whatever political persuasion.

An original Lucas 'Tower of Hanoi' puzzle of 1883, from the Hordem collection of puzzles.

Why did Lucas invent this particular puzzle? Well, he might have invented it as part of his inveterate interest in mathematical recreations; combinatorial puzzles have always intrigued people and many authors of books on mathematical recreations, such as Ernest Dudeney and Sam Loyd, invented very many that have become equally well-known. But Lucas was also a professional mathematician who did a lot of original work in number theory, particularly on recurrence equations and on large primes. He wrote an introductory textbook on elementary number theory, which is notable for its engaging didactic style and its inventive examples and illustrations.

Now, powers of two play a large role in such topics as perfect numbers and Mersenne numbers, the latter involving finding primes which are one less than a power of two (for example, $2^{216,091} - 1$, the largest such prime known to date – 1988). If you wanted a nice way of introducing pupils to such topics, what neater way could you imagine than offering them an amusing example that generates the sequence 1, 3, 7, 15 . . .? Lucas' puzzle does just that: he used it straight as a pedagogical device in one context, and dressed it up with a story for another. We may wish to use it for other purposes in the classroom today, but it is still the case that *doubling* is an important and fundamental notion and the puzzle could be called upon for specific and thought-out *mathematical* purposes, rather than as yet another item in a miscellaneous collection of things that might be tackled sometime, somewhere, somehow.

It is perhaps significant that another very popular situation for investigation is also due to Lucas (who might well be turning in his grave, considering the way his puzzles are sometimes being used). His *Jeu de pions* was described as a chessboard game with pawns in Rouse Ball's collection. Variations in which the elements were in a circle were then given by Dudeney, with various cover stories involving grasshoppers or frogs. The present writer first came across the game in 1951 when it was played in pubs with matchsticks, those on the left having their heads aligned opposite to those on the right. It was called *Frogs* in an ATM pamphlet on pegboard games and was being played in schools in the 1960s. It was then played with pupils themselves as the combinatorial elements, notably at various mathematical weekends that were organised by ATM in the 1970s.

Lucas' second game was mentioned earlier as one of the items in the second ATM collection of investigations. It is a natural, and almost always popular, combinatorial situation which offers a multiplicative growth pattern as compared with the exponential growth of the first game. In its simplest form, it generates a sequence that is one less than the 2nd power of n, contrasting with the formula of the first game – one less than the n-th power of 2. The game does also lend itself very readily to many of the process objectives that are currently being identified.

There are, however, a number of teachers who have reported that, although many of their pupils master the inductive generalisation involved (a double induction in the most general case), they do not seem to be able to formulate a general proof of the patterns that they detect in the accumulating evidence of particular cases. This is not normally a problem, for instance, in the situation of finding numbers of shortest routes on a square grid, referred to above. Here, the general additive pattern can be inferred by arguing from a particular case, and pupils can often do this in a way that does not invoke the particularity involved. Thus, to get to this point (say, three across, three up) I have to come either from this point (three across, two up) or that point (two across, three up); so the number of ways is the sum of the ways to here and the ways to there . . .

Why is the general pattern not so easily inferred – rather than guessed – in the case of *Frogs*? It *can* be, when teachers are prepared to ask certain key questions that point to a way of approaching the issue. For example: what different sorts of moves can the rules permit? If you are one of the elements (counters, matchsticks, frogs, pegs, people) how many others do you have to jump over? How many times do you think you will have to move into an adjacent place? Taking everybody into account, how many moves altogether? Even if this is answered in terms of a particular number of elements, the thinking is being directed in a way that ignores the particularity.

It is, of course, this element of *direction* that is the ideological crunch. For a variety of reasons, not always consistent, there is a developing disinclination by teachers, or perhaps by the influential teacher-training establishment, to be seen to be too heavily 'directive'. Pupils are to be encouraged to work at 'their own mathematics', at mathematics which is variously seen as being culturally dependent, gender independent, and struggling to be free from the shackles of tradition. Wallis' investigative method has somehow in recent times acquired the accompanying restriction that it has to be virginal – innocent of other than self-created knowledge. Although it is – rightly – sometimes considered a virtue to share with fellow learners, pupils are not always so obviously encouraged to share with tradition, with textbook, or with teachers.

It remains unclear – or, at any rate, not explicitly stated – why anyone should wish to work at Lucas' combinatorial games or, indeed, many of the situations currently offered to pupils for 'investigation'. They can be useful vehicles for logical thinking, and ordered ways of tackling problems, in which case they might be more usefully superseded by more worldly-wise activities like gardening, bread-making or making money. They can be ways of passing time – pastimes – in which case they do not seem to be as attractive to many people as doing crosswords, playing card games or watching television. Or they can be tools which a teacher might use in order to offer pupils access to such mathematical content as function, rate of growth, combinatorics, and so on, in which case these signposts might be made more explicit. Whatever the case, we need to be a bit clearer about these issues – for Lucas' sake.

Dick Tahta was formerly Lecturer in Education at Exeter University.

Index